METTERNICH,
REORGANIZATION AND NATIONALITY
1813-1818

AMERICAN EDITION

THE UNIVERSITY OF TENNESSEE PRESS
KNOXVILLE
1964

METTERNICH,
REORGANIZATION AND NATIONALITY
1813—1818

A STORY OF FORESIGHT AND FRUSTRATION
IN THE REBUILDING OF THE AUSTRIAN EMPIRE

BY

ARTHUR G. HAAS

FRANZ STEINER VERLAG GMBH · WIESBADEN

1963

TABLE OF CONTENTS

LIST OF ILLUSTRATIONS

PREFACE

The publication of Heinrich von Srbik's imposing biography of Metternich in 1925 not only presented a new portrayal but made plain various aspects of the Austrian statesman's career still worthy of the historian's attention. In reviewing Srbik's work, Hans Rothfels had emphasized especially one thought regarding internal policy: more important than the question of Metternich's deeds is that of his ideas. He referred particularly to Metternich's post-war internal program, some of whose features Srbik had indicated well enough on the basis of published material. It remained to document and to describe fully the extent of both Metternich's ideas and deeds in regard to internal policy during the Congress Era, to ascertain this policy as a whole in its aims and denouement. Beyond this remained the intriguing question: what would an archives investigation reveal of this formative phase of Metternich's career, in which he apparently meant to intervene in matters of internal reorganization? This book, originally written as a doctoral dissertation at the University of Chicago under the guidance of Hans Rothfels, is the result of such an investigation. To Professor Rothfels, whose interest in the problem of nationality inspired mine, I shall be ever grateful for the encouragement, counsel and help he has always so kindly given me.

The research undertaken for this work made necessary a long stay in Europe. This was made possible through the grant of an extended research-fellowship from the Institut für Europäische Geschichte in Mainz, to whose director, Professor Martin Göhring, I owe so much. There I was ably assisted by K. O. Freiherr v. Aretin, Fritz Kallenberg, Gottfried Schramm, and Ernst Schulin. At the Viennese Haus-, Hof- und Staatsarchiv I have become indebted to its very capable assistant director, Anna Gräfin Coreth, who, in her gracious manner and with a saint's patience, so often helped me with difficult documents or in learning the intricacies of various collections. The archives director, Richard Blaas, and the managing editor of the *Mitteilungen des Österreichischen Staatsarchivs*, Erika Weinzierl-Fischer, frequently went out of their way to make my work easier.

In Chicago, Professor Louis Gottschalk generously gave me both the benefit of his far-ranging experience and a good amount of his time. Professor S. William Halperin's kindly-made suggestions led to important improvements in the text. Miss Carol Rearick's thoughtful advice and cooperation in correcting the manuscript I appreciate very much. To them, I am especially grateful.

Finally, I would like to thank those who helped me with the correcting of proofs – particularly Hugo Lacher and, above all, my aunt Lydia Haas, who – by this time – probably knows this book better than I do.

Mainz, July 1962 A. G. H.

INTRODUCTION

QUESTIONS AND STARTING POINTS

The problem of nationality — the demand for national self-determination, the difficulties involved in governing and satisfying a self-conscious nationality unhappy under "foreign" rule — this is an issue which has played a decisive role in modern history and which has not yet lost its significance. In that patch-quilt of nationalities which is Central Europe, the problem contributed much to the frightful drama of its recent past. In no state was the problem so acute as in Habsburg Austria: the inability to solve it caused the empire to burst asunder. Far from being settled, the problem remained, dispersed among the very nationalities which were themselves just "free" and faced at once with their own dissatisfied national minorities. The Habsburg failure, so extensive in its consequences, has drawn considerable attention from historians. Yet, research on the nationality problem has been devoted by and large to the reigns of Ferdinand and Franz Joseph — to times in which the problem was obvious and most solutions smacked of hindsight. Was there not an earlier time in which a reform of the empire's internal structure might have had a steadier basis and thus have enabled it to cope successfully with much of what was to come?

There seems to have been no better opportunity than after the downfall of Napoleon, when a victorious Austria was occupied with reincorporating large tracts of territory amounting to nearly a fourth of its total area. Therewith the Vienna government had the task before it of reconciling several million "liberated" non-German subjects to a rule which some of these peoples could have considered scarcely less foreign than that of Napoleon. With the need for attaching anew to the House of Habsburg the loyalties of peoples whose independence had frequently been promised and even briefly asserted, with the need for making these peoples' membership in the Habsburg "family of nations" attractive, the situation certainly called for the formulation of some sort of "nationality" or "autonomy" policy: but were the Austrian authorities then aware of these needs and this call upon their statesmanship? Thus the main question to be answered by this work — which will concentrate on the years between Austria's declaration of war against Napoleon in 1813 and the effective installation of a permanent government in its recovered provinces early in 1818 — is: during this unique opportunity to achieve within the multinational empire an inner balance while the movements destined to destroy it had not ripened, did the Austrian government — and especially Metternich — recognize such problems as nationality and foreign rule, and if so, what steps were taken to find a suitable solution and with what success?

In the numerous histories dealing with the Coalition against Napoleon, the Congress of Vienna and the Congress Era, the name of Metternich appears on nearly every page. It is intimately connected with Austria itself. More than its first diplomat, Metternich was also the constructor of Austrian foreign policy; to him belongs a good share of the credit (or discredit) for the European settlements. Moreover, since the problem of nationality — definitely in the case of Poland and in some form or other in Italy and Illyria — was relegated as an internal affair to the various states concerned, then it would not seem unreasonable to suppose that in Austria the highest political office — the Metternich-led state chancellery — should have had its say in the matter of dealing with such nationalities.

Yet, in the few works devoted principally to internal policy and administration, the man presumed to be Austria's most powerful statesman and the initiator of the "Metternich system" stands conspicuously in the background. There has been no attempt, on the basis of archival evidence, to analyze internal policy during the Congress Era for possible clashes of political and administrative interests; neither has been investigated, on this basis, the extent of Metternich's influence on or cooperation with Kaiser Franz in internal matters. To be sure, both Heinrich v. Srbik and R. W. Seton-Watson touched upon these points as they dealt with Metternich's domestic policy. Both, however, used mostly published sources in crediting Metternich with some original ideas and with some initiative in trying to bring his reluctant master around to badly-needed reforms. Srbik, and before him Krones, had recognized Metternich's lack of influence in internal affairs; but this observation was usually related to Metternich's rivalry with Count Kolowrat, to years beyond our concern. While few historians would wish, by denying Metternich's authority in internal affairs, to exonerate him for the evils of the regime or for 1848, some have emphasized such authority in order to fix responsibility and Viktor Bibl, Srbik's constant adversary, even went so far as to lay the blame for the disintegration of the Habsburg Empire in 1918 at Metternich's feet. Indeed, the stereotype Metternich image — a dogmatic reactionary defiantly challenging progress and thus steering Austria toward tragedy — has resisted complete erasure despite Srbik's efforts and has remained a special convenience for those still championing the German national and "liberal" tradition. Even if one accepts this sort of image, the question remains whether it is applicable to Metternich throughout his career, and if not, then whether one can find a point where it begins to fit. Ironically, Metternich himself liked to emphasize his life-long consistency. Reminiscing as an old man, he more than once marked the year 1815 as a dividing point in his career and insisted that, thereafter, his principles had remained unchanged. Even Srbik accepted this statement at face value as he undertook to rectify the Metternich image. Consequently, all too easily the Metternich of Karlsbad and Verona or even of the *Vormärz* is made to appear as early as 1815. Furthermore, it should not be too surprising that an effort, such as Srbik's, to arrange a statesman's political principles into a definite set of axioms might neglect development and change.

To understand properly the Metternich of the period from 1813 to 1818, one must also examine his role in internal affairs and consider several questions: Is it possible that the Vienna government — in this case Kaiser Franz and a group of his organizers — regarded the incorporation of the new lands as just an administrative affair beyond the concern of Metternich's Staatskanzlei? If they did, what was the reaction, if any, of this office? Were there possibly two camps of opinion? Then, if dissension on post-war reorganization led to the first failure of the Austrian Empire to cope with its nationality problem, what were the roles of Kaiser Franz and Metternich in this failure? And to what extent was Metternich really responsible for the organizing of an A u s t r i a n administration in Lombardy-Venetia? This last question can be broadened to include the two factors upon which depended the extent of Metternich's influence: the defined competence of the Staatskanzlei which he headed (he was not state chancellor until 1821) and the force of his personality in dealing with his sovereign.

Is there any justification for presuming that Metternich — the central figure in this work — recognized nationality as a problem or that he had anything to contribute in the way of a solution? Up to now, what little we know of Metternich in this regard has been derived from two proposals, published in his memoirs, which he made to the emperor in 1817. One calls for a new administration of the interior which was to include regional-national chancelleries, the other for greater autonomy for Lombardy-

Venetia. These documents, admittedly somewhat out of harmony with the usual selections from Metternich's writings, have had little particular significance attached to them except by Srbik. Certainly they reveal a far more understanding and a far less understood Metternich. Although such documents surely are not isolated monuments but rather products of a policy, almost nothing is known either of their background or of their fate. What became of these proposals by Metternich had been so thoroughly forgotten that even Metternich's son Richard, the publisher and co-editor of his father's memoirs, could not inform the reader correctly. These pieces stand in curious contrast to known Austrian administrative practices before and after, and this apparent contradiction immediately raises a new question: If Metternich attempted in vain to carry through his own interior policy in the reincorporated territories, then what was the nature of this policy and what stood in its way?

So much for the theoretical starting points: a practical — although often difficult — starting point lies in the nature of the available source material. As far as the questions raised in this investigation are concerned, a large amount of the relevant sources has hitherto remained unused. Except for specific archives investigations of Metternich's diplomacy (among others very recently, Nada, de Bertier, and Schroeder) nearly all of the literature on Metternich — including the works of Srbik — relied on the published memoirs or on the various published collections of correspondence representing only a small fraction of the documents in archives.[1] Conversely what archives research was done on internal development has skirted Metternich and the Staatskanzlei, confined itself to areas of only partial concern here, or neglected important collections. Such recent historians as Rath, Antoljak, and Walter, and before them Lemmi and Helfert, have investigated — either in a general or selective manner — the structure, installation, or functioning of Austrian administrative machinery; however, the problem of nationality — as a political concern — has not been the focal point. Furthermore, scarcely any archival investigation, with the exception of Professor Rath's thorough research on the Austrian administration in Lombardy-Venetia, has attempted a "wide sweep" through the relevant material at hand. Thus, with regard to Metternich and interior policy, a systematic check of all pertinent files — of the Staatskanzlei (especially the *Vorträge* and *Interiora),* of the imperial office, of the deliberative, administrative, and organizing agencies, of the embassies and even of various individuals — was to be largely a novel undertaking.

Moreover, the possibilities of research on Metternich were broadened recently as the Prag government at last made available to the Vienna

Archives — by way of single microfilm rolls — specifically requested material from the formerly private Metternich Family Archives, previously in Plass, Bohemia.

LIMITATION AND CONCENTRATION

This investigation of reorganization and nationality is necessarily broad because it can not be confined to just one province, agency, year, or even Metternich himself. The problem of nationality has no neat file of its own, and references to it, unfortunately, are surprisingly scarce. However, some limitations of material, time, and area impose themselves. The span of five years selected for this work is not arbitrarily chosen but is marked at the outset by the reconquest of the Italian and Illyrian territories in 1813 and at the close by Metternich's renewed preoccupation with external affairs and the so-called "final establishment" of a new interior structure in 1818.

The internal areas to which Metternich and his Staatskanzlei could direct their attention were those presenting political problems on which the emperor called for the Staatskanzlei's counsel. On Bohemia and Inner Austria, which had long been administered by the *Vereinigte Hofkanzlei*, and on Hungary and Transylvania, which had chancelleries of their own, Metternich and his state chancellery had little to say. These areas were not involved in a reorganization; they were of interest to Metternich only in a general overhaul of the empire's entire interior structure — and it is only in this regard that they will be dealt with in this work. The German provinces do not, of course, present any problem of a subject nationality, and Hungary and Transylvania, instead of receiving insufficient privilege, enjoyed — according to Metternich — such an overdose that the very constitution of the Habsburg empire was threatened. The remaining areas — Lombardy-Venetia, Illyria, and Galicia — did have reorganization problems and, at the same time, populations which one could expect to feel sensitive to any want of respect shown their nationality by the central government. These areas will present the main scenes for this work.

Naturally enough, the extent of the Staatskanzlei's and Metternich's competence determined the bulk or scarcity of the material in the Staatskanzlei's files on any particular issue. Therefore, whereas there are no more than a few cartons on Bohemia or Hungary, there are dozens on Lombardy-Venetia. Similarly, the files of the *Central-Organisierungs-Hof-Commission* (COHC) or the state councils are largely devoted to the Italian provinces or to Illyria. Conversely, of those areas requiring reorganizing, exactly those with the most advanced political and administrative standards made the highest demands and posed the severest problems, which were, in turn, matched by corresponding exertions of the Austrian authorities — exertions which resulted in mountains of paperwork. The simple fact that the administration of the Italian provinces drew the widest attention from the Viennese authorities accounts for the disproportionate deposits in the archives.

Setting the necessary limitations to the chosen topic sometimes called for a Solomon's judgment. To free Metternich, for the moment, of his strait-jacket — the "system", to trace a change from versatility to immobility and from expediency to legitimacy, to differentiate between the Metternich of the Vienna Congress and the one of Karlsbad would be an engrossing study. Yet, such an effort, demanding a painstaking comparison of at least all his many public and private sets of correspondence, would simply be too far-reaching. Nevertheless, I hope to show in four chapters a less-known Metternich and to discuss in the epilogue the change to the more familiar figure and, on the whole, to illustrate a period in Metternich's life in which he was capable of submitting original ideas on reshaping the empire's inner structure.

The analysis of a complex and many-sided character like Metternich's presents some hazards; certainly it can lead one far afield. It is often difficult enough to sense the purpose behind one of the minister's documents, let alone his real feelings. Unlike excitable romantics, he usually preferred restraint and graciousness, and was adroit enough to have his contemporaries think what he wanted them to think and not what he really thought. Unfortunately for the researcher, such gifts of diplomacy were not only confined to conversation. Moreover, it does not seem very rewarding to affix labels to Metternich, to demonstrate that he was an eclectic or a systematizer, a moralizer or a *Realpolitiker,* a doctrinaire or a savior, a liberal-in-comparison or true conservative or die-hard reactionary, a pleasure-seeking Rhinelander or citizen of the world, a pseudo-Austrian or a real European statesman and so forth.

More important but also more intricate is the question of Metternich's relationship with the emperor. The minister Metternich never allowed himself to criticize his monarch Kaiser Franz, and only occasionally, confidentially and lightly, did he touch upon this subject. Thus in a moment of almost boastful self-confidence he once wrote to the Countess Lieven that Kaiser Franz did as Metternich wanted but only because the minister wanted what the sovereign should do and that even though Metternich knew what he himself wanted, he also knew what he might allow himself to want in relation to the emperor.[2] There are no records of imperial indisposition causing ministerial annoyance; perhaps one can say that Metternich understood very well how to shrug off unpleasantness from that high quarter.

There are accounts enough to supply the background necessary for understanding both monarch and minister. Let us consider here only the main points: although both men had cosmopolitan backgrounds, Metternich was more at home in the world than Kaiser Franz, whose parochial Viennese manner often ran counter to his Florentine up-bringing. Metternich's cosmopolitanism, rather than preventing him from respecting the rights of nationality, enabled him to appreciate them much in a way that Herder had done, just as it brought him to despise nationalistic pathos and bluster. Because of their very marked differences in character, experience, and perception, Metternich and Kaiser Franz were quite different pupils of the Enlightenment. For the former, not only were the rights of a nationality specified within the rights of humanity as a whole but also to violate something so organic and natural was simply political folly. On the other hand, Kaiser Franz's enlightened despotism suffered precisely from a lack of monarchic "enlightenment". He could not comprehend that rationalization of government was a continuous process and did not end with paternalism and administrative absolutism but rather demanded as a next step the modification of that concentration of affairs in the ruler's hands which had been required in the previous step. The emperor was as loath to delegate authority as to abandon the thought of centralization. This reluctance, coupled with administrative absolutism, meant for the emperor that, since the imperial administration was to be just and righteous for all subjects, there was no justification for a nationality's claim to special consideration and treatment. Since no province was better than another, he reasoned, and if the administration was to be equally efficient in all lands, then it should have the same form in all lands.

Admittedly, Kaiser Franz recognized some dangers. He never lost his dread of Hungarian defiance, and the failure of his uncle Joseph's experiment was one of his long list of nightmares. Metternich and his monarch were both horrified by revolution and its violence, though the minister saw its dangers for the world while the emperor saw only the threats to his throne. To be sure, few sovereigns had such a reign behind them: ever since Franz, as a frightened and immature youth, had suddenly been invested with the ancient imperial insignia in 1792, there had been war after war, loss after loss, humiliation after humiliation. His weird fear of every change doubtless was derived from those troubled times in which change usually meant for him another catastrophe. With Metternich it was otherwise: his political career was an increasingly imposing list of spectacular personal successes. In 1813 - 1814, while a young and triumphant Metternich was busy with the affairs of Europe, a relieved but sober Kaiser Franz devoted his efforts to the one field which he could direct to the last triviality — administrative organization. Experience had taught him to entrust foreign and financial affairs to those more capable than he; but in exercising his prerogatives, Kaiser Franz had his own ideas, about which he could be adamant. Finally, if, in addition to such background, one compares Metternich's far-ranging and quick intelligence with the emperor's mediocre, unimaginative but tenaciously bureaucratic mentality, then one can expect to meet widely divergent attitudes and approaches toward a reorganization policy.

Of course, the fate of any proposal by Metternich depended on the emperor's reaction. The minister could not foresee such reactions despite a good knowledge of his master's attitudes — a fact borne out by the frequency with which Metternich's hopes were disappointed. All too often the motives of such reactions were anchored in preconceptions against which, at times, all of Metternich's reason and influence could not prevail. But the minister was clever enough not to exceed his own limits. Perhaps his greatest diplomatic achievement was this very one of gradually winning the lifelong trust and friendship of such a difficult master. To accomplish this end meant patiently convincing the emperor of the "correctness" of his leading statesman's policies. It also meant, in at least one important instance, that Metternich had eventually to abandon a program which he knew to be in the future interests of the monarchy but against the present inclinations of the monarch. It is doubtful whether the historian can ever learn how much Metternich compromised at the expense of his private convictions in order to secure the favorable relationship with his sovereign and thereby his own position and comfort.

The influence on Metternich of some experienced officials like Marshal Bellegarde, General Bubna, or Count Goëss should not be overlooked. It is to Metternich's credit that he was able to recognize quickly the merits of their arguments and then dutifully to advance them, along with his own comments and views, to the emperor. Obviously not all of Metternich's proposals originated with him; in such an instance his service consists in seizing upon the essentials of specific suggestions made by men better acquainted with local issues and then fitting these essentials into his own political conceptions. While this work can not occupy itself too closely with those men who earned Metternich's confidence, it will attempt, whenever possible, to give them their due.[3]

Administrative details have been included here only when necessary to illustrate matters of nationality or territorial integrity. The dispatches of the lower ranks of the Austrian administration — revealing though some of them might be — must concern us here less than the interpretation given them at the higher levels, and public activity and opinions or direct police reports thereon can be only secondary to political evaluations of such activity and opinion. Certainly public opinion was important for the Austrian authorities; it served them as a constantly observed and occasionally tampered-with political barometer. Whether their readings were accurate (they usually were) is of less interest than the actions which those readings inspired.

Nationalistic strivings — whether the momentary independent political initiative and aspirations of 1814 or the later independence movements and secret societies — are vast topics in themselves and can only be referred to here briefly; the real concern of this work is, once more, the problem of nationality as seen by the Austrian authorities. In Lombardy-Venetia, this problem was concentrated, for these authorities as well as the population, in several specific semi-political institutions which symbolized a special *national* status: the Italian chancellery in Vienna, an Italian supreme court for the Lombardo-Venetian Kingdom in Verona, and the Italian viceroy in Milan. In Croatia and in Galicia, political attention was focused rather on the provincial estates as traditional political rallying points and sounding boards of *national* sentiment. In Italy there was a more recent tradition of direct home-rule and thus the viceroy was always more important to the Milanese than the provincial congregations.

GENERALITIES AND TERMS

Because some concepts and terms in this work — such as *reform, administrative necessity, constitution, masses, nation,* and *nationality* — occur frequently and can have various meanings, it might be well to comment briefly on some of the uses and implications prevalent in the Austria of the Congress Era. Usually but not always, the sense in which a term was used becomes obvious in context. Some terms — such as *constitution,* for example[4] — the men of the times had troubled themselves to define; but often, then as now, interpretations fluctuated to the extent that one word was able to evoke a whole scale of attitudes from one individual.

Few words were tossed about more than *reform* — demanded as necessary, acknowledged as unavoidable, disdained as a dubious slogan, feared as the first step toward revolution, depending on its proponent, its object, its method. Although Austria's advocates of reform were not as fiery or adamant as Stein and his like, there were nonetheless a number of clairvoyant men aware of an urgent need for reform within the Habsburg empire's entire governing apparatus. Among these one might count Kübeck, Dietrichstein, and a Metternich better acquainted than the others with any proposal's practicability. It was one thing to have brilliant ideas; it was quite another to submit them in a manner acceptable to the emperor. Thus, Metternich's proposals for changing the administration of the interior were cut to assure the monarch that his minister's suggestions in no way involved exactly what they really did involve — reform. To the minister, reform in Austria meant a step by step introduction of necessary new policies, institutions, routines, and general improvements, all the while adhering to professed fundamentals. Kaiser Franz regarded any reform with deepest suspicion, not the least of his reasons being that *per se* it cast criticism on an existing order of things for which he felt personally responsible; it could be taken into consideration only as a carefully planned and minimal *re-forming* of that already at hand — hence Metternich's obvious and continuous lip-service to such an interpretation. There could be no question for both monarch and minister but that reform might emanate only from "above" — from the highest legal authority. The very challenge to the monarchic principle inherent in a demand for reform from "below" condemned it to be ignored — officially at least — regardless of its content or urgency. When such demands for reform, moreover, were coupled with nationalistic and constitutionalistic ideas, a scornful Metternich could refer to reform as "the shibboleth of the liberals".

In an administrative sense, the object of reform was primarily the state machine. With an excellent administration, the emperor sought to reconcile his non-German subjects to Austrian rule. A more far-sighted policy of reform was aimed less at administrative efficiency than at a political reorganization which would satisfy subjects concerned more with the idea of "foreign rule" than with a good administration. A politically satisfied populace might well accept an administration less than perfect whereas a politically dissatisfied one could always find fault with even the most laudable intentions. Ultimately it mattered little that the Austrian administration in Lombardy-Venetia could pride itself on being the best in Italy.

To be sure, in Austria, reform was an administrative necessity which even Kaiser Franz could recognize on occasion. Metternich, in order to make his proposals more palatable to his monarch, skillfully tied the need for reform of the state machine (by decentralizing government and by delegating responsibility) together with his aim of increased regional-national autonomy. He preferred to agree with his sovereign that the hour for reform might strike only in the most peaceful and untroubled times. Metternich was not one to presume in the emperor's presence that such a time had arrived; however, he held before him the prospect of an agitated future in making the relatively calm present of 1817 more suitable for "small changes". With his monarch, the minister could only stress that improvement or reform was incidental to the establishment of proper fundamentals. No human institution supported by proper fundamentals, he claimed, could fail to improve itself in the course of its natural development; in this sense, at least, Metternich was ready to believe in the inevitability of progress.

In 1813 and 1814, reports came to Vienna from the reconquered territories — especially Illyria — that the population expected "reforms on a grand scale". By the Austrian authorities such "reforms" were generally taken to mean improvements over the state of things prevailing under the previous war-torn regime: an end to conscription, abolition of crushing taxes, broader consideration from Vienna for local wishes, etc. On the need for widely applied economic alleviation, the Austrian authorities usually agreed — notwithstanding some concern for the strained state of the imperial treasury. "Popular measures" were planned to meet the population's desires and needs, with an eye — of course — on the possibility of arousing thereby a favorable public response. However, such measures did not follow a definite reform program but were, rather, a haphazard attempt to answer the plaints of the populace. In time, after some observation of the social structure showed how different the needs among the various ranks were, a more specifically aimed program was discussed; especially in Lombardy-Venetia the question was asked: how were the various classes to be satisfied and won?

When Austrian officials spoke of "the mass of the population", they usually meant the majority of the population; the expression *the masses (die Massen, les masses,* but also frequently in the singular — *die Masse, la masse)* was used to denote a general majority or, specifically, the lower classes (who were of course a majority in themselves). Sometimes, however, *the mass* referred to a select majority of those holding political opinions. *The masses* as such were presumed to be, politically, "sleeping dogs" better left alone. Their cares were those of an every-day existence; here a program of *panem et laborem* was felt to be sufficient *(circenses* could hardly have

been expected from Kaiser Franz). The politically conservative ranks —
most property owners, the clergy, and all but the most impoverished
nobility — were to be kept loyal by receiving honors and some participation in court and governmental affairs.

Upon these classes, as well as on the satisfied *masses,* so the Austrians
felt, depended the Austrian position in Italy; upon them would rest a
système conservateur which upheld the monarchic principle. Extending some
sort of political function to the conservative ranks through meetings of the
estates seemed prudent to Metternich, but Kaiser Franz regarded such
bodies as a possible challenge to his imperial prerogatives and was reluctant
to revive even the traditional estates abolished by the Napoleonic regime.
Metternich, on the other hand, claimed to have gone as far as to propose a
central assembly for all of Austria — a proposal which the emperor apparently kept shelved his whole life long.[5] Yet, with his monarch's
acquiescence, Metternich pressed for a reconstitution of estates in the
various German states; he was even prepared to concede to such bodies a
right to determine budgets and taxation,[6] to forestall the demand for a representative constitution which would have brought to the political arena
the middle class with all its "dangerous" ideas. In the post-Napoleonic
period, this class, which carried the germs of nationalism and constitutionalism, presented a problem for Austria only in Lombardy-Venetia; but
there, few Austrians were optimistic about winning this class over as a
group. One hoped only to mollify its various components: the businessmen
by commercial privileges and encouragement of trade, the intellectuals by
recognition and by subventions of the arts and sciences, the civil employees
or army officers by guarantees of extended service or full pensions. Those
Austrians really acquainted with the Italian scene recognized soon enough
that the politically-minded could be satisfied, if satisfied at all, only by
a program demonstrating sincere respect for "national character", *i. e.,* by a
grant of "national institutions" which the population could feel were their
own.

Modern meanings of *nation* and *nationality* do not always match those
used one and a half centuries ago. Moreover, the word *nation* could mean
all sorts of things to the Austrian authorities of the Congress Era. It could
refer to a large ethnic whole, or *Kulturnation,* such as the Italian, Polish,
or German "nations", or to a smaller organized ethnic or religious group
such as the "Serbian" or "Illyrian nation" within the territory of Hungary or
the Military Frontier; it could refer to a large traditional territorial entity
within the empire such as the Transylvanian, Bohemian, or Hungarian *nation* or even to a new construction such as an "Illyrian nation" composed

of the former French Illyrian Provinces; it could refer to a pure *Staats-nation* lacking a definite and natural territory but with a fairly homogeneous population such as the Bavarian *nation*. However, it was generally considered as an anomaly to designate as a "nation" a realm composed of several "nations" such as the Ottoman or Habsburg empires, although, on rare occasions, the phrase "Austrian nation" is used to mean the Austrian state and its peoples. Despite such variety, it is usually possible to ascertain, within a given document, the sense in which the term *nation* was meant. It was no longer common in 1815 to apply the term to an *Adelsnation*, that is, the estates; even if one could still have referred to an *Adelsnation* in Galicia, one could hardly have done so in Lombardy-Venetia. The ethnic and cultural interpretation began to be used as frequently as a political interpretation. When Metternich or his contemporaries referred to the Italian or Polish "nation", they meant the people who thought themselves to be of Italian or Polish nationality; when they spoke of the Lombard or Illyrian "nation", they meant a distinct *Volksstamm*, a part of a people distinct in itself, organized in a regional territorial unit large enough to warrant the designation *nation*.

In this work, the terms *national feeling, national spirit,* and *national pride* appear often simply because these were the phrases resorted to most by Austrian officialdom when referring to a people's national consciousness and expressions resulting from it. In order to understand *national feeling*, one might distinguish, first of all, between it, patriotism, and nationalism. The first two could be classified under what Carlton Hayes took to be "humanitarian nationalism"; the third would include "Jacobin" and the later forms of nationalism. All are emotions based on an awareness of something in common — be it tradition, culture, language, religion, purpose, or destiny. Patriotism, a love for the fatherland, presumes a willingness to make personal sacrifices, a readiness to stand by one's country; men prepared to risk their own well-being to protect or to free their fatherland are patriots. There were many Austrians who sadly conceded to Federigo Confalonieri and his fellow-prisoners on the Spielberg this honorable designation. For Metternich, gracious and helpful as he was to the prisoners' relatives, Confalonieri was not much more than a pitiful beguiled Italian liberal stubbornly seeking martyrdom in a false cause; for Kaiser Franz he was simply a conspirator and a traitorous subject. Nationalism, however, does not necessarily mean patriotism and is conceivable without unselfish activity. As used in this work *nationalism* is not synonymous with *national feeling* or *patriotism*. While national feeling — and this would include true national pride — is essentially introverted, sensitive, and defensive, nationalism, while proceeding from the former, goes beyond it and is extroverted, assertive, and offensive. While national feeling demands due respect for nationality, nationalism demands control over a nation's destiny and a suitable role for that nation in the world; while the one is more concerned with preservation, revival, or even hallowing of national institutions and cultural heritage, the other uses these as implements in a political program. To be sure, the same national feeling could produce simultaneously an admirable patriotism and an intolerant and intolerable nationalism. The Hungary of 1848 is a good case in point; however, Metternich could have singled out some examples in the Germany of 1813.

If patriotism requires a fatherland, then national feeling and nationalism require a nation, whether a *Staatsnation* of the historic (or the more recent) territorial type, or a *Kulturnation*. Although modern historians frequently — and to some extent rightly so — describe expressions of national feeling in Germany, Italy, or Poland during the Congress Era under the rubric *nationalism*, the word *nationalism* itself was hardly heard in those times. In this work, I prefer to reserve the words *nationalism* and *nationalistic* for the demands for a new unified national state. In the first decades of the nineteenth century, the advocates of such a program represented but a small minority of the entire population; it is with the national feeling or national sensitivity of a larger segment of the population that the Austrian authorities had to concern themselves. To be sure, in contrast to Lombardy-Venetia, there was only a scant bourgeoisie in Croatia and Galicia and there national feeling was represented largely by the members of the estates who continued to see in themselves *the nation*. One can not find a general Austrian national feeling throughout the empire as a whole comparable to an Italian or German national feeling. Rather, there was evident, in addition to a genuine Austrian patriotism in German Austria, a strong affection for the monarch, the *Landesvater* Franz, who was the ruler and unifying symbol of many "nations".

The Austrian authorities could regard only national feeling or national pride as civic emotions calling for positive notice on their part. Demands for national independence, as all activity directed against the existing order of things, was seen of course as illegal and less as a matter for political consideration than one for the police. Whether wounded Italian national feeling in Lombardy-Venetia was to be soothed at all by a grant of separate status and whether a regional-national *esprit*, based on particular pride, was to be cultivated — these were questions which presupposed all-out efforts before any affirmative answers could be hoped for.

Certainly, Metternich knew better than to expect complete sobriety after a generation of so much upheaval; he knew that the idea of nationality, which had begun to blossom during this generation, would not wither on the vine. He understood this idea although he was hardly a nationalist; he had caught its spirit in a German guise in 1809 but had, in Golo Mann's words, "overcome it".[7] Yet, despite his cosmopolitanism, he considered himself a German — a fact which once he had to call to Napoleon's attention. The multinational Austria he called his "moral fatherland"; there he sought to channel the idea of nationality into politically suitable reservoirs: *regional nationality*. Thereby, all major entities of the empire were to be given an equal opportunity to develop their unique "national" stamp and an inner balance was to be achieved within the Monarchy by arranging such new "nations" as Inner Austria, Illyria, Galicia and Lombardy-Venetia alongside such historic ones as the all-too-mighty Hungary, Bohemia and Transylvania. Metternich's conception of nationality in the post-war years was cultural as well as political, although what may be considered his nationality policy went beyond a concern for cultural autonomy in making provisions for administrative and even political home-rule. As perceptive as such a policy might have been in most parts of the empire, in Lombardy-Venetia it was already behind the events. There the political climate remained disturbed not so much by a struggle for cultural autonomy, which was hardly threatened despite all fears to the contrary, as for a political or at least an administrative autonomy. Indeed, when measured against more recent acts of suppression, some of the Italian charges of "Germanization" might appear as overburdened, but this does not diminish their weight for that time. If "foreign rule" in Italy meant a Viennese emperor's troops on the peninsula and some German-speaking officials at the higher levels, of course, it was bad enough; but at least Italian national feeling, injured though it was by exaggerated administrative formalism, did not have to suffer from German nationalism: there was no attempt to force Italians to learn the German language or to put up German street signs in Milan. Within the empire, the Italian language enjoyed an eminence beyond Lombardy-Venetia's borders as no language other than German did. The great majority of administrative officials in Lombardy-Venetia was Italian. Yet, as the Austrian commander in Italy, Marshal Bellegarde, so often emphasized, it was necessary to "flatter Italian national character". Such flattery would have required a few subtleties and a bit of political psychology — something of which the minister was well capable, but not the monarch.

One final and brief comment on "national character": because of the broad concern of Austrian authorities with Italian affairs, their correspondence contains frequent opinions on supposed Italian traits. These opinions are usually in remarkable agreement; they range from an admiration of cultural achievements to a disdain for a singular lack of discipline. Thus, while the Italians were conceded intelligence, wit, talent, capability, facility, imagination, perspicacity, and esprit, they were accused of levity, superficiality, and impatience. Their preference for quick action was supposed to be accompanied by a dislike for thoroughness (a more honest word might have been *pedantry*). Their eloquence, their passion for talk, was taken to mean in the last resort profuse but empty words which only hampered decisive action for the country which, admittedly, they loved so deeply. Their demands and wishes resulted in a tireless complaining and seeking of objects for disparagement. Their very appreciation of the arts and the beautiful seemed to make them ostentatious, pompous, vain, sensitive, and delighted with ornamentation and display — something which they sorely missed in the slower and comparitively sober Austrians. On the other hand, although considered quarrelsome, jealous, envious, hot-tempered, fiery, and defiant, they were also thought to be lazy and willing to wield everything but the sword; a most consoling observation for the Austrians was that the Italians were unwilling to fight for their independence. This last point was perhaps the most important because, no matter how right the Austrians may have been on all the others, they could not afford to have been wrong on this one; but, ultimately, they were.

FRANZ I. VON ÖSTERREICH

CHAPTER I

CONQUEST AND CONFLICTING ORGANIZATION
POLICIES: 1813—1814

ITALY AND ILLYRIA. THE APPEAL TO NATIONAL SPIRIT
AND INDEPENDENT POLITICAL INITIATIVE

With the passing of midnight the armistice had expired and in the first minutes of August 11, 1813, Metternich ordered the lighting of signal-fires which meant that Austria was at war with France. Now the balance of power shifted decisively against an already shaken French imperium. Napoleon's position in Central Europe grew ever more precarious, while French might south of the Alps — soon cut off from the main force — dwindled rapidly. Upon Bavaria's turn-about to the Allies, the "Inner-Austrian" armies occupied a Tyrol in rebellious ferment and soon they filed across Alpine passes into valleys leading to the Italian plain. To the east, other contingents were able to enter the French Illyrian Provinces; they overcame initial checks in Carinthia, and after an insurrection of Croats in the Fiume and Karlstadt area had opened the way for them, they were able to reach the sea. Thus hampered in front and threatened in the rear, the viceroy of the Napoleonic Kingdom of Italy, Eugene Beauharnais, was forced to abandon a projected thrust into Austrian Croatia and had to fall back to a more consolidated line within his realm. After some two months of hostilities, Napoleon lost the battle of Leipzig, the Austrians took Laibach and Spalato, and were investing Trent and Trieste. Both fell on October 30.

In Dalmatia, Zara and most of its surroundings were in Allied hands by late autumn. Aided and supplied by a British squadron under Captain Hoste, Habsburg troops commanded by General Tommasich had quickly moved down the Eastern Adriatic coast. Complications accompanied these successes. From various quarters efforts had been made to spur Croatian national pride and feeling into an open rising against the French, and to establish influence — especially in the faction-torn former republics of

2 Metternich

Ragusa and Cattaro — after the capitulation of the French forces. While Austrian commanders had appealed to Croats and Dalmatians to reaffirm loyalty to the House of Habsburg, Captain Hoste of the Royal Navy and Colonel Nikitsch of the Imperial Russian Army had arrived upon the scene promising freedom and protection to the inhabitants.[1] Such activities, as well as the deftly-organized intrigues of the politically ambitious Metropolitan of Montenegro, caused the Austrians in Dalmatia no end of annoyance.[2] Furthermore, there had been a strange undertaking of Archduke Ferdinand of Austria-Este. This bright but rash brother-in-law of Kaiser Franz had led on his own initiative and cost a landing on the Dalmatian coast in the autumn of 1813 in the hope of turning the population against the French occupiers. However, this unauthorized adventure was considered inopportune and produced for the emperor a distaste akin to that felt four years earlier during the unsanctioned Tyrol uprising. Equally unenthused was Metternich's Staatskanzlei, which had taken scrupulous caution before the commencement of hostilities to avoid any disturbances on its southeastern frontier, especially among the "Illyrian nation",[3] and did not welcome unlooked-for and unnecessary bother in this area even if in the guise of a patriotic undertaking. The meek explanations of the would-be-hero archduke to Metternich and also to the Staatskanzlei's "second-in-command" — Hudelist — found little sympathy;[4] the concern of the Austrian foreign minister regarding Dalmatia had concentrated largely on establishing Viennese authority and on requesting his British and Russian colleagues — Castlereagh and Nesselrode — to recall their respective agents there.[5]

Long before the Allies, the French had recognized the potentialities inherent in Croatian and Illyrian "national feeling", but their early efforts to gain confidence and affection through the favoring of the Croatian language were all too soon forgotten. Their attempt to create among the troops levied in Illyria a Croatian *esprit de corps* soon buckled under the burdens of war; what finally emerged was an *esprit* not at all to French liking. In the end, the Illyrian Provinces were bled white — so it seemed at least to the Austrians entering these stretches of land. According to General Lattermann, the Austrian commander in Illyria and a man quite sensitive to Illyrian problems, the most unfortunate victims of the French regime had been Croatian youths who had often and deliberately been pressed into service far from their home for no other reason — so Lattermann assured Metternich — than "to nip in the bud their national spirit".[6] The general's indignation was justified at least inasmuch as the Austrians did not intend such action. But on the other hand, after having taken possession of the Illyrian Provinces, they did not intend to encourage national feelings either, whose consequences they were to encounter soon enough.

During the drawn-out Italian campaign, Austrian, British, and, later, Neapolitan commanders had been even more free in their appeals to "national spirit" as a useful weapon against the French. Especially the British commander in the Mediterranean, Lord Bentinck, had long unveiled the prospects of liberation and national independence to the Italians. Nor did the Austrian generals Nugent and Hiller hesitate to resort to similar exhortations during their advance on the peninsula, apparently without realizing the political implications of such tactics. But then, there was no clear and definite policy even in the highest political reserves, since this depended largely upon the outcome of the military operations. Just as Allied diplomats revised the future limits of France with every battle, the swift turn of events in Italy had often deprived many avowals or declarations, which allied representatives generously had made, of the official backing of foreign ministries already moved to new positions. Lord Bentinck, for example, followed in time an ever more independent course by stubbornly clinging to his personal convictions and acting accordingly. With such divergence of purpose, in spite of political directives issued to area commanders, one can understand that an abundance of promises — while not necessarily implying falsehood — often enough awakened false hopes.

Partly at least, such divergence was due to the slow correlation of aims between the incongruous forces now bent upon the overthrow of Napoleon in Italy. As has happened more than once in the run of history, a mobilization of all forces to insure victory of what seemed a just cause sometimes included partners of questionable character. Because they appeared indispensable, they became acceptable and thus it was with the marshal-made-king, Joachim Murat. Unlike the other Napoleonic lieutenant in Italy, Viceroy Eugene, who withstood all Allied offers to the end, King Joachim did not hesitate to desert his brother-in-law Napoleon in order to keep the crown which he had received from him. After the battle of Leipzig, he made overtures to the Allies; Metternich entered into negotiations with Murat as readily as Bentinck did reluctantly. Now, paradoxically, but as was to be expected, Bentinck's old adversary became the loudest proponent of an independent Italy — to be united of course under King Joachim I. With the need to check the Napoleonite effectively, the British attitude came to acquiesce in seeing a stronger Habsburg hand in Northern Italy, and as a consequence, abandoned the thought of Italian independence as a serious political consideration — a thought which might have fared differently had Austria remained the sole power factor on the peninsula.

By late autumn, the campaign in Italy had bogged down. In the second week of December, Field Marshal Heinrich Bellegarde was given command of the inadequately equipped Austrian forces in Italy; on the 15th he arrived at headquarters in Vicenza. Four weeks later, Murat had signed a treaty of alliance with the Austrians. The Neapolitans soon had Rome, Bologna, and various Apennine passes in their hands, and now moved further into Tuscany; they failed, however, to effect a junction with the Austrians who, on February 8, had become involved in the heaviest engagement of the Italian war through a vain attempt to cross the Mincio. However, Murat's presence in Tuscany had embroiled him in such disagreeable squabbles with Bentinck that he began to think of a rapprochement with Napoleon. At this time Nugent, Bentinck, Murat, and even Bellegarde were separately calling upon the Italian population not only to recognize their respective forces as liberators but to fight for its national independence. The general enthusiasm and spirit of the campaign was such that even the usually cautious Marshal Bellegarde permitted himself to be carried away, proclaiming on February 4, 1814, from Verona that Italians would enjoy the bounties of national independence and that the Alps would resume their ancient function of natural boundaries.[7]

Naturally, as the military strength of the enemy diminished, the individual political interests of the Allies came to outshadow the urgencies of military cooperation. Finally, after a sufficient exertion of diplomatic pressure and a reminder from Castlereagh to Bentinck "that the object is to promote union and to put aside every minor consideration",[8] a concerted effort against the viceroy was gotten under way. It finished the Italian campaign as the war in France ended. On April 11, Napoleon had abdicated and five days later his stepson Eugene had capitulated (Convention of Schiarino-Rizzino). The viceroy was permitted, however, by the terms of the convention, to dispatch envoys to Paris to plead for the preservation of his kingdom. On April 28, an Austrian contingent under General Neipperg entered Milan.

The frequency alone of appeals to "national spirit" in Italy and Illyria attests the Allies' confidence in finding many ready listeners. Certainly, in both lands a good number of politically articulate individuals — although of quite differing social strata and conviction — were stirred by more than just a desire to shake off the French and were aware of their people's common tradition, language, customs, and history — in short, aware of a national identity. This realization led, in the moment of interregnum, to independent political initiative which had for the Austrians onerous consequences, first because Austria had to suppress it, and secondly, because it was never quite forgotten. Accompanying such difficulties of a political nature were economic ones. Both gave rise to discontent already widespread before the Austrians were really established in the territories now in their charge.

Indeed, any thought of political dignity for Illyria was confined for the most part to the Croatian estates or to prominent spokesmen such as Bishop Vrhovac of Agram. But then, nation-conscious Croatian Illyrians recalled a great Croatian kingdom in times past and the special separate status occasionally accorded the "Illyrian nation" within the Habsburg empire in the previous century. They had not forgotten their grievances against Hungary and had begun to take an interest in the southern Slavic tongues. The French party among the Illyrians had scarcely been significant and had quickly evaporated after the evacuation of the forces they had served. The Croatian estates now hoped to gain from the emperor of Austria — whom they had more reason to trust than the king of Hungary — a confirmation of old rights which they now asserted.[9] The proud representatives of the "Illyrian nation" did not realize that they had hoped for too much until a stiff attitude from Vienna caused them to waver between a resigned compliance and a rebellious defiance.

According to the reports of the police administrator, Baron Haager, a good majority of the Illyrian population was pro-Austrian during the spring of 1814 and expected a return to an Austrian administration — although to an improved one.[10] A deputation was sent to the emperor; its address to the monarch was filled with expressions of relief, felicity and hope. It put forth the wish of "the nation", now freed from foreign oppression and joined once more to the grand *Völkerfamilie*, to benefit from the considerate and mild rule of a fatherly monarch and stated confidently that an application of imperial welfare would heal the Illyrians' wounds, enabling them "to forget that [they] were for a time unhappy".[11] As long as his subjects' desires were confined to such declarations of homage, Kaiser Franz was disposed to answer kindly. His reply, duly edited by Metternich's Staatskanzlei, was typical for the occasion:

The severest sacrifice to which I, as ruler of a great Empire, had to acquiesce during a long row of stormy years was the separation of loyal provinces from the main body of the state. Only a system based on the destruction of all concepts of order could have required such sacrifices as Mine. Nature herself has destined the southern provinces of Austria to be an essential part of a blessed whole. Now that the evil is rooted out, its painful effects shall also disappear. You shall return for ever more under the scepter of My House. You have demonstrated during years of trial that you — true to the memories of your fathers — can face any test. I shall keep My special attention on your welfare and shall get your provinces to flourish once more. A pleasant prospect opens before us: Europe shall enjoy many years of peace, and a few shall suffice to heal your wounds. You are sure to find in Me the same well-meaning father to whom you have given so many — and never unnoticed — examples of touching loyalty.[12]

Such soothing phrases, however, had little concrete meaning, and enthusiasm at deliverance and new prospects waned quickly with the waiting for improvements long in coming. This enthusiasm, volatile in its very nature, was often tied to sometimes conflicting desires and sentiments which the Austrian authorities could not always approve; they soon enough found themselves in embarrassing situations: in parts of Carniola, for example, some groups refused to pay *Urbarialabgaben*, insisting that the French law still in force had abolished feudal servitude.[13] General Lattermann was obliged to deny publicly the validity of such assertions.[14] Naturally, occurances of this sort only played into the hands of those pressing for an immediate reintroduction of the Austrian law code into the Illyrian territories. Moreover, certain circles of the population were becoming, according to Haager, increasingly disgruntled with still unrevoked French administrative and legal practices.[15] Furthermore, premature and naïve hopes for a quick reduction of taxes led to loud murmuring and even louder tumults.[16]

The estates in the meantime had begun to press for a restoration of their old *Landesverfassung*.[17] General Lattermann in Laibach was soon confronted with what the Viennese authorities labelled an "Illyrian insurrection", and fell into temporary disgrace for failing to prevent the gathering of a general congregation of Illyrian Croats in "the spirit of the Hungarian constitution". This action, which took place at Karlstadt in March, 1814, was of course against all imperial wishes, and Lattermann was hard put for explanations, which — as was to be expected — found slight acceptance.[18] The independent attitude which the Illyrian estates were capable of showing culminated on June 24, 1814, as they balked at rendering a new oath to "the promotion of the weal of the Austrian Empire". Further, they appealed to the "King" (of Croatia) not to separate them from their brethren across the Save nor to place them under a German administration. Emphasizing their national tradition, they lamented their fate:

It breaks our hearts that we, the purest descendants of those Croats who settled this land in the year 648, we descendants of those who established over 1000 years ago a free kingdom, we who had to give everything for the defense and security of Your Majesty, we who suffered so much in Byzantine, Venetian, and Turkish wars and who suffered the loss of a greater part of our kingdom to save other lands, we who have in so many ways shown our unshakeable loyalty to Your Majesty's illustrious House, that we should find ourselves, as a result of the pains and tried loyalty of our fathers, on the brink of destruction — torn from our brothers and stem, until we shall shortly even suffer in similar fashion the loss of home, our people's name, language, and tradition. One denies us not a favor but our own good rights.[19]

Italians too had their traditions and an especially strong awareness of their cultural heritage. Yet the very things which could make them proud to call themselves Italians could remind them that they were Venetians, Lombards, Florentines, or Romans. Historic particularism was still a compelling force on the Italian peninsula — a fact which came to form a premise of Metternich's Italian policy. True, the very name *Regno d'Italia* had had a magic ring for many — but not for all. A Venetian, for example, might well have wondered: what had his Venice really gained from being a part of this Napoleonic structure? Had not the French ruler destroyed the cherished (if moribund) republic, partitioned its old domains and finally annexed Dalmatia to the French Empire? Had he not wrecked what was left of Venetian commerce and prosperity with his abominable continental system and had he not humiliated the proud city of San Marco by subordinating it to Milan? The Lombard city, to be sure, was not spared the exactions of the Napoleonic wars. Many of its banking houses had collapsed, many of its best families were on the brink of ruin,[20] and many of its sons had not returned. But in contrast to Venice, Milan had tasted splendor. It had been a European capital and had housed a royal court; it had been the site of an extensive administrative apparatus which had provided rank and dignity to thousands. Having experienced an upsurge of activity and importance, it was unthinkable that it might sink once more into provincial insignificance. No wonder then that the Milanese welcome for the Austrians lacked the jubilant tones heard in Venice. But the tinge of reserve occasionally noticeable in the royal city was not due to any particular love of the French. There had existed a vigorous Francophile faction in Milan to the very end, but the majority of the population — disillusioned as it was — had, by then, come to scorn the French as foreigners quite as much as did other Italians. Many had welcomed the French as representatives of a great power which not only held the fate of the world in its hands but which would change the world, and especially Italy, for the better. This wonderful vision was dispelled for some sooner, for others later, and many who dreamed of a united Italian kingdom were constantly reminded that a Frenchman was king of a patch-work Italian state and that some of the fairest stretches of their peninsula were classified as departments of the French Empire.

Such feelings did not prevent many Italians from expressing admiration for the clear logic of French ways, for the dispatch of the French administrative system, and for the concise, lucid single body of French law. The Declaration of the Rights of Man had still excited many in a time when its application had already been conveniently limited. Ostentatious public works, support of various cultural activities, display of all sorts had been popular. The dash and flair of the eager and confident French once had delighted the Italian temperament — something which in later times was perhaps wistfully recalled in dealing with a sober and pedantic German officialdom. Even more, French initiative in establishing an "Italian" state had earned Italian gratitude.[21] Italian taste for French faculties was all too often forgotten by the incoming Austrians, who assumed that Italian distaste for French presence was sufficient to assure them the affections of those they had liberated.

Inasmuch as the Austrians were the harbingers of peace and order, they were hailed by all who had sickened of revolution and two decades of war. In this role the Austrians sincerely believed, and in the fulfillment of its duty they saw the justification for their presence south of the Alps. Then, too, numerous Italians were at the moment more concerned with their day-to-day existence than with political contemplations; they could only turn to Austria in their hope for quick alleviation.[22] But despite either political apathy or even sympathy for Austria, Italian national consciousness re-mained — even more formidable after its French supports had fallen away. The center of this consciousness continued to be Milan.

Although it is beyond the scope of this work to describe fully either the extent of Italian national feeling or independent political initiative among Italians north of the Po, some epitomizing might nevertheless be appro-priate. The strength and popularity of the "so-called Italian spirit" was such that discerning Austrians, and especially Metternich, could not help but feel uneasy. Desperate hopes had accompanied the brief moment in which independence had seemed a possibility; once past, the hopeful re-signed to the inevitable — disappointed and chagrined. Those who had hoped the most carried the deepest scars, and later on lifted the loudest voices. That, on the other hand, the vicissitudes of defeat and collapse had temporarily burdened with personal cares a great many Italians otherwise eagerly concerned for national dignity may have let it appear as if the expressions of national sentiment were but those of an easily-handled minority. Many less perceptive Austrians were thus misled; some never came to realize that there were men not content simply with peace and order.

National and liberal sentiments had grown rapidly throughout the peninsula. They had been fostered for two decades — multifariously and paradoxically — by French influence and rule, at first approvingly, then despite it, and had furthermore found sympathy and support in British pronouncements. These sentiments had produced since the outbreak of the French Revolution a voluminous amount of patriotic literature — among it a series of definite and sometimes far-ranging proposals for establishing a new order of things.[23] The primary aim of such projects was invariably some form of Italian political coherence. Of secondary rank were the questions of form and constitution, of the source and initiative and sponsorship of such undertaking, and of the title and name of this structure's head. Here the Italian idealists explored every possibility, drew upon the most diverse institutions, sought parallels and inspiration from the widest areas, and came to the most dissimilar conclusions. Such projects were discussed and stirred imaginations; some found acceptance with various political groups as concrete programs.

In the spring of 1814, there were in Northern Italy various parties whose strength now was determined by the shifting power-relationship between France and Austria. The French party and those whose fortunes were tied to Eugene's saw the Italian idea expressed somewhat sufficiently in the French-created Kingdom of Italy. All their efforts were directed toward maintaining the existing regime, with or, if need be, without the viceroy. For this goal they had sought to gain Allied approval. After the April-uprising against the French in Milan, such aspirations were fairly well dispelled and with them the French party as a political factor. The two important groups remaining were the so-called "pure Italian" (*Italici puri*) or independence party, and the Austrophile faction *(Austriacanti)*. Emboldened by the stroke against the French regime, the "Italian" faction took control and set out to realize their program of independence for at least the area of the former kingdom.[24] As it became clear that this was impossible, opinions grew divided, and the more realistic began to work for some sort of compromise with Austria and thereby came close to the program of those pro-Austrian Lombards and Venetians who wished for an extensive autonomy within the Habsburg empire.

The increasing number of those who looked to Austria were, of course, not all of the same blend. There was the older generation and especially those of the old nobility who had lost privilege and status through the French. This group in particular could recall a period of benign Habsburg rule which, after twenty years of disorder, seemed like golden days. Perhaps their nostalgia hindered them in understanding neither the harsh problems with which the Austrians came to be faced nor why the Austrians now did not rule with the facility of former times. Nor could they understand their sons who did not share their fathers' memories, who looked to the future instead of the past and refused to be content with the thought that order and justice as administered by Austria were sufficient to assure an Italian happiness and prosperity. The house of the Counts Confalonieri provides a touching example of how such dissension could strain the relationship between father and son.

At best, the "nationally-minded" who turned to Austria necessarily or willingly had hoped for an independent realm ruled over by a Habsburg prince. At least, they desired an autonomous entity governed by an Austrian archduke-viceroy whose position and status was to equal Eugene's. Upon this latter wish, Metternich came to form his policy for Lombardy-Venetia; as it failed to materialize, an ever-swelling group was to abandon all confidence in Austria and leave it with an ever-dwindling number of supporters in the Italian territories. The disenchanted ultimately were to turn to the irreconcilables, who had never given up their program for national union, independence, and a constitutional regime.

Independent political initiative in Northern Italy was a much more serious matter for Austria than it had been in Illyria, not only because it extended itself to broader levels of the population, but because it had become a matter of international attention. As Milan lay in political twilight, representatives of the still existing governmental institutions proceeded to act as free agents. Already on April 18, two days after the capitulation of the viceroy, the Senate of the Kingdom of Italy had voted to dispatch three of its members to Paris to plead for the integrity of the kingdom and to put in a good word for Eugene. However, the mission never reached France. One of the delegates, strangely enough, was to have been the reluctant Count Guicciardi, who had little sympathy for the viceroy's cause. At the same time, demands began to be heard that Italy follow the example of Spain and Germany in throwing off the French yoke.[25] Popular sentiment began to run high against what was called the French regime; its opponents insisted that not the Senate — handpicked by Napoleon —, but rather the electoral colleges possessed authority to speak for the "nation".[26]

On April 20, 1814, public emotions in Northern Italy reached the bursting point. On that day the French finally handed Venice over to the Austrians. As a spirited crowd shouted acclamation to the Austrians, some enraged groups gave vent to their pent-up feelings, accumulated during a six-months' siege; these shouted vengeance against the French and began a hunt for French personnel still remaining in the city until Austrian troops stopped them. Such an outburst — especially among a people accustomed to show its feelings — might easily have swept away all order and authority. But in Venice, whose future had already been settled by treaty arrangements,[27] the presence of Austrian forces prevented an emotional eruption from assuming serious political character. On the same April 20, after some seething and plotting, Milan's population furiously turned against the remnants of the French regime. In the Lombard city, whose future still seemed an open question, there was at this moment no Austrian force to hold down popular passion; here an emotional flood provided the opportunity for the mob to lynch the finance minister Prina and for a small but resolute group to grasp the reins of their "nation's" fate. The Senate was deprived of its authority. Initiative and control fell to the electoral colleges, which convened on April 22; on the next day delegates were hastily sent off to the Allied commanders on the peninsula and to Allied headquarters in Paris to negotiate for recognition and independence of the provisionally governed *Regno d'Italia*.

During the following fortnight, the project of an independent state, ruled possibly by a prince of the Habsburg House or perhaps even under English protection, was the general topic of conversation.[28] On April 25, the Milanese Count Porro-Lambertenghi broached this subject to Field Marshal Bellegarde as he was requesting Allied protection for his government. The marshal's reply, just as the inclination and tone of the British representatives, seemed so well disposed that the provisional government could allow itself some optimism.

On April 26, Viceroy Eugene bade his cherished Italy farewell. His exit was coupled with the entrance into Milan of the first Austrian officials — Sommariva and Strassoldo, arriving, it is well to note, in the name of the Allied Powers.[29] Two days later, 14,000 Austrian troops followed. On that day, a delegation was sent to Bellegarde, still in Verona, which reaffirmed the generally held sentiments regarding independence and an Austrian prince.[30] On May 4, the colleges in Milan, encouraged by what they took to be British acquiescence, unanimously proclaimed independence, not knowing that by this time they no longer held their fortune in their hands: in Paris, Lombardy had already been granted to Austria.[31]

On May 3, Federigo Confalonieri, a member of an independent Milanese deputation in Paris, knew that the game was up. The day thereafter, in a letter to his wife, Teresa, he mourned a dream:

A month ago we were still in time to take some step toward our political existence, now nothing remains for us but to implore for it. Will it be granted to us? Austria is the arbitress, the absolute mistress of our destiny. Thus has been changed the scope of our mission. There is no question any more of demanding from the Allied Powers a liberal constitution, independence, a kingdom, etc. etc., there is only the question of imploring for that which a patron will be willing to grant![32]

By this time, Bellegarde apparently knew too.[33] He already considered the problem of reconciling public opinion to the abolition of the electoral colleges. On May 6, Count Litta, who had been commissioned by the Paris deputation to lay its cause before Prince Metternich, was courteously received by the Austrian minister. To his implorations, however, was given the one reply which dispelled all further pretensions of independent political initiative: the right of conquest. Nevertheless, Metternich agreed that an autonomous kingdom of Italy, under Austrian rule and administered by an Austrian archduke, might well be admissible.[34]

It is debatable whether one may take seriously Metternich's professed reluctance at the incorporation of Lombardy and with it Milan, the hotbed of Italian national feeling. The urgent necessity of "rooting out Italian Jacobinism in Milan" and of safeguarding other Austrian possessions in Italy — the minister later let it be known — had forced him to acquiesce to this measure.[35] Indeed, Milan as a free rallying point of nationalistic intrigues against the Habsburg Empire would have confronted Austria with a really threatening if not impossible situation. News of Milanese turbulance possibly influenced — or justified *post rem* — the Allied decision to award Lombardy to Austria.

On May 7, the Paris delegation was granted an audience with Kaiser Franz, who made clear the way things stood: "You belong to Me . . . by right of conquest. I cherish you as My good subjects and as such, nothing shall be dearer to My heart than your welfare." Yet, he too, deigned to favor the idea of a kingdom which he thought to name after the ancient Germanic Langobards.[36]

All additional endeavors or discussions were anticlimactic. In Milan, continued expressions of the desire for national independence were received by Austrian officials with patience but also with mounting irritation. As

soon as Bellegarde had entered the city on May 8 at the head of 12,000
men, he was sought out by various delegations[37] to whom he could but say,
as kindly and as sympathetically as he might, that he was competent only
to refer their requests to a higher authority. Soon Sommariva and Strassoldo were compelled to act against all-too-freely voiced demands for national independence. Then, however, definite word came from Paris, and
finally on May 24 the president of the provisional regency admitted that
all further efforts toward independence were useless; rather, future efforts
should be dedicated toward obtaining the widest possible self-government:
the Italian territories should rank as a kingdom; they should be accorded
"national representation" and laws conforming to the customs and needs of
the inhabitants.[38] This program was no longer a diplomatic matter but an
internal affair; it was also a last hope: the consequence with which Metternich attempted to have it realized shall be a major concern of this
work.

On May 25, Bellegarde officially took charge of Lombardy in the name
of His Imperial and Apostolic Majesty. He had the provisional government and, with it, the electoral colleges, abolished. On June 12, 1814, in
Milan, the Peace of Paris was made known and the annexation was proclaimed ("Le vostre provincie sono definitivamente incorporate all'Impero
d'Austria"). On that same day, the deputation in Paris disbanded.

FORMATION OF POLICY FOR THE CONQUERED
TERRITORIES

The Emperor

Although Kaiser Franz left most political thinking to Metternich and
devoted himself largely to dynastic and administrative affairs, he nonetheless held firm notions on the composition of the state and the position
of the monarch within it. Inherited from the "enlightened" policies of his
illustrious predecessors, but carefully tempered by bitter experience, these
notions assumed with him in time an inflexibility which precluded any
innovation. As applied to problems of reorganization and nationality, they
made for a rather singular approach against which Metternich's complete
skill could not always prevail. Because Kaiser Franz scarcely distinguished
the interests of the Austrian state from those of the Habsburg House, and
because of inclinations of his character, his conception of state was a very
personal one. With remarkable frequency the adjective *My* accompanied

every sort of official designation. Because for the emperor the prerogatives of the monarch could only be conceived of as cloaked with unchallenged authority, and because all authority and initiative could emanate only from the monarch, no sort of independent political initiative could be tolerated. Provincial assemblies or estates were allowed to exist only through the pleasure of the monarch and only with the right to approve imperial measures. In upholding imperial authority, Kaiser Franz could range far in his choice of arguments. Whereas he often either refused to recognize outright French enactions or only occasionally and grudgingly conceded them merit, he readily recognized the validity of a French abolition of such institutions which might have encroached upon his prerogatives or which he otherwise was not anxious to revive. In this manner, he flatly dismissed any discussion of a self-undertaken restoration of the Illyrian estates.[39]

Furthermore, any other self-asserted rights or claims to legitimacy based on tradition or continued existence, as well as demands for the re-establishment of former assemblies or *national* chancelleries for Italy or Illyria, were discounted on the grounds that conquest by the emperor's armies had in effect created a *tabula rasa.* Thus he reasoned in shelving Hungarian claims to the former coastal possessions now part of the Illyrian Provinces or in expressing his will on the future of still existing institutions of the former Kingdom of Italy:

> Since these lands have been conquered, there can be no discussion of constitution, Senate, or any other bodies or representations. Consequently, the electoral colleges, in so far as this has not already been done, are to be dismissed, and no one, other than [Bellegarde] or the Provisional Government are to make decisions or give orders in My name.[40]

Therefore, the emperor held all claims made in the newly-won territories as lacking legal foundation. All other questions regarding the extent, privileges, title, and rank of the territories within his realm the emperor reserved for his own convenient consideration and disposal.

To be sure, Kaiser Franz, on his part, took pains to show the absolute monarch as a paternal and benevolent father and to display sincere concern for the welfare of his subjects. In his addresses to deputations from his various lands, allusions to this concern were seldom lacking. All the emperor's efforts were bent on establishing an exemplary administration: could not the maintenance of a rigid but enlightened absolutism be justified in the long run by a happy and prosperous populace? National feelings or political implications inherent in such feelings were beyond the horizon of Kaiser

Franz, who almost from the beginning occupied himself chiefly with matters usually reserved for administrative officials of medium rank but not for the ruler of a vast empire. His conceptions of state, especially regarding the future status of the new territories within his empire, were peculiarly formalistic and were seconded by a small group of advisors as devoted to centralism as he was.

Metternich

"We are negotiating as bravely as the army is battling," remarked Metternich with some self-satisfaction, as Allied diplomats were deliberating Napoleon's prospects and contemplating the manner of Europe's reconstruction.[41] A brisk activity was spurred on by the coming end; yet the exhilaration at achieving victory was dampened soon enough by the sobering reminder of all the unsolved and burning problems which waited around the corner. These problems involved not only claims to compensation or restoration of previous standing through a statistical accounting of souls and square miles but also the fate of whole peoples, and brought into question the future of unpopular and compromised regimes which had nonetheless managed to hang on to their existence. "How can these peoples, aroused as they are to the utmost," Metternich had asked anxiously, "ever be brought back again to accept regimes which they despise beyond all bounds?"[42]

The agitated and even alarming atmosphere prevailing on nearly all of the Habsburg frontiers meant, as far as the Austrian foreign minister was concerned, that the task of pacification was by no means confined to pushing back the French might beyond the Rhine. Even more than in Italy, a war of liberation had torn open German sensibility to common bonds and greatness; even more than the Germans, the Poles wished for one political structure for all their countrymen[43] and had numerous spokesmen — as did the Italians, especially in London — to court official and public opinion for a restoration of national independence; more than the Poles, the Serbs had shown themselves ready to risk their all in a bitter and smoldering rebellion, which Hudelist had likened to a Vendée,[44] to cast off the Turkish yoke. And yet, the dilemma was that a yielding to such still unbridled political passions would have spelled the dissolution of the very concentrations of power which had made possible the liberation of Europe from the French imperium, and which alone could guarantee, outwardly at least, the stability of the peace in the coming years.

Above all, the so-called "spirit of the times" haunted any conscientious meditation on a recreating of European order. Gentz, whose correspondence with Metternich had grown during this time to an almost daily exchange, had brought up the possibility of having to give ground somewhat to the "stream of the times",[45] and Metternich himself had even professed as his eternal and fundamental principle that "events which can not be hindered must be led!"[46] Whether the minister referred at this particular moment to two main tributaries of this "stream" — the striving for national union and independence, and a fancy for constitutions — we can leave to conjecture. We shall see that in time Metternich not only dedicated special attention to them,[47] but sought to channel these currents into modified and acceptable forms. Such currents were not, of course, to be restricted to one area; their universal character made for an eventually spreading pattern, and often enough nationalists of one people came to draw upon the struggles of another for their inspiration — a disturbing thought for any Austrian minister. During the last phase of the Italian campaign, the young but observant aide-de-camp of Bellegarde — Baron Hügel — had noted among Italians a large number of men with whom the idea of an "Italian nation formed into one great Italian state" had taken root. If this people could carry out this idea, so he mused prophetically, then perhaps "the German people would follow the example."[48]

Certainly Metternich and field-commanders like Lattermann or Bellegarde knew how to distinguish between what they took to be "allowable" national desires and the more radical programs — the one earning as much sympathy as the other disapproval. Of immediate concern in the newly occupied lands, then, was the intensity in general of national spirit, and the strength in particular of groups advocating a course of action contrary to Allied dispositions. It remained for the Austrian minister to see to it that the supervision of such groups was carefully coordinated and that their isolation was rendered effective by barring all encouragement from without. If Metternich had to resort to diplomatic pressure to deter the activities of foreign personnel in the Illyrian Provinces, the same was true on an even larger scale in Italy.

On the Apennine peninsula, Metternich had from the beginning urged accelerated military operations[49] so as to have something in hand. His general aim had been to see Habsburg might and influence fill the vacuum resulting from the collapse of the French imperium while keeping British and Neapolitan influence down and, simultaneously, to coordinate Allied policy, insofar as it existed, so that any Austrian demands could be carried forward with full Allied approbation. Various circumstances, however, had caused Metternich to relegate Italian matters to the sidelines. Not only had the fate of Napoleon drawn most of his attention, but the slow progress of Austrian arms beyond Venetia and the still problematic position of Viceroy Eugene had made for a certain delay in decisions; and early in 1814, Metternich could still feel that it might be just as well if, for the time being, "the fate of Italy were to remain in a state of suspense".[50] It seemed sufficient to have Field Marshal Bellegarde appear as a liberator of the Italians from foreign oppression.[51]

Nonetheless, even in the first phases of the campaign, the doings of Murat and Bentinck had begun to worry the Staatskanzlei.[52] Bentinck's lip-service to the idea of Italian union, an Italian constitution and a great Italian state,[53] and reports of his displaying banners inscribed with the words "Independence for Italy and liberty for the Italian people!"[54] especially forced Metternich to firm action. He was able to convince Lord Castlereagh that an urgent admonition of the British commander was in order. How much value the moderate British minister set on Allied accord is evident in his unmistakable language to Bentinck.[55] The happy relationship of complete mutual trust between the Austrian and the British statesmen — each frequently entrusted his dispatches to the other's courier — was the special delight of Metternich.[56] His satisfaction with Castlereagh and at having reached, as he thought, such perfect harmony of opinion was sometimes accompanied by a good dose of self-satisfaction as well.[57] Yet it was one thing personally to secure the agreement of Castlereagh and quite another to secure the obedience of the far-away Bentinck. The latter's independent actions persisted and it is no wonder that they brought Baron Hügel to express a general Austrian attitude: "It appears as if the English wish for a state of things in Italy quite contrary to our own interests."[58] Only slowly, and after the definite annexation of the Italian territories by the Habsburgs, did the activities of the English agents subside, but by then the damage had been done. Despite Metternich's and Castlereagh's efforts and despite the officially restrained British course, British liberal sentiment — with its open sympathy for the Italian cause and as expressed by British representatives on the peninsula — had contributed its measure to a further whetting of Italian national consciousness.[59]

For Metternich, one of the irritating things about Bentinck was not just that his conduct could be disdained as that of a "revolutionary fool" deserving every reprimand,[60] but much more that his misdirected idealism had led him to assume quite falsely that the Italians everywhere were capable of expelling the French in great part through their own efforts.[61] Thereby was implied not only that the Italians were able to coordinate their political aims, but that the Austrian presence in Italy was deprived of

3 Metternich

a legitimate *raison d'être*. Bentinck and such irritations aside, Metternich believed in April, 1814, that the general prospects for Austria south of the Alps had become attractive indeed,[62] at least as far as acquisitions and influence were concerned. It would be, so he stated, but a matter of the emperor's forming *sur les champs* Italian governments in a land which had — as Metternich claimed — "in every sense of the word become a *res nullius*".[63] However, he had already come to regard the Italian issue as a "moral question" of a most delicate nature and had joined to this observation the thought: "but I don't fear it as long as there occur no *große Dummheiten*."[64] Therewith Metternich's solicitude for Italy struck as early as the spring of 1814 the note which, in varying degree, it was to sound henceforth: a pleasant outward optimism accompanied by a disharmonious overtone of apprehension.

At the beginning of May, 1814, the territorial regulations in Italy having been settled, Metternich formulated the basic points from which his Italian policy would now proceed. After necessary deliberations and concurrence, both monarch and minister sent on May 15, 1814, instructions from Paris to Bellegarde in Milan.[65]

Metternich also dispatched some copies, including his own comments, to Hudelist in Vienna, thus informing the two men most closely associated with a successful application of his views. (The imperial instructions had made Bellegarde accountable for the moment for civil as well as military matters in Lombardy;[66] Hudelist was entrusted with running the Staatskanzlei in Metternich's absence and represented it at the meetings of the state conference.) As expected, the emperor's main care was to acquaint the marshal with territorial dispositions, administrative procedures, assertions of imperial authority, and denials of independent political action in the manner already noted — arguments which Metternich could only underline. The minister reserved for himself observations which might supplement the imperial message and serve as points of departure for Bellegarde's future official deportment; they can be reduced to one subject: Italian national feeling — its weight and counterweight.

First of all, Metternich drew Bellegarde's attention to the existence of a state of mind in Italy which could in no way be supported by Austria. This "Italian spirit", which Metternich was usually careful to label "so-called" was cultivated to a large degree, he pointed out, by such non-Italians as Napoleon, Murat, and Bentinck; he was even compelled to admit that "a few of our own people" had had an effective hand "in this business". As a result, the emperor was faced with a deputation calling itself "Italian" (to be sure, it was admitted only as a Milanese one) which did not hesitate to request recognition of an independent kingdom. Then, failing in this, the group wanted to have the emperor assume the title "King of Italy". It was of course out of the question, Metternich declared, that the monarch accept such a hollow and incorrect title — one which would not only stir up fantasies and cause disorders in the neighboring states, but which implied pretension and encroachment, and thus would perpetuate a chronic instability upon the peninsula. To assure the pacification of the peninsula — and this was always to be the prime aim of Metternich's Italian policy — it was mandatory above all to render innocuous what he called this "*prétention italienne*". Here Metternich advocated as an effective counterpoise "*le morcellement de l'Italie*" which, he hastened to add, was quite in conformity with the position of the Allied Powers and which merely recognized an age-old situation. His favorite and, as he thought, convincing premise was that perpetual local hates and jealousies in Italy had always prevented or survived any attempt at integration.[67] Conversely, the Italian situation being as it was, it would only be sensible for Austria to take advantage of it. To combat the "Italian spirit", Metternich emphasized, "we shall try to rekindle the Lombard spirit." The emperor thus intended to take the title "King of Lombardy",[68] to preserve the "Order of the Iron Crown", and to add this ancient Lombard royal symbol to the imperial coat-of-arms.

But the very premise which served to support the argument for Italian regionalism also was able to threaten the attempt to create an effective regional esprit for the entire Austro-Italian area. The predicament arising from the fact that Austria possessed Venetia as well as Lombardy did not escape Metternich. Should the proposed Lombard Kingdom — as quite naturally the Milanese would wish — be extended over Venetia or should it be confined to Lombardy proper? The answer to this important question was to be based on the wishes of the inhabitants.[69] However, even if the recent importance of Milan spoke for a solution in its favor, so he added, its awkward geographical position and the undeniable "worth" of Venice — whose state of mind he described as "less corrupt" than the Milanese — spoke against it. In any case, the Lombards had to know beyond a doubt that their future was tied completely to Austria. As a last thought, the minister enjoined the marshal to direct his attention to the isle of Elba which, he thought, it was difficult not to regard as a potential volcano.

The idea of an archduke-viceroy, which both Metternich and Bellegarde regarded favorably[70] and later championed fervently, was not mentioned; perhaps it was inopportune to do so in conjunction with the imperial instructions. Furthermore, Metternich remained silent on methods of administration. From Bellegarde, at least, he had no reason to fear a reactionary course capable of arousing popular feeling and threatening anew hard-gained peace and order. His anxiety over such a possibility elsewhere had induced him more than once to urge various Italian governments to moderation.[71]

Since the issue of the newly-acquired territories' political status within the framework of the empire remained undecided, immediate dealing with their populations was confined to the administrative level. There, unless a politically conceived formula for some regional autonomy was soon to be forthcoming, would be the only meeting ground where such populations might expect consideration for national character and customs and where, in return, the Austrians might gain some affection. There, then, was to take place a crucial encounter which determined whether Italians and Illyrians were to regard their new rulers as alien or not. Thus the question now before us is: what principles guided the Austrian authorities as they set out to provide an administration for their newly gained non-German subjects?

ADMINISTRATIVE CONSIDERATIONS

The Emperor

The anarchy following French withdrawal from Italy and Illyria called for quick preliminary measures to restore order. Sometimes the Austrians were able to revert to tried practice. In Dalmatia, they dusted off institutions of Venetian heritage which had been useful during the earlier occupation of 1797. But in doing so, they did not fail to distinguish between the Italianized trading classes of the coastal cities and the Croatian peasant stock of the hinterland; proclamations, for example, were usually printed in Italian and Croatian.[72] The Austrian commanders in Illyria realized only too well how confusion bred discontent; unfortunately the lack of directives and of on-the-spot authority prevented them from organizing as they felt necessary. Complaints of a steadily worsening state of affairs resulting from administrative floundering continued to reach Vienna and Allied headquarters.[73]

Since it was assumed that at least the Illyrian territories would fall back to Austria, basic questions regarding their eventual administrative and political disposition soon had occupied the Staatskanzlei and the conference of state: What form of administration should be erected and what should become of the French laws still in force? Beyond this, would part of the

Illyrian Provinces be returned to the Hungarian crown or would they remain as an intact unit within the empire, and if so, what form and rank would be granted them?[74] As it turned out, some of these questions waited over two years for an answer — others even longer.

In November of 1813, the emperor took the first steps in organizing the lands occupied up to that time by his southern forces. On November 14, the direction of Italian and Illyrian affairs was removed from the hands of the *Armeehofkommissair* Freiherr v. Baldacci and entrusted to the collective guidance of a special core of the state conference *(Enge Conferenz)*;[75] it was not a very successful measure. Nonetheless, Baldacci continued to be one of the emperor's closest advisors on Illyrian matters,[76] and within a week he reported to Kaiser Franz upon the causes for Illyrian difficulties and on the hopes for better treatment — especially in regard to Hungarian claims.[77] On November 28, 1813, the emperor announced the provisional military occupation of the conquered Italian and Illyrian territories.[78] Two principal and yet conflicting motives of action not only underlie the contents of this document and similar ones of later date, but underline much of the cross-purpose found in administrative doings in general: r e l i e f   v e r s u s   r e v e n u e ; on the one hand there was a sincere desire to lighten the lot of the inhabitants, and on the other, the pressing need to draw upon these lands as quickly as possible for the replenishment of empty coffers.

At the same time the emperor bade his commander in Italy to care for the winning of public sentiment and to ascertain popular wishes.[79] Since the thought of a good administration and, thereby, a satisfied population was so important to him, he naturally took an active interest in the state of public opinion. Here he and Metternich were of one score; hardly a government accumulated such a mass of detailed and even inflated reports on the mood of the populace. One may suspect that for the interest of Kaiser Franz, more than for Metternich, a sense of precaution and apprehension was as much of a mainspring as genuine solicitude. While the emperor was interested not only in probing but in mollifying public opinion, his imagination in this respect did not range very far; usually it was up to Metternich to submit ideas capable of packing popular fancy.

In his atrophied rationalism, the emperor could well appreciate the forms but not the spirit behind Josephinian reforms; for him it was simply self-evident that the ideal administration was a highly centralized one in which all channels would lead to and unite at the source of all authority as directly as possible. In the pursuit of this ideal, there stood about him such prominent men as the Counts Saurau, Zichy, Ugarte, and Lazansky, all of whom had come from the same "school" as he. As applied to the organization of the annexed Italian and Illyrian lands, the emperor's aim was to place the organs of the new administration under the direct control of Vienna, and — as stated on November 28 — simultaneously to arrange for conformity with administrative practices already existing in the German provinces. The key words of most imperial decisions pertaining to administrative organization in the new areas during the period prior to the Congress of Vienna are: *Möglichste Gleichstellung, Gleichsetzung,* or *Gleichförmigkeit.*[80]

Kaiser Franz, always suspicious of French measures, was inclined to give a ready ear to reports — mostly from the Illyrian Provinces — of a dislike for French laws and of a desire to return to an improved Austrian administration. There was no question as to the eventual abolition of Napoleonic ordinances; however, a realistic approach called for an equally gradual dismantling of the French structure and erection of an Austrian one. Consequently, in spite of some opposition, the emperor felt compelled to retain temporarily those parts of the French administration which he deemed indispensable for good order.[81] In the spring of 1814 things had advanced to the point, however, where Kaiser Franz began to stress his desire for conformity. On May 12 he declared flatly: "It is hereby My determined will to keep steadily in eye the attaining of conformity [in Dalmatia] with the way things are in My German provinces."[82] Two days later, he summarized even more emphatically the core of his entire incorporation policy into one grandiose sentence which, as an illustration, deserves to be quoted in the original:

Da meine Gesinnung dahin gehet Meine neuen Staaten in Italien, und das zurückerhaltene Illyrien so viel möglich Meinen übrigen deutschen Erblanden in ihrer Organisierung gleichzustellen, was Meine Absicht in den Mir vormals angehörigen venetianischen Staaten war, und so wie Ich jetzt vernehme, ohngeachtet es noch nicht ganz bewerkstelliget war zur Zufriedenheit der dortigen Inwohner gereichte, und dieses nachdem Ich die französische Verfassung eingesehen habe, nicht schwer halten dürfte, ja sogar mit grossen Vereinfachungen, Verminderung der unter diesem Sisteme bestandenen Beamten und Erleichterung der Untertanen hervorbringen wird, so will Ich, dass hiernach genau geachtet, die Sache mit allem Eifer auf dem kürzesten Weg und mit der möglichsten Schnelligkeit angegriffen, daher mit einer eigenen aus den betreffenden Hofstellen und den geschicktesten hiezu geeignetsten Beamten zusammen zu setzenden Commission, wovon die Glieder und der Präsident Mir von der Konferenz vorzuschlagen, und der alle hiezu erforderlichen auch

staatsräthlichen Akten mitzuteilen sind, vorgenommen, und von dieser
die Vorträge an Mich erstattet werden, welche Ich sodann in der Konferenz unter Meinem eigenen Vorsitze, da Mir so sehr am Herzen liegt,
auch Meinen neuen Untertanen die Wohltat mit Meiner Monarchie vereinigt zu seyn schleunig empfinden zu lassen, vornehmen werde.[83]

Since the equalization or conformity policy also called for the introduction of the Austrian law code into the new territories, provisions were
made for its translations into Italian and "Illyrian" (Croatian).[84] On July
11, 1814, the emperor extended this policy to the Italian and Illyrian school
systems, with a now oft-occurring stress on speed.[85] On August 1, the
Austrians in Illyria were able to declare the entire body of French law and
administration null and void.[86]

Theoretically, equalization with the German administration did not
necessarily mean Germanization; however, it is difficult to imagine how
this was altogether avoided in practice. Especially the conduct and fervor
of some officials gave rise to frequent charges that the Austrians wanted to
Germanize everything. Perhaps it was all too often overlooked that many
Italians never could be made to feel as equally privileged citizens of the
Habsburg state as long as they were subject to German law, and that in
consequence they could not help but consider themselves under an alien
system and foreign rule. Certainly the emperor took pains to see that his
officials, if not indigenous, were fluent in the language of the land in which
they were to serve. Particularly in Italy he made sure that all court
officers and judges knew Italian — a language officially recognized for
judicial proceedings.[87] Applications of candidates for Italian and Illyrian
posts show that most were proficient in Italian or "Illyrian" or even
"Carniolan" (Slovenian) if not in all of these tongues.[88] Yet this concern
was a recognition not so much of nationality as simply of the need to
assure close contact between population and officialdom.

However, the emperor sometimes went so far in the interests of im-
partiality as to select purposely non-local and — as he thought — therefore
non-partisan candidates; such a practice was little understood and even
less appreciated in the non-German areas.[89] Usually, men of experience and
unassailable reputation already on the scene were welcome, and as long
lists of prospective officials — often meticulously drawn up in Kaiser
Franz's own hand — reveal, indigenous names predominate for all but the
highest posts, and even there they were well represented.[90] The guiding
lines for selecting officials in Italy and Illyria were prescribed by the
emperor in his edict of November 28, 1813. Especially scrupulous attention

was expected for those posts which had direct influence upon the well-being of the people; an even greater exercise of care was required to exclude anyone capable of harboring motives of revenge, or anyone politically compromised.

Progress in administrative organization proceeded at an unequal pace through the two separate *gubernia* at Milan and Venice;[91] especially in Lombardy it was slow. The initial imperial instructions for the Illyrian-Italian areas had been in time extended to Lombardy and were gradually adjusted to local conditions. There, however, not only was the conformity policy confronted with serious obstacles in its application, but on a theoretical level its political expediency was ever more put into question by a number of high functionaries connected with Italian or organizational matters. Moreover, in Lombardy the Austrians had had a late start and the French administration remained in many cases intact; the means for removal or replacement were not yet adequate to allow for a smooth and rapid introduction of an Austrian system. At any rate, brave efforts were made to render relief measures purposeful — never forgetting thereby the currying of a public opinion dangerously depressed by calamitous shortages. At least the pleas of Bellegarde and Reuss succeeded in preventing a circulation of Austrian paper notes from making things still worse.[92] Even more than the economic situation, the political climate received special attention; a main concern of Kaiser Franz was to have his police keep a close watch on public mood and illegal groups. Generally, to judge from public reaction and police reports from Italy, the Austrian authorities quickly got off on the wrong foot.[93]

Easier progress was achieved in the Illyrian Provinces. There was less cultivated sensitivity among the general population and less debate about the necessity or desirability of retaining the French administration, which had not taken such deep root as it had in Italy. Then too, in some parts of the Illyrian Provinces direct government from Vienna had long been practice. Furthermore, a strong "national feeling" — insofar as this existed beyond the circles of the estates — could of course be noted only in the Croatian parts of the Provinces, and, if it was directed toward Austria, then not so much in antipathy as in anticipation.

The territorial composition of the former French Illyrian Provinces was subject to immediate modification. In addition to the transsavian Croatian lands (military and civil Croatia, on the right bank of the Save), the Provinces were comprised of Dalmatia, Ragusa, the bay of Cattaro (Austrian Albania), Carniola, Austrian and Venetian Istria, Gorizia without Gradisca, the Carinthian Villach circle minus Tarvis, and East Tyrol. The last named, as well as the Italian speaking (Trentinian) South Tyrol — which had been parts of the Kingdom of Italy — were promptly rejoined to Tyrol proper. Originally parts of the Illyrian Provinces, Gradisca and Tarvis had been attached to the Kingdom of Italy in 1810. As Kaiser Franz learned that the German and Wendish (Slovenian) speaking inhabitants of the Tarvis area had suffered discrimination — especially in regard to language — during the four years under an Italian administration, he readily granted on March 30, 1814, their request for reunification with Carinthia — i. e., with the Illyrian Provinces.[94] The Gorizian frontier was readjusted in July.[95]

A definite step toward the internal regulation of the Illyrian lands was taken on March 9, 1814, as the emperor named Count Saurau *Hofkommissair* for this area.[96] The main purpose behind this measure, so the emperor had emphasized, was his resolve to impart upon his subjects there the benefits of a better administration and to mitigate well-grounded complaints.[97] Saurau's confidential mission was simply to get the organization of the Illyrian Provinces on its feet[98] — something which his unique authority enabled him to accomplish in six months. Already on April 25 he presented proposals which he and Baldacci had worked out jointly.[99] For the coastal lands, he suggested a special *gubernium* at Trieste, with *vicegubernia* at Fiume, Zara, Ragusa, and Cattaro. As far as he was concerned, the parts of Croatia — with the exception of Fiume — which now formed part of the Illyrian territories might be returned without delay to Hungary. Not the least reason for this move was to eradicate thereby the embarrassment resulting from the "extorted constitution" in Illyrian Croatia which had placed Lattermann and all other Austrian officials connected with that affair in such a predicament.[100] In addition, Saurau put forward various relief plans such as unrestricted trade for the ports and the exclusion of paper currency.[101]

Because these proposals were right in line with the emperor's views, he approved most of them, adding as a last thought the desire that Saurau might submit a confidential opinion upon the feasibility of re-erecting the estates in Carniola and Gorizia.[102] Saurau received the free hand he wanted and was responsible alone to the emperor (in case of his absence, to the *Enge Konferenz*). Although the Croatian lands which had once belonged to the crown of St. Stephen were for the time being not returned to Hungary, clearly any consideration of an Illyrian special status was ignored by the emperor and his organizer in Illyria.

On July 23, 1814, appeared the imperial decree officially proclaiming the annexation of the Illyrian Provinces; it contained the usual promises of a better administration.[103] In the following week, Kaiser Franz constituted the *Central-Organisierungs-Hofcommission* (COHC) — with Count Lazansky as its president[104] — to carry out the incorporation into the Habsburg state of all the territories gained through the victory over Napoleon.[105] In his definition of the commission's functions, the emperor once again spelled out his policy of equalization or conformity.

After the first Peace of Paris, and the return from London in July, 1814, Metternich had for the first time the occasion to turn for a moment from foreign to domestic affairs. To what extent would his views coincide with the administrative course which the emperor had more or less independently initiated and followed?

Metternich

We have seen how the political implications of the Italian and Illyrian acquisitions drew the increasing heed of Metternich and his Staatskanzlei. Two crucial problems of interior policy, as far as this organ of the state was concerned, were the cultivation of regional *esprit* as an answer to what were considered excessive and impermissible national strivings, and the selection of proper principles and methods of administration. As early as the beginning of May, Hudelist hinted in a letter to Metternich that the Staatskanzlei might have notions on administrative policy other than those prevailing. His satisfaction at finally witnessing some action was not without premonitions:

> Things are at last getting started — the Lord be praised — with the administration of the Italian provinces. That things move quickly is an indispensable condition for keeping the lively Italians satisfied. One cannot coin everything with a German stamp; rather, every nation will render that which one is justified in asking of it only if it is governed after its own fashion and the forms used are suited to its national character.[106]

In the meantime, at the end of May, Metternich could well be content with his work in Paris; he spoke optimistically of achieving the *Lieblingsidee* of his foreign policy: a steadfast system based upon the cooperation of the Central Powers which the maritime nations could join as a natural course of things. "With a few good furnishings in our interior," he added, "good prospects shall open before us."[107] But by the middle of July the situation, instead of improving, had developed to the point where Hudelist lamented to Metternich that he considered every further delay in Italy as a calamity.[108]

On July 30 Metternich presented to his monarch his opinions on the creation of the COHC.[109] Whereas he agreed fully to the need for this measure, he could not agree to the manner in which the deliberations thereon had taken place;[110] his representative and chief assistant — Hudelist — had not been included or consulted. This inexcusable disregard of the chief political agency of the state — the Staatskanzlei — on an issue which could affect "its innermost driving wheels", so he insisted, was but a further demonstration of how mandatory it had become to avoid a planless and arbitrary composing of the conference of state.

Furthermore, Metternich showed a striking and fundamentally different attitude toward the organization policies pursued up to that time. Thereby two interpretations of interior policy confronted each other: both aimed ultimately at internal security and a contented populace, but the one, its vision narrowed by administrative formalism, lacked the perception of the other. Whereas the first proceeded from hardened rationalistic principles and presumed to achieve its aims mainly through a centralized system of perfectly administered welfare, the second advanced further by recognizing not only the utility of institutions and laws already adapted to a people's needs but also the significance of the emotional factors inherent in a people's attachment to such institutions and laws. Whereas the first interpretation could mean inconsiderate levelling, the second insisted that a realistic interior policy of a heterogeneous state must seek not an elimination of diversity but rather a judicious conservation of all elements capable of contributing to public order and contentment — whatever their heritage.

Thus, for Metternich, equalization and conformity were not the prime objectives of administrative organization; he proposed that the words which called for the equalization of the administrative system in the newly acquired areas with that already existing in the German provinces should be modified to the following:

The purpose of this commission should be to appraise carefully the present conditions in the newly acquired areas, and to take the proper initial steps so that their incorporation into the whole can occur in the most efficient manner; at the same time its aim shall be to preserve the assets to be found in previous administrative practices and, insofar as necessary, to fit them into the forms prevalent in the other parts of the Monarchy.

Here we see the beginning of Metternich's efforts to draw the over-all organization and administrative policy toward a moderate and tolerant line — one which denounced "Germanization" as it promoted greater understanding between Italians and Germans, one which discouraged unwarranted centralization as much as it encouraged a healthy regionalism, one which would grant (as he thought) fuller consideration to "national feeling", one which in its last consequence attempted a reorganization of the lands in the Empire according to the nationality of the inhabitants.

In concluding, Metternich suggested that the emperor might appoint an official of the Staatskanzlei — Freiherr v. Wessenberg — to the vice-presidency of the COHC; Wessenberg, who was to receive the title of *Geheimer Rath,* would then act as a mediator and link between the commission and the Staatskanzlei. Thereby Metternich hoped to prevent any further disregard of his office in an activity whose eventual consequences could well be portentous for the well-being of the monarchy. Furthermore, he wished to make sure that his own views were heard among the deliberations of the commission. His magnanimity on Wessenberg's behalf may be explained by the fact that the latter was about to submit a report on a special mission to appraise the Italian situation with which he had been entrusted and which he had now completed. That Metternich could subscribe wholeheartedly to Wessenberg's conclusions — which later on were submitted in confidence to the emperor as those of an independent and qualified fact-finder — gave all the more weight to the Staatskanzlei's challenge of the conformity policy prescribed by the emperor. Kaiser Franz approved the appointment and promotion of Wessenberg; on the other items of Metternich's *Vortrag* he had nothing to add or to comment.

That it was to take the Austrians several years to replace fully the laws and administration left behind by the French with their own has often been made a point of reproach. However, the undeniably confusing and unsatisfactory state of things resulting therefrom can not be attributed merely to inefficiency and inadequacy, for beneath these failings lay an administrative policy at odds with itself. The emperor's wish for the introduction of a thoroughly Austrian administration as soon as possible was opposed by such men as Metternich, Wessenberg, and Bellegarde, who felt that such a course might antagonize Italian sensibility at seeing "everything Germanized" to the point where all provisions for a good relationship between authority and population would be rendered ineffective. As repeatedly as such voices cautioned against a thoughtless discarding of existing practices, they pressed for a quick declaration of permanent status so as to dispel the uncertainty which strained the nerves of all. Whether they were right in supposing that the Italians cherished most institutions of French origin as if they were their own is another matter. At any rate, neither the one nor the other line of administrative policy was followed in any consequence and as the organization of the new areas seemed to straggle along with one foot on the sidewalk and the other in the street, it could not help attracting scoffs and scorn — and not merely from those always ready to abuse all things Austrian.

To summarize: A widespread appeal to "national spirit" in Italy and Illyria during the military operations was followed by a flaring-up of independent political initiative on a "national" level during the time of turnover. Such action was regarded by the emperor as a direct challenge to his prerogatives and was in no way to be tolerated. At the same time, a definition of the newly acquired Italian and Illyrian territories' political status within the Habsburg Empire remained in suspense. The decisive encounter between the populations of these acquired lands and the Austrian state was transferred for the time being to the administrative level where, however, as most Austrian officials had to admit, things were from the beginning not in the best of order. Metternich proposed to counter nationalistic strivings — unsupportable because they transcended and disregarded the existing political system — by cultivating a regional tradition and *esprit*. The minister made a determined bid for a voice in matters of internal organization and administrative affairs and challenged the emperor's centralistic policy of conformity as politically unsound and in need of modification in order to avoid offending the feelings of the newly acquired but "nation-conscious" subjects.

CHAPTER II

WAITING, WARNING, AND WAR ONCE MORE: 1814-1815

THE WESSENBERG MISSION AND THE CONFORMITY POLICY

After the First Peace of Paris had been signed, Metternich looked forward to accepting an invitation from the British Prince Regent to visit England along with the other organizers of the victory over Napoleon. He was to represent there his emperor who, despite all pleading, had declined. Kaiser Franz had become increasingly discomfited outside of his own realm and shied at the thought of sharing the acclamations of London's crowds with the popular "heroes" of the day — Alexander of Russia and Frederick William of Prussia — and at celebrating all too openly the defeat of his son-in-law. Much more, he yearned anxiously to set foot again on home ground[1] where grateful subjects waited with an enthusiastic welcome.[2] For his part, Metternich hoped to use his sojourn in England to work for some sort of understanding among the Allied monarchs on the issues which would face them at the impending Congress. But just prior to his departure in the first week of June, Metternich turned once more to matters south of the Alps.

In a dispatch containing a copy of the peace treaty and an exact definition of the Italian territories, Metternich requested the commander in Italy, Bellegarde, to assure everyone of the emperor's personal occupation with the organization and welfare of his Italian lands. Bellegarde, in turn, was to report to the emperor on the manner in which imperial instructions had been carried out.[3] In a separate message, Metternich informed Bellegarde that Baron Wessenberg was being sent on a special fact-finding mission to the Italian provinces, a mission which the marshal was asked to assist in every possible way.[4]

Soon after arriving in Milan, Wessenberg sent a report of his first impressions to Metternich, reserving details for his return to Vienna. Pointing to the need for correlating political considerations with administrative ones, he insisted that the responsibility for handling the organization of the Italian provinces, at least until the establishment of a permanent administration, should be given to the Staatskanzlei. Such a step, he felt, "was imperiously demanded by the political situation." The principal questions concerning the administration of this "beau pays" were for him the following: Should all the Italian provinces be placed under one and the same administration? What would be a suitable form for the representation of government? Which principles were to be followed in the administration as such? Most pressing, of course, was to remove the state of uncertainty so disquieting for the populace. He realized well enough that this had to await the final settlement at the Congress, but at least preparations for such a time could be launched presently, and with this in mind he had set out to assemble all the material which might be needed in Vienna. He assured Metternich that the Italians — although naturally excitable — were much more manageable than generally believed and that, with some tokens of esteem and consideration, one would find a ready response. One could really have the best of the bargain, he thought, if only one were to treat them as a respected nation; but, he warned, were they to encounter only disregard and disdain, then one would have them as enemies. These Italians, he concluded, were not those "which we knew in 1790" and among the progressive Milanese, once known as the Bœotians of Italy, there were enough intelligent and enlightened men, and, moreover, "quite honest ones".[5]

Wessenberg's urging of a speedy end of the provisional status was to become a familiar and common refrain. Somewhat akin to Metternich's and Bellegarde's views was Wessenberg's judgment of the Italian character and his cautious optimism which he made dependent upon a due respect for Italian nationality and custom. An even more striking similarity of attitudes is displayed by Wessenberg's elaboration upon his return to the capital and Metternich's *Vortrag* of July 31, 1814. It is quite likely that Wessenberg, who had come back to Vienna at about the time that the COHC was established, had had some preliminary exchange of opinions with Metternich which possibly influenced the minister's stand against the imperial policy of conformity and centralization.[6]

To the first part of August, 1814, belong several memoranda by Wessenberg on the general political and economic picture in Italy.[7] He contended that the turmoil of the past years had taken no lesser toll in blood and ruin in Italy than in France. More than that, it had awakened there the hope of seeing for the first time in "twenty centuries" a unification of the peninsula into a single national state. The old system had been swept away without too many regrets — if one excepts some appreciation for Habsburg enlightened despotism in Italy — and most Italians had welcomed the new methods of the French, for which Wessenberg could not conceal a certain admiration.

In a report on the organization of the Italian provinces submitted to Metternich on August 13, Wessenberg insisted again that the only real line to follow was a prudent combination of the chief political and administrative viewpoints: the first was that Vienna must win the affections of the Italians in order to be sure of them; the second concerned itself with the most efficient use of the provinces for the good of the empire. Here, Wessenberg's strongly pragmatic concepts came to the fore — after all, the financial question was an essential part of his assignment — and set him apart somewhat from Bellegarde, who could plead the Italians' cause on purely benevolent grounds, and Metternich, who did not state administrative objectives in terms which Italians might have regarded as denoting exploitation. It follows that Wessenberg would devote much of his attention to the methods by which the Monarchy — i.e., the Austrian state — would be brought "as quickly as possible to the usufruct" of its new acquisitions; political considerations were important insofar as they could aid or hinder the attaining of this goal. Decided without delay therefore were to be the internal arrangement of the Italian provinces, the setting up of the *gubernia*, and the form and nature of the taxes. Regarding the first, he believed, as did Bellegarde and Metternich, that stringent reasons suggested the retention of the French departmental and cantonal system. He failed to see how this might be detrimental to the Austrian administration, especially in view of the considerable cost and effort involved in a change of more than just nomenclature. At any rate, he was certain that, as far as the yield from the Italian areas was concerned, one could hardly get more out of them than did the French system. Thus it might be wiser to consider its retention — with due modification naturally — rather than to risk the upheaval of a complete change which would not only deprive the Monarchy of gains one had every right to expect from these areas but which would necessitate supporting them. In following the only feasible course, Wessenberg insisted, one would soon come to realize that past and present conditions in Italy, as well as the character and political tendencies of its inhabitants, made for quite a different picture than some of the organizers had originally imagined:

A complete conformity of the administration of the Italian provinces with those of the hereditary lands — at least at present — would correspond just as little to the interests of the Austrian state as to those of the said provinces. Such a conformity would in any case require a long period of time during which a great many other advantages would be

BELLEGARDE

lost and some of the good now existing could not be preserved for the future.

A final memorandum of Wessenberg found its way to the imperial desk some time later, and from there to Lazansky's — the president of the COHC. This unsigned document came to grips with the issue clearly enough: "In order to gain the trust of the Italian people, it is above all necessary to avoid worrying them with the thought that one would want either to Germanize Italy or to treat it simply as an Austrian colony."[8] The ample amount of acute self-esteem which the writer observed among Italians could, he noted, be just as useful as dangerous for the Austrian government. Unhappily, this self-esteem had already been slighted through ordinances and laws issued by a "Bohemian Commission" — the Italians' name for Lazansky's COHC.

Precisely this sensitivity had brought about the insistence of Italian departmental deputies then present in Vienna to be admitted to the COHC; perhaps they recalled that Kaiser Franz had assured the Confalonieri delegation in Paris, during a second audience on May 27, that he would undertake nothing in Italy without consulting the Italians.[9] To be sure, the Vienna deputation so concerned for a voice in its home affairs presented a marked contrast to the Paris one in its aims as well as its membership. It was composed largely of Lombardo-Venetian noblemen faithful to the House of Habsburg — such well-known persons as Guicciardi, Mellerio, and Porcia were among them. Inasmuch as these three afterwards attained high posts, one might think that some individual wishes of the deputation were respected. Of course, such concessions hardly impressed the *Italici puri*, who did not expect such servants of the Habsburg cause to represent Italy's true interests, or the emperor to select for service in Italy anyone whose devotion to his person and state might be questioned.

Wessenberg recognized the mounting dissatisfaction in the Italian provinces as concentrated among three groups which had everything to lose: the former military and civil employees, the acquisitors of national property (*biens nationaux*), and the *rentiers*. He well understood how instability accompanied anxiety, especially when that anxiety arose from the collapse of a regime to which was owed position, property, or pension. The urgent need to calm spirits and banish fears could best be served, he thought, by retaining not only as much as possible the previous administrative system but its employees as well. This proposal reveals a lack of acquaintance with the emperor's nature. To think that Kaiser Franz would sanction such a blanket acceptance and not suspect therein some sort of curtailment of imperial prerogatives, that he would approve lock, stock and barrel an entire bureaucracy without being able personally to probe into the qualifications of each, was too much to expect from a monarch who often delighted in scrupulously going over lists of candidates and applicants, deciding which to appoint what, which to place where. Wessenberg's views on what to do with employees of the former regime were also shared by Metternich and Bellegarde. The latter, being on the scene, understood the misfortunes which beset many such persons. Once, upon hearing his aide Rosetti remark that "we don't need half of these [former state employees]", the marshal rejoined: "Perhaps you are right in saying that we do not need them, but I think they all need [us] as much as [we] need the first half."[10] Yet it is probable that the sympathetic Bellegarde was not frightened, as Kaiser Franz surely must have been, primarily by the thought: Who would pay the unneeded half's salaries? Wessenberg's assertion that such costs would be less than those resulting from the chaos of a complete changeover, if unconvincing for the emperor, must at least have added to the latter's irritation at encountering more and more arguments — political as well as financial — against his wish to achieve conformity.

Furthermore, Wessenberg insisted that the *biens nationaux* must be guaranteed and state obligations honored when possible. Perhaps he did this because the emperor's opinions on this displeasing question had not been reassuring, despite the fact that the monarch had calmed the delegation in Paris in regard to this point with the words: "I am not fond of promising much, but what I promise, I do. . . . I recognized Napoleon as a legitimate sovereign, . . . and therefore must recognize his legitimate works."[11] But then, the fear was not unfounded that Kaiser Franz might feel unable to afford such generosity and find it out of place to assume another's burdens.

Wessenberg had harsh words for the provisional authorities, whom he accused of acting "wholly against the intentions of His Majesty." Their lack of understanding and their zeal to alter all existing practices, especially financial ones, had contributed to the sad fact that Austria had gained nothing from its Italian acquisitions up to then. This enthusiasm for housecleaning might well serve the interests of some individuals, he thought, but through it Austria's name became hated and administrative business became disarrayed. Once more Wessenberg repeated his objections to the conformity policy in almost the same words as in his report to Metternich, pointing to the wide disparity between the German and Italian provinces and the serious difficulty, disadvantage, and imprudence which an attempt at conformity would bring. Finally, he asserted that the whole matter was not one of creating a province useful to the empire out of a

land lacking all culture and organization — as he considered Poland to
have been — but rather, through the establishment of an efficient permanent administration, of profiting from the surplus which one of the
fairest and richest lands of Europe had to offer. It was simply hard to
believe, he added, that a state such as the former *Regno d'Italia* — which
had everything required by a well-ordered and amply-provisioned land —
could have had an organization so faulty as to be discounted without a
second thought.

The significance of Wessenberg's reports lay not in the validity of his
particular arguments nor in the practicability of his proposals nor in his
comparisons and retrospections (which require some qualification) but
rather in that his overall views on a new course of action substantiated for
the first time Metternich's misgivings on the conformity policy which the
emperor initiated some time before. In addition, the opinions of such a
qualified observer, who had informed himself on the scene, could not
lightly be dismissed. Wessenberg's high rank (as second plenipotentiary, he
signed with Metternich almost all documents concerning Austria at the
Congress) and his well-known strength of character (this was exactly
what led to his difficulties and break with Metternich in later years) point
to his being more or less an independent fact-finder rather than simply
an agent. Probably both discussed Wessenberg's mission before his departure, and in all likelihood Metternich felt that he could be sure of Wessenberg's open-mindedness. His confidence seems reflected in the effort to
have Wessenberg, as representative of the Staatskanzlei, appointed vice-
president of the COHC.[12] Although this move was successful, it ultimately
meant very little, since Wessenberg could be spared from the Congress no
more than Metternich; but it can be considered, along with the "anonymous" report to the emperor, as an attempt to give the Staatskanzlei a more
authoritative voice in matters of internal organization. That the conclusions
of Wessenberg's memorandum did not exactly please the emperor may be
taken for granted. He kept it for nearly two months before sending it to
the COHC's president for evaluation.[13] Its warnings, coupled with those
now arriving from Bellegarde in Milan, would seem to have made necessary some sort of reappraisal and the issuing of new directives. But instead,
there was only an issuing of opinions on opinions and debate and delay.

BELLEGARDE AND METTERNICH

Marshal Bellegarde in Milan had never overcome the feelings of uneasiness which had beset him on first encountering the desperate pleas for Italian independence. The summer had come, but the dissatisfaction was far from gone, something which overeager police officials were the first to suspect; indeed, their well-being appeared almost to depend upon an ability to discern behind every door subversion and conspiracy. The marshal complained of being submerged by misleading police reports. He was convinced, however, as he wrote to Wessenberg shortly after the latter's departure, that all the agitation would cease once the Congress had produced a final clarification and once it had been decided to "caress somewhat national spirit and public fancy."[14]

Bellegarde had welcomed Wessenberg's mission; he had, moreover, every reason to maintain a cordial contact with the latter. The marshal soon must have realized how distressing his own position had become if he had to witness developments in his command of which he disapproved but which the confusing criss-cross of authority prevented him from correcting as he would have wished. If Wessenberg were to attack the thoughtless conduct of the provisional authorities in Italy, then Bellegarde — although in agreement with Wessenberg and of the best intentions — would scarcely be able to dodge all criticism and responsibility. He had gone to some pains to make clear to the Staatskanzlei's fact-finder the very delicate political atmosphere prevailing and the need to respect "national feeling"; he had attached much hope to Wessenberg's reports to Vienna. The investigator on his part showed some sympathies for the marshal, realizing that he was sick at heart and did not wish to remain in Italy. He had even asked Metternich for a few kind words for Bellegarde, since "it would be too bad if we were to lose him completely."[15] Yet, strangely enough, in all of Wessenberg's reports, there is no attempt really to single out either Bellegarde's opinions or his conduct as apart from that so markedly criticized.

The less-than-satisfactory news from Italy brought Metternich to the point where he was forced to admit that, even after a quarter of a year, Austrian authorities and Italians had not yet come to understand one another. Smooth progress under such conditions was hardly possible, and he soon was compelled to offer public opinion abroad — especially in England — some indirect apologies. Thereby he complained of a "most disagreeable state of tension" in Italy, which, even if incapable of altering the fact of Austrian rule there, often enough hindered the realization of well-meant ideas and projects "conceived for the happiness of the Italian subjects."[16]

Repeatedly throughout the remainder of 1814, and usually after reading Bellegarde's dispatches, Metternich stressed to Kaiser Franz the urgency of winning public opinion in Italy and of making the name of Austria popular among the Italian population through various inexpensive acts of generosity and liberality.[17] He even proposed subsidizing La Scala in Milan and encouraged recognition and support of well-known and deserving artists to demonstrate to Italy that Austria knew how to appreciate its culture.[18] At the advice of Bellegarde he brought before his monarch the request of former Italian officers to keep their old uniforms and the pension-plea of the famous poet Monti, suggesting thereby that such small gestures would reap bountiful political dividends.[19] But the emperor, who also wanted to win public opinion but who could not overcome his formal sense of justice, refused to make any exceptions for either the veteran officers or Monti.[20] At the same time, reports continued to come from police president Haager on the mounting dissatisfaction, disappointment, and distress, especially among the middle class.[21] From the beginning, Bellegarde had wanted to make evident to all in Italy that Austria was capable of consideration; he even urged the emperor to mitigate his desire that various Italian areas, impoverished as they now were, should come up with the costs for Austrian troops stationed there.[22] The marshal reserved his greatest trust for Metternich, whom he knew to be sympathetic; but he also directed to him the most pointed warnings.

At the beginning of autumn, Bellegarde had as yet refused to believe in the specter which came to haunt Austrians in Italy throughout the years: that of a general national conspiracy.[23] Rather, he imparted to Metternich, all the commotion and unrest on the peninsula had the aim only of provoking the Austrian authorities into a false move and thus into discredit. He persisted in hoping that Metternich and the Congress would do much to tranquilize spirits in Italy. At this time, he saw the malcontents there divided into two groups which extraordinary circumstances could unite: *les amis* of Italian independence with their hopes of English aid and the adventurers who attached their fortunes to the schemes of Murat. Oddly enough, the chief obstacle to the King of Naples remained Lord Bentinck, whose attitude toward championing Italian independence had not changed, even if the official stand of his own government had.[24] The efforts made against Austria, Bellegarde let Metternich know, would be fruitless if its administrative and political conduct were such as to win public opinion, but in the same sentence he warned that the future would give cause for disquiet if Austria wished to bring to Italy its laws and institutions, which were in no way suitable to the land or its customs, or if the government encouraged commerce and industry in the German provinces at the expense of the Italian ones. The large Italian population necessitated, so he thought, that the Austrian government should occupy itself with means of providing work for the poorer class and of opening civil-service careers to the middle class. If "we know how to hold and cultivate the attachment of the property owners as well as the masses and the clergy" — which he regarded as decided Austrian partisans — then, he assured Metternich, "we shall have nothing to fear but a small group of intriguers who are today powerless and who can gain only through our own mistakes."

It was not long, however, before Bellegarde, along with the rest of the world, began to despair of any early benefits from the Vienna deliberations. "Who knows when the Congress will end?" he sighed, fully aware that as far, at least, as the Italians were concerned, the real organization of their land seemed somehow dependent upon the Congress' results. Simultaneously he observed an ominous resurgence of the independence movement,[25] nourished as it was through uncertainty and delay. At the same time also, he could only be skeptical of the Lombard deputies' efforts to achieve something in Vienna with Kaiser Franz.[26] Toward the end of the year, the marshal came to be more outspoken both in giving details of general dissatisfaction and subversive activities in Italy and in stating his personal discontent at his own position: dissatisfaction threatened to billow because of the uncertainty regarding the disposal of former "national property" and because of the "cherished phantom of independence."[27] In such intolerable circumstances, he felt powerless and, not wishing any longer to jeopardize his long and honorable public career, he wrote both to the emperor and to his foreign minister, requesting to be relieved of his command.[28]

What can be said of Metternich during this time? Certainly he relied upon and valued Bellegarde's opinions more than others; he passed them on to his monarch, adding his own sometimes revealing comments — such as that independence and union under one regent were the Italians' *Lieblingsideen*,[29] and again that it would be necessary to work against such ideas with the utmost purpose.[30] But other than to gild items of Bellegarde's solicitude with his own personality and prestige, to present them to the emperor in a proper focus and perhaps a more palatable form, he had at this time little original to add — either in thought or initiative. In view of the many urgencies in Vienna, he could hardly have done otherwise.

Even before the Congress convened, he had endeavored to effect a badly needed overhaul of the central organs of the state machine whose methods of conducting business were at times chaotic.[31] This serious run of things arose from a dilemma: how could the monarch of an absolute and paternalistic state, who through theory as well as through the makings of his character felt compelled to decide personally issues of even the most astounding triviality, delegate his authority? Since it exceeded the capacities of any human being to attend to the entire stream of state business, some of it had to be channeled aside. Yet the problem of divesting the sovereign of some of his burdens was never satisfactorily regulated.[32] From the beginning, Metternich faced all kinds of opposition; at least he had hoped to relieve the emperor somewhat through a clarification and definition of functions between legislative and executive, between ministerial and administrative spheres.

Once the diplomats had gathered, Metternich was involved in the most serious difficulties — political as well as personal — so that he could devote not more than token attention to matters south of the Alps. His delicate and tacking approaches past such diplomatic shoals as Poland and Saxony led not to accord but to outcry and charges of playing a double game. Misunderstood and suddenly peltered by reproaches from all sides — whether the indignation of the Russian czar, the disparagement of the Austrian empress, or the angry sputtering of the Prussian Hardenberg — he could only trust that his monarch would stand behind him — which, of course, Kaiser Franz did. But after the breakdown of negotiations and the violent clash with Alexander, the minister could ill afford to endanger further his already somewhat weakened position by pressing his views on Italy, which were in any case quite well known to the emperor. For his part, Kaiser Franz had little enough time to spare from his duties as host to an agreeable if not agreeing international congress; he took due notice of Bellegarde's and Metternich's admonitions, but relied on the COHC to iron out the situation in Italy satisfactorily.

BELLEGARDE, THE COHC, AND THE COLLECTING OF OPINIONS

On August 17, 1814, the COHC had requested Bellegarde in Milan and Reuss-Plauen in Venice to submit comprehensive general data as well as ideas on the organization of an administration in their respective commands.[33] Bellegarde set to work immediately and sent in his report nine weeks later.[34] From Reuss-Plauen nothing was heard despite reminders; it was well known that he longed to be relieved.[35] By mid-October, however, the emperor had become impatient with the slow progress of the commission — a feeling which he was to see return with regularity — and as he was wont to do now and then, he turned to his confidant, Baldacci, for an opinion.[36] The latter, now chairman of the Bureau of Accounts (*Rechnungsdirektorium*), favored an on-the-spot organizer and singled out the example of Saurau, who had managed to get things going in Illyria within half a year.[37] That circumstances in the Illyrian Provinces were not quite the same as those in the Italian ones was a point which Baldacci did not bother to emphasize. The only effect the Baldacci report seemed to have upon the emperor was to keep him from making an early decision.

Bellegarde's thorough account did not confine itself to Lombardy — the marshal was after all not only commander in Milan but of the entire Italian area as well. It was passed on to Hofrat v. Kübeck of the COHC, who used it as the basis for his elaborations.[38] At least those few political considerations which the marshal felt he could allow himself in a largely statistical report were in general accepted by Kübeck. Bellegarde, like Wessenberg, admired the clarity and precision of French methods and, even more, was struck by the strong impression which their successes had left upon the population. Now, Kübeck held to the marshal's views in stating that it "should not be too difficult to erect a good solid administration based on Franco-Italian fixtures and suited to local conditions as well as to the prevailing practices of the Monarchy." For Kübeck, the chief question upon which the organization of the Italian provinces ultimately depended was whether the Italian territories should be considered as an autonomous whole or simply as integral parts of the Austrian lands.[39] All the while, he added, it should be kept in mind that the emperor desired "to make the bonds with the Austrian state more fast and intimate than before and to entwine the interests of Italy with those of the Austrian state through a common code of laws and a similarity of administration."[40] Kübeck proposed a division of the provinces into an East and West Italy separated by the Mincio and then a formation of these lands into a kingdom which would be bound directly to the Habsburg empire in the same manner as Galicia or Bohemia.

Outwardly at least, the young but clever Kübeck was a compromiser and cautiously — perhaps skillfully — appeared to move in the direction of the imperial wishes. He proclaimed as his and the commission's views what had been the very words of the imperial prescriptions; the commission must pursue these, he wrote, so that "within a few generations the idea of self-assertion among various provinces and small states might be eliminated while the name of an intelligent and highly cultured nation would be preserved by tying it inseparably to the power, protection, and laws of Austria."

Regarding the matter of assemblies, both Bellegarde and Kübeck recommended recreating at least a central congregation within each of the two areas so that the interests of the politically articulate population might be represented. Members were to be chosen from the landed nobility, the (property) tax payers, and the citizens of the privileged cities. However, to suggest for the congregations any sort of real prerogatives was out of the question; they were to resume the advisory capacities of former times while the selection of members was to remain the emperor's privilege.

Kübeck's proposals were translated into Italian and transmitted to the Lombard deputies for their study. They wanted, for one thing, that the central congregations select a president from their own ranks rather than, as advocated, that the governor of the provinces should assume this position *ex officio*; for another, they wanted local assemblies within all the districts. These wishes were written off by Kübeck and the commission — by the latter with the argument that then no fewer than four bodies would meet in Milan: the city council, a general and a patrimonial congregation for city and district, and finally, the central congregation for Lombardy.[41] Thereupon, all the accumulated opinions were referred to another expert, Hofrat Patroni, who added his own before returning all the material to Kübeck and the COHC for necessary rebuttal. Finally, on January 11, 1815, after sufficient discussion at a full gathering, Lazansky — as president of the commission — submitted its proposals to the emperor: basically they were those of Kübeck along with summaries of all the other opinions.[42]

On February 22 followed the imperial resolution:[43] the emperor decided to raise the acquired Italian lands to the rank of a kingdom; however, he remained undecided as to its name and referred this question to the Staatskanzlei. In general, he acquiesced to the commission's proposals. Simultaneously, he appointed the new civil governors of the two *gubernia*: to Milan Count Saurau, who had already returned from Illyria,[44] and to Venice Count Goëss, who had been up to then governor in Lemberg. Furthermore, he emphasized that, in the filling of posts for the two *gubernia*, as much consideration as possible should be given to competent nationals. In addition, Kaiser Franz consented not only to central congregations but to the district congregations desired by the Lombard deputies. The nominations of members he reserved for the time being to himself; later on, candidates might be put forward by the congregations for the emperor's sanction. As before, the assemblies were limited to advice and approval. On the last day of February, the emperor guaranteed all legally acquired possessions of "national property".[45]

No doubt, Kaiser Franz regarded these concessions as appreciable. Yet in all the commission's somber proceedings, reminiscent rather of a canonization than an organization, no problem was approached with a feeling of priority for those so-called "Italian national wishes" which any sort of political prudence could and would have respected. Neither the commission nor the emperor considered Kübeck's first alternative — Italy as an autonomous whole — with any seriousness. There was no provision for Italian self-rule in Milan, despite the fact that praise enough was reserved for the enlightened Habsburg administration in Lombardy of days gone by. There was no mention of a revived Italian chancellery in Vienna. Thus were overheard the pleas of the Austrophile Italians as well as the admonitions of those few influential men solicitous of the welfare of the Italian provinces — those whom one might call the Italophile Austrians. The only government organ from which the commander in Italy could have expected some insight was the Staatskanzlei, but its two top men were occupied with other matters. Simultaneously, there appeared for the emperor to be no compelling reasons for abruptly revising his views; indeed, it seems as if his only — and then not always successful — teacher would remain disaster. After some ten months of drawn-out and ponderous deliberating on administrative details rather than on political requirements, the fundamental form of the new organization in Italy was decided — almost too late.

THE MURAT CRISIS AND THE PROCLAMATION OF THE LOMBARDO-VENETIAN KINGDOM

The news of Napoleon's disappearance from Elba and landing in France rushed over Europe like a shockwave. Seldom had an event so stunningly stirred imaginations, hopes, and fears; seldom had reaction so suddenly forged unity of purpose and resolve where before had stood irreconcilable interests. Often outward calm hid deep concern, or empty boasts preceded flight; and especially in France, professions of loyalty were as touching as transferable.

Metternich had always feared French influence on the Italian peninsula, be it through might or ideology.[46] But now a dreadful prospect not lightly to be dismissed was a three-fold attack on Austrian Italy: from the west by Napoleon, from the south by the ambitious and restless Murat, and from within by a rising of the Italians themselves, grieved as they were — in Baron Stein's words — at "the loss of nationality and at the shortcomings of the Austrian administration."[47] No wonder then that the general concern for Europe's fate was accompanied for many by a particular fear regarding Italy. Few, during those anxious first weeks, could have known that the crisis in Italy was to evaporate quickly, although afterwards some claimed to have taken — all along — Napoleon's or Murat's initial successes as but the overture to their final downfall.

Early in March of 1815, the uncertainty regarding Napoleon's objectives or Murat's designs brought Bellegarde near dilemma. Would he really still be needed on the Italian scene? On March 11 he expressed relief at Saurau's appointment as civil governor and at the news that General Frimont was bringing an army corps to Italy. He thanked Metternich for all his efforts and repeated his request to be relieved. But it was the last time he was to mention this subject for some time. His main concern now was a measure which had become for him, if not a magic formula for Italian stability, the only one which seemed to promise political effectiveness: the raising of the Italian provinces to a semi-independent political unit with the rank of a kingdom. He urged Metternich to accelerate this matter as well as all others pertaining to the future of Italy; he reminded him that neglect here could destroy the work Metternich was conducting far away.[48] It was not long before the marshal's feelings of responsibility ushered his personal wishes out of consideration. He realized only too well that no one had better qualifications or, what was more important, more sincere intentions than he to convey to Vienna the need to do justice in Italy, not only to its inhabitants but also to Austria's position there. Of this the emperor or his minister were not unaware; they were only too happy to have Bellegarde remain — especially in view of the marshal's popularity.[49]

As March drew to a close, the situation was tense. Napoleon had taken up his old quarters in the Tuileries and Murat was on the move. Still there was no word from Vienna on the matter of proclaiming a Lombardo-Venetian Kingdom which was so close to Bellegarde's heart and now perhaps the only means for Austria to counter that which would surely come: a sweeping appeal from the King of Naples for Italian national independence. Then, Bellegarde feared, Austria would need not only an army to combat Murat but another to keep its own provinces in obedience. There was not a minute to lose, he pleaded, if it was not too late — already the entire peninsula was covered with Murat's agents. The emperor must take the title "King of Lombardy" and give some meaning to this act which, Bellegarde claimed, was so ardently desired in Milan; this, the marshal wrote in an appeal to Metternich, might be the sole means "of preserving us from catastrophe!" This small concession was for the emperor only a crown to be added to those he already wore, and if the emperor decided to do this, the marshal was convinced, then there was hope enough that Italy would remain with Austria. However, he went on, "I can't hide the fact that this is an urgent matter which I beg you to submit to the emperor's attention without delay." If for some reason the emperor would refuse this crown or not attempt to win the affections of the Italians personally, then at least a prince of the House must be delegated for this purpose. "After all," Belle-garde reminded Metternich, "one can't leave men out in the cold in a time like this; one must capture their minds and their imaginations . . . [It is necessary] to caress their vanity and to give the Italians a bit of hope."[50]

In the meantime, things took their course in Vienna. Six days after the imperial decision of February 22, Lazansky requested from the Staats-kanzlei an opinion on the naming of the new kingdom.[51] During the fol-lowing month Metternich and Hudelist devoted some attention to this problem. Various drafts and suggestions were drawn up and went to and fro: Lombard kingdom or Langobard kingdom — apparently nothing new had occurred to anyone since this question was discussed in the previous spring.[52] In the earlier drafts on this subject, it is interesting to note, Met-ternich emphasized the heterogeneous status of the new state. Of those fundamental principles upon which he proposed that the new kingdom should be founded the very first was that "the imperial Austrian Italian lands form a separate state with the name Lombardian Kingdom." Only the second one declared this kingdom to be united forever with the Austrian Empire; the third that a viceroy would represent the monarch there.[53] At the end of March, neither the question of the kingdom's name nor that of its precedence within the imperial title-row was decided; furthermore, whatever its exact name, should it rank before or after Galicia-Lodomeria? To this seemingly petty matter, as with Illyria later on, the emperor and his minister attached some significance — although for very different reasons. For the latter, it was less a matter of legal precedence than of not offending a sensitive nationality; precedence before Galicia would be preferable insofar as it would be in the "interest of the Italians" not to place their kingdom behind all the others, especially since "the ideas of the Italians deserve more indulgence than those of the Galicians." But within a few weeks, he was to plead for the Galicians so they might not feel slighted at seeing the Italians receive special favor. On the other hand, he added, one must bear in mind that Lombardy was the youngest member-state of the "family" and that, above all, Hungary would be displeased if Lombardy got ahead of it in line.[54]

On April 1, after some last-minute changes in which the Venetians were once again remembered, the emperor resolved to call his Italian provinces the "Lombardo-Venetian Kingdom".[55] A few days later Bellegarde was promoted to deputy (*Stellvertreter*) of the viceroy yet to be named.[56] On April 5, Kaiser Franz and Metternich together set down the marshal's new functions: he was to be responsible directly to the emperor and to supervise and, when necessary, to coordinate the activities of the military and civil authorities in both Milan and Venice, who in turn, were to conduct their affairs with the *Hofkriegsrat* and the COHC respectively. Reports of special importance were also to be submitted to the viceroy or his deputy.[57]

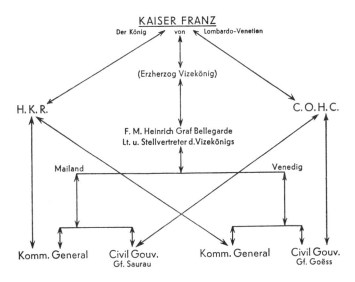

In the accompanying somewhat simplified diagram, there are recognizable two quite different possibilities of channeling official business between the imperial *Kabinettskanzlei* and the civil and military authorities in Milan and Venice. The one led through the office of the viceroy; upon it was concentrated all anticipation of some sort of Italian autonomy: much depended upon whether this channel would serve as a practical instrument or remain ornamentation, whether the flow of business would really be conducted through it. The other set of channels represented the simpler and more effective method of direct rule and administration through the *Hofstellen* concerned — the *Hofkriegsrat* and the COHC. The emperor's

preference could, however, hardly have been to place some of his authority
into the hands of the one of his brothers who would become viceroy. Yet,
the very existence of the "viceroy" channel, even if largely on paper and
even if extorted from a grudging monarch by precedence and prudence,
was nevertheless a first step; it was the foundation upon which an effective
national autonomy for Lombardy-Venetia could have been erected. As
such, it became a focal point of interest, discussion, pleading, hope and
chagrin, not only for the Italians who still wished Austria well and expected it to keep its promises, but for Austrians like Bellegarde, Metternich,
and, later, Bubna, who for Austria's sake stressed time and again the need
to satisfy Italian expectations. Actually, three years went by before a viceroy arrived, and by then Bellegarde — the deputy — had long departed
from Italy. Ironically enough, Bellegarde, as lieutenant to a non-existent
viceroy, was a more effective intercessor for Italian autonomy than the
viceroy himself ever was — but few Italians understood this unintended
subtlety.

On April 7, 1815, there was proclaimed in Vienna the Lombardo-
Venetian Kingdom, whose king was to be crowned with the age-old Iron
Crown — a symbol's symbol, so to speak.[58] Six days later, the two *gubernia*
of the new Lombardo-Venetian Kingdom were instructed to make use of
the Italian language as much as possible.[59]

That the atmosphere in Italy was laden and that Murat's agents were at
work spreading the idea of a coming great all-Italian kingdom was known
in Vienna well enough.[60] For this reason, it is all the more strange that
Bellegarde had to resort to such earnest and, as it seems, lonely pleading.
But until the last minute, few were ready to believe that Murat would be
so rash as to risk his now legitimized throne in an open attack on Austria.
As he changed his allegiance for the second time within little over a year,
his desperate gamble for all or nothing was made — on March 30 he issued
at Rimini his dramatic appeal, so immediately overwhelming, so deeply
touching:

Italians! Now you can have an independent nation! Throughout the
land, everywhere, is heard the cry for independence. This is the right of
every people — by what other right do foreigners deprive you of it?
They rule and occupy your fair land; they take your riches and your
sons to die far from the graves of their fathers. Nature has endowed our
Italy with barriers and boundaries — yet what good are they? And an
even greater delineation exists — the sharp distinction between our Italian culture, customs, language and character, and those of other peoples.
And how are these distinctions respected? Liberate Italian soil, you, who

once were masters of the world! You, who have suffered centuries of foreign oppression! Now 80,000 Neapolitans are led by their king northward, sworn to free all of Italy — and all of Italy is behind him. He appeals to all true Italian hearts! Now is the time to decide whether Italy shall be free or again be submitted for centuries to a foreign yoke. How free with their promises, how perfidious your present masters are! Experience has shown you how little you can trust them. Italians, you are called upon to unite so as to receive a government of your choice and a constitution worthy of the times and of yourselves which shall guarantee your freedom and welfare as soon as your independence is attained.[61]

How could Bellegarde answer such an appeal — so compelling that only a heart of stone could remain unmoved, so dangerous since almost every patriotic plea in this superb piece of propaganda contained a bit of truth? He could only peel from Murat's phrases their gilded coating and reveal the ugly uncertainty which lay underneath; he could only stir where a people weary of upheaval were most sensitive — the fear not only of yet another forfeit of security but of yet another and even greater disappointment.

On April 5, after sufficient time had been allowed for the first effects of Murat's proclamation to subside, the marshal made his counter-proclamation in the tone of a well-meaning but sobering second thought:

Hardly have the hopes and efforts for a lasting peace been realized, after so much hard work, when suddenly they are interrupted by the unthinkable ambitions of a single man from whom Italians have all already suffered. Murat, who owes his existence to Austria, now attacks it and brings war and destruction to Italy. He is new and foreign to Italy as well as to those who rule. Thereby he uses words which one could have expected from an Alexander Farnese or an Andrea Doria. Now he has made himself the head of the Italian nation. But your emperor and king, as was his House, was born and raised in Italy and rules his lands there, as he does his many other nations, with paternal affection. Murat, who is ruler of only one end of Italy, seeks to lead astray the minds of people with the fantasy of an Italy bound by natural boundaries. But where, one may ask, would be the capital of such a state, of a land which contains so many natural divisions? Not the extent of its territory nor the number of its inhabitants nor the strength of its armed might but rather good laws and respect for honored customs and uses make for the happiness of a people. For this reason, the inhabitants of Tuscany and Lombardy remember gratefully the names of Maria Theresia, Leopold, and Joseph. Murat attempts to seduce and betray the less thoughtful and careful with false hopes of independence. The Allied Powers will show you how little they sympathize with Murat. On the other hand, the benificence of the emperor speaks for itself. Austria has tried to unify all parties and to treat all, even those who were led astray, as truly its sons. Austria is by its very nature peace-loving. It has promised peace, quiet, security, good government and paternal care, and all this it will render! Compare the happy days before 1796 with that which you have had to endure afterwards. That which you have suffered was the result of and was built upon the same pronouncements which are put before you now, to urge you to new tribulations and upheavals. You have been disappointed before. Be wiser and more careful this time! Folly now will cause you much greater injury than before. Be calm and be loyal to your monarch, who is worthy of your affection, and be loyal to your fatherland![62]

On April 16 Bellegarde made officially known in Milan the creation of the Lombardo-Venetian Kingdom. Thereby he assured Austria's Italian subjects that "their nationality which they rightly love so much would be safeguarded and conserved."[63] But Bellegarde was already crossing the next bridge. All this was not enough! He was acquainted only too well with the emperor's habits as with the short patience of the Milanese. Three days before, he had written to Metternich, warning him that delay in nominating the viceroy would thwart the success expected from the emperor's new measure. Otherwise the ill-intended would not hesitate to call it a brazen sham presented to the Italians in order to amuse them, to nurse their favorite idea, to quiet them. They would insist that, *mutato nomine,* all would remain as before, that there would be no royal court to give lustre to the capital, that all the inconveniences of a far-off bureaucracy would continue, that the Italian nation would no longer be a "national body" as before, that false hopes would be the only fruits born from the prestige of a kingdom with which one beguiled their vanity and their credulity. Bellegarde called to Metternich's attention that such observations could easily come to the minds of all Italians — proud, skeptical, and defiant as they were — and lead to extreme feelings of humiliation and alienation. Surely the minister would recognize the justness of these reflections aimed at preventing consequences which could be as troublesome as inevitable. That Bellegarde's words in his proclamation of April 5 were not empty, one can gather from those directed to Metternich eight days later:

We won't gain a thing by stringing this people along. We must show them in deed that we are seriously occupied with their well-being and their political existence — which is their mania — that minister and government share the affection and well-meaning intentions which the sovereign has for them. [Only this sort of conduct would] dissipate the idea of a foreign yoke and the contempt attached to it . . . and bring back Austria's good name, which was almost lost and, finally, conciliate those passionate spirits who are as susceptible to attachment and enthusiasm as to hate and vengeance.[64]

THE FINAL RESTORATION OF ITALY: OPPOSITION
AND ITS IMPLICATIONS

At the height of the war, as if to bolster feelings of responsibility and pride for the new kingdom, Kaiser Franz decreed a convening of the Lombardo-Venetian central congregations.[65] At the same time, Saurau was given — in addition to his duties as civil governor in Milan — the position of army minister in Italy for the duration of the conflict. He was to care for the needs of Austrian troops on the peninsula and to organize provisional regimes in those reconquered areas which the troops would occupy.[66] Within a week, the COHC's president was concerned with a drawing up of definitions between Bellegarde's and Saurau's respective spheres of authority,[67] and Metternich had issued specific political instructions.[68] Their main theme was that, since Murat had destroyed the tranquillity of Italy, and Austria was obliged to shoulder the burden of restoring order, those states which would owe their liberation to Austria and thus be obligated to it for this service, should then accept Austrian guidance in establishing a new collective security on the peninsula.

Thereby Metternich had, at long last, a good chance of realizing a pet project: an Italian Confederation similar to the German one. This was to be the final foundation of his European structure; as in Germany, Austria was to be the keystone. The idea of gathering the Italian states together into some sort of frame had appeared ever since the French invasion in 1795 — then, to be sure, French and not Austrian leadership was intended.[69] The idea was revived with the defeat of Napoleon, but stipulations in the First Peace of Paris (art. IX) were discouraging to it; discussion on this subject had been avoided at the Congress of Vienna for fear of stirring up difficulty at what seemed a most inopportune time.[70] Now, Metternich felt, the time was ripe "to form under our shield a federative defense system in Italy."[71] Within the next two months, he brought up the idea repeatedly.[72] Unfortunately, Metternich's well-founded speculation in regard to the

5 Metternich

gratitude of liberated states was not to be extended to Sardinia, which came to be the real obstacle to the scheme. It had no feeling either of obligation or of a need for Austrian protection; much more, it feared a curtailing of its ancient practice of straddling the Alpine barrier — if not geographically, at least politically.[73] In Turin, expected distrust and misgiving was soon evident.[74]

Bellegarde also supported this plan with enthusiasm but was much more outspoken in the methods of urging the Italian princes to acquiesce. It was strong stuff indeed to advocate using the dissatisfaction of subjects as a diplomatic lever against their ruler. The marshal declared that Austria could compel to compliance the restored but reactionary and reluctant princes in *"belle Italie"* by holding before their noses the discontent of their subjects, a discontent which arose, so Bellegarde claimed, in large part from insufferable practices revealing an unwillingness or incapability to recognize the progress of man's thinking within the last quarter-century. Such arguments as well as the threat inherent in the fact that — as Bellegarde insisted — the opposition in Italy represented the majority, could well be expected to be persuasive. In any case, the Italian Confederation would be so popular, Bellegarde assured Metternich, that it would gain for Austria all the voices of the nation, "since without a doubt all institutions which tend to bring together the different peoples of Italy and unite them in the sense of the German Confederation could not help but please all sides extremely."[75]

In such a confederation, therefore, Bellegarde as well as Metternich hoped to visualize a frame for the Italian nationality. In this sense it was as much a concession as purely a means of consolidating Austrian hegemony. This attempt to endow the expression "Italy" with more than geographical significance — and not the so-called "morcellement" — represents the true line of Metternich's Italian policy. The splitting up of Italy into various fiercely independent, reactionary, and even hostile states was the last thing which the Austrian minister wanted. The reason for drawing the Italian states together under the eyes of a watchful but in no way expansionistic Austria was simply that it could not afford a recurrence of disorder and turmoil.

Furthermore, Bellegarde reminded Metternich, an Austrian primacy in Italy expressed through an Italian Confederation could even claim an altruistic and beneficial aim. As planned, such a primacy would give Austria more force and weight than that which the presidency of the German Confederation offered and "despite efforts made by the Italian courts to circumvent it, this Austrian primacy would prevent them allowing their

peoples to relapse into that state of absolute feebleness to which are ascrib-
able the recent misfortunes of this land." The inner repose of Italy, by no
means safeguarded, would be in every sense Austria's burden. "It is easy to
see," the marshal maintained, "that if we do not succeed in giving to these
governments an energetic impulse, they will lose in a very short time all
support except of those who had remained loyal during the French regime."
And if this were allowed to happen, the result would be a public completely repelled by the present order of things. In the end, it would mean a dissatisfied Italy which could be held in control only through military might
and this would be nothing but a "replacement of the system of terror" of
which Bonaparte had availed himself.

But what of popular opposition? Bellegarde was the first to realize that
the campaign's happy outcome had not eradicated this unhappy problem.
Experience had shown, he observed to Metternich, that it was no longer a
question of dealing with a few dissatisfied here and there as he had thought
previously. Rather, it was a numerous group, contained only by force. It
was composed of diverse elements but united in despising the *status quo*,
which it saw sustained only by the grip of Austria. Consequently, its
members fastened all their hopes upon the time when a crisis would cause
Austria to weaken her grip and enable them to strike forth. This notion,
one may add, was the first premise of the belief in a "national conspiracy".
In examining the structure of this group, the marshal singled out the urban
populations as its breeding ground; he lamented the non-existence of a
reliable landowning countryfolk. Those living on the land, belonging for
the most part to city dwellers, led a drab life and were, on the whole, indifferent to "national events". Opinions in the cities, and especially in the
capitals, were therefore decisive in any judgment of the political atmosphere; precisely there the most significant changes had taken place. The
formerly so reliable old nobility and the clergy had never quite recovered
from spoliation and ruin. But during Napoleonic times, a new extensive
middle class of civil and military officials, commercial entrepreneurs, and
intellectuals had made careers and fortunes, appropriating thereby more
and more land. Of course Bellegarde knew that one could not expect all of
those who had benefited from the previous regime to become friends of the
Restoration. His analysis, made as it was some fifteen months after the
capitulation of Eugene, indicated that the sudden revulsion against the
French, the joyous relief at peace, and the warm welcome for Austria were
emotions long spent and forgotten; indeed, many began to recall better
days before the end had come. In a wry understatement, the Austrian
commander noted that "considering the demoralization bound to arise un-

der a government pursuing private [rather than public] interests, those individuals are the exception who disregard their own losses and nevertheless are satisfied with the return of a government which destroys their hopes, and for many, even their existence."

Apparently Bellegarde feared those who harbored grudges as more severe and dangerous foes than those idealists to whom could be ascribed somewhat honest if contrary political convictions and what he called "a better morality". To the latter group he counted those who, supported and encouraged by the English Opposition, dreamed of an independent Italy united under one monarch. Whereas those now deprived of an accustomed or barely attained status of comfort would logically supply the nucleus of the discontented, the marshal realized that aggravation through new factors continuously fired up new tension. Some of these factors could, regrettably, not be avoided: the financial straits, debts, and obligations inherited from the previous regime; the present needs of exhausted states; the resulting disappointment at the maintenance of taxes at almost the former rates; slow recovery from economic ruin; serious crop failures and the ensuing hardships, especially for the lower classes; stoppage on a large number of popular but extravagant public projects; and the necessity of continued conscription and of stationing large contingents of troops on Italian soil.

But what could be avoided? In view of the frequency with which posterity has applied the designation "reactionary" to Metternich, it appears ironic that he, just as Bellegarde, should have been so adamant in condemning reactionary rule. Considering themselves as up-to-date apostles of the Enlightenment, both felt that such rule would not only violate the ethics of responsible governing but would taunt revolution into reality. First and foremost, this serious threat was to be avoided in an Italy which Bellegarde had aptly likened to a momentarily dormant but by no means extinct volcano. It was all the more deplorable, therefore, so thought Bellegarde, that many of the restored governments had ignored their original manifestations so soon and proceeded to drag back all the despised practices of yore. In all this forgetfulness that things had changed, they came to alienate even those among their own supporters to whom some sense could be attributed. Upon returning to their thrones, some of the Italian rulers had been compelled to accept principles of moderation — the only applicable ones, as Bellegarde insisted — in order to prevent immediate and excessive reaction. But even if this had won over a number of the not completely hopeless, the irreconcilables were hardly impressed. Yet instead of working to gain badly needed support, too many of the restored governments could show only a gain in the number of the malcontents.

At this point one might ask: what did the Austrian commander in Italy and representative of the viceroy have to say about Austrian Italy? He was prudent enough, of course, not to be too specific or to include the King of Lombardy-Venetia in his bitter disapproval of the Italian princes' resented conduct. In his painful admission that there was at present scarcely any opposition on the peninsula as strong as in Lombardy-Venetia itself, he left little doubt of his misgivings. For more than a year now he had pleaded for concessions to Italian national feelings, for a kingdom, for a viceroy with some real authority. Now he spoke of an Austrian obligation not only toward Lombardy-Venetia but toward the rest of Italy, now free at last of Murat. If Austria wished to win active support and influence on the peninsula — despite the princes — then it must first of all be able to serve its own Lombardo-Venetian Kingdom as a model for the other governments. But even this step had a prerequisite: "We can gain the attachment of the others only in gaining first the affections of our own subjects." To do this, he emphasized once more to Metternich that "it would be necessary above all to centralize much more the administration of the provinces of the new Lombardo-Venetian Kingdom [about Milan] and to render it more national and less dependent in its affairs on the capital [Vienna]." Yet on this point there was so much left to be desired; Vienna did not seem to be able to loosen its reins. Moreover, even if Austria should have been expected to set an example, it was forced — and particularly in Milan and Venice — to battle the most haunting specters of times gone. Opposition in Austrian Italy was so formidable, according to the marshal, because the previous *Regno d'Italia* had been incomparably more "flattering to popular vanity" than the present kingdom. One should not forget, he added, that in the former, the Italians had after all succeeded in removing the French and winning for themselves most of the high posts.

Of all the immediate and burning causes of grievances in Lombardy-Venetia, perhaps none stung Italian dignity so sharply as the announced revamping of the judicial system. Although long determined by the emperor, his Italian subjects could not bring themselves to accept this basic change; the abolition of the *Code Napoléon* and the introduction of the Austrian civil law was being undertaken, in words of Bellegarde which echoed the sentiments of most Lombardo-Venetian citizens, "without taking into account the customs and habits of the nation." Moreover, the Milanese were to be deprived of their high court of appeal (third instance) by transfer of its jurisdiction to Vienna — and this court had been a privilege of autonomy enjoyed under the Habsburgs before the Revolution, a fact which Bellegarde had felt necessary to call to Lazansky's attention.[76]

Protests accumulated and in time doubts were heard even among the highest Austrian circles against this judicial policy, which was not a life-and-death matter for the Habsburg monarchy, but which well affected the lives of all in Lombardy-Venetia.

The far-reaching cultural and political implications which such a course might have, and also the state of the Italian provinces in general, were the subjects of two discourses sent to Metternich's Staatskanzlei some time in the middle of 1815. Their author was Freiherr v. Sardagna, an Austrian well qualified in judicial affairs; he stood close to Bellegarde and wrote with his full approbation.[77] Moreover, he seems then or not long thereafter to have won the confidence of Metternich. Like Bellegarde, Sardagna proceeded from the primary and deeply disturbing questions: "Why are we obliged to admit that [in spite of the best intentions] our government is not liked in Italy? Why . . . must one pronounce the sad truth that at present the might of one of the better monarchs is only sustained by military force and that nearly the only partisans upon which he can rely in case of danger are to be found in the barracks?"

In taking up the Italians' grievances, Sardagna also delved into the many possible factors behind them; he accused the present administration of such sins of omission and commission that it compared quite unfavorably with either the former Austrian or French administrations in Milan. Like Bellegarde, he had some notions on a social and economic program which included public works, rises in civil service pay, creation of new and important offices, cajolery of the nobility through various honors, and a severe crackdown on well-known troublemakers. Even more, he was keenly aware of the cultural differences and national sensitivities, the respect of which was a prerequisite for a successful organization policy in Italy. But above all, he showed that he understood the proper composition of a multinational state to be one of equal and interdependent partnership.

To be sure, many of his proposals regarding Italy were taken from past example. Seen together, the better aspects — at one time or another — of previous autonomy had amounted to a great deal. They were now made the measuring points not only by Sardagna or Bellegarde but by all Italians who still were expecting something from Austria. Nonetheless, Sardagna's proposals represented by and large the limit of the attainable under existing circumstances. They contained in essence nearly all that was said and done in the ensuing years and most of the ideas which Metternich came to accept as the only possible solution for the Italian difficulties as soon as he himself was on the scene.

In analyzing the distribution of discontent among the various social

levels, and in weighing the political potential of various classes, Sardagna
could only agree with Bellegarde; he too, not in disdain but as a simple
matter of fact, discounted the unpropertied masses as a political force —
even though, as Sardagna claimed, they had shown themselves during the
campaign as more pro-Austrian than the others simply by having ignored
Murat. Among the groups stirred politically, he saw not an attachment to
the House of Habsburg — all the more reason, he thought, to follow the
Napoleonic example of creating a reliable party — but a persistence of the
hope for national independence and union. Such ideals he recognized as the
vehicles for the ever more ominous secret societies, which were to be considered as the result of already existing opinions and not as the creators of
the opinions which they propagated.

For the fact that on each day dwindled away not only the attachment
still remaining among the Italian subjects but also the influence which Austria could exercise, there could be for Sardagna only one main reason: the
present administration of Lombardy-Venetia had failed; it simply did not
suit the country; despite some concessions, it was after all German in its
form and character. Is there not discrimination, Sardagna asked, if Lombardy-Venetia has been handed over exclusively to the Austrians who made
up the COHC? No Italian was more serious or more fervently open-mind-
ed than this Tyrolean as he said that, no matter how liberal-minded or un-
partisan the commission's members might consider themselves, they could
not help being partial to the welfare of their German fatherland nor could
they deliberate on measures for Italy without considering thereby advantages for the old provinces of the monarchy. As discerningly as Sardagna judged human nature, it must be admitted that his attitude on the
commission was only a sincerely meant repetition of an oft-heard charge,
one which even Metternich was to take up later just as sincerely, despite the
fact that it was not quite true. Nonetheless, this and all the inconveniences
of an inconsiderate policy — not to mention the introduction of the Austrian law code — had now to be endured. Recalling Milan's recent past,
Sardagna could show how the present Habsburg regime suffered through
comparison: a nation once accustomed, as he imagined, to display in the
administration, to magnificence in public works, to the luxury of a brilliant court, to a representative of the sovereign cloaked with real powers,
now found itself left empty-handed. Instead it felt only the reins retied all
too tightly between it and a people whose language and customs were so
very much more different from theirs than those of the French.

Like many Austrian officials, Sardagna sentimentally recalled the
benefits of enlightened Habsburg rule in time gone by. Had the Austrian

heritage, he asked, been completely forgotten in Lombardy? The future generation in Lombardy-Venetia would accustom itself as little as the present one to an absolutely foreign regime, one which is a far cry from the Austrian administration under which Lombardy had prospered in better days. Then, the dignity of the residing archduke and his minister had also been enhanced with an imposing authority, and what was more, Germans did not direct Italian affairs exclusively from Vienna. Furthermore, the position of the Italian possessions as part of the rest of the peninsula had wisely been taken into consideration. For this reason, if not also to smother all hopes of amalgamating the Lombard administration with that of the German provinces, he remembered, Lombardy had been placed — just as Belgium — under the immediate direction of the Office of Foreign Affairs.

The problem of Lombardy-Venetia's position within the monarchy did not raise a wholly new problem regarding the state's structure as a whole. For Sardagna, one of the most important sets of institutions which the Habsburg empire possessed were the *Hofkanzleien* of Austria and Bohemia, of Hungary, and of Transylvania. In his opinion, these chancelleries were such an effective form of mediation between the monarch and his peoples that they might well be given credit for preserving the Habsburg empire from "the constitutional mania". In carrying out imperial resolutions, these institutions modified them according to the needs of the different populations which they represented. He emphasized that each of these chancelleries was composed, moreover, either of nationals of the provinces whose affairs they, in the last resort, directed or of persons who, having served there for a long time, were avidly and particularly interested in their well-being. But instead of such an institution, Lombardy-Venetia had its COHC with all its shortcomings. The next necessary step was logical and clear enough:

An Italian *Hofkanzlei* composed of nationals who could plead their country's cause before their sovereign [would] see to it that his orders were executed in the fashion and forms best suited to Italian customs and mores. Well constituted, it would take notice of that which had occurred during the last eighteen years and would be there, not for itself, but for a higher and more sacred purpose — to combine the interests of the Lombardo-Venetian Kingdom with those of the Monarchy.

Not only did Sardagna point to the wide cultural dissimilarity between Germans and Italians but also to the latter's cultural achievements as being in every way equal if not superior to those of the former. It was therefore all the more irresponsible, in his opinion, to force upon the Italians a law code which — far from proven more efficacious — exhibited noticeable defects, to treat the land as if it were a colony, and to exercise a cultural paternalism which — at most permissible with primitive peoples — was wholly uncalled-for in Italy. Sardagna's broad and specific condemnation of a policy advocating conformity and what he called *amalgamation* — a condemnation which he insisted was heard often in Austria itself — was coupled with the admonition that it would certainly be more politic to encourage diversity among the Austrian family of states. Obviously then, disregard for national customs and traditions, the brazen imposition of a form equal to but not equally suitable to all, was not the way to win affection. But more than anything else, this Austrian jurist challenged the assumption of German guardianship over the other nationalities in the Habsburg empire: "None of the peoples is numerous or mighty enough to be able to claim for itself with any right predominance over the others, and particularly the Germans, who possess the capital, least of all."[78]

KAISER FRANZ AND METTERNICH: FROM VIENNA
TO PARIS ONCE AGAIN

At the Congress, the problem of nationality had been an important theme in the discussions on Poland; it had been left more or less in the lobbies regarding Germany and Italy; it was mentioned only fleetingly among those observing Serbia and Greece. Whereas the plenipotentiaries of the major powers paid their respects to Polish nationality, and whereas the British and the Russians especially could well afford a generous solicitude for nationalities of other states, it was principally Metternich who had already to concern himself with the negative sides of the nationality problem. As the first minister of a multinational major power, he could hardly help but be sensitive to possible dangers to the existing political structure which might result from excessive national feelings, wherever they might appear. For example, a struggle for independence on the part of Serbs or Greeks could threaten the existence of the Ottoman empire, which, if nothing else, at least screened off Russian expansion toward the southwest. Austria now had every reason to sustain this ancient adversary, Metternich had often emphasized,[79] not the least being that if a polyglot state's right of existence could be cast into doubt by "just" national aspirations, then the doubts which could be applied to the Ottoman empire today could be applied to the Habsburg empire tomorrow. This unfortunate dilemma, among other things, kept Metternich from sympathizing openly with national and "Christian" uprisings against Turkish rule and forced Austria to continue material aid to the Porte even in the face of a possible extermination of the "Serbian nation".[80]

Since Czar Alexander espoused all sorts of "liberal" causes, gave comfort to those hoping for Italian independence, and fancied himself as champion and protector of the Polish and Greek nationalities, he always remained an object of Metternich's special vigilance. The minister even at this time labelled him as "one of the most active implements in the liberation of the Greek nation". Even though the czar did not see in this dream any Russian aggrandizement, what made his attitude nevertheless so dangerous was — according to Metternich — that he simply wanted a Greek empire for the Greeks just as he wanted an Italy for the Italians.[81]

Even prior to the Congress, Metternich had been compelled to adjust his Polish policy to the czar's high-sounding aims, and at one point declared himself ready to support a free and independent Poland to prevent Alexander from pocketing the entire Duchy of Warsaw.[82] Also, he soon came to fear that the czar's efforts to arouse and rally Polish national feeling about his standard as King of Poland might extend its magnetism across the frontiers and attract the Galicians of Polish nationality to the goings-on in Warsaw. This fear was rendered all the more acute by the fact that such inhabitants had less to expect in comparison from an Austrian administration whose interest in Polish customs and language was not particularly warm.

As the regulation of the so-called Fourth Partition of Poland became certain, the participating powers, as well as Britain, seemed to outdo one another in expressing concern for the Polish nationality. On January 12, 1815, Castlereagh had come out for treating the Poles as Poles and granting them the necessary institutions. This the Russian foreign minister, Nesselrode, could only underline, since thereby Russia could, now more than ever, step forth as guardian and protector of the Polish nation. On January 30, Hardenberg had followed suit for Prussia. During the meeting of February 21, Metternich presented his opinions.[83] The Austrian emperor, he declared, was in complete accord with the contents of Castlereagh's communication and was far from being disquieted by that which pertained to Polish nationality in general. On the contrary, it was claimed, Austria had never viewed a free Poland as a rival or as an enemy, and only imperious circumstances, quite apart from the wishes of Austrian sovereigns, had compelled them to take part in the partitions. And then, the emperor had always sought to promote the welfare of his Polish subjects, a fact attested to by comparing the present cultural niveau and prosperity of Galicia with that of former times. Now, Metternich continued somewhat glibly, the emperor had once more subjected his own desires for a free and independent Poland with a national Polish government to the considerations of the other powers. However, he would not cease, for his part, to watch over the happiness of his Polish subjects with that paternal care which he dedicated with equal justice to all peoples of different origins which Providence had placed under his scepter. In that regard, the emperor was declared to be in no way behind the liberal views of the czar in favoring national institutions for his Polish subjects.

Such notions from a ruler bent on achieving conformity might strike us as strange indeed, were it not that behind the kind sentiments which the minister attributed to the emperor and which may be regarded to some extent as diplomatic embellishment, one can discern Metternich's own convictions. Metternich often, and with some presumption, presented personal views as those of the emperor — a practice which the following statement (taken from the above-mentioned note) might illustrate: "His Imperial Majesty is convinced that the first guarantees of repose and of the strength of states are found in the happiness of their peoples, and that this happiness is inseparable from the just deference which governments must have for the nationality and habits of those under their administration."

But at the same time Metternich had to forestall the spreading of Polish nationalism in Galicia. The question of what to do there had brought him together with the head of the police, Baron Haager, and the former governor in Lemberg, Count Goëss, who had just been transferred to Venice. As Metternich reported to Kaiser Franz, there was quick agreement regarding police measures: secret agents might ascertain nationalistic activity in Galicia's neighboring states as well as the connections of their inhabitants with those of Galicia. On this point, Metternich had nothing to add. The aim of political and administrative measures was also clear enough: to fasten ever more securely the loyalty of the Galicians to the Habsburg empire. Here, Metternich concurred wholeheartedly with Goëss in regard to method: may it never be attempted to make the Poles with one stroke into Germans; before anything else, they must become real Galicians so that they may cease to regard themselves as Poles. Thus Metternich resorted once more to a means which he had already advocated in Italy in order to discourage a general nationalism of a people divided by various frontiers: the encouraging of a regional-national character and spirit.

Furthermore, Metternich supported the establishment of a "*National-repräsentanz oder ständischen Verfassung*". Quick assent to such an estates-

constitution, he thought, would do much in winning the adherence of the
Galicians; the proper time for making this known might well be in conjunction with the forthcoming publication of the pacts between Austria,
Prussia, and Russia on the dissolution of the Duchy of Warsaw and the
definition of respective boundaries. Also, Metternich found Goëss' suggestions on administrative measures to the point and to his liking: important
posts for deserving nationals, expansion and alleviation of Galician commerce, reduction of obligations, amnesties, and, finally, a personal appearance of the emperor. All this would help to gain public opinion, although
Metternich felt that Galician wishes would be fulfilled, at least to some
extent, through the aforementioned pacts' provisions for their nationality.

One other matter remained which Metternich's sensitive concern for
equilibrium within the monarchy could not leave unmentioned. He recalled
that just a few days before, the emperor had granted the new Lombardo-
Venetian Kingdom privilege and favor. Consequently, he cautioned, much
care and insight were now necessary to avoid giving the Galicians the
impression of being less deserving or even slighted, especially in regard to
the dispensation of imperial benefaction. This was all the more important
in that also in Galicia "the very desirable conviction might arise that with
the justest of monarchs, devotion and loyalty would always be answered
by paternal care, affection, and mildness."[84]

On May 3, 1815, both Austria and Prussia signed treaties with Russia
on the regulation of Polish territory; these included stipulations guarantee-
ing to their respective Polish inhabitants national institutions, which,
according to the Russo-Prussian pact, were to assure the conservation of
the Polish nationality. The Russo-Austrian treaty, moreover, provided for
a representative body for Polish citizens.[85] In the Final Acts of the Congress of Vienna, the paragraphs calling for representative bodies and
national institutions were repeated for all three powers. To them was reserved, however, the way and manner of carrying out such measures.[86]

The fact that the czar held the greater part of former Polish territory
enabled him to appropriate the name of *Poland* itself. Thereby he was able
to fulfill the program of national institutions on a much broader and appealing basis than could his neighbors, who possessed smaller stretches of
Polish land. As King of Poland he could claim that Poles had only him to
thank if Poland retained a proud place among the European society of
nations. With this make-believe and, as Hudelist complained to Metternich,
by using all "the weaknesses of the nation", the czar had apparently won a
great deal of ground with the Poles.[87] Especially those who had placed

desperate hopes on Napoleon and who were now stunned by his final downfall became susceptible to Russian propaganda. At the same time, the Galicians could not be expected to remain immune to all this; Metternich was soon warned that he might have to take action to prevent an epidemic of "hotheadedness" in Galicia.[88] Indeed, the firing up of Polish national feeling under Russian auspices had given rise to an idea as absurd as it was discomforting for Austria — that Galicia should be detached from the Habsburg empire in order to enlarge Congress Poland to its "proper extent". More alarming than anything else was the enthusiasm which had accompanied this rumor on both sides of the Galician frontier.[89] But even in view of such developments, the emperor did little more than to entrust matters of external interference to the foreign ministry, and of internal security to the police. As for a Galician program, Kaiser Franz seems to have been content with a policy of watchful waiting.

While in Milan Bellegarde and Sardagna were attempting to fit for Lombardy-Venetia as best they could a national autonomy policy consisting of patches, Kaiser Franz and Metternich had seen the Congress of Vienna disband at last after a ceremonious final signing; once more they had set out to follow victory to Paris.

In the meantime, uncertainty and rumor continued to hover over the Italian scene — even the possibility of an Italian chancellery was making the rounds.[90] After the Second Peace of Paris had been signed, both emperor and minister began turning their attention to the Italian situation with which they had almost lost touch; recent reports from Milan had been far from encouraging in their accounts of slow progress, and of opposition, not to mention severe criticism of administrative policy. Moreover, Metternich complained that the otherwise so conscientious Bellegarde "had not answered a single point."[91] The marshal, for his part, resented hearing that administrative progress in Milan lagged behind that in Venice and was especially distressed because the monarch himself had more than once complained of this: after all, Venetia had been organized, so to speak, back in 1804, whereas Lombardy had learned of its final territorial limits only after the Congress, and of its territorial subdivisions not even at the hour of his writing. In addition, he protested to Metternich, "I am not at all informed nor kept up to date on what is going on down there [in Venice]." Feeling the need to justify his tenure in Milan once more, Bellegarde went so far as to minimize discontent there which, he claimed, "had not troubled public tranquillity for a single instant" despite the many adverse circumstances — a fact which he felt must surely reflect favorably upon the Milan *gubernium*.[92] In view of the marshal's earlier warnings, Metternich may have been vexed at this and even slightly annoyed at Bellegarde's sincerely meant reminder that the minister could not — by his own admission — be expected to rectify or contradict such facts and ideas as Bellegarde presented and that Metternich was insufficiently informed on details too long and wearisome to elaborate in correspondence.[93]

Certainly this must have aggravated an atmosphere at imperial headquarters already made somewhat sultry through the incomprehensibility of the Milanese situation.[94] Accumulated imperial displeasure finally burst forth in *Allerhöchsten Resolutionen* to get things going and in a reprimand for the authorities in Milan, which Lazansky deftly passed on to Bellegarde. This brought forth all kinds of explanations, especially from the latter's aide Rosetti,[95] and a bitter protest to Metternich from the marshal himself.[96] Of course the sensitive Bellegarde was stung by this rebuke which he rightly considered uncalled for and irreconcilable either with his position or his long and distinguished service. To receive such a censure through the ordinary channels of the COHC must have been especially humiliating for the lieutenant and representative of the viceroy. In such a capacity, Bellegarde correctly countered to Metternich, it was not his obligation to prod on *gubernial* affairs of which *"messieurs les gouverneurs"* simply kept him in the dark. More than that, the one matter which must be his real concern was the viceroyalty, but this vital question was the very one the emperor had himself postponed to be arranged personally upon his sojourn in Italy. Bellegarde thus could only hope for an early arrival of the emperor and his minister to straighten things out and thereby to restore his honor.

This unfortunate development resulted from the disparity between the monarch's and the marshal's views on what a viceroyal representative's role should be. Because Kaiser Franz saw in Bellegarde not much more than a sort of ornamental administrative referee who was conceded responsibility only in the case of failure, because Bellegarde's office was circumvented and deprived of the dignity which not just he but the Italians as well expected to see attached to it, his status had become doubtful and he was himself discouraged: no matter to what degree the hampered marshal might have shared the blame, it all landed at his feet. All the while, however, the emperor had grown more than anxious, as Metternich expressed it, "to observe from close up the unknown — the working of the Milanese *gubernium*." Whereas outwardly the purpose of the Italian journey might have been the reception of homage, the primary incentive had become the urgent need to detect and remove difficulties there so that the administration could at last function smoothly.[97] Metternich knew that any future measures could strike a positive response only if reflecting some of the so-called national sentiments; only if issued by a concerned and well-meaning emperor on the scene, could they stem rising dissatisfaction and consolidate loyalty to the House of Habsburg. As Metternich looked ahead to the Italian journey, he was beset with a strange mixture of high expectation and foreboding. Everything would depend on the effect of the imperial presence: Could the sober monarch capture the hearts of his imaginative Italian subjects? Would he keep to the course which Metternich had, with some apparent momentary success, so earnestly urged upon him? "God grant", the minister had written shortly before departure from Paris, "that [the emperor] carries out there what he has in mind here."[98]

To summarize: The Wessenberg mission substantiated Metternich's objections to the conformity policy and helped to extend the Staatskanzlei's voice in internal affairs. However, both Metternich and Wessenberg, as Austria's plenipotentiaries at the Congress of Vienna, were occupied for nearly a year almost exclusively with foreign affairs. They were unable to devote much more than a token attention to matters of internal organization — an issue which Kaiser Franz left to the *Hofkommissär* in Illyria, Saurau, and to the COHC. The commission plodded along a course close to the emperor's original policy and skirted all proposals for some sort of separate status for the newly-won lands. On the scene, Bellegarde repeatedly warned Metternich and the emperor that the organizing authorities must pay more respect to Italian "national wishes", that the long-awaited proclamation of the Lombardo-Venetian Kingdom was not enough and that the new kingdom must be given a much greater semblance of national autonomy — which meant first and foremost a viceroy with substantial powers. The marshal shared Metternich's enthusiasm for an Italian confederation, being certain that any institution capable of bringing the Italian people closer together would be appreciated by all. In such a confederation Bellegarde saw a means for Austria to fulfill its obligations to the Italians — not only through protection and pacification but also by preventing reactionary rule, which he regarded as a chief contributor to discontent in several Italian states. He knew that Austria could only win the respect of other Italians and their governments by serving its own Lombardo-Venetian Kingdom as an example and that it could do this only after winning first the affections of its own Italian subjects and finding friends other "than those in the barracks." Yet, he charged, this was made impossible by the present Austrian organization policy in Italy. Bellegarde and Sardagna fully realized the harm done by the notion of foreign rule and by the impression that the Germans took upon themselves the right to rule over other nationalities. Thus they deplored the imposition of alien forms and the very evident disrespect for Italian national character and customs. In the meantime, although Metternich had paid his respects to Polish nationality, he was soon faced with the negative aspects of the nationality problem in Galicia. For this region he proposed the same policy as he already had advocated in Lombardy-Venetia: encouragement of a regional-national consciousness so that ties beyond the frontier might be forgotten. Finally, in Paris, aware that things had gone wrong in the Italian provinces, Metternich had urged upon the emperor a new course of action.

METTERNICH

CHAPTER III

ON THE SCENE AND THE DELAY OF A SATISFACTORY
SETTLEMENT: 1815-1816

METTERNICH, LOMBARDO-VENETIAN AUTONOMY,
AND THE COHC

Kaiser Franz and Metternich made the journey to the lands south of the Alps separately. In November 1815, while the emperor had already enjoyed a jubilant welcome and was engaged in a series of resplendent receptions in a setting which only Venice could furnish, his minister was still finishing up diplomatic matters in Paris. Metternich finally departed late in November and, proceeding through Switzerland and Lombardy, joined his monarch on December 5. Although he likened Venice to a grandiose structure whose impoverished owner was forced to dwell in a small hut adjacent to the monument of his former glory, he was satisfied more than ever with public sentiment there. To overcome the city's economic stagnation by stimulating trade, he saw no alternative but to have Venice declared a free port.[1]

After a fortnight there, during which he already seems to have occupied himself with the more pressing problem of Milan,[2] he went ahead to prepare the monarch's entry into a city still proud to have been the capital of the "Kingdom of Italy". This event all sides keenly awaited. Whereas it was generally expected — recalling the spring of 1814 — that Milanese enthusiasm would not match that of the Venetians, it was hoped nevertheless that dazzling social events attending the imperial presence might dim memories of Eugene's elegant court and, moreover, that such activity might relieve Milan's high-society of a dangerous boredom and satisfy at last its longing for display. Just as in Venice, public entertainment and lavish illuminations were prepared. A festival air was to bring the public into gay spirits, thereby compensating to an extent for what the sober-minded monarch lacked in flair.

Indeed, public enthusiasm, even if occasionally spurred, could well be spontaneous — as Austrian authorities often insisted — and in the case of

Venice, we do not need to dispute them. Yet they must have known only too well the ephemeral nature of such enthusiasm, and especially in Milan it mattered to make the most of the opportunity while still good. However, although the monarch's entry into Milan on Sylvester Day lacked neither solemnity nor pomp, it did lack real warmth, something only too openly admitted.[3] In spite of a considerable turn-out, it remained a welcome for an emperor of Austria but not for a king of Lombardy-Venetia entering his capital. The inevitable comparison with Venice caused Kaiser Franz some time later to reflect glumly: "In Venice I was among my children, in Milan I saw only subjects."[4]

Throughout this period, Austrians were wont to accept as a matter of fact a difference in attitudes held in regard to the two cities — a difference which led to the conviction that Venice was but a serious economic concern whereas Milan was a serious political one. Demonstrations of loyalty were certainly easy when publicly-voiced aspirations involved only economic concessions which stood a fair chance of fulfillment; it was something else when aspirations involved political concessions where the prospect of fulfillment seemed discouraging to say the least. On this point, Metternich now set out to concentrate and, if necessary, to correct Vienna's policy toward its Italian possessions.

No sooner had Kaiser Franz arrived than Metternich had ready and waiting for him a report on the situation in Lombardy.[5] For Metternich, the past few days in Milan had marked one more turning point in his career; for the first time in years, the minister for external affairs began to devote serious and extended attention to internal problems — to responsibilities which could have been regarded as beyond the Staatskanzlei's proper province of foreign and political matters. If the whole Italian business was only an administrative affair, then nothing could be said against those resentful of the Staatskanzlei's "extension" of its jurisdiction. For Metternich, it was not even a debatable question; too much time had been lost already. Energetically and proficiently he sought information from all quarters, not hesitating to contact all sorts of individuals acquainted with Italian grievances. Comprehending the essentials correctly, he saw that a mass of arguments supported his opposition to centralization and conformity. Much of what Metternich was now to carry forward was a summation of all that Marshal Bellegarde had pleaded for since assuming his duties in Italy. He stressed to the monarch that his views were shared by various officials of high rank; he in turn could only praise Bellegarde as well as those members of his staff who had earned appreciation among the local population.

Although Metternich foresaw the introduction of the Austrian law code on the first of the year with some misgivings, he echoed Bellegarde's belief that even now the price for popularity was still at a bargain level; surely the emperor, who had already shown some good will, would not deny a few reasonable concessions. Moderate individuals would eventually grant that Austria could not be expected to perform the impossible such as conceding to the wishes for independence but, by the same token, such individuals could never forgive Austria were it to leave the possible undone. Metternich realized this only too well — and one was not asking for the impossible: "One could do so much good so easily," he urged, "without sacrificing the interests of the Monarchy as a whole." As a preamble to his observations, the minister underscored the dissimilarity of the Venetian and Milanese situations in terms of civic-mindedness, pointing to the intense interest and participation in public affairs apparent in the Lombard capital. "Everything is lively here," he noted, "and the activity of the few incites the many."

Metternich's major concern actually embraced three levels: the people, the city, and the land. He came to recognize the social factors and problems underlying much of Lombard discontent and to share Bellegarde's solicitude for the mass of civic employees facing an uncertain future. In speaking for them, he could not avoid good words for the French administrative system they had once served, echoing therewith Wessenberg's and Bellegarde's admiration. For him, too, it had been progressive, its forms had been carefully ordered and selected, it had overcome the problems with which it had been faced. Of course he could not ask the emperor to reinstate this system, but he did urge him to seek a reasonable middle way, so as "not to increase the number of the discontent to infinity." But why this compliment to the French administrative system already written off long ago? First, it was an indirect way of saying that the Vienna organizers need not always suppose that what was good for Vienna was necessarily good somewhere else. Second, it served to illustrate the connection between the disparagement so commonly expressed for the alien "Austro-Bohemian" system and the very real concern for material security. Metternich realized that Austria could never expect an easing of the situation in Milan if a formidable left-over bureaucracy trembled at seeing all old administrative forms "being tossed over in a heap", and, if a considerable number of businessmen and workers, who had staked out their lot in the relative prosperity of the last decade, now feared that the ground would be pulled out from under them.

All individual cares were summed up in the general fear that Milan might lose its lately won position, "that it might degenerate to a poor provincial town." Actually, from what one could call a purely Viennese point of view, a diminishing of this bothersome frontier-city's importance and prestige on the Italian peninsula could only be welcomed with feelings of relief. Yet it was the Austrian first minister who argued that the city "may not be allowed to become a Brünn or Graz and thus sink behind Turin and Florence" because he knew that, aside from inevitable revenue losses, Austria could not afford the bitterness bound to result from such a development. Metternich realized that the obvious program of fostering prosperity while discouraging politics might be thwarted by the large number of superfluous, dissatisfied and politically-minded public servants. Nevertheless, a partial answer at least was in the offing: ultimately, for civil servants, the form of administration mattered less than its ability to assure them employment. However, an extensive administrative apparatus seemed warranted only by the presence of a high and independent authority or by a prince of the imperial house. Thus a telling social-economic argument was added to the others favoring the location of a viceroy and his court in Milan. Socially at least, Metternich insisted, all the requisites for such an arrangement were present. Milan could claim a nobility more numerous than that of Vienna as well as a society so well recovered from recent vicissitudes that Metternich, in all seriousness, contended that it "did not fear *having to pay* so much as not being able to spend." Whether Kaiser Franz understood that under such conditions the virtues of *Sparsamkeit* might not be appreciated and whether he was impressed by such premises (already advanced by Wessenberg and Bellegarde) is difficult to say. Even if the emperor was aware of the natural desire to resume a more sumptuous life, he also knew that the state could contribute little to such a cause. Since he was wont to keep an anxious eye on the imperial treasury — the always ailing child of the Habsburg state — very likely he countered, with a mere shrug of the shoulder, Metternich's assertions that the pleasure-loving but politically dangerous elements of Milanese society would mind bills for luxury less than an austerity program.

Metternich then took up the "legitimate" political wishes which might, to some extent, have safeguarded an Italian autonomy. They centered in three oft-mentioned institutions: a viceroy and court — the surest symbol of a special if only seeming sovereignty; a high court of "third instance" — a means of retaining a certain independence in judicial spheres despite the introduction of Austrian law; and an Italian chancellery, whereby "the Italians were to be represented in Vienna" and whereby a separate status for the Italian possessions was to be assured on the highest level, thus making Italian affairs relatively independent of the central administration. It is noteworthy that Metternich usually used the word "Italian" where he actually could mean only "Lombardo-Venetian".

To be sure, all the above-mentioned institutions had a claim to tradition. Previously they had been an administrative convenience for a dynastic power ruling over scattered lands; now they were anything but that for a state rebuilt as a rounded-out territory and bent on achieving a centralized administration. Metternich was clever enough to recognize that they had now become a political convenience, if not more — a political necessity. Of these three institutions, the most important because potentially the most effective voice in government affairs and the truest embodiment of a national consciousness was the Italian chancellery. Indeed, the creation of such an office was inevitably the first and most sensible step in Metternich's efforts to reconstitute the lands of the monarchy along more national lines. But here in Italy it was more than just a Metternichian project; as he insisted to Kaiser Franz, the wish for such an intermediary organ between emperor and "nation" was "unanimous". Off-handedly but decidedly, Metternich disclaimed any desire of the Staatskanzlei to assume this intermediary role. It was less a matter of prestige than of competence, and he was honest enough to admit that with an Italian chancellery there could be no such skirting of issues. Not often had the minister taken a stand with more conviction and feeling; he could not urge the emperor strongly enough to act on the imperative need for installing an Italian chancellery in Vienna. Certainly, he felt, for a statesman determined to absolve his government from the charge of "foreign oppression" there was just one course to insist on: "These lands m u s t   b e   g o v e r n e d   h e r e , and the governments here m u s t   t h e n   l e t   t h e m s e l v e s   b e   r e p r e s e n t - e d   i n   V i e n n a ."

Even if such insight resulted from conscientious listening and reflection, it demonstrated quick and intelligent perception. Now reduced to its barest terms, the question of a Lombardo-Venetian autonomy was to be made palatable to a sovereign unsympathetic if not incapable of comprehending the issues involved — and this in a sphere which he considered as his own field of competence. The situation was not the same as in foreign and diplomatic concerns where Metternich had a relatively free hand. The minister was compelled, as so often, to disguise an internal problem of far-reaching political implications as an administrative trifle: "The whole question reduces itself actually to the following: should Vienna be bothered every month with 500 or only fifty issues from here? In the first case there would be a back-log of 400 which would cripple the course of things here."

If all local business were to be dragged to Vienna, Metternich put forward with all earnestness, then Kaiser Franz would shortly be unable to "extract as much as a penny from these lands and everything would bog down." If this dark threat — perhaps the most effective argument in dealing with the emperor — were not enough, the minister hastened to offer a rosy alternative: "If on the contrary, Lombardy and Venetia are governed here under a *strong* governor and in line with principles announced and controlled — of course — in Vienna, then Your Majesty will have repose, happiness, and peace spread over the lands beyond the Alps." The need for such finesse (or primitive assurances) to overcome the imperial predisposition might seem slightly amusing were it not for the note of tragedy it sounds for the future of Austria. On this major document on Austro-Italian relations, the emperor made no other comment than the usual *"Dient zur Wissenschaft* (Acknowledged)".

After Metternich had expressed himself on what should be done in policy, he turned to what had been done in practice. His apprehension and displeasure mounted as he discerned how the COHC's shortcomings threatened the delicate balance upon which hung a still favorable acceptance of Austrian rule. He qualified his initial praise for Austrian officials organizing the Italian provinces; unlike them, he did not have to fear being explicit. Bitterly he blamed the provisional government and the COHC for all the confusion and misunderstanding that hampered a smooth transfer of administration.[6] Naturally, he could not very well implicate his master; blandly he went about as if the emperor's intentions had always coincided with his own. These intentions had been, he stated, to change only that which was revolutionary and incompatible with the principles of the monarchy and, simultaneously, to examine thoroughly existing institutions for their present worth and possible retention. Thus he repeated precisely that which he and Wessenberg had formulated some eighteen months before as the necessary modification of the COHC's announced organization policy. To carry out these imperial intentions was not the task of the military and provisional governments but rather of the COHC; the commission in turn was not properly organized and, therefore, could not perform what was expected of it. Instead of an effective Commission for Organizing, he charged, it had become an organizing office with a membership of some forty-two persons. Legislative and executive functions — which Metternich was always keen on keeping strictly separate — were hopelessly mixed; a profusion of half-measures was inevitable. Such faulty organization attempts and a lack of definite provisional laws had simply lamed any administrative endeavors. He deplored the commission's superficial efforts, its losing track of its objectives. Considering the loopholes and insufficiencies apparent everywhere, he exclaimed in consternation: "The organization of the Italian Provinces [has] scarcely earned this name." But worse, not even its personnel could be regarded as proficient. While conceding to its members experience with regard to Vienna or to the hereditary provinces, he berated them "for not having the slightest knowledge of the lands which they were called upon to organize." Even acknowledging Metternich's ill humor — to which a serious eye ailment may have contributed — such a severe attack ran over all customary forms. Yet Metternich knew that he could risk such a wide swinging blow if Kaiser Franz could be made to feel that the men he had once trustingly selected had let him down. Professing duty and discretion, the minister was of course careful enough to request the emperor to regard the matter as most confidential.[7]

Since arriving in Milan, Metternich had made himself a spokesman for the wishes of the Italian population and had not spared his countrymen in his criticism. Now, the balance had to be drawn: Austrian action in Italy had at last to be brought into c o n f o r m i t y   w i t h   I t a l i a n   e x-p e c t a t i o n s . His intervention was to end once and for all Kaiser Franz's old policy, which meant c o n f o r m i t y   o f   a very different nature. The minister sought, as he put it, "to correct the evil at its source" — an evil which he discerned both in theory and application. There should have been all along, he felt, a central Italian office, separate from the COHC, to administer the Italian provinces. Now, reminding the emperor that they had agreed completely on all major issues only the day before, he sought a change of direction. He insisted that no further alteration or introduction of administrative practices be undertaken without express imperial permission. Moreover, all future activity of the commission was to be more attuned to the wishes of the inhabitants; the monarch had after all accepted or, at least, not rejected these wishes, yet they were so neglected and measures for the people's welfare so ineptly executed that the public had become embittered. "It is quite clear," Metternich concluded, in his occasionally displayed tongue-in-cheek manner, "that the orders of Your Majesty have either not been followed or are badly carried out, and that the sentiments of Your Majesty have either not been made known to the public or this has happened in a manner which offers the well-disposed no peace of mind but rather leaves the ill-disposed a free field for their machinations."

Realizing that all the signs of maladministration had to be removed before a new start could be made, the minister deemed necessary a thorough and detailed study of past and present practices. Therefore he suggested that a comprehensive report be drawn up; he expected that the unsatisfactory answers by the responsible authorities would be proof enough of their incompetence. Furthermore, since all the relevant persons of the commission — from Lazansky on down — were present in Milan, they could all be called to account. Certainly Bellegarde would have his piece to say. Finally, the minister told his monarch flatly that it was up to him to be consequent and to make sure that the nature of the new organization would be clearly determined and understood by all.

The emperor's reaction was livelier this time; immediately an ominous imperial message was dispatched to the president of the COHC:

> Within eight days you shall provide Me with details on the following points: 1. What has been ordered in My I t a l i a n   S t a t e s   r e - g a r d i n g   a new organization? 2. What measures have been decided upon to make possible required c h a n g e s without however damaging those institutions destined to remain temporarily or permanently? 3. What measures have been directed to the Milanese g u b e r n i u m or, insofar as these fell within its own competence, issued by the g u b e r - n i u m   itself, to insure the transition from the previous routine of business to the newly ordered one without delaying business? 4. What steps has the local g u b e r n i u m already taken and which does it intend to take in order to enlighten the p u b l i c   s p i r i t as to My true intentions?[8]

Doubtlessly, Metternich wrote this billet for his startled monarch — the finely expressed faultlessness ("My true intentions") attests to that. It represents the high point of his battle against the emperor's conformity policy.

But even this belated although apparently resounding victory proved to be illusory. When not in Metternich's presence, Kaiser Franz hesitated. He just could not bring himself to abandon his old concepts altogether and, to make matters worse, he remained close to his centralism-minded advisors. Thus, without the monarch's determination to embark upon a new course, the minister's vigorous new start was like a gust of fresh wind into unfurled sails.

The very tentative nature of Metternich's influence was perhaps most pointedly summarized by an independent observer — the British ambassador to Austria. Lord Stewart, a halfbrother of Castlereagh, had accompanied the imperial court down to Italy and was certainly informed about the Milanese situation by Bellegarde and Metternich himself. His dispatches to Castlereagh, the British foreign secretary, contain comments on policy conflicts which — even if heard for the most part from the marshal and the minister — reveal criticism of the emperor and his circle hardly to be found in Austrian communications.[9] Because of personal inclinations and of the oft-expressed British benevolence for the Italians, Stewart's opinion of the centralizers came close to contempt. Conversely, he sympathized with Metternich's endeavors, becoming as convinced of Metternich's good intentions as of the validity of his arguments. Thus he assured his brother that "if Prince Metternich's long indisposition [the eye ailment] had not impeded his active Exertions, he would have brought about a greater Liberality in Arrangements for the Emperor's Italian Subjects and have prevented much of the ill Temper and dissatisfaction that exist" and, further, that the Prince "is disposed to see Things in a point of View infinitely more liberal and congenial to the Sentiments of this Nation". At the same moment, Stewart singled out the crux of the problem: but the minister "has a party to manage whom he cannot always overcome".

Who were the leaders of this "strong party" which answered the plaints of the Italians with the words "they might submit quite as well as the Hungarians or the Bohemians to a general Arrangement under one Government", which was willing to concede only a viceroy "without Influence, without Power, without Credit, and without Money, thus placing him in the most painful Situation", which was responsible for "the vexatious Inconvenience of sending every Point to be judged to Vienna", which was "endeavouring to germanize every Concern here" and which, thereby, let discontent "manifest itself in a thousand ways"? There was the reportedly "corrupt", "profligate", "generally unpopular" and "obnoxious" Saurau who "pleases the Emperor however by his strict and regid Austrian Ideas"; there was the "extremely disliked" Lazansky and, finally, there was Kaiser Franz himself, of whose pettiness and "particular Turn of Mind" Stewart complained often enough.[10] With such a sovereign surrounded by such a clique, the immediate measures Metternich had hoped for were awaited in vain and Stewart expressed a general feeling of gradual impatience as he noted, in the middle of March, "I w i s h I c o u l d s a y t h e A u s t r i a n g o v e r n m e n t b e c a m e m o r e p o p u l a r b y t h e i r A c t s i n t h e s e S t a t e s ."[11]

THE ITALIAN PROVINCES: PLEAS, PLANS, AND PRACTICES

Unfortunately, the emperor's prime interest was directed toward hearing explanations rather than acting on the ideas in Metternich's proposals. But beside the chorus of excuses there were other voices — and these are of immediate interest here — less concerned with past errors than with definite measures to conciliate Austria's disgruntled Italian subjects. Especially two men in high positions supported Metternich and urged an Austrian policy more considerate of Lombardo-Venetian feelings. One was a somewhat neglected member of the COHC — Marchese Ghisilieri, a man dutiful to Austria, devoted to Italy, and desperately hopeful of a better relationship between them. He had taken the occasion of the emperor's visit to Milan to write down his views on Austrian rule in Italy,[12] views which closely paralleled Metternich's; probably Ghisilieri was one of those with whom the minister had talked at Christmas time. He stressed four main points: conformity must be avoided; real autonomy in Lombardy-Venetia must be granted if only to render the Austrian government respectable in the eyes of the Italians; a high court of third instance was indispensable; finally, an Italian chancellery in Vienna was a prerequisite to any hoped-for improvement. He omitted the viceroyalty — presumably because it already existed on paper.

The other rejoinder came from Bellegarde — his farewell message before leaving Italy. The marshal had been increasingly unhappy with the course of things there. Feeling unappreciated, and with still no viceroy in sight, he gave in to despair. His departure depended only on an opportune moment;[13] it came early in March when a viceroy was at last named even if not sent, thus theoretically making a representative superfluous. At the same time, Bellegarde was promoted to *Obersthofmeister* to the crown-prince Ferdinand.[14] The Italians had reason to regret his going, for, although he had not been able to achieve much for them, he had never tired of pleading their cause.[15]

However, as it turned out, there had already appeared on the scene two men who were to carry on in Bellegarde's spirit. At the end of November the new military commander in Milan had arrived to replace General Frimont; he was the capable and sympathetic Count Bubna, as accomplished a diplomat as general. His efforts to promote understanding and good will were no less sincere than Bellegarde's. Well acquainted with Italian affairs, Bubna soon came to be Metternich's main informant on conditions in Italy. His intelligent assessment so impressed the minister that he extended their exchange of views from a normal correspondence through regular channels to a highly confidential one.[16] At this time also, the civil governor in Milan — Saurau — called to Metternich's attention the importance of the governor's central position for observing all of Italy. To make effective use of it he wanted a reliable assistant wholly versed in Italian customs and forms; for this task he had had in mind Freiherr v. Sardagna, who had excellent recommendations from Metternich and Bellegarde.[17] Saurau's request was granted and Sardagna was named *Legationsrath* to the Milanese *gubernium*.[18]

The marshal had considered as his last duty, prior to departure, that he should lay before the monarch an exposition of his basic principles on Italian policy and, as he called it, of "the necessity of carrying them out."[19] His last report was simultaneously a convincing and ably presented apology of his activity and a summation of his unchanged views. Regarding the former, he recalled the innumerable difficulties which had faced him. There were those of a political nature: the appealing memories of the *Regno d'Italia* and the brief moment of independence which Milan had enjoyed during the interregnum in 1814, and then the persisting Italian spirit and hopes for a unification of the entire peninsula. Especially among the remnants of the Italian army were such feelings discernible; for these old soldiers Marshal Bellegarde showed ample sympathy. It had been his idea to keep Italian troops under Habsburg standards separate from other Austrian forces and on the same footing with those of other Italian states — this on the assumption that an Italian Confederation would soon come into being. The emperor had, however, turned thumbs down on this project for Austrian-furnished Italian Confederation troops. The administrative difficulties which beset the marshal were no less severe: the unavoidable changes in personnel, the reduction of the number of employees, the resulting hardships. Under such circumstances, discontent was to be expected. Nevertheless, Bellegarde — who had wanted above all a smooth and considerate transition — had succeeded in turning a good part of the once independent governing authorities into a well functioning Austrian *gubernium*. One may well agree that this was no mean achievement. Furthermore, he insisted that through his mildness he had done Austria more good in the long run than might at present be noticeable. At least — he could not help mentioning with some pride — during the critical Hundred Days, there had been no attempt to take advantage of the situation in the area under his command.

Three premises provided the foundation for Bellegarde's views on Italy. First of all, he insisted that the Austrian Italian provinces always must be regarded as a part of the rest of Italy — a thought, he said, aimed not so much at the present as at the future. Secondly, Austria's presence on the peninsula carried with it the obligation of providing Italy with security and a positive example of Habsburg rule. Sad to say, here Austria was confronted with the dilemma of having to support an undeserving lot of unexemplary princes, as often as not at odds with their own best interests. Such weak rulers were unreliable and remained a serious liability and, as such, a cause for concern. Thirdly, Austria might win public opinion in Italy by being able to demonstrate enlightened rule and consideration in the Lombardo-Venetian Kingdom. For Bellegarde, this was to be done only through real magnanimity, by granting a real and meaningful separate status:

> Italy must be treated always as a body completely different from the other lands of the Monarchy. Its firmest attachment to the whole must be attained and manifested in that this region shall be governed with entirely different forms and methods, and that all unnatural attempts at bringing these lands closer to the German ones shall be forestalled. It is not sufficient to dupe such an intelligent people with a few insignificant measures or empty forms. I can only say with the deepest conviction, now that I soon shall cease to have any influence upon the administration of this land, that it is absolutely necessary as well as unavoidable to give up once and for all any idea of an eventual conformity, no matter how gradual, with the German forms of the Empire, and along with this idea, also the plan of an eventual assimilation — which even the Emperor Joseph failed to accomplish, and at a time when loyalty and obedience had not been shaken.

The emperor's reaction to such determined pleading may be measured by imperial resolutions on the three aforementioned institutions upon which a Lombardo-Venetian special status depended. That he viewed the viceroyalty as irksome and meaningless became ever more apparent. On the first of the year, the new law code had gone into effect; on January 2, orders went out to end the provisional regency (whatever that meant); a whole new government had come into being, but its supposed head — the viceroy — had, though long promised, not even been named. Finally, on March 7, 1816, Kaiser Franz appointed his reluctant brother Anton,[20] bringing forth an almost touching Milanese enthusiasm. Saurau conveyed to the emperor the general gratitude for this eagerly awaited appointment as well as for the granting, at last, of a Lombardo-Venetian supreme court of justice.[21] That such a favorable turn in public opinion must be seized upon immediately and exploited to improve relations even more was something Kaiser Franz heard from Metternich often enough. In this instance, however, the feeling that enough had been done already led him to answer: "It's good to know that the Milanese are thankful and appreciative of what I do for their welfare," and let it go at that.[22]

By June, rumors were spreading that Archduke Anton might not come at all because his elder brother refused to assign him a respectable role. Kaiser Franz had revealed his disinclination as well as his lack of interest in the office of viceroy as its spheres of activity were being deliberated: "It is not My will that the viceroy of the Lombardo-Venetian Kingdom should delve into administrative affairs and thus infringe on the governor's efficient conduct of affairs." After all, the emperor bluntly admitted, the appointment was to be "a viceroy intended merely as a symbol and as a conspicuous gloss".[23]

At the same time, the initial session of the *supremo tribunale di giustizia* at Verona had been postponed to the first of August. At least, this institution was to function then. Surely mirroring the general feeling, Ghisilieri's satisfaction at this advance was coupled with the reminder that an Italian chancellery was still lacking. Such a shortcoming would prove to be, he thought, "a fatal barrier in good relations between the emperor and his zealous ministers and Italian subjects." The argument that other lands of the empire were able to get along without a chancellery was irrelevant to Ghisilieri, in view of Lombardy-Venetia's special character and the vast differences apparent between this kingdom and the German provinces. The example of Galicia was equally inapplicable although, as he thought, some members of the COHC acted as if there were the greatest resemblance between Poland and Italy and their peoples. Just as inappropriate, he continued, seemed the contention that under the present regime other new territories had been organized without recourse to a chancellery; the organization of Galicia — "if it can be called that" — had taken years; moreover, Austria had had eight years in which to attempt in Venetia an organization *à l'allemande* and had hardly managed a provisional system by the time it lost those lands again. In recalling that, on the other hand, Austria got things going again within three months after it had recovered Lombardy in 1799, Ghisilieri ignored the fact that Austria had not had to start there from scratch. As a final admonition, he made — like Bellegarde — a point which, one would think, struck deep. "If loyalty to the throne is the most important thing," he wrote, "then it would be wise to recall the generous policy of Maria Theresia, whose various peoples — as different as they can be among Europeans — stood by her in her time of troubles."[24]

Although Metternich had frequently raised the subject of an Italian chancellery — along with a similar proposal for Illyria — Kaiser Franz simply could not make up his mind on an institution which he saw as awkwardly interfering with the channels of a centralized administration. As often before, he turned for advice to one of his cronies. He presented to Count Wallis a question containing alternatives which really represented the two opposites of organization policy: "On the one hand, might it be more purposeful to establish such a chancellery for Lombardy-Venetia, a kingdom so different in language and constitution, and, if so, how? On the other hand, would it not be better to achieve the uniformity so very much desired within the political administration and to erect at the *Vereinigten Hofkanzley* merely a separate department for Italian affairs, and, if so, how? And in the latter case, should the affairs of Tyrol and Illyria be handled similarly?"[25] Unfortunately, Wallis' reply has not been found. Suffice it to say that for the time being neither the one nor the other alternative was decided upon; the matter rested in suspense until Metternich forced action on the creation of national chancelleries in the later part of 1817.

From an administrative viewpoint — and this was largely that of the emperor and his organizing commission — respect for a nationality's individuality was a meaningless consideration where fair and equal treatment for all citizens precluded any possible discrimination. In truth, the Austrians can hardly be accused of really having wanted to make the Italians into Germans, although some Germanizing of administrative procedure alarmed the sensitive Italians into regarding this modification as but a first step. Certainly there was not, nor could there have been, a mass influx of Germans into Italy or a Germanizing of Italian names or a proclaiming of German as the official language. If respect for nationality may be measured by two important criteria — the proportion of nationals within the local administration and the care given to the native language and schools — then the Italians did not fare badly. Aside from the fact that the emperor made a point of honoring a number of prominent Italians by appointing them members of the newly created Order of the Iron Crown and bestowing on a few deserving ones the title of "royal chamberlain",[26] one may mention that the new "cabinet" at Milan under governor Saurau consisted solely of Italians. Furthermore, of the counselors at the Milanese Court of Appeals, sixteen of twenty had Italian names; in Verona, ten of fifteen; and at the supreme tribunal at Verona, five of ten. Kaiser Franz wished to see Italians considered for the lower posts at these courts; however, in each court two individuals capable of understanding German were to be employed.[27]

We have seen that the emperor demanded from his civil servants a knowledge of the language spoken in their area of activity. Applicants with insufficient qualifications were turned down[28] while the fluent received every advantage. Partly for the purpose of providing better training for his civil servants, Kaiser Franz approved the study of "native language" at the various institutions of higher learning throughout his empire. Thus the COHC could request, in November 1815, the establishment at Laibach of a chair for the "Slavonic language", referring thereby to the existence of such chairs for the cultivation of the *Landessprache* in Bohemia and Moravia. Moreover, it was mentioned, there already was at Laibach a chair for Italian.[29] Furthermore, the commission asked for a chair for German at Padua and at the *lyceums* at Venice, Treviso, Udine, Vicenza, and Verona.[30] In 1817, Kaiser Franz sanctioned a chair for Polish — as an elective course — at the University of Lemberg, stipulating that its professor should be subjected to the same provisions as the professor of Czech at Prag, the professors of Italian at German universities, and those of German at the Italian ones.[31]

The regulation of the Lombardo-Venetian school system — of the public schools, the *lyceums*, the *gymnasiums* and the universities — was carried out during the summer and autumn of 1816 in accordance with proposals made in the springtime by *Hofrat* Jüstel.[32] He followed necessarily the line set down by the emperor, which called for the most possible conformity of the Lombardo-Venetian school-system with the one in the German provinces.[33] Jüstel thought that a modification should be allowed only "where made mandatory by physical and political differences of things in general and of the national character". The emperor approved these suggestions. At Lombardy-Venetia's two universities — Padua and Pavia — the curriculum in philosophy was to be the same as in the German lands. Regarding the *lyceums*, Kaiser Franz ordered that "instruction in the German language, as in art, must be offered — although only as an elective subject" and further, that "all branches of philosophy shall be taught at the *lyceums*, without exception, in the Italian language." Such measures show clearly that the Austrian administration, despite the emperor's persisting wish for conformity, was a long way from forcing on the Italians a diet of purely German dishes.

However, even the best of well-intended programs could not secure success for the Austrian administration if suspicion and prejudice hampered relations between Italians and Germans. The government's obvious duty was to promote good will and to acquaint itself with the ways and workings of the Italian mentality; some steps were even taken in this direction. While the emperor showed a fatherly concern (by employing one of the

COHC's talents — the same Jüstel mentioned above — to investigate the causes for cursing in Venice and to offer suggestions for its elimination),[34] more inspired Austrians sought to win Italian intellectuals for an exchanging of ideas. As early as 1814, Bellegarde had had the notion to found a literary journal to be entitled *Biblioteca Italiana*, partially to emulate the patronage of arts and sciences conspicuous under the French regime.[35] He succeeded in persuading the well-known poet and playwright Ugo Foscolo to participate — a notable achievement, since Foscolo had been a loud proponent of Italian freedom and unity and now risked the reproaches of the *Italici puri*. The whole project nearly collapsed as Foscolo, undergoing a change of heart and allegiance during the Hundred Days, slipped away from Milan. The project was revived towards the end of 1815; Saurau turned to Metternich — both by that time in Milan — for support. Since discontented intellectuals continued to regard the Austrian regime as stifling to all intellectual life, the governor argued, the government would do well to subsidize such a literary undertaking — all the more so since thereby public opinion might be positively affected.[36] After returning to Vienna, Metternich recommended the idea to the emperor, beginning with the following words: "During my sojourn in Italy I reflected on every . . . means whereby one might increase understanding between Italians and Germans and remove the deeply-rooted prejudices the former hold against the latter. It appears to me that literature, whose moral influence has become such a mighty lever for governments these days, would be the proper way to bring both nations closer together."[37] The matter was not resolved by Kaiser Franz but by Archduke Ludwig who, acting in his imperial brother's stead, gave approval. The publication's full title was *Biblioteca Italiana ossia Giornale di Letteratura, Scienze ed Arti, compilato da una Società di Letterati*; although in its first issue it could boast of such distinguished contributors as Monti and Mme. de Staël, the journal's initial success was shortlived. Its reputation damaged by internal rifts and lacking appeal, it soon became, if not a bore to the Italian literary public, a burden to its Austrian supporters.

METTERNICH AND THE STATUS OF ILLYRIA

In May, 1816, Kaiser Franz and Metternich proceeded from Lombardy-Venetia to the Illyrian Provinces, stopping for some weeks in Trieste and then in Laibach, prior to returning to the capital in June. Both had been anxious to reach some understanding regarding these territories before their visit there. Furthermore, action on this point was spurred by reports of dissatisfaction with the still unsettled political status of these lands and their division into separate *gubernia*. Administrative affairs had been regulated — formally at least — some fourteen months previously by Saurau. Already on April 25, 1815 — within a fortnight of the proclamation of the Lombardo-Venetian Kingdom — this issue of external form had been up for discussion; since then, it had occasionally been referred to, but nothing more had been done.[38]

The problem of the future status of the Illyrian Provinces consisted of two main points: that of territorial composition and that of political rank and privilege. The first devolved into two principal questions: should Hungarian claims to an Adriatic outlet finally find satisfaction and should Dalmatia remain part of the Illyrian territories? There was considerable sentiment favorable to the Hungarian cause; especially some close associates of the monarch, like Count Zichy, had openly expressed their chagrin at his refusal to return the Fiume area to the Crown of St. Stephen.[39] The emperor had shoved aside such appeals with the retort that the Emperor of Austria and his armies, and not the King of Hungary, had reconquered these lands. The Dalmatian issue involved less drama. Kaiser Franz's main concern seemed to be preservation of his title "King of Dalmatia". The second point — that of rank and privilege — also devolved into two principal questions: should the Illyrian Provinces be elevated to a state of royal rank and should this state then receive "national representation"? As a primary political matter, this point was relegated to the Staatskanzlei for examination.

On February 1, 1816, Metternich wrote his opinions on the various questions regarding the Illyrian matter.[40] Referring to the minutes of a meeting held in the previous April, he was convinced that, first of all, retention of the name "Illyria" would be advantageous in every way. Furthermore, he recommended that these Illyrian territories should be designated a *Kingdom*. The designation *Province* would be awkward, he thought, "since it offered no analogy to the other regions of the Monarchy and because a *province* consisting of provinces would provide a real anomaly"; moreover, the designation "Kingdom of Illyria and Dalmatia" for the entire land would take into consideration the various claims attached to the emperor's title "King of Dalmatia" and would — since the Illyrian Provinces were to form two gubernia — correspond to a well-established precedent of "double-kingdoms"; there existed already, similarly designated, a Lombardo-Venetian as well as a Galician-Lodomerian Kingdom.

To the proposal of returning coastal areas, now a part of Illyria, to Hungary Metternich said a decided "No". In this opinion he concurred with the majority of the conference. He was aware of possible counter-arguments to which even his "second", Hudelist, subscribed. Nevertheless, the legalities which granted to the emperor the right to dispose over these lands once lost and now reconquered were paramount and indismissable to Metternich. But the minister presented another argument against a new projection of Hungary to the sea across Croatian lands. "As inclined as I always am to subordinate small and partial advantages to greater considerations," he stressed, "I can not help doubting whether in this case His Majesty's efforts to show good will to the Hungarians by returning to them a part of Croatia would bring a proper reward. For me, one really preponderant reason for non-incorporation is that the welfare of a majority of the inhabitants would deteriorate [as the consequence of such an act]."

Having stated his case, Metternich elaborated his views once more in a conference held on February 17.[41] As the Hungarian question was again discussed, he emphasized that the Illyrian lands belonged to the empire as a whole and as such they had a right to a political designation of their own. Moreover, he did not hesitate to reveal his feelings about the Hungarian art of administration. The Illyrian population, he declared, deserved a better fate: not only would the general well-being regress, but public institutions — especially schools — would suffer from the antiquated Hungarian constitution; everything, so he thought, would soon find itself in the same deplorable state as in the lands across the Save. Yet even these strong words did not persuade everyone. The Staatskanzlei's Hudelist and Pfleger, who were still stirred by memories of the difficulties which a rebellious Hungary could conjure up, held to their conviction that, as a conciliatory gesture, at least a part of Civil Croatia should be re-allotted to the Hungarian crown.

Metternich insisted that Dalmatia should remain a part of the Illyrian territories and then proposed that this territorial unit should be raised to the rank of a kingdom; in so doing, he championed the idea of a "greater Illyria" within the frame of the empire. According to him, not only did "higher reasons of state" speak for the retention of the historic name "Illyria", but the name "Kingdom of Illyria" would have "a pleasant sound for the great majority of the inhabitants". In advocating the territorial integrity of Illyria-Dalmatia, the minister pointed out that the character of its people differed markedly from that of their German and Hungarian neighbors. Finally, Metternich revealed remarkable foresight by hinting that the creation of such an Illyrian kingdom, proudly ranked with the other great units of the empire, would present an effective counterweight against Russian influences and machinations among the population there. Not all members of the conference, however, approved of such a large territorial unit, and Lazansky objected that such "nations" as Carinthia and Carniola would lose their "national names"; but then, Metternich had no cause to lament the loss of such petty provincial "nationalities". Just in regard to Dalmatia he had denounced an ultra-particularism capable of jeopardizing not just the effective administration but the very existence of larger and more vital territorial bodies within the empire.[42]

The question of "national representation" remained undecided. Metternich was known to favor it, as he had in Galicia and Lombardy-Venetia, to enable the population to develop regional pride or *Stammesstolz*; even if symbolic, a national assembly was always an expression of national personality. After all, only through a voluntary profession of such "nationality", only through a preference for being a member of the Habsburg family of "nations" could such peoples as Lombardo-Venetians, Illyrians, or Galicians loosen ties with their brethren beyond the frontier. That this meant, above all, abandoning any thought of "Germanization", Metternich emphazised often enough.[43]

What, then, were the underlying aims of Metternich in advocating the raising of the Illyrian Provinces to such dignity? From an administrative viewpoint this plan provided neither convenience nor advantage to the central government. There was, of course, no justification for a mere revival of traditional heterogeneity and, even less, for a mere play of blocks with territories. His aims were necessarily political and concerned the structure of the entire empire: not only would the admittance of Illyria into the company of such territorial nations as Bohemia, Galicia, Lombardy-Venetia, and Hungary go far toward earning the gratitude and loyalty of the population to the House of Habsburg, but, moreover, a political balance would be maintained among the states of the monarchy by forcing Hungary to make room for one more partner. Finally, one more step might be taken in the minister's effort to reconstitute the empire into an indissoluble bond of six or seven equal members.

Yet Metternich's plans for Illyria in 1816 implied even more. In view

of his notions on the encouragement of regional nationality in Galicia or
Lombardy-Venetia, it would not seem unlikely that he had taken into
consideration a gradual awakening of the Southern Slavs to their nationality. To have attempted, while there was still time, to guide such national
feelings into forms not only acceptable but even beneficial to the monarchy
would have been a policy of admirable astuteness. How better to achieve
such an aim than by establishing for this nationality its own Southern
Slavic realm within the empire? In the latter part of May, at the first
opportunity available after having completed a survey of the Illyrian
lands, Metternich presented just such a proposal to the emperor:

> In carrying out Your Majesty's intentions, I have brought up the
> question of the "Illyrian Kingdom" with several individuals, including
> old Goëss,[44] and can assure Your Majesty that it should and must find
> acceptance with all reasonable people. The majority of this nation here
> is of Slavic origin and naturally harbors a predilection for [Slavic] stock.
> A S o u t h e r n S l a v i c r e a l m can bring only advantage, especial-
> ly where this nationality coincides with the Roman Catholic religion.
> I refer then completely to my first idea — in this matter there is s o m e -
> t h i n g g o o d but a b s o l u t e l y n o t h i n g b a d — thus there is
> certainly one voice f o r i t . Since there is no objection to the retaining
> of the provinces anyway, then Carniola can just as well be a province
> of Illyria as of Inner-Austria. Consequently, I am convinced that Your
> Majesty would do better to hold to the basic idea than to depart
> from it.[45]

It is especially striking that Metternich not only used the term *nationality* in a cultural sense, but that he alluded to the Roman Catholic faith
as a unifying (if not rallying) factor among Illyrian Slavs. The fact that
here the political frontier ran somewhat parallel to a denominational one
made it all the more feasible to encourage Catholic Southern Slavs to
identify their interests with those of Catholic Austria and thus, in effect,
to draw them away from their Orthodox and Moslem brethren. Religion as
a differentiating factor provided in Illyria a much more solid foundation
for a true regionalism than in Lombardy-Venetia or Galicia, where the
absence of such a strong factor made the cultivation of a regional feeling
much more difficult.

Apparently Metternich had broached this project to the emperor previously, as his reference to his "first idea" indicates. Whether the "basic
idea", the "first idea", and the thoughts expressed in the foregoing *Vortrag*
were the same or present a development can not be determined; decisive is
that Kaiser Franz did not "hold to the *Grundidee*" as Metternich would

have wished. The significance of the Slavic nationality was lost on him. Whereas the emperor usually did not disagree with Metternich's political propositions, he would often enough demonstrate his incomprehension by executing them as fully altered administrative measures. One can see to what extent Metternich had to take into account such shortcomings of his master by the manner in which he cloaked a meaningful political move — keeping Carniola within Illyria — as a mere administrative question. How very much the idea of a Southern Slavic realm escaped Kaiser Franz, how differently emperor and minister thought, is evident in the imperial resolutions to the proposals brought forward both by Metternich and the COHC.[46]

These resolutions were confined to the questions of territorial composition and rank. In the listing of territories which were to constitute the new kingdom, no mention was made of Dalmatia, although the emperor had declared: "I have decided that all of the lands belonging to the French possessions in Illyria should be left under that name."[47] It seems somewhat paradoxical that while the order of rank (immediately behind Galicia-Lodomeria) and the proposed coat-of-arms of the new kingdom were already being fixed, uncertainty should remain as to its territorial extent. Lazansky had to seek assurance on this point in a note to the Staatskanzlei on June 22, asking whether he was correct in assuming that Dalmatia was meant to be excluded from the new kingdom. The answer, which must have reassured him, serves also to illustrate the baroque chancellery style flourishing even in 1816:

Was die in Beziehung auf Dalmatien gemachte Anfrage betrifft, so ist die Geheime H. und St. Kanzley vollkommen mit der Meinung einer löblichen k.k. Zentral-Organisierungs-Hof-Ko'on einverstanden, daß diese Provinz nach dem Wortlaute der Allerhöchsten Entschliessung nicht unter die Bestandteile des neuen Königreiches Illyrien gehöre.[48]

Thereupon, Lazansky drew up the draft for an imperial patent which was presented to the emperor three days later[49] and was approved on August 3, 1816. The official proclamation of the Kingdom of Illyria was issued on the same day.[50] All in all, it was but a partial success for Metternich; but it was not his last try.

ITALY: GENERAL SECURITY AND NATIONAL
CONSPIRACY

Kaiser Franz's hesitation in committing himself to a generous policy of Lombardo-Venetian autonomy had a sobering effect on Metternich. However, another development, the threat of an Italian "national conspiracy", awakened among Austrians once again old anxieties.

Unlike Illyria, Galicia or other regions of the empire, the Austrian Italian possessions had become a cause for concern to Vienna because of the apparent disharmony between nationality and government; furthermore, their fate continued to draw international attention. In any consideration of the Italian situation on the part of the Allied cabinets, the acceptance of Austrian might on the Apennine peninsula as a guarantee of peace and security was necessarily paramount. The dissatisfaction of Italians chafing under inept rule or yearning for an independent nation, regrettably, could only be a second thought. To be sure, it was not a forgotten thought: there were enough voices raised to recall it. Moreover, to a larger degree than other Habsburg nationalities, the Italians could claim a growing politically interested and literary-minded public, which, consequently, was also more susceptible to fresh ideas and influences from outside. Aware of such things, Metternich made it a point to make credible abroad — especially in England — Austria's good intentions and accomplishments. Simultaneously he sought to counteract what he considered to be pernicious influences discernible within the spheres of Austria's interest. Usually he used his spokesman in London — Ambassador Prince Esterhazy — to explain Austrian policy in Italy; this was quite necessary, he maintained seriously, since in the wake of the most violent upheaval in the history of the civilized world, the people demand a reckoning from their governments as to what had been done to assure repose.[51]

Repose and moderation were the keywords and presuppositions for any optimism in Metternich's outlook, especially regarding Italy and Germany. He presumed that the vast majority of the population in both lands was satisfied and politically moderate. He was sure that the troublemakers in Germany would find an insurmountable opposition in the *bon esprit* of the German people; in Italy, the *esprit public* had not given rise to concern during the year following Murat's defeat, he wrote to Esterhazy, since the emperor's "wisdom and moderation" had isolated those partisans of the Revolution who thought to adorn themselves with the name "Italians". Such expressions of wishful thinking may fall within the line of a statesman's duty and were surely more what Metternich wanted others to believe than what he dared believe himself. Indeed, the Italian situation still left much to be desired from an external as well as an internal aspect. The minister's hopes for creating an Italian Confederation on the model of the German one were dissipated by Sardinia's persisting in its old independent ways, unmindful in so doing — Metternich reproachfully remarked — of the fateful consequences such conduct might have on the peace and stability of Europe. Confident of Castlereagh's understanding, Metternich requested Esterhazy to lay this issue before the British foreign secretary and to prevail upon him to apply pressure on Turin.

If a *Lega Italica* was not to be realized, how then should Austria consolidate its own power position and simultaneously assume its responsibilities toward and act in concern with the lesser states of the peninsula? Hegemony need not be based merely on physical power, a method as crude as it was impractical; when based on "moral power" — a favorite Metternich phrase — it could prove much more effective. Some of Metternich's associates, to be sure, did not wish to rely alone on moral influence based on good example; for Hudelist, a real Austrian protectorate over the smaller Italian states seemed indispensable.[52] In any case, subtle efforts were made to bring the Italian states more effectively under Austrian supervision. Thus, Metternich proposed the creation of various permanent interstate institutions which would "protect this Italy — constituted to some extent as a political whole — against attacks from outside as well as disruptions from within". Along this line, the establishment of a common postal system (naturally under Austrian auspices) was to be an important step, as Metternich neatly expressed it, toward "consolidation of the moral domination over Italy . . . which will in future times guarantee the maintenance of the political domination."[53] Another such step might be the retention, under a different name, of the *Monte Napoleone* — the bank and credit institute of the former Kingdom of Italy. The Staatskanzlei's Hudelist championed this move, in the face of opposition based on financial considerations, as a sure means of providing Austria with a controlling hand in Italian affairs.[54] Still another step was to be an all-Italian police observation network centered at Milan. Nevertheless, Metternich professed aversion to an Austria in the role of protector either in Germany or in Italy.[55] Rather, he stressed that Austria's *"système essentiellement conservateur"* should inspire the other governments of Italy.[56] Such conservatism was based upon repose and was meant to be moderate; it abhorred extremism, be it that of discontented or evil-thinking radicals or that of contented or non-thinking reactionaries. The excesses of the Ultras in France could enrage Metternich[57] as much as the narrow-mindedness of the regime in

Tuscany. He blamed the grand duke's conduct for "being the cause of all complications" and more than once besought Kaiser Franz to admonish his brother.[58]

At the beginning of the Italian visit, Metternich's sense of security and optimism reached heights never again attained. Beguiled by the favorable impression acquired in Venice,[59] he was sure that "Austria's possessions in Italy . . . how beautiful they are I hardly need to say . . . would be as firm as a rock". But all depended upon the Austrian government's doing its part; "if only half-reasonable and adroit, there is truly nothing to fear" since, he was convinced, the matter of "Italian independence has sunk to almost nothing" in Lombardy-Venetia.[60] Thus, given a fair administration in Lombardy-Venetia, there remained only negative outside influences to worry about. However, these were most difficult to control. The Italians-in-exile, mostly in London, continued to be the loudest agitators for national independence and naturally they had their contacts at home. Repeatedly, the minister warned Esterhazy to keep a careful eye on their activities.[61] Moreover, even if the publication of unfavorable works such as Abbé Pradt's which termed Austrian dominance in Italy one of "*les profondes et éternelles douleurs de l'Europe*", was something to be taken in stride,[62] the presence of foreign agents in Lombardy-Venetia was not to be tolerated under any circumstances. Yet, despite repeated remonstrances to various governments and despite determined police activity, Milan continued to be a focal point of international intrigues.[63]

Besides persistent agitation for independence, a disturbing development in Italy came to be the noticeable predilection for constitutions. Metternich regarded this "fancy" as a companion to the national independence idea and as a "plague" which one simply had to endure. He was especially annoyed by the Sicilian constitution and never tired in ridiculing this effort of the headstrong Lord Bentinck to transplant English institutions to a Mediterranean isle in disregard of local traditions and needs. Nevertheless, he was anxious lest this constitution's influence might cross to the mainland; once established there, it would represent a serious threat to the entire complex of the Habsburg states and dependencies where government was based on the principle of absolute monarchy.[64] Thus, during the summer months of 1816, he warned that "the first state in Italy which grants a constitution throws the apple of discord into its own interior and into the midst of the other governments of the peninsula."[65] In addition, the Staatskanzlei was particularly discomfited by the promised constitution which Czar Alexander was ready to grant to his Polish subjects in 1816. Hudelist termed it "a real *habit d'arlequin* with the one bad difference that the colored patches were not even sewn together"; in effect, he claimed, it satisfied no one, but it did stir too many imaginations.[66] However, its impact on Galicia proved to be negligible and within a few months Metternich could report that intriguers were making little headway while *l'esprit public* in Galicia was never more calm, and that our grand proprietors are satisfied with the idea of repose."[67] Now, paradoxically, the news of this constitution had evoked a lively response in Italy, not only from the reading public but also from a disconcerted governor Saurau in Milan. Wishing to cool some of the ardor displayed, he thought of ways to present the other side of the medal. He hit upon the idea of planting an article in the newspaper of Lugano, carrying a Warsaw dateline and replete with praises for the Emperor Alexander. But then, all the weaknesses of the constitution were to be carefully exposed and the reader was to be persuaded that mankind would fare better under a "mild absolute monarchic government" than under any constitution yet devised. This article was then to be taken up by the Milanese journals.[68] However, such a trick was simply too obvious for Metternich; he brushed the idea aside, thereby proving himself a superior master at manipulating public sentiment. The minister advised the governor that efforts attempting a frontal attack on ideas momentarily favored by the public fail to produce the originally desired effect. "The constitutional mania", he wrote, "must be regarded as *la maladie du temps* and I always fear that in treating the question in a polemic manner, we should soon be faced with a refutation to which we then would be compelled to respond anew." He concluded that this constitution, "miserable in every aspect", was not worthy of a public debate and that the efforts of its impact would prove themselves ephemeral.[69] Nevertheless, this incident of February, 1816, illustrates Metternich's determination not to let ripples distort the illusion of repose reflected upon the surface of the Italian scene — the same determination which led to his quick response once he felt that disturbances called for action.

During Napoleon's exile on Elba, the strength of the Bonapartist group and the extent of dissatisfaction on the peninsula had nourished among Austrians the fear of a "national conspiracy" to overthrow legitimate rule and to gather together the Italian nationality into one great state. This fear had subsided somewhat after the failure of Murat's rash grasp for all of Italy. It reappeared, however, as the malcontents found themselves again and, moreover, received encouragement and support from various quarters, especially England. Reports from Central Italy told of misrule, murmuring, and potential troubles. At the same time, while planning a reorganization of the Lombardo-Venetian police system, Baron Haager and Count Sedlnitzky had emphasized that a "fanatical yearning for national independence" abided among Italians — even among those people in Lombardy-Venetia who could be considered loyal to Austria.[70] Toward the end of February, 1816, Saurau had news of underground activities; Metternich reacted calmly but had to admit that an odious agitation was making itself felt once again.[71] In the meantime, the minister had castigated the organizers of the Italian provinces for their ineptitude and had sought to convince the emperor of the need to grant some sort of home rule. But all too often, as he reminded Kaiser Franz that a worsening situation in Italy might be eased by a show of imperial magnanimity, the monarch simply replied: "Notify My Police Director".[72]

In the first days of April, 1816, Metternich was notified by the Austrian envoy in Rome — Count Apponyi — of the existence of a widespread conspiracy. A plot to remake all of Italy into a single independent nation ruled by a single monarch under a liberal constitution had been hatched in Rome and supposedly had found adherents in every part of the peninsula. Apponyi claimed for himself some credit by having won the confidence of a certain Duke of Brindisi, who seemed as eager to place himself under Austria's protection as at its disposal.[73] The reliability of such an informer, so willing to make disclosures, made him suspect from the beginning — certainly he was an idealistic but confused turncoat yearning for acclaim and prone to exaggeration. A reserved Metternich recognized this fact perhaps more readily than Apponyi, who after all had little desire to diminish his own "achievement". Much of what Brindisi purveyed was obvious fantasy or wishful thinking; completely unrealistic was the utter dependence on England affirmed in the conspirators' oath, which, according to Brindisi, ran thus: "I place myself under the protection of England and swear to it faithfulness and dedication for the purpose of achieving the independence of Italy. To attain this goal, I shall not shirk from any means. I pledge secrecy, and should I break this pledge, then I empower my comrades to end my life." Desiring to ingratiate himself, Brindisi turned to the tactic of promising still further revelations. Even Apponyi was stunned by the preposterous proposal that Brindisi's influence might be used to turn the Italians' keenness for a single independent nation to Austria's benefit: after union of all parts of Italy had been accomplished, this single state was then to call upon the Emperor of Austria to be its new ruler. Unclear as his expositions were either in regard to the "plot" or his motives and political views — he seemed especially intent upon a new Europe which included an independent Italy — there nevertheless appeared to be substance enough in his story to warrant a hearing. Moreover, one could not ignore assertions regarding a plot whose eventuality had long been dreaded or accusations, not merely against various Italians throughout the peninsula, or against the English along with their government, but against many Italians holding high and trusted positions in Habsburg service. Such charges, as unbelievable as many were, required nonetheless a tedious thorough checking.

Did Metternich believe in a "national conspiracy"? Hardly, at least not to the extent described by Brindisi, although he did concede that the whole affair merited full attention. Even more, he admitted, as Bellegarde had done over a year before, that the ferment in Italy was kept in check only by Austrian might. Nothing illustrates more clearly the lack of progress toward improving the Italian situation than this repetition of the marshal's lament. The minister had done his part to urge a considerate and prudent government and administration at home and abroad; now he felt called upon to obviate danger more directly. The best means to render possible troubles innocuous, he thought, was not only to detect the troublemakers but to place Austrian agents into the midst of the independence party, a chapter of which was active even in Milan.[74] However, his concern over an actual "national conspiracy" dwindled gradually and he became certain that no dangerous plot prevailed.[75] In the autumn he assured the emperor categorically that, even if some sort of conspiracy had existed, none existed at that time; but he was careful to add that this did not mean there might not be one in the future.[76]

The volume of correspondence exchanged for more than a year between Metternich, Apponyi, Bubna, Guicciardi, and others as a result of the Brindisi affair is astounding. Again and again the catchwords *plot, independence, national union*, and *liberal constitution* appeared in all sorts of reports on the activities of secret societies, on the effect of English influences, on the causes for dissatisfaction in Italy in general and in Lombardy-Venetia in particular. Once more it had to be said that the reorganization of the Italian provinces was taxing everyone's patience, that not enough was being done to soothe "national pride". The question which arose from all this was: how could one effectively cope with such a "national conspiracy" should it ever really come into being? The obvious answer was: the only means of combating all-Italian secret societies and conspiracies would be through a highly-coordinated all-Italian police system.

That the police system now at hand was inadequate for the task of tracking down subversive activity across the borders or of drawing an all-Italian political weather-chart became plain as the details and implications of the Brindisi affair were being examined. Thus Metternich informed Count Diego Guicciardi of Milan that *"nous croyons nécessaire d'y établir une surveillance centrale et un centre d'observation, qui, pour être utile, doit s'étendre sur toute l'Italie"*. Guicciardi himself had been selected by the emperor to take charge of this operation which was to function under the name Central-Beobachtungs-Anstalt (Central Observation Agency).[77] The greater part of the CBA's interest, as Metternich's, was directed toward areas beyond the Po where the "disturbers" were most numerous; the motto of the whole undertaking, for which now various plans and suggestions were being made, might well have been: Keep an eye on potential trouble-makers and prevent them from making trouble.[78] Saurau had proposed a secret police apparatus directly responsible to Metternich but in practice probably in his own hands. The minister rejected this idea, sarcastically advancing the argument that the monarch would disapprove of a police system not in conformity with the forms usual for the other provinces of the empire. A more surreptitious reason may have rested with Metternich's antipathy toward the Milanese governor and the desire not to burden the Staatskanzlei with such responsibility and odium. Saurau was to submit his reports to the President of the *Polizei Hofstelle* but, Metternich added, might well send some now and then to the Staatskanzlei.[79] In the mean-time, Guicciardi seemed to have developed some misgivings regarding the entire project. However, Metternich persisted that the CBA was indispens-able for the peace and security of the peninsula.[80] This point he kept ex-pounding for the remainder of the year, even as the organization of the CBA encountered some obstacles,[81] until he was able to say with some satisfaction that the surveillance had extended its scope sufficiently to make any future plot difficult.

Why had Metternich taken this matter so to heart? Certainly not be-cause he was eager to introduce a police state into Italy. Endangered were the quiet conditions so needed for developing a better relationship and understanding between Italians and Austria, for cultivating regional — especially Lombardo-Venetian — pride, for bringing the emperor to agree to a new organization of the monarchy which would take into account the nationality of its various regions. The CBA was meant by Metternich to be no more than a safeguard; it was aimed not at a whole population but at a small group. The decisive difference between 1816 and later years lay in the fact that in 1816 the majority of the Lombardo-Venetian inhabitants still harbored some expectations regarding their wishes for special status and that Metternich had not yet exhausted his efforts in that direction. Later, as it was realized that Austria had nothing more to offer, discontent spread irresistibly. Only then, as police activity was devoted ever more to suppression, might the designation *police state* have had· some justification. But from the time of the Brindisi affair until the Italian revolutions of 1820, Metternich's views on Italian security remained relatively moderate; their salient features were the following:[82]

Discontent and "mauvais esprit": The number of malcontents on the peninsula was considerable and swelling. The ineradicable resentment and agitation against the existing order were traceable to remote and immediate causes. The former were to be sought in the upheavals of the French Revolution; during the campaigns, pledges of liberation had been loosely flaunted — especially by the English who had recklessly invoked national spirit and promised national independence. More immediate causes for dissatisfaction were the incompetence and imprudence of the various restored governments in Italy; Lombardy-Venetia, although better run than its neighbors, was not absolved of this charge. Discontent of a political nature manifested itself mainly among the middle class and the educated. Active behind the widespread general discontent were the more radical elements, small in number but all the more difficult to detect — sworn enemies of legitimacy working for an overthrow of the present regimes. Austria's first duty was to remedy abuses wherever possible; since combat against *mauvais esprit* could not be conducted merely in a negative fashion, Austria must be able to offer a positive program.[83]

Conspirators and sects: The general discontent provided the milieu for sects and troublemakers. To pretend that these did not exist, as some naïve optimists did, belied the facts and was a gross self-deception. All conspirators had one great aim: the overthrow of legitimate rule, the union of all Italy into one state, and a national government according to a liberal constitution; they awaited only the first real opportunity, the first sign of Austrian weakness to strike out. Thus Austria must remain strong and purposeful and must take care not to be led astray by any adventure. Austria's responsibility for keeping Italy immune from all European disturbances was, unfortunately, not made easier by conspirators and *secteurs* who had connections beyond the peninsula and received aid and sympathy from various English groups as well as from Russian agents. Therefore, the Austrian government was called upon to protect Italy from outside interference by means of a vigorous and vigilant police and to protest in a polite yet forceful manner to Austria's allies against such interference.[84]

Areas of danger: As bad as internal "evils" were, external ones were really to be guarded against. That the comparison between Lombardy-

Venetia and the other Italian states was favorable and thus a consolation on the one hand, meant, on the other, a concern for the state of things among Austria's neighbors. Austria needed to keep a watchful eye on them because inconsiderate or even provocative governing would spur disloyalty and plotting. Moreover, "*le mauvais esprit chez nos voisins*" led to fears that "pernicious" influence might spread into the Austrian provinces. This would be just the opposite of what should be: Austria must have a good influence upon its neighbors.[85]

Surveillance: The continuously stressed need for careful surveillance was applicable to two fields: public opinion, where immediate causes of discontent could best be perceived, and underground activity, of which the Austrian police constantly had to keep abreast. Even better, of course, was to be one step ahead and to "seize the evil by its roots" by knowing beforehand all plans, projects, and ramifications.[86]

Prospects for tranquillity: In spite of potential trouble, there was for the moment no real immediate danger and thus nothing to fear. The maintenance of tranquillity could be assured through an effective surveillance. The repose required, as Metternich was fond of saying, "to calm spirits" was to be had if Austria would only do its share and if Providence would grant a few quiet and undisturbed years. More specifically, the peace of the peninsula was to be eventually secured if there occurred no sudden interruption from without or no serious eruption from within.[87]

These views reveal that Metternich had learned from Bellegarde. Unlike the marshal, however, he refused to grow discouraged either at the course of things in Italy or at the emperor's intransigence. Ascertaining causes of dissatisfaction and supplying some sort of remedy became for him a frequent but largely futile chore. Upon repeated request, Metternich received one report after another on discontent and public sentiments which he then submitted, conscientiously commented upon, to the emperor.[88] The minister was as ready to admit the administration's faults as he was to promise amelioration — something he surely did sincerely, knowing well what was at stake. He took up and brought before the emperor all kinds of suggestions from Bellegarde and, later, Guicciardi and Bubna. Among other things, he recommended a streamlining of routine by eliminating unnecessary referrals to Vienna — the deplorable backlog of two thousand cases jamming the Lombardo-Venetian courts was a case in point. He urged economic stimulation and came out for a broadened work program — specifically for the Venice Arsenal district, which was one of the severest "depressed areas" of the times. Furthermore, he advocated an abolition of irritating inland tolls — such as the one between Lombardy and Venetia along the Mincio — and a reduction of certain taxes and imposts to promote commerce.[89] At least, with such proposals Metternich did not have to approach the emperor as carefully as when dealing with Italian autonomy, a Southern Slavic *Reich*, or broad powers for the viceroy.

The various social problems which contributed so much to discontent remained unsolved and, despite Bellegarde's warnings, the Austrian administration was not able to claim improvement in that direction, even in 1817. In the few instances when there was a will there was no way and when there was no lack of means, then there was lack of determination. Since the middle class was never considered reliable, it must have been all the more disconcerting to perceive dissatisfaction among those classes from which Austria had hoped to draw support — the nobility and the clergy.[90] Equally distressing, the lower classes — in a political sense still in the category of "sleeping dogs better left alone" — had begun to be stirred by their economic needs; here an immediate welfare and charity program was required to avert trouble.[91] Sad to say, the Austrian administration's alleviation measures often came too late. That such measures should be issued before and not after expressions of popular discontent is hardly disputable. However, Kaiser Franz was wary of granting measures which he thought might yet prove to be unnecessary; often such wariness was overcome only after the proper moment for effectiveness had already passed.

No wonder that under such circumstances Metternich was dissatisfied. In view of what he had hoped for, the visit, in 1816, to the lands south of the Alps had yielded at most only partial results. Despite his efforts, it had brought no appreciable betterment, whether in the public attitude, the efficiency of the administration, or the emperor's understanding of the underlying issues. In his reappraisal, Metternich was beset by several formidable questions: How now to make the most of his obviously limited authority so that the emperor might yet concede to "national wishes" and win therewith an already dissatisfied and not easily satisfiable Italian population to the idea of enjoying membership in the Austrian family of nations? How to achieve a structural reorganization of the empire which would actually demonstrate that Illyria-Dalmatia and Lombardy-Venetia were equal partners of the other territorial nations within a great and historic empire? How to re-interest a surely reluctant Kaiser Franz in such basic considerations of vital problems which the monarch, if he regarded them at all, might very well regard as his own but not the foreign minister's business?

To summarize: Coming to see the situation in Italy "from a point of view infinitely more liberal and congenial to the sentiments of this nation" (thus Stewart), Metternich had immediately taken up the cause of meaningful Lombardo-Venetian autonomy. He strongly urged the emperor to grant effective home rule and to establish an Italian chancellery in Vienna. At the same time, he bitterly criticized the activity of the COHC and demanded a thorough reappraisal of the commission's make-up and policies. Like Bellegarde, he emphasized that an elimination of prejudices between Germans and Italians, thus a better understanding between these two peoples, was a prerequisite to any improvement. The pleas of Metternich, Bellegarde and other concerned Austrians for an Italian chancellery, for a viceroy with authority, and for a Lombardo-Venetian supreme court of justice were met with imperial indecision. Only the last-named institution was approved by Kaiser Franz in 1816. In addition to a fairly autonomous Lombardo-Venetian Kingdom, Metternich proposed an Illyro-Dalmatian Kingdom — "a Southern Slavic *Reich*" — for the peoples of Southern Slavic nationality and of the Roman Catholic faith. But Kaiser Franz did not accept this proposal and acquiesced only to a small Illyria comprised merely of the northern part of the former *Provinces Illyriennes*. There, as in the Italian provinces, respect and care for native language was practiced — albeit as an administrative necessity. Moreover, an attempt at thorough "Germanization" was more a matter of fear than fact and, despite the monarch's disinclination to grant his Italian subjects home rule, a considerable proportion of nationals served in the Lombardo-Venetian administration. With the good example of a well-governed and well-satisfied Lombardy-Venetia, Metternich had wished to bring the other Italian states to follow Austrian leadership. As it became clear that an Italian Confederation was not to be realized, he began to seek other means to assure some coordination among Italian states. Especially as the Brindisi "disclosures" rekindled old fears of a nation-wide conspiracy to achieve national union under a constitutional regime, the need for some all-Italian controls was made obvious. Although soon played down, the "plot" helped in establishing the Central Observation Agency, a bureau designed to spot trouble throughout Italy and which, so Metternich hoped, would help safeguard the Italian repose that Austria needed in order to fulfill its program and promises. Because obviously the emperor's visit to Italy and Illyria had resulted not in those positive measures Metternich had hoped for but rather in increased discontent, the minister felt called upon to seek a new approach to a general solution.

DIETRICHSTEIN

CHAPTER IV

A PERMANENT BUT IMPERFECT SOLUTION: 1817-1818

ITALY AND THE NEED FOR A PERMANENT SETTLEMENT

Early in 1817, the betrothal of Kaiser Franz's daughter Leopoldine to Crown Prince Dom Pedro of Portugal and Brazil had been arranged. After her marriage by proxy in Vienna, she was to journey to Italy, spend a few weeks there with her sister Marie Louise, and then proceed to Livorno, whence a Portuguese naval squadron would carry her overseas to Rio de Janeiro. As official chaperon and commissioner charged with "handing her over" to Portuguese authorities, her father appointed none other than Austria's minister of external affairs, Metternich. Beyond the pleasant prospects normally associated with a June sojourn in Italy, this assignment offered him the opportunity of contacting directly various officials in Lombardy-Venetia and other states regarding the various problems of the peninsula and the monarchy. As luck would have it, a revolt of Brazilian forces in Pernambuco repeatedly delayed the arrival of "that devil of a squadron" and permitted Metternich to mix a good deal of pleasure with his business — something for which the invigorating baths of Lucca and the lovely Tuscan countryside were appropriate enough. Of course, he had his conferences with Guicciardi, Saurau, Bubna, and Goëss on his way down and again after the departure of the archduchess finally took place in mid-August. He returned to Vienna during the first week of September.

These discussions touched not only upon the usual topics relating to Italian security — the increase of discontent, the extent of outside influences, the shortcomings of the administration of one's own and other provinces — but on the need to turn at last the provisional status of the Austrian administration into a permanent one.[1] Metternich had outlined his views on the European situation in general terms: the understanding between major governments was good enough; that between some governments and their own citizens was not. The whole line of his expostulations indicated the folly of separating external and internal policy; Austria could maintain its position as a major power and as a bulwark against revolution only if "morally strong in our interior".[2] Such phrases, repeated often enough, might have served to bring the emperor to eventual insight and agreement to Metternich's proposals for changes in the inner administration. Apprehension regarding the European scene had perhaps some basis if one considered the real weaknesses of the empire — above all, the arbitrary handling of internal policy, which resulted in a makeshift inner structure and an imbalance among member states.

In the summer of 1817 Metternich began to display an occasional edginess. There were moments when he saw apparitions in every corner, complained of the activity of various sects in Central Europe, and deplored the spreading of liberal and "pernicious" ideas;[3] at the same time, he warned the emperor of the dangerous atmosphere upon the Continent and of the results which a reactionary administration could bring.[4] It was little comfort to imagine, as Sedlnitzky and even Bubna were sometimes wont to do, that the Italians were as faint of heart as strong of voice and were unwilling to shed blood for the independence which some yearned for so demonstratively.[5] Certainly the minister was not prone to having illusions — he himself had warned too often against such a mistake. It must have been sobering to have Bubna point out to him (a half-century before a king of Sardinia became king of Italy) that the Italians were casting their eyes on the House of Savoy as the one real Italian dynasty capable of taking up the cause of national independence and that the independence party in Milan was reacting accordingly.[6] This meant that all future trouble in northern Italy would somehow have its contacts with Turin — a hypothesis borne out within four years. For the present, however, it meant that Kaiser Franz had dissipated his own and Austria's chances in Italy by having failed to convince the Italians that — even with his Italian birth and upbringing — he was an Italian prince or, at least, acting in the Italians' interests.

Since an improvement of the Austrian administration in Lombardy-Venetia would have had a direct bearing on the political situation in Italy, Metternich's feelings that something must be done grew as Italian public opinion deteriorated. Of course, both the emperor and his commander south of the Alps had sought to govern in such a manner that all Italians might become convinced of the benefits of Habsburg rule. For three years this aim had been more or less thwarted by an interior policy at odds with itself. If now Austria wished to show others its resolution and capability to snuff out any movement threatening to public tranquillity, then what Metternich called "internal moral strength" was a *sine qua non*.[7]

The very evident deterioration in public mood since 1816 was making itself felt in Lombardy-Venetia as in the other parts of Italy. Metternich knew to distinguish between general and local factors; the latter were always more acute because they offered more concrete objects for feelings of grievance. Although Lombards and Venetians enjoyed an administration in every way superior to those of other Italian populations, they demanded as a matter of course an administration intricate and efficient enough to conform to their advanced standard of living. Consequently, they were more articulate and pointed in their criticism than other Italian peoples. When referring to such a disagreeable topic as Lombardo-Venetian discontent before his monarch, the minister usually was wise enough to apply soothing ointment; the comparison with other Italian regions — where things were much worse — seldom failed. It did matter to keep Kaiser Franz in a frame of mind receptive enough to accept those propositions which Metternich might make.

Metternich's severest reproaches were levied at the middle-Italian states. Especially "the daily blunders" of the Tuscan government — a land ruled by the emperor's brother Ferdinand — roused his displeasure; its administration he denounced as "the most miserable in existence".[8] The minister's vehemence may have been intended as a round-about way of opening the emperor's eyes once more to malpractices at home. There could be no doubt that the failures of the Austrian administration lay behind much of the discontent among the Italian subjects. For Metternich, Austria's responsibility was as serious as simple: "To prevent dangers which can only be pernicious for us, it suffices to dispose of the causes of discontent at home and to convince all the peoples of Italy that those we rule are well-governed."[9] But if these words were to have any meaning, then a new effort to streamline the administration was mandatory. All too often in the past, Metternich complained to Kaiser Franz, the good and well-planned was spoiled by human failures and shortsightedness: "The result then is that usually the grandly and well-conceived is applied pettily and the common and petty is raised to grand chicanery. In these few words lies the history of the administration of the Italian-Austrian provinces."[10]

In addition, the unappreciated and disliked COHC had now been in existence for over three years. Moreover, as even the Archduke Rainer (another of the emperor's brothers and a future viceroy) complained in August of 1817, the commission's president, Lazansky, was still "seeking, more than the circumstances in the [Lombardo-Venetian] land would allow, to make everything conform to practices existing in the German provinces."[11]

Now, one and a half years after the imperial visit to Lombardy-Venetia and Illyria, how stood the issues of an Italian or Illyrian chancellery and a viceroy for Milan? Kaiser Franz had simply shelved them. The viceroy had been requested in 1814, promised in 1815, named (Anton) in 1816, and was now, in the summer of 1817, nowhere in sight. Not only the Italians but also Austrian officials were bewildered at this inexplicable delay. Early in 1817, for example, the usually well-informed Sardagna had applied for the job of secretary to the viceroy-soon-to-arrive.[12] He, like the Italians, was still waiting, not just for the viceroy or the Italian chancellor but for some slight sign that Vienna would grant the Italian provinces real status within the monarchy. Now, during his Italian visit, Metternich promised Austrian officials there that the emperor would certainly nominate a viceroy by the end of the year with sufficiently extended powers to do good on the spot and that he would establish direct communications with the Italian authorities independent of the other departments. In words recalling those of Bellegarde some two years before, Metternich felt sure that Austria would attain its aims as would the Italian population—i.e., "the wishes and hopes of all honest and intelligent men would be fulfilled and Austria would save Italy from the dangers which menace it."[13] The need for reshaping the government in Lombardy-Venetia in order to regain lost ground and the meaningful reorganization of the central administration of the entire empire from the highest to the regional level were joint issues which were now the objects of Metternich's main efforts. How much hope was attached to these coming changes one can gather from the repeated assurances exchanged between Metternich and Austrian officials in Italy. Perhaps typical was Bubna's assertion to Metternich that the situation in Lombardy-Venetia was already improving now that hints of changes were in the air.[14]

Metternich had long prepared himself on the Italian issue. In the process he followed his oft-expressed axiom that one might attempt to provide corrections and remedies only upon being thoroughly informed. During the establishment of the CBA in the autumn of 1816 he had set out to obtain for his own information reports on Italian problems. Specifically for this task he had commissioned Tito Manzi, an able man with multiple connections whose wide experience eminently qualified him for such an assignment; on the other hand, Manzi's loyal service in the Napoleonic *Regno d'Italia* had aroused the misgivings of Saurau, the Austrian governor in Milan. Nevertheless a confident and trusting Metternich brushed aside Saurau's warnings;[15] instead, he eagerly awaited Manzi's extensive report. He received it some time after his return to the capital in September. Thereupon the minister based his own commentaries which he prepared simultaneously with his proposals for a general overhaul of the central administration. The material on Italy and Lombardy-Venetia he submitted to the emperor on November 3, 1817.[16]

Metternich stressed that it was precisely the dissatisfaction prevalent everywhere on the peninsula that had led him to gather the information from which he now wished to profit. He could then impart helpful advice to other governments and hope to gain, moreover, some points for improvement within Austria's own Italian provinces. The minister quite agreed with Manzi's views on the extent of the discontent and its direct relationship to poor administration, especially in Tuscany. Again, he reassured the emperor that it was only a matter of internal improvement to keep the revolution away.

Yet Metternich apparently considered over-alarming the emperor as bad tactics; it was much more important to persuade him that circumstances were at last favorable enough to permit Austria some slight revamping which might render the Habsburg government more popular. Thereby Austria might possibly win even the attachment of the neighboring peoples, none of whom, he reminded his monarch, was happy with its present government. Turning to Lombardy-Venetia, Metternich began by presenting the brighter side of the medal. To set the emperor at ease, he declared that the superiority of the present Austrian administration in Italy was admitted even by the most devoted partisans of the "previous regime". Only in Lombardy-Venetia, he insisted, were all classes of the population equal before the law, only there did the nobility and the rich not have the upper hand, only there was the clergy kept within bounds, only there was no one persecuted for his political past. So much for a tactful tribute to efforts at enlightened rule in Lombardy-Venetia! However, Metternich continued, be the principles of the Austrian administration ever so just, police reports from Austrian Italy revealed that there prevailed an extensive discontent, caused principally by an alleged desire to give these provinces a German cut. Just as an example, Italians were offended by the allocation of judicial posts, where they suspected all too many German magistrates — a grievance which Metternich suggested eliminating by simply employing more Italian nationals. He could only repeat what the emperor had, in one form or another, heard so often before:

From a political point of view, the faults and weaknesses of the administration in this interesting part of the Monarchy must be remedied as quickly as possible; the course of affairs must be made more active; national esprit and national self-consciousness

m u s t b e m e t h a l f - w a y i n t h a t t h e s e p r o v i n c e s r e -
c e i v e a f o r m o f a d m i n i s t r a t i o n w h i c h p r o v e s t o
t h e I t a l i a n s t h a t n o o n e w i s h e s t o t r e a t t h e m i n
j u s t t h e s a m e m a n n e r a s t h e G e r m a n p r o v i n c e s ,
a n d t h u s , s o t o s a y , t o a m a l g a m a t e t h e m w i t h
[t h e G e r m a n p r o v i n c e s] .

For Metternich, all depended on a judicious conduct of the Vienna
government. To prompt his sovereign to action, he hinted, in the couched
and sometimes awkward language occasionally used when addressing the
emperor, that the day was near "on which Your Majesty shall find Your-
self moved actually to bring into reality the salutary proposals which the
Same All-highest Majesty has intended for a long time in order to establish
the welfare of those provinces on a permanent basis". Metternich was convinced that the new "course" he sought would be a grand work and that
the measures meant for Lombardy-Venetia would — in his favorite phrase
— contain "everything good": if only carried out properly, all or almost
all might be won, since, as he insisted, they "would fulfill the just wishes
of a nation."

PROPOSALS FOR A NEW INTERIOR ORGANIZATION:
A CENTRAL MINISTRY AND NATIONAL CHANCELLERIES

To harmonize the apparently contradictory principles of unity and
diversity had always been a primary problem accompanying the integration of the Habsburg lands. Yet, this very prudent harmonization — so
often stressed by Metternich — called for a careful balancing of institutions
which, however, was seldom attained. Usually, during the many phases of
Habsburg history, dynastic and state policy inclined toward one or the
other of these principles. Until the reign of Joseph II, a tendency to
respect heterogeneity prevailed. The very manner in which various territories, often historic entities, had come into the Habsburg collection of
states usually required a maintenance of special status and accepted custom.
This seemed the only feasible way to avoid either the risk of offending
local estates or the unwelcome task of providing a new administration.
Generally, heterogeneity and territorial chancelleries — such as for Transylvania, the Banat, or Illyria — were even encouraged to check what were
felt to be excessive Hungarian pretensions. Conversely, the idea of special
status and diversity ran counter to rationalistic and centralistic concepts

of state which guided "enlightened" rulers in the modernizing of their governing apparatus. Thus, the Illyrian chancellery, reestablished by Leopold II on the advice of Kaunitz, was abolished again by his son, the young Kaiser Franz, once accord with Hungary was reached. All pleas to revive it remained unanswered.[17] There had been other chancelleries which were not revived in 1814: the loss of Lombardy in 1797 had meant the end of the Italian chancellery established under Maria Theresia and the loss of Dalmatia in 1805, after seven years' possession, had made the hastily erected Dalmatian-Albanian *Hofstelle* superfluous.[18] Now, in 1817, there remained only the *Vereinigte Hofkanzlei* for the Austrian, Bohemian, and Galician lands and then the Hungarian chancellery, to which the Transylvanian one was, in effect, subordinated.

In the years following the downfall of Napoleon, the need for reorganizing the administration of a restored Austrian empire presented a unique opportunity to achieve an inner political balance. Conceivably this could have resulted in the equal partnership of all regions upon which depended the stable existence of such a "family of peoples" as was the Habsburg Empire. However, in the general hope of achieving unity, those taken in by the theoretical merits of a centralized state proceeded unmindful of the practical difficulties — and even more unfortunate — of the political dangers involved in applying Viennese norms to all parts of the empire. Certainly the failure of Joseph's attempt to Germanize his lands left behind bitter memories and some caution — caution all the more justified by the fact that since Joseph's death, the Habsburgs had acquired millions of non-German subjects. Yet, the appeal of a general conformity — at least within the non-Hungarian lands — was one which Kaiser Franz had not been able to resist.

Although the COHC had to act under imperial directives clear enough in their expressed wish for conformity and equalization, there had always been some individuals bold enough to insist instead on a recognition of multiplicity and on a respect for other nationalities. They of course were the first to admit the need for some coordination and centralization. The seemingly obvious solution — centralization at the very highest level only, autonomy for the various regions — was not altogether new and had been heard in one form or another since the failure of the Josephinian experiment. Again in 1815, it had been propounded in a *Vortrag* of the COHC's subcommission on Tyrol, submitted in conjunction with a memoir by the organizer of that province — Baron Roschmann — on the reintroduction of the former estates-constitution.[19] The authors of the *Vortrag* felt called upon to emphasize in their recommendations the following points: the Habsburg Monarchy was not one nation nor one people but a multinational empire in which no people, whether Germans, Slavs, Italians, or Hungarians, might presume predominance over the others; in this great empire of many nations, all differing in customs, needs, industry, language, morals, and opinion, such variances as well as each people's special character had to be honored and respected; the government of such an empire had to surrender any thought of achieving uniformity or even conformity; rather, it might bring about unity only at top echelons while leaving particular issues to regional authorities. As so often, tradition was called upon — a frequent practice in which, however, admired past examples did not always apply precisely to the present. The authors emphasized that a system of tolerance and respect had proven itself in the fiercest of times because it had bound together all nations of the monarchy in loyalty to the throne; they denied that such a system had ever displayed any disadvantage.

Such opinions, however, had little bearing on an already determined course. To be sure, this course was gradually modified through the pressure of practical difficulties. It never demanded the degree of Germanization and centralization desired by Joseph, but, unhappily, its insistence on a conformity of non-German peoples' institutions with those at hand in the German or hereditary provinces amounted, as far as these peoples were concerned, to nearly the same thing.

Now, in October 1817, Metternich was preparing his proposals for a reconstitution of the Austrian central administration through the erection of a ministry of the interior and national chancelleries. He had not only sounded out the emperor but had undertaken to explain the proposals' purpose and scope to some of his friends and associates. One of the listeners had been Prince Dietrichstein, Metternich's longtime friend and neighbor. Unable to express his opinions on the occasion of Metternich's exposition, Dietrichstein did so, apparently after a week-end's deliberation, in a letter written on Monday, October 27, 1817.[20] This document is extraordinary: it alone provides us with information on the proceedings preliminary to the minister's proposals as well as with an independent and surprisingly frank appraisal. It permits us to reconstruct, somewhat, the substance of what Metternich had had in mind before submitting his ideas to the monarch. Its outspoken candor can be ascribed to Dietrichstein's peculiarly critical and searching mind and was unthinkable in any but such an informal communication employing the familiar *Du* as address.

Metternich had broached the need for a new inner structure of the monarchy by pointing, first of all, to the critical problem of securing the empire's future. This problem, Dietrichstein agreed, in itself would demand a regulated interior system capable of functioning smoothly even under adverse circumstances and under inept rule. Such a reference to the eventual accession of Kaiser Franz's son Ferdinand had not been intended to question the succession but had merely served to underscore the seriousness with which Metternich wished his proposals considered. The admonition to Kaiser Franz was to be clear: it behooved precisely a superior monarch to take special care to consolidate his legacy. However, Dietrichstein objected to such a motive for change and reorganization — "This one inducement which you want to use with the father regarding his son" — although he was otherwise in general agreement with Metternich on the value and the necessity of the proposals. Such argumentation helped little, Dietrichstein insisted, since behind Metternich's premise lay only the wishful thought that his regulation, his answer to the uncertainty of the future, might remain certain and inviolate. This, alas, seemed to Dietrichstein just too improbable and too much to expect, since the "misfortune which stands before us can only be checked by something really unalterable; yet, actually, just one word from someone of influence would suffice to alter the whole procedure." The misfortune Dietrichstein alluded to was, of course, the reign of Ferdinand; all the danger that it threatened could be successfully confronted only, he wrote to Metternich, "by [some kind of] a *constitution* which, however, neither you nor I shall propose and for the proposal of which, moreover, they would send us both strolling." Because of the impossibility of a proper constitution, the future would remain dependent on the whims of fate. This did not mean that Metternich's efforts would be in vain. On the contrary, Dietrichstein assured his friend, all that he might achieve until this time came would be considered a great service to his country, "all the greater, the more time we have, because it will make us and others more capable of defying and adjuring storms." Accordingly, Metternich could only secure his new program by the force of his personality, something possible only were the emperor to continue reigning for some time.

Dietrichstein found Metternich's proposals "excellent". Left unmentioned was that, without Kaiser Franz's wholehearted approval, Metternich's program stood little chance of remaining intact even during the present reign, to say nothing of the "storms" — the difficulties inevitable after Franz's demise. Both Dietrichstein and Metternich knew that it would require some skill to convince the emperor that present practices were inadequate for the internal management of a mighty empire or that Metternich's proposals represented the right means for improvement.

Like the minister, Dietrichstein recognized a fundamental need: to get away from the absolute though patriarchal rule of one man who, in a more modern age, could not possibly cope with all that was theoretically required of him. To end the system which permitted huge backlogs and interference from imperial special commissioners designated on the spur of the moment and which was really a patchwork routine getting along as best it could, there seemed to be only one way: responsible ministries for all aspects of governmental duty. Dietrichstein did not share Metternich's reserve in suggesting a whole series of new ministries at once; if he were in his friend's place, he wrote, he would propose seven: exterior, interior, war, finance, justice, police, and finally, culture and education. It is striking that, in the Austria of that time, Metternich's confidant should urge a ministry of education because "it is important *enough* with us to warrant *also* being independent." The same distinction, he sought, was also due to the police, especially in what he called a "constitutionless" state.

Of course, the main point of discussion had been the ministry of the interior and the various national chancelleries to be ranged under it. Whereas Metternich had proposed six such offices, Dietrichstein came out for seven — one for each of the seven natural territorial or ethnic regions of the empire: 1. Bohemia-Moravia-Silesia; 2. Hungary; 3. Galicia; 4. Transylvania; 5. Austria (Upper and Lower Austria, Salzburg, Tyrol and Voralberg, and Styria); 6. Italy (Lombardy and Venetia); and 7. Illyria (Carinthia, Carniola, Croatia, the Littorale, Dalmatia, and Albania). Metternich had planned a single chancellery for Bohemia *and* Galicia and thus, in effect, proposed chancelleries for areas in which Germans, Italians, Northern Slavs, Southern Slavs, Hungarians, and Rumanians were predominant. Why Metternich had combined Bohemia with Galicia into one clumsy block is a matter of conjecture — perhaps it was to present the Northern Slavs as a combined block akin to the Southern Slavic one or, perhaps, to avoid three chancelleries representing largely Slavic populations. At least, the Illyrian chancellery Metternich had wanted in 1816 had also been meant for a similar combination of largely Slavic populations. Dietrichstein protested against such a Bohemian-Galician combination as "ridiculously large" in contrast to the "ridiculously small" present Illyrian Kingdom (only half of what Metternich had envisaged as his *Mittägliches Slavisches Reich*) and proposed that it should therefore be split into its two more natural components, both of which, he could have added, were still larger than Illyria. Here, however, Dietrichstein ignored the fact that a Lombardo-Venetian chancellery would have administered an even smaller territory than would have a chancellery for a combined Illyria and Dal-

matia. Yet, on this point he demonstrated his remarkable gift for pre-
diction: even the small Illyrian kingdom, he believed, could not remain
intact the way it was; it would not be able to hold on to Fiume and
Croatia "*contre le serment du Roi d'Hongrie, contre l'intérêt de l'état et
contre le sens Commun*". In less than five years he was to be proven right.
Dietrichstein correctly foresaw the political tact required in subordinating
"national" chancellors to the new minister of the interior — the representative of central authority and the symbol of the empire's unity. Thus he
deemed it prudent not to invest the new minister with the old title
Supreme Chancellor which was then applied to the director of the United
Chancellery for the Austro-Bohemian lands. He was sure that the Hungarian and Transylvanian chancellors, as well as their proposed new colleague
from the Italian provinces, would object out of purely traditional grounds
to serving an official bearing such a title. The new title — *Minister of the
Interior* — by itself needed not to offend, however. Certainly Dietrichstein
had a talent for spotting possible points of trouble: at Kaiser Franz's court,
where titles always were in abundance, this new one would have had its
special significance and justification. Yet, the monarch showed from the
very beginning that he preferred the old one to the new.

Dietrichstein had not hesitated in approving Metternich's "entire idea"
but, simultaneously, he warned Metternich: "Don't count your chickens
before they're hatched."[21] He meant that Metternich naturally had approached the whole matter from the aspect of the institutions needed and
not of the personnel available. However, this practical point was the very
one that concerned Dietrichstein, who emphasized that the persons were no
less important than the project and that the best project might be ruined
by the wrong people. The big question for him was: who would be the
coordinator and representative of central authority over the various
chancellors — i.e., who would be the minister of the interior? Prior to
departing for Italy, Metternich had gone over this problem with Dietrichstein; whereas he had already decided upon the office, he had not done so
on its occupant. At that time, in order to get things started, Dietrichstein
had suggested the selection of Archduke Rainer; there seemed to be no
other choice, Metternich himself agreed and had arrived at "the ingenious
modality: Minister of the Interior — *Minister vacat* — temporarily represented by His Imperial Highness the Archduke Rainer." However,
Metternich had known that only Rainer would come into consideration as
the long-overdue viceroy and that he would most likely be appointed by
Kaiser Franz at year's end.[22] Later Dietrichstein came to accept the fact
that no alternative remained but to send Rainer to Milan because, as

he put it, "we once *promised* the Italians an archduke as viceroy instead of leaving them Bellegarde and because, since then, we have treated them badly." Apropos, he added, it might be well if Count Strassoldo (now with the COHC) were to serve with the viceroy in Milan and Count Mellerio as Italian chancellor in Vienna.

The question of the ministry's occupancy had remained unsettled. Such a key post, representing not only an important symbol but involving real and delicate duties, required, in Dietrichstein's words, "a man of thick skin". But then, the list of candidates available for the new ministry was reducible to almost nothing; most of the prospects he swept away in a flood of sarcasm: Ugarte? — wishy-washy, ridiculous, a satire! Wallis? — No, God be praised! Lazansky? — insufficiently cultivated! Kolowrat? — lacking in strength, a rare quality nowadays! Baldacci, Mittrowsky, Chotek, or Goëss certainly did not come into consideration. Zichy? — not much better than Ugarte! Stadion? — unsuitable even if replaceable as finance minister. Hauer? — possibly in ten years' time. Saurau? — perhaps he had some of the necessary ingredients although not *"pour le commencement"*. Then, in a light vein, Dietrichstein brought forward his own name only to dismiss it as the silliest thought of all. As sharp as his comments were, they came fairly close to the mark, and Saurau did get the post. As for himself, Dietrichstein professed no interest in any sort of governmental service, excepting perhaps "one of the seven — or, as you would have it — six chancellorships!" His own interest, he added, would depend on who the minister of the interior would be. In conclusion, he entreated his friend to think over impartially what he had written since "perhaps I am not wrong after all."

The draft as well as the final copy of Metternich's *Vortrag* on "Changes in the Inner Administration" also bear the date of October 27, 1817.[23] It consists of two parts: an introduction and the proposals themselves. In the first, in order to prepare the emperor, Metternich employed a threefold tactic: to explain and to characterize the proposals, to reassure and to placate the monarch, and finally, to warn and to point to the future.

The proposals were to be but an initial step, he wrote, containing "at first appearance little and yet everything essential." This statement was surely meant to satisfy Kaiser Franz that there would be no unpleasant surprises later on; it also meant that Metternich had intended to water down his proposals much like distasteful medicine to a reluctant patient. This alone prevented Metternich from following Dietrichstein's advice even had he wished to do so. He had long learned where the dividing line between imperial condescension and indecision lay. To come forward with all his contemplated suggestions at once was hardly wise; apparently he had decided in the last minute to secure first of all a bridgehead. Thus in limiting himself to the attainable and in wishing to avoid possible difficulties which might snarl even the beginning, Metternich deferred all treatment of Hungarian and Transylvanian matters to a later date.

Turning from his first to his second tactic, the minister characterized his proposals as simplicity itself. He had to assure his sovereign that they represented nothing unnecessary, nothing revolutionary, nothing bold, nothing new, nothing hastily conceived; instead, all was the result of long and careful planning. He recalled the many conversations during which the monarch had not shown himself unreceptive on this subject. Just this fact reveals why Metternich could not have carried forward Dietrichstein's suggestions: what would be the emperor's reaction were Metternich now to come up with something new and different? Not only did the minister find it expedient to allay Kaiser Franz's misgivings in regard to the proposals but even with respect to their author. Had not the emperor always been satisfied with his minister in the past? Surely he had come to know Metternich through long experience as a man of moderation far from wishing to indulge in risky ventures, as a man always concerned with order — and now in particular because "disorder must ensue from an administration internally too complicated". Although this compelling phrase was one truth which Kaiser Franz certainly understood, there was the possibility that he might have considered Metternich's proposals as an even further complication — thus the stress on simplicity and on the fact that all proposed institutions were to be built on foundations already at hand. This necessary testimonial to the existing system was reason enough not to dispute the emperor's desire to retain the title *Supreme Chancellor* even in view of Dietrichstein's essentially correct objections. To the monarch, Metternich had stressed purposely that within his proposals reform meant only *re-form* and not innovation; it must have been otherwise with his discourse held in Dietrichstein's presence. That discourse had stimulated Dietrichstein to reply in a spirit of innovation although tinged with pessimism and modified by some awareness of realities.[24]

In approaching Kaiser Franz on a reformation of interior affairs, Metternich had to make the most of his vaunted tact. He could hardly have criticized the state machine in its essence without offending its superintendent. He could, at most, mention certain defects; moreover, in order to undertake improvements and repairs on the state machine, he had — first of all — to reassure a fearful Kaiser Franz that it was solid enough not to be impaired by such tinkering. This he did by emphasizing that foundations so well laid by "the glorious reign of Maria Theresia", "the theoretical endeavors of her successor", and finally, by the present "most fortunate lawgiver for the happiness of his people", would require little serious alteration and no great exertion to achieve "everything good". That, for all its good foundations, the present system was inadequate for the modern needs of the monarchy, Metternich could not bring himself to say in straight language. He preferred circumlocution and described his own feelings of duty regarding the need for internal improvement rather gingerly: "The cause for existing ills (and where are they not?) must be sought and examined; the results of this investigation must be reduced to simple terms. This task I had taken upon myself on a day when I felt enlightened enough and thus strong enough for it." The minister's repeated efforts to show confidence and conviction do not, however, conceal the uncertainty with which he advanced on this particular issue. But behind all such superficial assurances remained a key argument: reform was an administrative necessity.

For a long time now, Metternich claimed, he had not only kept an eye on the evils within the administration but had considered some of the solutions. Why the delay? Because he did not wish "to pronounce lightly, without reflection or examination, that which might be so momentous in its consequences". We may assume that it also took many months to sound out and to belabor the emperor. Now, the minister could submit his first proposals, convinced of his "I dare say it — surely true maxim" and of the most satisfactory results of a painstaking groundwork. Scrupulous not to gainsay any of the emperor's preconceptions, he conceded that "no time is less opportune than the present for undertaking reforms within any state", but, he added within the same breath, "fortunately the state machine is already constructed on such a sound basis that, in the extended sense of the word, there is nothing actually within the machine to overturn." All that he proposed, he went on, "would deal with the main springs of the whole. And here one would need not even to introduce a reform aimed at an overturn of standard forms but only an ordering of parts and, indeed, only of the already existing organic parts of the central administration of the state." "Nothing to overturn", "not even a reform" — the need for such reassurances in a matter calling for plain language shows up Kaiser Franz's pathological aversion to reform or any internal reorganization. It demonstrates clearly that Metternich was not master of internal as well as external affairs.

In looking ahead, Metternich was far from maintaining that his proposals might be the cure for all future ills; he was certain that "the good" could be attained only through a clear understanding of the proper attributes of the government's highest authorities. In an interesting allusion to the inevitability of progress under certain conditions, he indicated that "there exists no human institution which, when based on plain and fundamental principles, would not improve itself naturally as a matter of course, just as still greater laming and confusion would be the unavoidable consequence [should such principles be lacking]". This truth alone, he affirmed, was one of the chief reasons why the emperor had to act to reorganize his central administration accordingly.

The minister had been determined to impress on the sovereign the obligations owed to his successor; in appealing to the father as well as the ruler, he allowed himself a somewhat more forceful tone. That the state machine managed to function was no real argument against a proposed overhaul; that it did so despite the negative effects of an overly-centralized administration could only be attributed to well-organized and regulated lower echelons and "to a monarch able to govern". How little this would be the case even in the slightest catastrophe which the monarchy would surely some day face, the emperor had to know well enough — both as monarch and as father. For such a time, Metternich warned, the monarch was called upon to provide. There could be but one real way: still under Kaiser Franz's supervision, the highest echelons of government must be reorganized in a manner which would guard most efficiently against deviations and mistakes. He asked his monarch to imagine the present course of affairs without Kaiser Franz's presence and authority — the authority upon which such a course was "almost exclusively based". Years were often not much more than moments in the lives of states: the important thing was to act now! In such a work as Metternich had in mind, a mere establishing of principles did not suffice. It was necessary above all that the various governmental levels concerned might get used to their new spheres of activity — and this would take time. On this point he issued his sharpest warning: "Your Majesty shall have done nothing for the future should Your Majesty wait until the last years of Your Majesty's lifetime to decree some grand measures for ordering the future . . ." The emperor had, in other words, to assume responsibility for grooming the new system to such working order that "a weak successor" could not jeopardize a good and thorough government or, much less, think of replacing it.

To comprehend the nature and the purpose of the proposals themselves, Metternich thought it necessary to consider at first three topics: the character and actual strength of the monarchy, the organizational possibilities, and the composition of the highest levels of the central government. Let us take each of these in turn as well as the proposals themselves, and outline thereby briefly Metternich's main thoughts:

A. *The character and actual strength of the monarchy:*

1. Obviously the monarchy was not up to its full strength — the result of an improper organization of the highest governmental echelons.
2. What was the nature and position of the empire in
   a. a political-administrative aspect? Because of its multinational character, it was and should be a federative state. Moreover, most of its parts had old, respected, and still existing estates-constitutions (*Landesständische Verfassungen*). With calculated flattery Metternich contended that Kaiser Franz had approved a policy of deferring to differences in language, custom, and mores in such lands as Tyrol, Galicia, and Lombardy-Venetia. Such differences deserved the profoundest governmental consideration because in them the nationality of each of the various regions of the empire asserted itself.
   b. a political-geographic aspect? As a great but vulnerable landmass with few easily defensible borders, the empire must find its strength in a common public spirit and interest encouraged through a good common political, military, and economic system.
3. If Austria required more effort at self-preservation than any other state save Prussia, then the real strength it needed could only be the result of clearly conceived and firmly applied correct principles of government. In its precarious position, Austria could not afford a haphazard government.

B. *The organizational possibilities:*

1. The total fusion of all diverse elements into one form of government and administration had been the daring Josephinian solution. Such an attempt might have been applicable to a homogeneous state, but not in an empire of so many peoples and languages. It was doomed to fail; it could only have been achieved by a veritable revolution from above. Yet such a turn-over was always accompanied by dangers which only the extremest rigor could avert. As if this were not enough, Metternich unveiled to the emperor an even more frightful prospect: in the present state of things, a try for fusion might result in a demand for a central representative assembly.

2. The only alternative to consider was that of a fair and reasonable preservation of diversity — the various regions' special and peculiar rights and standings which were based on uniqueness of heritage, custom, and language — under the guidance of a strong and efficiently organized central authority. In the pursuit of this alternative, there arose a twofold question: how could the Austrian state be strengthened most efficiently

  a. with the least possible modification of already existing practices?

  b. with due consideration to the nationality of the inhabitants and to the existing constitutions of the various regions? The policy of the central government toward its various nationalities had to be uniform to prevent a disharmony dangerous to the inner balance of the state. Yet, in Austria one had to observe extremes of such a policy — i.e., too much and too little respect for nationality — being practiced simultaneously. This idiosyncrasy, Metternich might have added, mocked any thought of uniformity:

    i. Hungary presented the classic example of exaggerated deference to national character and aspirations. Whereas it and Transylvania enjoyed privileges sufficient to hamper the state machine, the distinctions between other entities, different in local needs and administration, were increasingly and excessively obliterated. While Hungary claimed rights bordering on independence, the noteworthy nationality of other Austrian states was dissipated in friction between the central government and the provinces — and this to the disadvantage of the state as a whole.

    ii. Even if nationality was respected at the lower level of the administration, there persisted at the higher level an undeniable tendency toward fusion. This tendency resulted in tie-ups and friction; it perverted the real purpose of centralizing governmental power into a passion for delving into local details that was deadly to the "enlightened spirit" with which the highest central authorities should be imbued. One word from the monarch would suffice to end such error and to establish the proper pattern on which the government could develop its true strength.

C. *The composition of the highest level of the central government:*

1. The executive arm of the government was divided into diverse branches of activity similar in most modern states of that time.

These were listed by Metternich as: external affairs, internal affairs, finances, war, justice, police, and budget and expenditures.

2. Each of these branches was again divided naturally into two sections which were, however, to remain strictly separated:
   a. the "moral", which conceived and carried responsibility;
   b. the "technical" or "manipulative", which carried out the will of the first and was to be subjugated to it. The decisive distinction between the designations *minister* and *president* (of a *Hofstelle*) had always to be kept in mind. Although a president had executive power he remained foreman of an agency whose deliberative and collegial character tended to obliterate individual responsibility. A minister, on the other hand, could be burdened with full responsibility without excluding such collegial procedure as might be desirable to retain.[25]

3. This logical separation of the ministerial office from the largely administrative *Hofstelle* had already been practiced in two branches of government: external affairs and finances.

4. Thus it should also be with justice and the interior; the police and budget control, in Metternich's thinking, did not deserve such eminence. On an education ministry, he kept silent.

D. *The establishment of the ministry of the interior and the national chancelleries:*

1. The head of the administration of the interior was to receive the title: *Supreme Chancellor and Minister of the Interior.* He was to be the guardian and representative of the unity of the state and government.

2. Directly under the minister were to serve four chancellors who, together with the minister, would then form the ministry of the interior. The chancellors' spheres of activity were to be determined by the nationality of the inhabitants and the local needs of the respective provinces under their jurisdiction. The chancellors were to represent within the ministry regional considerations and feelings; in their respective lands, they were to stand for the principle of unity of government. The officers to be appointed were:
   a. a Bohemian-Moravian-Galician chancellor for the lands named.
   b. an Austrian chancellor for both Austrias, Styria, Salzburg, and Tyrol.
   c. an Illyrian chancellor for the Kingdom of Illyria and [sic] Dalmatia.

    d. an Italian chancellor for the Kingdom of Lombardy-Venetia.
3. The effect of such an organization would be to bring the Hungarian and Transylvanian chancelleries down from their present elevated standing to the general level of the four chancelleries now proposed. Therein would lie the initial step in an eventual redefining of both lands' status — a complex operation which should not be mixed with the easily improvable.

Alongside such changes in the executive sphere, Metternich had had in mind similar ones in what might be called "the legislative" one. A logical corollary to the ministry of the interior as a symbol of a single central authority over somewhat autonomous parts would have been a central assembly — a *Reichsrat* — composed of delegates from the various provincial estates. Such a project was advanced by Metternich at about the same time as his other proposals. We know of it only through an autobiographical fragment written in his later years.[26] It was in line with his policy — based on the maxim: "Events which can not be prevented must be guided" — of pressing for the introduction of the estates-form of constitution *(Landesständische Verfassung)* wherever possible to forestall clamor for the more radical representative form which was the angel of death for absolute monarchy. Thus he used all of his influence to compel laggard German princes to comply at last with Article XIII of the Acts of the German Confederation, which provided for the establishment of such a *Landesständische Verfassung* within all member states.[27] Whereas Kaiser Franz approved of Metternich's constitution policy within the German Confederation and although he even — according to Metternich — recognized the importance of the *Reichsrat* for the monarchy itself, he postponed action on the project from year to year. In 1834 he supposedly reproached himself for not having acted upon it before; his new resolve was brought to naught by his death soon thereafter.

    Unlike Metternich, Dietrichstein had not been forced to express himself in terms of a stepwise advance. Therefore, his letter to Metternich reflects, more than the toned-down proposals of the minister, the formula upon which the Austrian empire might have found its inner strength in a modern world. This formula, which Metternich of course had also in mind, meant the equal partnership of all of the six or seven natural regions of the empire through an enhancing of neglected members and the downgrading of the hitherto overly-privileged ones. An inner balance was to have been guaranteed by equally-ranked "national" chancelleries under the guidance of a superior authority representing the unity of the state. Surely, this formula was a more sensible solution for the internal structuring of an empire increasingly threatened by time than many of those advanced subsequently in more desperate days.

Metternich's proposals of October 27 and of November 3, 1817 — his most significant advance into internal matters — were the logical result of a policy at least three years in the making. Up to then, the high points of this policy had been the pleas for national autonomy in Lombardy-Venetia at the end of 1815 and for a *Reich* to embrace the Southern Slavic nationality in the spring of 1816. The proposals of 1817 climax his objections to an imperial reorganization policy founded on the ideals of centralization and conformity — objections expressed repeatedly since the organization of the COHC in 1814. The proposals were meant to effect an end and a beginning — an end of the COHC, now to be replaced by the ministry of the interior and thus the real end of the provisional government despite earlier imperial decrees to that effect — and the beginning of a permanent interior structure, especially for Lombardy-Venetia which now at last would receive its viceroy, its Italian chancellor in Vienna, and an Italian governor in Milan. Finally, these proposals, which give such a revealing insight into Metternich's relationship to his sovereign, were far from being all that he designed. They were, he emphasized, but a first step. What was to come was indicated clearly by the minister: the great work of fitting Hungary and Transylvania truly into the empire. How successful the ultimate work might be, however, depended on how well the initial proposals would fare; thus, it remains to be seen how this "first step" was carried out.

FROM THE PROPOSALS TO THE PATENT

The natural anxiety with which Metternich awaited the emperor's reaction to his proposals, so long in the making, must have come to the surface occasionally. Yet, as usual, there are no references to Metternich's feelings — if one excepts an expression of views on internal problems in a conversation which the usually blasé Gentz termed "remarkable".[28] The whole reorganization issue seems to have been kept on the imperial desk; until the week before Christmas brought a sudden surge of activity, there is no record of deliberation within such bodies as the *Staatskonferenz* or the *Staatsrat*.

Although we do not know the emperor's direct reaction to the proposals, several documents pertaining to the formulation of an imperial statement

on the new organization, as well as the published statement itself, show
that his misgivings made necessary telling alterations.[29] Two of these documents are Metternich drafts — one a revision of the other — for an official
announcement in the *Wiener Zeitung* which appeared on December 24,
1817. A third is an unused draft of the imperial edict; although composed
on the same lines as the Metternich drafts and containing some sentences
that were the very same, it is of doubtful authorship: it does not seem to be
Metternich's — perhaps it was Saurau's. Between the Metternich proposals
of October 27 and the drafts written in the middle of December, and then
among the drafts themselves, there are some striking differences. The word
nationality, frequently used in the October *Vortrag,* does not appear at
all in the Metternich pieces of December. To be sure, in the unused draft
of the imperial edict, *nationality* is referred to once, but very much in the
sense of Metternich's original proposals; perhaps the draft's author took
his cue from them and perhaps he was not as acutely aware of the imperial
qualms as Metternich must have been after experiencing the monarch's
initial reactions. According to the unknown author, a "system of unity"
was to lead all of the empire's lands and peoples to the same goals of
general and individual welfare; it meant applying principles of conformity
and equality to public duties and education. Concurrently, he proposed
that the emperor call for a simultaneous observance and due respect—when
necessary — "of the differences and singularities of the language, of mores
and customs, of climate, and of the inherited nationality".

Within Metternich's two drafts and the published announcement, there
is obvious a progressive dilution of the cardinal idea of unity *plus* multiplicity. In the first draft, Metternich put down as the emperor's conviction
that, in planning for the welfare of the empire and its inhabitants, two
aims must stand together a s a p a i r : attaining the greatest possible
unity and strength of the empire, a n d the so necessary deference to local
interests and needs. In the second draft, the equality of these principles
gives way to a definite subordination of the latter to the former: here the
emperor was to express the conviction that "in his great empire, the real
and generally needed strength of the government under the fundamental
concept of the entire state's oneness demands in its application due respect
to local conditions arising from the needs of the individual parts comprising the empire." In the published announcement, consideration for local
issues and interests is called for "in the most extended sense" (a favorite
Metternich phrase) but only within the frame of the primary aim of unity.
Thus was excluded the notion that respect for nationality was fully
equal in importance to the considerations of unity in consolidating the

empire for the future. This notion Metternich had vainly sought to retain
— albeit weakly — in his first draft, even after Kaiser Franz's objections
to what he took to be an overvalued nationality idea had become plain.

Moreover, Metternich's old hope of achieving some sort of ministerial
government was dissipated. He had cautiously brought forward the suggestion to raise the number of ministries to four through the creation of
two new ones: interior — his pet project — and justice. Kaiser Franz
rejected the latter — again an example of this already over-burdened
ruler's reluctance to do anything resembling a delegation of responsibility
and authority. He merely replaced Öttingen with Wallis as president of
"Meiner Obersten Justizstelle".[30]

The four chancelleries proposed by Metternich — Bohemian-Galician,
Italian, Austrian, and Illyrian — were now reduced to three: Bohemian-
Galician, Lombardo-Venetian (not Italian), and Austro-Illyrian. Why
this fatal combination of Inner Austria and Illyria? In view of Lombardy-
Venetia's small size compared to an Austro-Illyrian or Bohemian-Galician
combination, it is questionable whether geographic scruples, such as
had already beset Dietrichstein, could have been a decisive factor. If there
was any reason at all, then possibly because the emperor considered the
Austrian and Illyrian territories as one piece of ancient family property not
to be given out of hand. This assumption is strengthened by the fact that
Kaiser Franz never appointed an Austro-Illyrian chancellor; despite the
application of such an excellent candidate as Goëss, he satisfied himself that
this post would be sufficiently represented by a *Vizekanzler-Stellvertreter*.
An interesting sidelight is that the unknown author of the unused draft of
the imperial patent accepted the combination of these two chancelleries but
separated instead the Bohemian and Galician ones, thus keeping their
number at four.[31] In stating the emperor's motives for the establishment of
chancelleries, he again reflected, much more than Metternich in his drafts,
the ideas contained in the original *Vortrag* of October 27: in line with the
policy of respecting individual differences, appropriate chancelleries would
be provided for those provinces and groups *(Völkerstämme)* sharing either
a common historic origin or political background or closely related to
another in language and customs.

Needless to say, a combination of the Austrian and Illyrian chancelleries
undid much of Metternich's proposals. If formally at least a ministry of
the interior and three chancelleries were created, the underlying ideas and
the very principles behind Metternich's attempt — and these were the crux
of the matter — were relegated to the sidelines. Thus Metternich was
compelled to take back a good part of his carefully planned "first step".

Already Kaiser Franz's reaction in 1816 to Metternich's suggestion of a *Mittägliches Slavisches Reich* — for an area where were combined Slavic nationality and Catholic faith — made apparent his incomprehension of nationality as a factor in any reorganization of his empire. In these matters, Metternich felt able to approach him only by employing the terms of an administrative thinking which the monarch understood. That Kaiser Franz would then retort in such terms was to be expected; that he then might go beyond Metternich in a petty reshuffling of terms and thus distort all the initially underlying ideas — this was a chance against which there was no guarantee.

Acting at the emperor's bidding, Saurau had, on December 18, submitted his opinions on the new ministry of the interior. He interpreted the whole thing more or less as a simplification and concentration of the inner administration[32] and had few original ideas to contribute. He enclosed a copy of Metternich's proposals in which, unlike earlier versions, the appurtenances of the ministry of the interior were listed in greater detail.[33] On December 23, Saurau was informed by the emperor of his appointment as supreme chancellor and minister of the interior.[34] Thereby he received general instructions: his duties were to be performed always keeping in mind as a basic maxim the empire's oneness, yet observing and heeding the special character of its various parts where and whenever required by special position and circumstance. In outlining the functions of Saurau's new office, Kaiser Franz did not even deign to designate it properly and simply referred to it as *Hofkanzlei*. In its "legislative" capacity, the office had to draft all political laws concerning new administrative forms and structures, changes, or reforms. For this activity, it was to secure all the necessary material from the regional authorities (*Länderbehörden*); however, before being submitted to the emperor, all plans were to be referred back to the regional authorities for an appraisal of their practicability in regard to the province's special character. In its "managing" capacity, the new ministry was to supervise the regional administration's working but, at the same time, was to avoid meddling in details. Finally, as subordinates of the supreme chancellor and minister of the interior, Kaiser Franz appointed the heads of the three chancelleries: for the Lombardo-Venetian one, Count Mellerio; for the Bohemian-Galician one, Count Lazansky; for the Austro-Illyrian one, — as vice-chancellor and temporary representative of the unnamed chancellor, Freiherr v. Geisslern.[35] Thereby, Lazansky was informed that his old agency — the COHC — was dissolved and that the provinces formerly under its jurisdiction were now raised to the same level as those previously administered by the *Ver-*

einigte Hofkanzlei; Lazansky himself would remain *Hofkanzler.*[36] The entire personnel of the new ministry took their new oaths of office at 10:30 a.m. on Monday, December 29, 1817.[37]

If that presently realized from Metternich's original twofold program — a reorganization of the entire monarchy and a "national" administration for Lombardy-Venetia — seemed meager, the minister showed few signs of disappointment because, whatever his private sentiments were, he could hardly admit defeat openly. Even if a small and doubtful benefit remained for the empire as a whole, then Lombardy-Venetia at least seemed to draw apparent dividends from Metternich's endeavors in the form of the long-awaited viceroy and a special chancellor. Indeed, if the minister could claim this partial success, it was important to sound optimistic in making the most of it and to rally favorable opinion. Since Metternich expected or hoped that a feeling of gratitude would provide the foundation for an upsurge of positive opinion, then it was essential that Lombards and Venetians must immediately come to feel that they had grounds to be grateful. Much depended, therefore, on giving the new measures a propitious interpretation and, simultaneously, on making sure that expectations thus aroused would be fulfilled — in view of the circumstances, no easy task.

Consequently, Metternich made a special point of writing to those Lombardo-Venetian officials most concerned with what he called "a new system of organization for the interior": Bubna, Goëss, Guicciardi, and Mellerio.[38] Common to all these somewhat formally written communications — although in varying doses — is a bit of wishful thinking: these new useful measures for Lombardy-Venetia could not help but have "the most salutary influence" on both the course of the administration and public opinion; these well-meant measures were an example of the emperor's confidence in and solicitude for his Italian subjects and as such should be properly appreciated; these beneficial measures would satisfy all friends of order as they would frustrate all troublemakers; these long-desired measures, finally, would satisfy Italian wishes.

Varying reactions were produced as essentially the same Metternich letter was addressed to an Austrian confidant on the one hand and to two Italians in Austria's service on the other. To Bubna, the minister wrote encouragingly but with few illusions; to Guicciardi and Mellerio he wrote as a diplomat and not without glowing assurances. With the former, Metternich did not go beyond a request to acquaint the public with the true sense and advantages of the new measures; to Guicciardi and Mellerio, however, he represented the measures as "much more than meets the eye"

— being "infinitely more extended in their results than appears at first glance". Yet, behind such a remarkable profession of better things to come, there may have lurked some anticipation of a skeptical reception if not an unwitting admission of the present measures' inadequacy. Metternich had less need to provide Bubna with such allusions. However, although the minister could not guarantee that the emperor would be won over to a real Lombardo-Venetian autonomy, he did not scorn the hope that the new measures might still somehow be implemented to the satisfaction of Guicciardi, of the sensitive Mellerio, and of all their countrymen.

The official announcement's unmistakable emphasis on unity, centralization, and uniformity, Metternich explained to Guicciardi and Mellerio, did not mean that such aims alone were just and necessary. There would be also, he assured them, a proper consideration for particular and local interests. As they knew, the chancellors had been appointed to defend such interests against the central government; but even more, the emperor had done what the Italians desired by placing Italians in charge of Italians. This point Metternich had not bothered mentioning to Bubna, confiding instead the hope that these new measures might dispel a favorite rumor of the "evil-minded" — that Kaiser Franz sought to "Germanize" his Italian provinces.

Metternich also devoted some attention to the individual assignments and duties of his correspondents. With Bubna, his main concern remained the careful cultivation of public opinion and the surveillance so connected with the preservation of tranquillity. Guicciardi — Mellerio's successor as vice-president of the Milanese *gubernium* — received praise for his part in the surveillance program which was to continue unchanged; his secret reports to Bubna and Metternich were also to be dispatched as before and were to by-pass the new Milanese *gubernium* as well as the viceroy. Goëss — Mellerio's eventual successor as Lombardo-Venetian chancellor — was to remain in Venice although he actually preferred to become Austro-Illyrian chancellor — a post for which he was eminently qualified.[39] The reluctant and unconvinced Mellerio required special treatment. Metternich assured him that he would be complying with a direct request of the monarch who needed a man of Mellerio's stature and qualities; he would render his sovereign and country a service by agreeing to a stay in Vienna which would be limited to, at most, a year. Metternich knew that Mellerio's consent to lend his name — which, it seems, was primarily what was wanted — was conditional on whether the Lombardo-Venetian chancellor in Vienna and the viceroy in Milan were to be more than mere ornaments.

Announcing the long awaited coming of the viceroy was the most jubilant note in the Metternich letters; yet his confidence alternated with caution. He stated as a certainty to Guicciardi and Mellerio — but not then to Bubna — what he had mentioned five months before to the general as a sincere hope: the viceroy, with quite extended functions and powers, was to govern and to do good on the spot.[40]

Simultaneously with the installation of the new system, Kaiser Franz appointed, on January 3, 1818, his brother Archduke Rainer viceroy of the Lombardo-Venetian Kingdom.[41] Already a fortnight before, as a third brother -- Anton — had been officially relieved as viceroy-designate after some twenty months of unwillingness, the emperor's first care had been to delineate between the duties of the viceroy and the *Hofkanzlei* (as he persistently called it) and ordered both Metternich and Saurau to occupy themselves with this matter.[42] One of Saurau's first official acts as minister of the interior was a speedy compliance to an imperial billet to draw up — once again — temporary instructions for the viceroy.[43] Thus a three-year-old debate was renewed and continued for some time. All the while, the nature of the viceroy's functions was to form the subject of a spontaneous, eager, and endless speculation among the Lombardo-Venetians soon made all the more sensitive by the viceroy's arrival. Because, through the viceroy, Vienna had a last chance to gain the affections of the Lombards and Venetians, the results of the deliberations on vice-royal powers were to be decisive in shaping once and for all the relationship between Habsburg Austria and its Italian subjects.

THE DISILLUSIONMENT

Judging from all indications — especially *gubernial* and police reports — the reaction in Lombardy-Venetia to the announcement of the new interior organization was surprisingly favorable. That the Austrians in Lombardy-Venetia played up the impact of the December 24 patent is understandable; anyway, their wishful thinking in that regard did not last long. The sober warnings only a few months later indicate a fairly accurate appraisal of public opinion. Certainly, in the long run, Guicciardi and Bubna had little interest in deluding either themselves or Metternich. Rather, as the situation deteriorated, it was better to have the emperor know the worst. General Bubna, an Austrian who knew his Italians well, was not inclined to enthusiasm; however, he made an exception in describing the effect of the imperial patent in Milan.[44] For him the news was a sensation beyond all expectations. No government action since the time of Maria Theresia, he wrote happily to Metternich, had obtained such a complete success. Indeed, the minister deserved his due for having achieved "a grand *coup d'état* in disposing the emperor to take a measure which placed the Italian provinces up to the niveau of the other states of the Monarchy". Bubna could only share Metternich's sentiments in declaring the measures to be "analogous to the wishes and cares of the Italian people". However, he already added an afterthought which was to appear frequently in the future when alluding to this subject: "We shall have occasion to appreciate [these measures'] usefulness if ever we find ourselves in trouble."

The positive effects of the government's wise decision were so automatic, Bubna claimed, that he did not need to act on Metternich's request to help the public realize the measures' "true sense and advantages". This was unnecessary, he assured him, since "nothing escapes the natural perspicacity of the Italians. . . . They have analyzed the text of the decree in a true sense — one finds it very different from those rescripts [issued] by the COHC!" Even beyond the Po the good effects were making themselves evident — notably among the smaller states. There, Bubna knew, such consideration from local rulers was hardly to be expected; this situation made the contrast between what he euphemistically called the emperor's paternal benevolence and other Italian rulers' narrowmindedness only too apparent. This contrast tended to establish with public opinion, which Bubna felt to be more noteworthy in Italy than in other areas of the empire, the notion that Kaiser Franz was "the lone ruler of Italy in a moral sense." And this notion, Bubna added in disclosing once again his disturbing afterthought, "shall be of great support in more difficult times."

A large number of Milanese notables, including Mellerio, had been gathered at Bubna's residence as the new system was announced. The general had staged the scene effectively; his account is revealing even if slightly homilistic: "The joy of the well-disposed stood triumphant against the stunned silence of the adherents of independence who probably just a few hours before were still blabbering about the Austrian government never being able to act other than in the spirit of Italy's subjugation." Certainly these adherents were at a loss to explain how the House of Habsburg could sanction a measure quite incompatible with what they had taken to be the expressed policy of the court. Even more significant in Bubna's opinion, those usually indifferent were forming one chorus of approval with those now acclaiming Austria. Of course, it was too much to expect complete gratification; some complained from the start that Mellerio would lack the authority warranted by the position conferred upon him — a view which Mellerio seemed to share, since he — as even the Austrian commander admitted — displayed mixed feelings.[45]

While Guicciardi reported more soberly a general approval of the new organization of the inner administration,[46] Bubna claimed it to be the talk of the town at all social events and, of course, at and after the opera. The gratitude upon which Metternich counted was mobilized into official expression: the congregations assembled for that purpose on January 8; even a triumphal arch was dedicated to the founder and king of Lombardy-Venetia. It was surely a boon for previously distressed Austrian officials to be able to claim simultaneously such an unprecedented lifting of public morale and a letting up of public discontent. According to Bubna, just the impending appointment of the viceroy had sufficed to excite the Milanese to the point of forgetting their grievances[47] and, according to Guicciardi, once Rainer was named, curiosity and speculation about viceroyal powers let the commercial class cease its plaints.[48] Bubna rightly surmised that public opinion "is at the moment with us and . . . that from now on it can be kept that way at little cost and guided at will." He was ready to do his part in giving it direction; that the "little cost" might yet be too much for Kaiser Franz, he had no sure way of knowing.[49]

Putting before the emperor the reports of the positive reaction to the creation of the new interior organization, Metternich made the most of it — especially for himself. He strongly implied that the monarch should have had more trust in his minister's principles and that the whole business had not been a mistake after all. Self-assured, he let him know: "This first impression is certainly the true voice of all concerned. I always like to be sure that I have not been wrong, even if I have no doubts that a decision I have taken must be good in its consequences when based on a clear and correct idea."[50] It was especially satisfying that even the various diplomatic posts throughout the peninsula substantiated the favorable impression made, particularly by the appointment of the viceroy and the Lombardo-Venetian chancellor.[51] Naturally the emperor was pleased to hear about his role in extending Austria's "moral influence" throughout Italy.[52] However, Metternich reminded him gently that the momentarily buoyed-up public mood brought forth all kinds of expectations and that the favorable impression was increasing to the point where people were promising themselves "the most beneficial prospects for the future".[53] Although encouraging, such an observation was also portentous when considering a possible disappointment; then, the greater the hope, the worse the disappointment.

Metternich proceeded on the assumption that the viceroy, whose nomination continued to stir up enthusiasm,[54] would be granted some real activity. Thus, he sponsored the appointment of the patiently waiting Sardagna as viceroyal secretary for diplomatic correspondence. Kaiser Franz turned this application down, stating that the viceroy would not require such assistance. Unavoidably Metternich had to agree with the emperor's position that the viceroy should not carry on a diplomatic correspondence with foreign powers; however, he rejoined, the situation of the Italian provinces could not be compared with other parts of the empire where the governors did not indulge in such activity. Indicating clearly to the monarch his own magnanimous conception of the viceroy's role, he insisted that the viceroy of Lombardy-Venetia would need to correspond with foreign — and especially Italian — governments on "issues having a direct bearing on the kingdom entrusted to h i s s u p e r - v i s i o n ".[55] Nevertheless, the emperor persisted that such a secretary would be superfluous in view of the fact that *"Mein Herr Bruder der Erz- herzog Rainer, als Vizekönig Meines Lombardisch-Venezianischen König- reiches"*, would not engage in diplomatic activity.[56]

Metternich knew all along that Kaiser Franz jealously begrudged his brothers any independent popularity and that especially in Lombardy- Venetia this disinclination was compounded by the *idée fixe* of controlling affairs directly from Vienna. Yet, in view of what the minister had hoped for, this imperial answer was a set-back; it revealed that the deluge of favorable reports from the Italian provinces, far from moving Kaiser Franz to meet the expectations of his subjects there, only bolstered him in keeping to his set ways.

At the same time, the first signs of a break in the favorable opinion began to appear. At the beginning of April, Guicciardi notified Metternich that the patience of the Italians was wearing thin: some five months after the viceroy had been decided upon, his authority was still undefined.[57] Because the Lombardo-Venetian population trustingly expected all and every improvement to come from the hands of the viceroy and the chan- cellor in Vienna, speculation concentrated ever more on their functions. But the long and, as it now seemed, futile waiting made it difficult for those still hopeful to ward off the "I-told-you-so-s". The fact that grumbling of every sort was beginning to be heard again made obvious how threadbare good feeling had become. Metternich was almost at the point of shrugging his shoulders; whether the Lombards and Venetians would or would not consider the whole new system as but a farce with fanfare was at the moment solely up to the emperor. In a reply to Guic- ciardi, Metternich began to resort to a phrase which, for exhaustion of originality in a tedious matter, became a favorite refrain: when Europe is quiet and tranquil would be the moment for Austria to perfect its government in Lombardy-Venetia.[58] On the same occasion he also reminded Bubna of the difficulty in eliminating all the causes of discontent in a country "which had more than one motive for regretting the existence of the Kingdom of Italy". Bubna too was served a platitude: "With wisdom and perseverance we shall get the Italians to appreciate the real advantages of the paternal government His Majesty has promised them."[59] The general, however, was not yet ready to retort in similar fashion; he was succinct and implored Metternich to keep trying:

> Above all, I would like to ask you to call to His Majesty's attention at every opportunity that the Italian provinces can gradually reach that spirit of loyalty prevailing in the other provinces of the Monarchy only if they are ruled in accordance with the meaning of the patent of December 24, which has had such a magnificent effect on public opinion. Otherwise, there will be no real pacification and Italy remains no more than a subjugated province, the possession of which can be maintained only by armed might and which is, consequently, dependent on circumstances.[60]

This sober note reflected depressing reports from Italians in Vienna that the viceroy would arrive without either instructions or authority and that he would live in Lombardy withdrawn and privately until his functions might be regulated. The local population — so thought Bubna, in words similar to Guicciardi's — was accustomed "to be ruled with precision if not with too much haste" and could not hide its astonishment at the fact that nothing had been settled in the four months following the appointment.

Prior to departing on a spring-time trip to the Adriatic, the emperor had arranged for a meeting to discuss the powers of the viceroy.[61] It was held on April 13, 1818, under the chairmanship of Count Zichy; the Staatskanzlei was not represented — neither Metternich nor Hudelist was there. Before the conference lay a two-year-old opinion of Bellegarde. It warned that "the nation" would not be satisfied with a viceroy reduced in activity since it had been accustomed to seeing the previous one (Eugene) so active and, furthermore, that "this nation" was set upon having its affairs regulated within its own borders. The marshal's admonition was one which General Bubna often came to repeat: public opinion could not be won "if the nation could see no advantage in the nomination of a viceroy."[62] Nevertheless, it was decided that the viceroy would be bound by strict and limiting instructions. All existing administrative posts in the kingdom were to continue in their present functions, thus leaving the viceroy with actually nothing to do. As a small concession, some reports were to be allowed to be dispatched to the Vienna *Hofstellen* via the viceroy. From the beginning it was clear that the position of the viceroy was not to surpass that of a governor of the other provinces; indeed, he was not even endowed with a governor's powers. He was meant to be not much more than an arbitrator between the actual governors in Milan and Venice in the case of differences. Far from being above them in might and power, he was at most a feeble middleman more apt to be in the way — thus seen, a convincing argument for reducing his powers even more. Surely Kaiser Franz was thinking along such lines. Long detailed lists of instructions, revealing a scarcely concealed pettiness, were corrected and undersigned in the emperor's own hand. From the very beginning, his approach to this question was not: what aspects of state business should be considered as beyond the viceroy's sphere of activity, but rather: what morsel of the regular affairs might still be left to him? This "morsel" amounted to little more than to doling out pensions and honors and to pinning on an occasional medal.[63]

Based on the foregoing, the *Hofkanzlei* (the ministry of the interior) served its proposals to the emperor in accordance with his tastes: just as the *Hofkanzlei* had striven to limit the functions of the governor of Galicia, so no active or independent role was to be allowed to the viceroy. At least, in the recognition that "the eye of the [Lombardo-Venetian] nation" would be on the viceroy, a suggestion was made to limit his functions only gradually and inconspicuously. Thereupon, on May 2, 1818, Kaiser Franz ordered Saurau to draw up a final statement. He added the strict injunction not, under any circumstances, to make known to the Lombardo-Venetian provincial administrations the limiting of viceroyal activity.[64] The protocol then presented by the ministry of the interior on the scope of the viceroy's power was simply based on previous imperial directives.[65] Thus, with only a concern for secrecy and without having heard Metternich — whose attitude was probably all-too-familiar to him — Kaiser Franz decreed a viceroy who was just what the more cynical (and realistic) Italians were already saying openly — a sham.

The unfortunate viceroy's lack of initiative was to reveal how right such insinuations were from critics and outright enemies of Austrian rule. But until his impatiently awaited arrival in the latter part of May, Austrian officials had their hands full of trouble. As Guicciardi complained, the discouraging news emanating from Vienna rendered futile most efforts to kindle favorable public opinion.[66] Despite every assurance given to those besieging the Austrian administrators with one and the same question regarding the viceroy, disillusion began to fasten itself upon public opinion

like a spreading mold. Equally distressing symptoms were described by
Bubna in mid-May.[67] The general had just returned from Venice where he
had seen the emperor and Goëss. There, despite a sincere attempt to combat the economic stagnation, a dissatisfaction was making itself felt which
he classified as even severer than in Lombardy. He regretted that ill-feel-
ing on the part of Italians in Venice brought about a serious social cleavage
between them and the Germans — a severe disappointment to Metternich's
hope for promoting understanding between the two nationalities. Fortunately, Milan was spared such a development. There, Germans, especially
officers, continued to find acceptance — a fact all the more remarkable,
Bubna proudly related to Metternich, since this was not at all the case
during the French occupation. However this may be, discontent also grew
in Milan — mostly, of course, in the coffee-houses, those convenient
meeting places of the intelligentsia where one could encounter poets,
patriots, plotters, and sometimes the police.

Nonetheless, the broad preparations for the immediate arrival of the
viceroy — now three years after one had been promised — seemed to give
the Austrians a short respite. That in the air of festivity some enthusiasm
was regenerated was only natural. To impress even the unconcerned or unconvinced, as well as foreigners, Bubna not only provided for a show of
celebration and pomp but, by ordering all available troops into the city
planned an imposing show of strength.

As the embodiment of Lombardo-Venetian "national" status, Rainer
was received in Milan on May 24 with a warm and even joyous demonstration. The acclamations were genuine, Bubna insisted, and not bought,
as he thought them to have been under the French regime. Yet he knew
that this expression of enthusiasm, especially if taken as one of faith and
trust, might well be the last. He reminded Metternich again of the deep
anxiety, notably of all thoughtful individuals, over the viceroy's authority
and over the treatment of Italian affairs at the *Hofkanzlei* where,
it was wished, at least a pair of competent Italians familiar with the local
situation should be employed. This was another reference to the obvious
discrepancy between reality and the December patent's high-sounding
promises to use nationals within the chancelleries to represent the regional
viewpoint to the central authorities — a discrepancy which Bubna had
called to Metternich's attention a month before.[68]

Metternich relayed Bubna's report, along with his own comments, to the
emperor at the first opportunity.[69] The happy news of the viceroy's
jubilant reception was all well and good; it was, however, more important
that the emperor should be reminded once more how much the viceroy

BUBNA

meant to the Italians. In bringing forward Bubna's concerns, the minister agreed in believing that the duration of a still favorable impression depended on two conditions:

> The Milanese must first of all be convinced that the viceroy shall be left with a really sufficient elbow-room for his activity in order to do good there. The second condition is that the establishment of the *Hofkanzley* must correspond to those basic principles which Your Majesty had announced in the patent of December 24, 1817, and which already has done so much good merely by becoming known.

Metternich's plea was the last of a long line and in its essence repeated what he, Bellegarde, Bubna, and a good many others had said over the past four years. Pending the emperor's reply and return from Dalmatia, Metternich conscientiously informed Bubna that he had written to his sovereign, as requested, on the need of implementing the December 24 patent. He added rather dryly that it would be up to the viceroy to rally somehow the different classes of society to the government and that all one could do would be to wait for the viceroy's first measures as well as to keep an eye on public mood.[70]

The emperor's answer was definite and made clear that it was useless to approach him again on the subject of the viceroy or the chancelleries. Kaiser Franz insisted that an extension of the viceroy's very modest duties was out of the question since his activity "is so broad that I doubt whether he will be able to perform that put to him." The monarch's chief reaction to this serious matter was annoyance at all the fuss. Certainly it was neither necessary nor suitable, he felt, to let the viceroy's spheres of activity become known because in Lombardy-Venetia "everything is carped at and — even then — it may not have pacified anybody but rather have exposed the viceroy to demands which could not have been satisfied." Equally obdurate, Kaiser Franz reintroduced the Viennese (the strict Spanish) court ceremonial in Milan. He did so against desperate objections of the Lombard — and especially the more recent — nobility and against the better judgment of Bubna and Metternich. This act was one further example of how the emperor's determination to achieve conformity ran rough-shod over prudence even though in this case, the inevitable social reshuffling could have cost Austria the support of that very class upon which it relied the most. Finally, in the issue of Italian affairs at the *Hofkanzlei,* Kaiser Franz indicated that he would disregard the chancelleries as the highest regional agency and as a bridge to the highest central authorities — i.e., the so-called ministry of the interior. He held to his view that, as with the other provinces, it would be more convenient to have local affairs dealt with directly between competent men from the local *gubernium* and the *Hofkanzlei* proper.[71] In any case, Kaiser Franz was to show himself quite satisfied with the tranquillity reported from Milan. This was due to the new measures in effect there, he admitted to the British ambassador, Lord Stewart, but confided simultaneously that "only by a steady adherence to all the old forms and usages of his ancestors" had he overcome liberal and jacobinical ideas in his empire.[72]

In the meantime the minister had packed; in the first days of July he was off for Bohemia on a six-weeks' rest and watercure to "reestablish his health". Then he was to journey, via Frankfurt, to his lovely new possession — Schloss Johannisberg — on the Rhine, before going on, at the end of September, to the international congress meeting at Aachen. With that, Metternich's career entered into a new phase. His time and attention were devoted once more almost exclusively to external affairs — a field in which he was more sure of appreciation. From Bohemia he continued to send back to Kaiser Franz Bubna's reports which Hudelist had sent on after him, still admonishing from his baths that the new system of administration "must receive the fullest development, as is Your Majesty's intention, if its results are to correspond to its purpose" and still warning that Austria could not afford even the slightest blunder with the sensitive Italians.[73] Determined to shelve the matter on a somewhat agreeable note, he referred the emperor to Bubna's statements, which he enclosed with his letters, and from which one could gather the impression of a temporary improvement in public opinion. But that was only an illusion based on the public's last show of patience in waiting for the viceroy's initial deeds in the interests of his new "countrymen". The deeds never came and it was not Rainer's fault.

In midsummer, Bubna reported that order prevailed, not because of satisfaction but because of resignation. At times he too seemed overcome by such a sentiment, wondering whether, "after some twenty years of storm and change", one could really expect much more than that which one actually had. For him, as for Metternich, Austria's hope came to be time — time and order. If the addiction to independence waned, then only because the present was unfavorable to the upheaval sought by the revolutionaries and because the fundamental will — "the national spirit" — was lacking the necessary strength; but here the general misjudged the speed with which apathy could be cast off. He was sure that the masses, so occupied with a "pathetic animalistic life", would think little beyond their everyday needs, that the coffee-house romantics, with their brainstorms on constitutions and an independent state, could be kept in check easily enough.[74] That the middle class was alienated was not as important for him as that the masses might trust the government to supply bread and work. Nevertheless, agitation and criticism mounted; the main current of discontent continued to sweep about the lamentable viceroy and his questionable powers. Bubna shrugged off most of these plaints as simply inherent in "the national character"; their frequency and exaggerated nature he attributed in part to the fact that all too many indolent people gathered in Milan. It was no wonder, he disclosed to Metternich, that in an atmosphere of such thriving dissatisfaction a stranger might discern a revolution in the making before noting that actually tranquillity prevailed.[75]

The finishing touch to this description of a sultry situation was given by the remarks which Hudelist added in forwarding the Bubna reports to Metternich:

> Mellerio is threatening more and more with his departure; Saurau will not hinder him. Police reports are not favorable to Saurau. Moreover, Sedlnitzky is of the opinion that the public, although quiet, is sunk in deep apathy and is not satisfied with the administration of the interior. In the meantime, if we have *panem et circenses* the rest will probably be settled somehow.[76]

These few lines of Hudelist may end the story of Metternich's attempt to reorganize the Habsburg empire in a manner commensurate with the needs of nationality; they express only too well the new interior ministry's ineffectiveness and Vienna's failure to gain the affections of its Italian subjects. There was nothing more to offer, nothing more to expect. With this unnecessary failure, Austria lost for good any hope of popular support in Lombardy-Venetia, thus truly basing its rule there on sheer force — an alternative which especially its military commanders in Italy had always deplored.

To summarize: In 1817 Metternich resumed efforts to settle the Lombardo-Venetian problem satisfactorily and permanently, once again pressing the emperor to comply with "national wishes" for home rule and to appoint at least a viceroy and an Italian chancellor. Simultaneously, he stressed that Austria could maintain its position as a major power and as a bulwark against disorder only if "morally strong in our interior". He considered these two points as joint issues. The need for removing temporary authority — i.e., the COHC — in the reacquired lands and aligning them with the other areas of the empire under one central authority gave impetus to and was combined with an even more ambitious program: the reorganization of the empire's central administration down to the regional level in a manner best suited to strengthen the monarchy against the perils of the future. Here, the idea of centralization was ruled out except where demanded by a common purpose of the various member states. Moreover, according to Metternich, the empire's full strength was to be developed by an inner political balance resulting from equal treatment (not equalization) of all "nations" of the Austrian *Völkerfamilie*. A reorganization was all the more necessary because this was not the case, Hungary having too much, other areas too little to say. The idea *unity in diversity* and the equality of all regions was to be demonstrated by equally ranked chancelleries, designed to represent each area's special regional-national interests. They were to be subordinated to a ministry of the interior acting in the interest of the empire as a whole. According to Prince Dietrichstein (whose own proposals spelled out Austria's needs much more openly), Metternich originally proposed six chancelleries: for Bohemia-Galicia, Inner-Austria, Illyria, Lombardy-Venetia, Hungary, and Transylvania. But then Metternich decided to defer action on the two last named chancelleries to avoid jeopardizing what he emphatically labelled his "first step".

Kaiser Franz agreed to his foreign minister's limited program at most half-heartedly, and proceeded to despoil it of its underlying ideas by arbitrarily combining the Austrian and Illyrian chancelleries; he did not even bother to name a chancellor for this combination, and left the number of appointed chancellors actually at two — the centralist-minded Lazansky and the reluctant Mellerio. Moreover, the emperor refused to accept the fact that his *Hofkanzlei* had become a *ministry of the interior*. Only Lombardy-Venetia appeared to receive tangible benefit from the new system through the appointment of a viceroy and a chancellor. There especially, Metternich meant to make the most of the meager results in the hope of convincing the sensitive public as well as the distrustful emperor that all sides would benefit from the new measures. But neither the reports of a momentary enthusiasm in Lombardy-Venetia nor the fear of disappointing an expectant public moved the emperor to magnanimity. Despite frequent pleas from Metternich and Bubna to implement the December 24 patent, he refused to grant Viceroy Rainer or Chancellor Mellerio the authority their positions called for. That Austria had nothing more to offer its Italian subjects other than this imperfect permanent solution was considered a breach of faith; apathy, disillusion, a marked deterioration in public mood followed, and Austrian rule in Italy continued, more than ever lacking the consent of the governed.

CONCLUSION AND EPILOGUE

In late summer of 1813, as Austria's great moment of decision had come, few — and certainly not Metternich — dared hope that Napoleon would soon be banished from the Europe he had so long dominated and altered at will and that most of his political structures would vanish with him. Only as the Allies marched on to Paris did they also approach the full significance of their victory. They were confronted by an almost unexpected opportunity, unique in its scope and its moment, to lay the foundations of a new Europe. Never before had so much of the continent undergone simultaneously such violent change in political order; the statesmen of 1814 had behind them an unprecedented generation of extremes and innovations and before them a future, so one thought, bound to profit from experience and a recognition of new values. One such value was the idea of nationality: could it have been a factor in a European reorganization?

As victory was to mean an end of upheaval and disorder, so peace was to mean the reestablishment of order. As implicit as *past practice* may be in the concept *restoration*, the majority of European statesmen — even if not all monarchs — had learned that a restoration of *order* could not mean merely the restoration of the *old order.* Yet, to guarantee Europe peace and freedom from further aggression required bringing the guarantors to effective strength; since previous strength had not sufficed to ward off aggression and because serious losses had been suffered, adequate compensations were allotted. Moreover, since the continental Allies were not just outsiders triumphantly disposing of others' destinies but were themselves former victims now bent on securing their own good fortune, their vital interests had to be identified with any program for restoring order. Hardly any responsible statesman would have agreed that a Europe recovering from twenty years of war could then have afforded the experiment of submitting large zones like Germany, Italy, and Poland to the uncertainty and instability which completely new — if not revolutionary — regimes, institutions, and programs would surely have brought. That under such circumstances the politically-minded of some European peoples would be disappointed in their desire for a national political identity was sad but unavoidable; nationality could not be a determining factor if it meant cutting into those very states to which Europe owed its liberation and on which depended future security. That in this incompatibility of ideal and necessity might lie the seeds of even greater turmoil was a possibility then too remote to have been taken very seriously. Consideration for nationality — excepting the loosely constructed German Confederation — was referred to the individual states (with certain treaty provisions in the case of Poland) to be dealt with as an internal matter.[1] Thus, while international proceedings did not concern themselves with popular consent, Metternich was soon faced with one of the basic maxims of political prudence: to govern well, the consent of the governed is required. Certainly he knew that Austrian power had its obvious limitations and that it could do no more than impose and maintain a desired system of order; a *fait accompli*, to be sure, might be accepted as a situation of little other choice; but consent required wooing.

During the Wars of Liberation, various European powers had learned to fight the French with some of their own weapons; one of these had been the appeal to national spirit and the promise of national independence to various subject nationalities. That such appeals and promises were frequently phrased and interpreted to imply more than just freedom from French domination drew no objections until it became clear that such methods might be incongruous with political aims. In such areas as Northern Italy and Illyria, new control and a political program did not follow the French collapse firmly or quickly enough. This situation forceful men immediately exploited in order to assert independence or to demand satisfaction of national interests. Soon, however, the hard truth that Austria's intentions or power could not be prevailed against reduced manifestations of nationalism to more modest entreaties for national autonomy. Fortunately for Austria, such manifestations of national feeling were more regional than national in their extent — a fact which Metternich recognized and sought to turn to Austria's advantage by encouraging regional *esprit*. In this manner Austria came upon the need to reconcile several national groups to a rather dubious political fortune by demonstrating that membership in the Habsburg "family of nations" would be worthwhile.

Metternich realized that the unique opportunity to reorganize in Europe applied particularly to the Habsburg empire. First, however, came the practical problems arising from the reincorporation of lost or new territories. He knew that in Lombardy-Venetia an impressive French legacy would render difficult even a partial return to the old order but also that a preservation of Franco-Italian fixtures would go far in nourishing a particular Lombardo-Venetian regional pride. Surely Metternich was not mistaken in hoping thereby that a development of *Stammesgefühl* — a regional-national selfconsciousness — might help to loosen bonds with brethren across the empire's frontiers. He, Bellegarde, and others often pointed to the Italian population's preference for Franco-Italian forms which, they agreed, were better suited to Italian character than German ones. This fact alone would seem to weaken an occasionally-voiced supposition that a return to Theresian methods of administration, rather than to Josephinian intentions, might have saved Austria's position in Lombardy.[2] While both the minister and the marshal repeated the oft-told story of the successful Austrian administration in an Italy of long ago, they both at the same time admired and lamented the heritage left by the *Regno d'Italia*. Thus, the emperor was eventually persuaded to follow two traditions at once by appointing — as Maria Theresia had done — a chancellor for Italian affairs in Vienna and — as Napoleon had done — a viceroy for the "royal" capital in Milan. Metternich was not alone in advocating a reconstruction of the monarchy on the principle of "unity in diversity", nor in insisting on a cultivation of regional spirit and a grant of special status to the Italian provinces. Such ideas were based on political prudence — a quality, so it seems at times, monopolized by the Staatskanzlei; yet these ideas conflicted with the organization policy — based on centralization, on conformity and equalization, and on an introduction of a German administrative system — which Kaiser Franz had already set in motion.

Metternich had objected to this policy but could not follow up his intervention in internal matters, since he was soon occupied for a year with the Congress of Vienna. In the meantime, the COHC was not to be deterred from its course despite pressing pleas from Bellegarde, the Austrian commander in Italy, to desist from "Germanizing" Italy and to respect Italian national feeling. The dramatic events of 1815 accelerated at most the yielding of empty promises; the dismantling of the former Franco-Italian administrative structure continued. Metternich's hopes of bringing the emperor to greater insight while on the scene were disappointed and his urgent request for home rule in Lombardy-Venetia as well as his proposals for a "Southern Slavic Realm" went unheeded; Kaiser Franz even relegated to his desk-drawer the more immediate issues of naming a viceroy and a chancellor for the Italian provinces. With even greater disinclination he reacted to Metternich's broadly-conceived and farsighted proposals to strengthen the monarchy for the hard tests of the future, disregarding the basic idea of nationality and slighting the ministry of the interior and its chancelleries. Finally, after a three years' delay in sending a viceroy, he begrudged his brother Rainer all functions and activity which honor (to say nothing of political prudence) would have demanded and incurred thereby the major blame in the failure to win the affections of his Italian subjects.

Metternich must be credited with having the ideas and striving to open the emperor's eyes to an admirably sensible program — a program almost fascinating in the way it anticipated much of what was arrived at in futile hindsight decades — even a century — later. That this first official attempt to deal with the idea of nationality in the Austrian Empire failed does not deprive it of its own historic significance; it is really beside the point whether the conjecture — what might have been had Metternich's reorganization program been realized — leaves one with feelings of skepticism or of sadness at lost opportunities. However, although Metternich had the program, he could not sell it to his monarch. The question arises whether Metternich, had he mobilized all the force of his personality and authority, could have pushed his measures through despite imperial obduracy. To be sure, the emperor had admitted his limitations and yielded to Metternich in external affairs as bitter experience had taught him to do; it was otherwise with internal matters, where he discerned no urgency, much less crisis. At least with home affairs he intended to act the absolute and paternal monarch and to achieve an ideal inherited from his uncle Joseph: to conduct personally all affairs in his domain through a centralized administration. But with repeated, and mostly unsuccessful, approaches Metternich had reached the limit of the emperor's as well as of his own patience and the minister was not one to run full tilt against a wall. With all his charm, he would have been the first to agree that selfdenial — that is, risking his position for his convictions — was rather pointless if it meant depriving Austria of its one capable statesman, one to whom it owed so much. Anyway, Kaiser Franz was not to be argued with or threatened with resignation as Wilhelm I was to be by Bismarck; he would have accepted it, most likely, with regret but without hesitation.[3] The decisive point is that in these years Metternich was not all-powerful and that his lack of authority in internal policy fairly absolves him from its errors. Formally he was no more than foreign minister; Kaiser Franz did not name him state chancellor until 1821 — a time in which revolution and conspiracy had finally brought urgency and crisis even to Austria's internal affairs.

The year 1818 was, however, still one of calm and the eventuality of a national conspiracy in Italy had been forestalled — or so one had thought — by the CBA. Metternich had hoped that a final settlement in Lombardy-Venetia would approximate Italian wishes; as long as such a hope had some basis and as long as a good part of the public still believed it had something to expect, the revolutionary cells were hard put for recruits and police activity was confined to prevention rather than to suppression. But because after 1818 the Austrians obviously had nothing more to offer and thus left the Italian population dissatisfied, a negative relationship hardened. Nevertheless, a temporary *modus vivendi* was made possible on the one side by an administration trying its best under the circumstances and on the other by a resignation of the populace. Yet General Bubna clearly foresaw that any stir of outside troubles might shake off this resignation.

Externally, Austria's position in Italy was continuously embarrassed by the agitation prevailing in the smaller states, an agitation for which the ineffective governments were largely responsible. Such a situation did not exist with regard to Poland, which had been partitioned once more by three major powers. If one overlooks the Free City of Cracow, there were no independent Polish states as there were in Italy. In turn, the Italian states were not to be organized into a league on the German model. Internally, Austria's position in Northern Italy lacked some of the complications at hand in Galicia. The Lombardo-Venetian Kingdom was the successor — even if only a partial one — to the *Regno d'Italia;* Austria had the former capital in its hands and did not face a relatively "liberal" "Kingdom of Italy" beyond its frontier as Galicia adjoined the Russian Kingdom of Poland with its capital at Warsaw. But it turned out to be that Austria had its difficulties in Lombardy-Venetia long before it had them in Galicia; conversely, the Poles rose against the Russians long before they turned against the Austrians. In Poland as in Italy, there were strong national currents, but they ran in different channels. In Poland the concern was for the recreation of a historic state traditional within the European system; consequently Metternich was prepared, under circumstances, to champion a free Poland in 1814. In Germany and Italy there was no such tradition (romantic recallings of medieval structures aside); rather the traditional was reestablished. Thus a new national state, so thought the anti-nationalists, had to arise from the ashes of the traditional political structure and because such new states in Germany and Italy would then be erected at the expense of existing princes, they could only be anti-monarchic — i.e., democratic. Metternich, who could compromise easily in practice but not in theory and who foresaw so much, failed to foresee one of the great compromises of the later nineteenth century. This was to be the coordination of the principles of legitimacy and nationality — of the traditional *Fürstenstaaten* and a national German Empire which was even to become Austria's staunchest ally.

In Italy, national feeling was largely expressed by the bourgeoisie and a nobility which could almost be reckoned to it — classes absent in Poland, where national feeling was confined more or less to a widespread land-dwelling aristocracy. With its Lombardo-Venetian Kingdom, Austria was the leading Apennine power and could have set the example (a persistent Bellegarde plea!); in Galicia, it had either to follow or isolate itself against the example of Alexander's Kingdom of Poland. The imaginative czar, an absolute ruler in Russia, had no trouble in playing the liberal monarch to the Poles. The unimaginative Kaiser Franz was neither capable of such a split in personality nor of assuming a similar role in Italy. He did not possess the greater part of the peninsula and, in view of the various smaller states, did not consider it proper to claim the title "King of Italy". In Galicia, he had no intention of competing with the czar; he had his own methods.

Whatever influence Metternich had on internal organization was limited to those areas whose reorganization was to call for policy decisions or which were involved somehow in international questions. Because Bohemia, having survived the Napoleonic Wars as a violated but intact part of the Habsburg empire, was scarcely involved in either case, Metternich had little opportunity to concern himself with its affairs. An exception was the discussion in 1818 of this land's membership in the German Con-federation — a question which Metternich answered affirmatively on the grounds of tradition. The same question he answered negatively, however, in regard to Lombardy-Venetia — although recalling some old connections — because of the strong cultural differences between it and the German lands.[4] Galicia had been more affected by the Napoleonic Wars: Western Galicia, acquired in 1795, was lost permanently a decade later; the Tarnopol Circle of Eastern Galicia had been handed by Napoleon to Alexander at Pressburg in 1805 but was reacquired by Austria in 1815. However, this area did not come under the jurisdiction of the COHC. In Galicia proper, the estates in particular had wished for some "national institutions" as were then promised in the treaties between the partitioning powers and by Article I of *The Acts of the Congress of Vienna*. Even before these documents were signed, Metternich had, in April 1815, put forward this wish as politically expedient to fulfill; but a year later, in April 1816, nothing had been done and Hudelist complained that Galicia

— in comparison to the "favored" Lombardy-Venetia — was being "treated like a stepchild".[5] Finally, in April 1817, an estates-constitution was granted. The first assembly was opened by Kaiser Franz in person in mid-June (quite in contrast to the dramatic manner in which Czar Alexander addressed the Diet of the "Polish nation"). At this fulfillment of the provision for "national institutions", however, Kaiser Franz's displeasure was aroused because no German text had accompanied the Polish text of the agenda announcements.[6]

That the paternal methods of Kaiser Franz were not appreciated and that, instead, the government's "well-meaning intentions" were being met by a "deeply-rooted distrust", even the governor of Galicia, Hauer, had to admit.[7] The emperor himself, after having left the land, admitted to Metternich the difficulties and the "miserable state of things in Galicia", but hoped at the same time that an improvement would soon follow.[8] Yet, even if there was a gradual improvement, it was still insufficient — a fact which Metternich bitterly had to call to the emperor's attention in April, 1818. A few weeks before, the czar had spoken to the Polish Diet in Warsaw on Polish "national existence" and "liberal institutions".[9] Hauer had thought to overcome what he feared might be harmful influences by publishing (in French) his administrative report so that "the Galician nation, in comparing its situation with that of the Kingdom of Poland, might recognize the advantages." Metternich did not share this self-confidence and plainly advised the emperor against the project since "the improvements requested in 1816 are not yet so far in effect that one could speak of a satisfactory result." Such a comparison with the Congress kingdom the minister feared all the more since it would surely bring to light, as he suspected, the Galicians' predilection for a representative constitution.[10]

Since Czar Alexander monopolized the exploitation of Polish national feeling, Austria's only possible policy was to encourage a Galician *nation* and, in the words of Goëss and Metternich, "not to turn the Poles with one stroke into Germans, but rather, before anything else, into real Galicians so that they cease to regard themselves as Poles."[11] As Metternich still had plans for Lombardy-Venetia, he had taken care to remind the monarch that Galicia must not be treated less favorably — a consideration meaningless after 1818. The Staatskanzlei's chief concern in Galicia was the relatively intangible influence of Russian-cultivated Polish national feeling and, as in Italy, the more tangible activity of Russian agents;[12] against the latter it could raise diplomatic protest — the rest remained for local authorities and the police.

Between 1819 and 1821 the whole aspect of the nationality question was changed by events in Germany, Italy, and Greece; it became identified with a challenge against legitimate rule and won again international significance. Within the Habsburg empire, problems of nationality were left to be considered (or disregarded) at an administrative level. Little remained of the new interior organization Metternich had tried to establish. Mellerio had gone home, replaced by Goëss as Lombardo-Venetian chancellor. With a smoothly running and just administration, Vienna meant to satisfy the Italian population, the thought being: the efficiency of an administration is more important than its nationality. The government, while still considering occasional plaints and some pleas for deference to Italian national character, now concentrated on means to improve the dispatch of administrative affairs and the general economic picture; thus Metternich eagerly made known that the emperor had new remedies to dispense on his impending Italian journey in the summer of 1819.[13] Yet, for the Italians, the only noticeable change in administrative procedure seemed to be that significant proposals were no longer treated in a petty manner but that petty concessions were accorded undue significance.

Notwithstanding, both Bubna and Goëss knew that a policy of good example in Lombardy-Venetia was hampered simply because discontent increased faster than Austria's ability to govern well. Even more, the wish for an autonomous administration and, even worse, a persisting "preference for national independence" overshadowed all Austrian endeavors.[14] Thoughtful and well-meaning as were both Bubna and Goëss, they knew how limited were their own capacities to secure decisive improvements: they could only present what they took to be feasible ideas and suggestions to Metternich along with urgent pleas to prevail upon the emperor. But Metternich, although still receptive, was not much more effective than they were. In time, Bubna and Metternich became more and more inclined to sigh in resignation and to shift the responsibility for most troubles to developments beyond Austria's control. While on a trip to Italy in the spring of 1819 and following an exchange of views with the general, the minister had written to his monarch that the main reason for the recent deterioration in Italian public mood lay not in any blunder of the Austrian government; rather at fault were the harmful influences exerted by the current manifestations of the two ideological ills of the time: the constitutional movements in France and Germany and the "phantom of independence" at which the Italian "nation was continuously grasping". He followed Bubna in advocating a more apparent *Kulturpolitik* and such small but effective generosities as a subsidy for *La Scala* or a Milanese school for boys. Furthermore, he added rather glibly, "something useful and pleasant should be arranged for Lombardy and especially for Milan."[15] But such niceties aside, the real problem in the administration — as he saw it on the scene — had changed little since 1814 and this hard truth continued to arouse his displeasure; leaving Italy, he confided to his wife: "I do not believe there are two things less alike than Germany and Italy, and yet our sages in Vienna want, cost what it may, to make Germans out of the Italians. Well, they'll succeed marvellously."[16] But beneath such sarcasm was a bitterness at failing to prevent just that.

While in Italy, Metternich heard of Kotzebue's assassination. It sparked off what he came to call "the German Revolution" and it meant the beginning of a new era and, in a certain sense, a new Metternich. If the so-called "Metternich system" ever really began, then it did so during the first of a series of crises which now followed in rapid succession and shattered the repose which Austria so badly needed. A shocked Metternich became conscious of a new mission to save Europe from the upheavals of revolution through a "moral" crusade. With astonishing adeptness he distinguished between "the good" and "the evil". Kaiser Franz was awed as he should have been and was made aware of his complete dependence on his foreign minister Metternich, who, in "saving Europe", also preserved his empire. The close relationship between the two remained sealed on this basis — hence their mutual respect and even friendship.

The German crisis had induced the emperor to postpone his own trip to Italy — news which startled the Austrian officials but left the Milanese unmoved.[17] Before proceeding from Italy to Karlsbad, an apprehensive Metternich had written to Esterhazy in London that the German and Italian issues were fatally linked: much as Italian secret societies had the one aim of independence and reunion of the entire peninsula under a single constitutional government, a good number of German intellectuals wished to unify all of their nationality into one Germany.[18] Metternich saw clearly that the mutual sympathy expressed by nationalists on both sides of the Alps was merely one sign of the reciprocal influence of events; each group wished the other well and both hoped to see the fusing together of an Italian as well as a German nation. But in 1819 his main attention was devoted to Germany, now the fountainhead of both constitutional and national feeling. He understood that the passions which inspired so many Germans were the effects of the "glorious events of 1813" which had, as he put it, "recreated Germany and [through which] the Germans saw themselves given to the sentiment of nationality." From that moment on, he claimed, a battle took place between German courts and German people.[19] Defending the legitimacy of the various German states did not prevent Metternich from admitting that their inhabitants constituted, more than just a sum of populations, one German people. Indeed, by this time, the political exponents of this people were drawn from considerable elements among Germany's intellectual and middle class. This group, already infected with nationalism and liberalism, felt no longer satisfied by the existing order, either with or without an estates-constitution, and began to press for the representative constitution — i.e., government and representation in the name of the people. This development Metternich had foreseen and had tried to prevent. To wield power through popular mandate meant, after the people's membership had been defined, execution of its supposed will. Thus, for Metternich, a new representative constitution was bound to lead to a nationalistic assembly. For that reason, as minister of an empire of several entire peoples and segments of others, he was convinced that a representative constitution signified the inevitable destruction of the existing political-social structure just as much as did the principle of nationality when raised to an ultimate principle of political order.

A relieved Metternich was sure that his Karlsbad Decrees would not fail in their positive effects on Italy as well as Germany.[20] His concern for better propaganda in Italy went so far as to propose establishing for Milan a political bureau for publishing "in the Italian spirit" the government's point of view which, he lamented, was all too rarely heard. For this project, he had picked the poet Monti, now apparently once again reconciled with the Austrians. Moreover, he carried forward Bubna's suggestion to support Monti with an expanded Milanese Institute in his literary feud with the Florentine Academy on the matter of the Italian Dictionary. Why all this? One could not deny the unrest in Italy, he reminded the emperor, especially in Milan. Its intelligent population was particularly afflicted with what he called a "national characteristic": passionate occupation with some topic or other. Furthermore, the minister claimed, the independence party always dangled before the eyes of the impressionable Milanese "the hallucination [*Hirngespinst*] of the union of Italy". What could be better than to throw these intellectuals a bone and thus unobtrusively divert them from politics — a dish not meant for them. Such a feud between Tuscans and Lombards might lead to a severe split among Italy's intelligentsia, Metternich believed, and from such a development any number of political benefits could be drawn. It was a belated and somewhat naïve recourse to his old "Lombard spirit" idea.[21]

Paradoxically, just as the German "Central Investigation Commission" was to be set up in Mainz in 1819, the dissolution of the Milanese CBA was discussed. Soon, the optimism resulting from Karlsbad was added to reasons for its abolition; actually, the institution seems to have lost its effectiveness by having become too well-known. Metternich had been urged by Guicciardi, whose participation was obviously half-hearted, to bring the matter before the emperor. It was eventually decided that, in bowing out, Guicciardi was to turn over all papers to Bubna. The general, for his part, favored continuing some sort of "supervisory" activity beyond the border.[22] This idea was also to Metternich's liking; he advanced it to the emperor who decreed the dissolution of the CBA on March 13, 1820.[23] A year later, after the Milanese "conspiracy" had occurred, a new and more specialized institution, akin to the Mainz Commission, took its place: the notorious Milan Investigation Commission under the leadership of Salvotti — the prosecutor of Confalonieri.

At the same time, in 1820, another sort of institution — the new private Lancaster schools — had aroused Metternich's suspicions; he charged their instructors with being friends of the Revolution and desiring to educate Italian youth "after the principles of so-called nationality, of free constitutions, and the hate of foreign rule." This seemed to him to be an exploitation of the sense of nationality in a most negative way and even if Metternich could still admit merit in the novel teaching methods (class discussion), he had to condemn its fruits. To justify closure, he ordered a thorough investigation. One of the schools' chief proponents, Metternich pointed out, was Count Confalonieri, whose aims he thought to recognize — even then — as obviously against the government.[24]

In the spring of 1820, Sardagna had submitted to Bubna an analysis of Italian discontent. His solution: real autonomy — as complete a separation of the government in Milan from the one in Vienna as the framework of the monarchy would permit. On the whole, Bubna shared his conclusions, although warning on the side that the Italians' typical exaggeration and their extravagance in the use of words made judging public sentiment no easy task. But he did not know, under the circumstances, how to give the undeniably deplorable mood a better turn. Resignedly but realistically he wrote to Metternich:

I am far from believing that we have done everything to win the affections of the Italians, but whether this goal was to be attained at all is, to say the least, problematic. All parties had — in the last war, whenever it suited them — spoken to the Italians about their independence and thus roused them from their slumber. The idea, to unite under one head fourteen million people who speak the same language and to play a role among the European states is too attractive a thought to be forgotten and no form of government which does not fulfill this aim positively can still please them.

In an ironic frame of mind, he thought the Italians could be satisfied only at the expense of the empire's old provinces — that is, "if the present situation is turned about and all Slavic-German interests are subordinated and Milan would take the place of Vienna as central point of the empire." On the other hand, he might have added, even without such an extreme, Kaiser Franz had never been able to see why Lombardy-Venetia should receive broader privileges than his other lands. Yet, although Bubna pointed to some improvement — at least, he insisted, things were better than in the days of "the unpopular COHC" — and although he refused to see things as black as some, he prudently kept his guard up against any surprises. For that reason, he assured Metternich that, despite momentary quiet, "my sentries, reserves, and patrols are kept on the move as if we were in enemy territory." As if such care for security were not enough, Bubna reassured himself by asking: "Where is the liberal of sufficient influence and renown to unite to action this land where mutual envy and jealousy are taken in with the mother's milk? This superhuman work would require the sort of man whom Italy has not seen for centuries."[25] The founder of the *Giovine Italia* was to become known in less than a dozen years; the end of quiet came in less than two months.

The Neapolitan revolution was another serious blow for Metternich, who had just thought all once more under control. He viewed it as his gravest test;[26] this time his sense of urgency, mission, and even indispensability exceeded all bounds — perhaps necessary to move a startled but cautious emperor to quick and effective intervention.[27] A tense Metternich mobilized forces, prevailed upon friends, and pressed the monarch for more improvements in Lombardy-Venetia.[28] Happily the affair in Naples went well and the Northern Italian disturbances were dealt with. Again came a restoration in Italy, whereby pacification, repose, and a return to absolute but not arbitrary rule were fundamental issues.[29]

During the Congress of Verona, it mattered most for Metternich to show resolve and to set examples; indeed, somewhat irritated, he complained to his sovereign that things had reached the point "where more personal courage was required to come out for legitimacy and the monarchic principle than to undertake a revolutionary attack on the governments." Therefore, he could not support a course of clemency and amnesty as advocated by Sardagna in regard to those imprisoned in the wake of the various "national" conspiracies.[30] First there would be the severest punishment under the law; then, a generous monarch might allow for clemency — a pattern followed with Confalonieri and Andryane. Both men had their death sentences commuted; both were eventually released after years on the Spielberg. This tragedy contained some of the most stirring scenes in the dramatic story of Austria in Italy: Madame Bubna's supposed hurried warning to Teresa Confalonieri of her husband's impending arrest, Bubna's and Metternich's gracious comfort and help to two griefstricken yet determined women — Confalonieri's wife and Andryane's sister — and Metternich, the state chancellor, engaging in a secret and futile discussion with the prisoner Confalonieri.

At the same time, in 1822, Metternich set about to present to the world a vindication of Austrian rule in Italy. This he did in response to a request from his friend Lord Aberdeen — the former British ambassador in Vienna. Aberdeen's Tory party had been under severe attack from the Opposition for condoning the worst sort of repression in Italy and now Aberdeen turned to Metternich for material to use in refuting the charges and in defending Austria as well as his own party. Thus he had directed to Metternich specific questions on a comparison between the former French and the post-war Austrian administrations. Metternich was only too delighted to oblige; he would not always have such an illustrious forum. Scrupulously he instructed his subordinates to be carefully truthful in all which was chosen to be said. Elaborate statistics showed a favorable comparison in regard to education, public welfare, construction, commerce; with such matters as taxes, conscription, or student enrollment, Austria fared especially well since these could not have been much of an exhibit for a war-time regime. His underlined conclusion was: "*Que Le Royaume lombard-vénétien marche d'un pas, non précipité, mais sûr, calme, ferme et continuel vers un état de perfectment et de maturité.*"[31]

How little of Metternich's original policy for Lombardy-Venetia had materialized was made evident by the opinions of leading Austrian officials in Italy whom he had commissioned to report, during the Congress of Verona, on the Italian situation. In a common memorandum, they flatly stated their pessimism regarding a return to repose on the peninsula or in the Austrian provinces since "it is impossible to delude oneself that the Lombards do not share the common sentiment of other Italians whom they have not ceased and shall never cease to regard as their sole true compatriots." This statement might well be the epitaph for Metternich's attempt to rekindle the Lombard spirit so that "*l'esprit soi-disant italien*" might be forgotten. The parcelling up of Italy, the authors felt, simply would not allow for a reestablishment of calm and tranquillity; as a compensation they suggested an old idea: Italian national pride, severely wounded because of "the political nullity of Italy", might be salved, they thought, by an Italian Confederation similar to the German one. In any case, they emphasized, the chief complaint continued to be that the Lombardo-Venetian administration was too foreign; this meant that the Lombardo-Venetian Kingdom could not, at the moment, serve as the model for the other Italian governments. This fact was a bitter admission, all the more so when recalling Bellegarde's concern with this very point seven years earlier; it was also a painful point of honor since, as one of the authors — Ficquelmont — recalled, the Allies had also imposed an obligation upon Austria in entrusting it with Lombardy-Venetia. That the many proposals of these conscientious men were but repetitions is perhaps more significant than the fact that nothing came of them.[32]

More than ten years later it was not otherwise. Much had changed in Italy after the July revolution: the *Giovine Italia* had appeared and unquellable demands for national independence rang out everywhere. In 1833 Kaiser Franz was to receive a long anonymous essay dealing with the revolution in Italy, Austria's troubles there, and "the appeal of nationality — that most awful weapon in the hands of an opponent."[33] The author, Sardagna perhaps, denounced centralization and the abundance of German officials; he listed all sorts of methods by which respect for the Italian nationality and encouragement of Italian national pride could be demonstrated. He advocated reviving the dried-up *Biblioteca Italiana*, granting real and effective national autonomy and displaying the viceroyalty as the one institution through which Austria's Italian subjects could recognize their own "national" status. These were intelligent observations and appealing, even compelling, suggestions — all of which had been sounded fifteen to twenty years before.

The southern revolutions of 1820—1822 had challenged the Austrian empire to a test of strength which it triumphantly withstood. Initially, however, the danger was taken so seriously that special levies of troops and contributions were called for — even in Hungary — and Metternich appealed to his newly-won friend Czar Alexander for eventual military aid. Thereby the Hungarian nation realized anew that it represented the great reserve of Habsburg might and renewed its demands for a return of Illyrian Croatia and the Littorale. Although past requests had been shelved,[34] Kaiser Franz had never shown sympathy for the "Illyrians", be it from a political or a cultural standpoint. He denied the "Illyrian" (i.e., Croatian) language the rank which German, Italian, and even Latin held in a largely Slavic land; in 1822, he practically banned it from the Istrian Court of Appeals.[35] In the summer of that year, in view of Hungary's loyal attitude, the monarch could no longer stave off that nation's claims to an outlet to the sea; for the King of Hungary it was not a difficult decision.[36] Thereby Dietrichstein's prophecy came true: the little Kingdom of Illyria could not remain inviolate and Hungary despoiled it of one third of its Slavic inhabitants. Metternich reacted apathetically; possibly distracted by the preparations for the Congress of Verona, he even forgot to prepare the official patent announcing the change, causing considerable last-minute embarrassment.[37] The Kingdom of Illyria, reduced to a meaningless expression, was finally done away with in 1848.

Thus evaporated Metternich's endeavor to create for the Southern Slavic nationality a political entity of its own within the empire as early as 1816, a time in which the future leaders of the Illyrian national movement were just schoolboys. Then, a *Reich* such as Metternich envisaged would surely have earned Habsburg Austria the gratitude and attachment of its Southern Slavic subjects. Instead, the want of such a structure deprived their gradually fermenting political feelings of any vent and cleared the way for the fatal Austrian-Hungarian dualism. For the Croats subjected to Budapest, it meant suffering a bitterly resented policy of Magyarization; for the Habsburg empire it was a grandiose lost opportunity.

In 1823, the Bohemian-Galician chancellor — Count Lazansky — died. Kaiser Franz did not appoint a successor. In 1825 the remaining chancellors were officially listed merely as *Hofkanzler*.[38] It may be considered as the end of Austria's first ministry of the interior with its "national" chancelleries — after not even seven years of a more or less paper existence.

After 1818 Metternich undertook no further effort during Kaiser Franz's lifetime to revise the internal policy or structure. Even as the first state chancellor since Kaunitz, Metternich soon had, in Count Kolowrat, a formidable rival in internal affairs. After the manifestations of constitutionalism and nationalism during the "German" and Mediterranean revolutions, Metternich could only reflect soberly on the readiness with which the dissatisfied had risen against legitimate even if oppressive authority. The future demanded a firm hand; in his role as the supplier of principles to European politics, he was also concerned with a solidarity of the great powers against any disrupters of order — even if sentiment for a suffering nationality such as the Greeks placed the principle of legitimacy up to a severe test.[39] Hardly a state was immune to revolution; no state was as vulnerable as the Habsburg empire, which could not exist either as ·a republic or as a national state. With a nationality fully bent on a nationalistic program — where ultimately no concession would suffice — it was better to keep silent. However, that a multinational Austria could not dare to over-centralize or — even worse — Germanize at the expense of any nationality, he maintained to the end of his life.

APPENDICES

APPENDIX A

DOCUMENT SELECTIONS

1. Metternich to Bellegarde, May 15, 1814.

2. Metternich to Kaiser Franz, April 18, 1815.

3. Sardagna Memoir, Summer, 1815.

4. Stewart to Castlereagh, Feb. 4, 1816.

5. Metternich to Kaiser Franz, May 24, 1816.

6. Dietrichstein to Metternich, Oct. 27, 1817.

7. Metternich to Kaiser Franz, Oct. 27, 1817.

8. *Wiener Zeitung*, Dec. 24, 1817.

APPENDIX B

DATA ON AUSTRIAN OFFICIALS
APPEARING IN THIS WORK

APPENDIX A

DOCUMENT SELECTIONS

No. 1

METTERNICH À BELLEGARDE

le 15. Mai, 1814

... Il existe en Italie depuis des siècles beaucoup de haines et de jalousies locales. Ces haines n'ont jamais cédées à la réunion de tant d'élémens divers, et elles lui ont survécu. Le lot de l'Autriche se trouvant borné par le Tessin et le Po, rien n'empêche que nous ne tâchions de réveiller l'esprit L o m b a r d . Aussi S.M. est-Elle décidée à ajouter à Ses autres titres celui de R o i d e L o m b a r d i e . La couronne de fer entrera dans les armes de la Maison; l'Emp[ereur] conservera l'ordre, qui en porte le nom, en lui fesant subir des changemens dans la forme et les couleurs du Ruban.

Une question qui se présente tout naturellement en suite de cette détermination est celle de savoir — si le royaume de Lombardie doit s'étendre sur cette province proprem[en]t dite et sur le Vénétien, ou s'il doit se borner à la première. Les Milanois désirent beaucoup cette extension, parceu'elle assurera à leur ville un degré de prospérité particulière. L'Emp [-ereur] se réserve de se décider sur cet objet très important en lui même pour une époque plus reculée. Il veut sonder l'esprit et les dispositions de Ses nouveaux Sujets Italiens. . . .

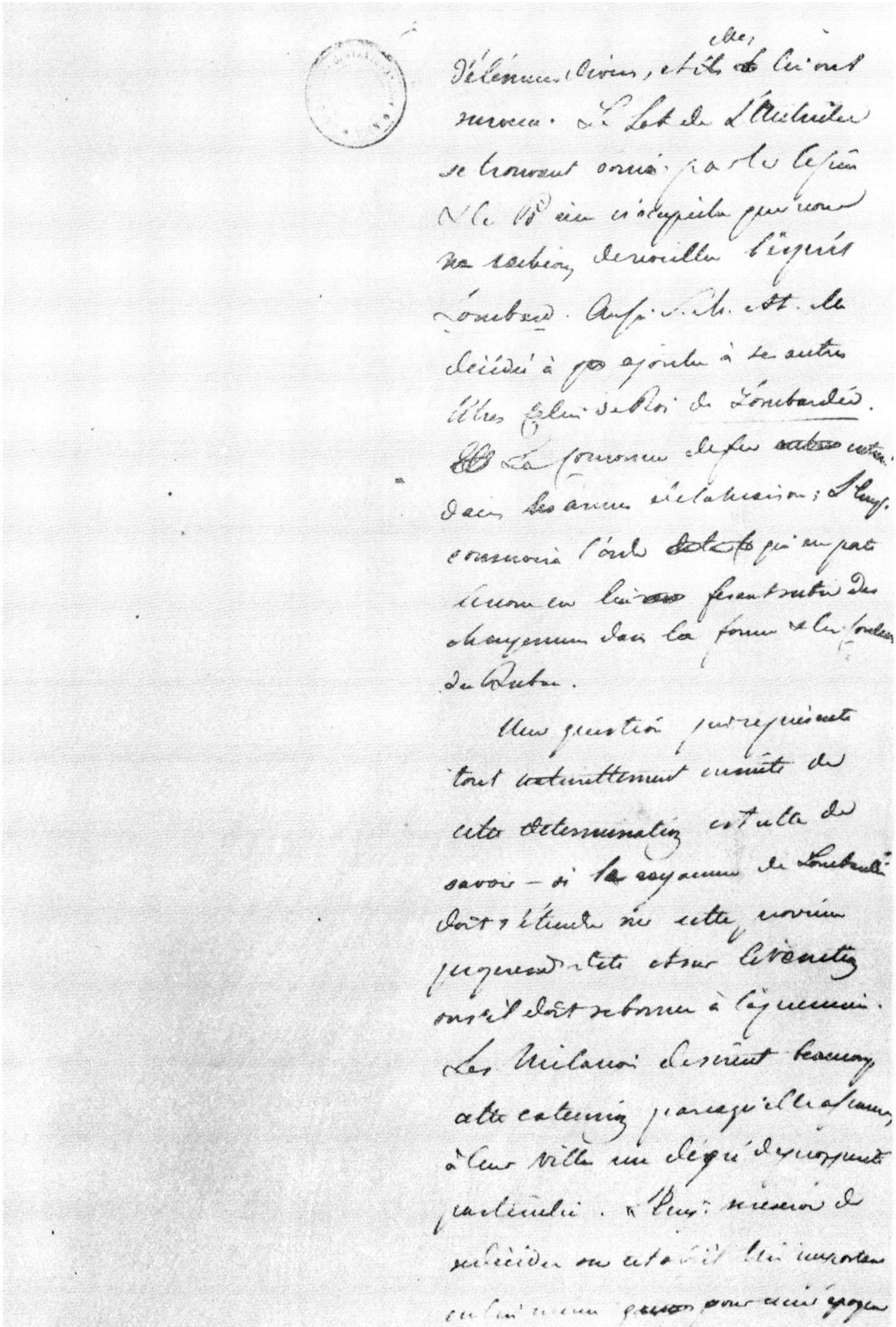

METTERNICH TO BELLEGARDE, MAY 15, 1814

No. 2

VORTRAG DES FÜRSTEN METTERNICH AN KAISER FRANZ ÜBER DIE SITUATION IN GALIZIEN UND DIE VON GRAF GOESS DAZU GEÄUSSERTE MEINUNG

18. April 1815

Eure Majestät!

In Folge der auf E.M. Befehl zwischen mir, dem Präsidenten der Polizei-Hofstelle und dem Grafen Goëss abgehaltenen Zusammentretung hat letzterer über die in Gallizien zu ergreiffenden Maßregeln mir den hier ehrerbietigst anverwahrten Vorschlag mit der Bemerkung mitgetheilt, daß Freiherr von Haager bereits davon Einsicht genommen und vollkommen einverstanden ist.

Die Anträge des Grafen Goëss sind von zweyerley Art: Geheime Polizei Einleitungen, um von dem was in den an Gallizien gränzenden Nachbarstaaten vorgeht, von den Verbindungen deren Bewohner mit diesseitigen Unterthanen, sowie von den Passanten schnell, verläßlich und ohne Aufsehen unterrichtet zu seyn; dann politische und administrative Anordnungen, um sich der Anhänglichkeit der Gallizier an den Österreichischen Kaiserstaat mehr und mehr zu versichern.

Ich finde bei den von Graf Goëss vorgeschlagenen Polizei Einleitungen so wenig etwas zu erinnern, daß nur der Wunsch übrig bleibt, Baron Haager möchte, wenn es nicht etwa bereits vom Grafen Goëss vor seiner Abreise geschehen ist, mit möglichster Beschleunigung die Individuen namhaft machen, welche mit den erforderlichen Eigenschaften und Gewandtheit zu der in Frage stehenden geheimen Beobachtung ausgerüstet als Kreiskommissäre in Podgowze, Tarnow, in der Gegend der Einmündung des Sannflusses in die Weichsel, in Lubieza, Brody und Podwolocziska mit voller Beruhigung über den Erfolg angestellt werden könnten.

Bei den politischen Anwendungen bemerkt Graf Goëss sehr richtig, dass deren Tendenz vorzüglich dahin gehen müsse, nicht aus Pohlen mit einem male Deutsche sondern vor allem erst ächte Gallizier zu machen — damit sie aufhören, sich als Pohlen zu betrachten, indem man nur durch diesen Stuffengang hoffen kann, den Endzweck zu erreichen, und jedes andere Benehmen der Regierung nicht nur davon ab-

führen, sondern in dem gegenwärtigen Augenblick
sogar gefährlich werden könnte.

Ich glaube mich nicht berufen, in das umständliche Detail der Organisierung jener National Repräsentanz oder ständischen Verfassung einzugehen, welche Graf Goëss sub No. 1 in Vorschlag bringt, bin
aber im Allgemeinen mit dessen Ansicht vollkommen einverstanden, daß
selbst schon die vorläufige Zusage einer solchen Verfassung sehr wesentlich beitragen würde, die Ge-
müther der Gallizier zu gewinnen.

Der schicklichste Zeitpunkt, ihnen die Allerhöchste Willensmeynung
hierüber vorläufig zu eröffnen, dürfte wohl jener der Publikation des
nächstens zwischen Österreich, Rußland und Preußen besonders abzuschlies-
senden Traktats seyn, in welchem die Auflösung des Herzogthums War-
schau, und die neue Abgränzung zwischen den drei Mächten ausgesprochen
wird.

Nur müßte nicht, wie Graf Goëss meint, von irgendeiner Bestätigung
der Vereinigung Galliziens mit dem Österreichischen Kaiserstaat die Rede
seyn, weil eine solche Äußerung leicht zu Mißverständnissen über die frü-
heren Verhältnisse dieses Landes Anlaß geben könnte.

Graf Goëss betrachtet als weitere Mittel zu Gewinnung mancher Einfluß habenden Familien und Individuen die Einführung einer allgemeinen
lebhaft gewünschten eigenen ständischen Uniform, die Wiederbesetzung
der in Gallizien beinahe durchgehend erledigten Landes-Erzämter
durch verdienstliche Nationale, die Aussicht für andere,
als Kreisräthe bei den Kreisämtern, als Friedens- oder Schieds-
richter in den Orten ihres Aufenthaltes ernannt zu werden, ganz vorzüglich aber und mit Recht eine Reise E.M. in jene Gegenden, wenn die
Zeit-Umstände einmal gestatten werden, das Land mit der Allerhöchsten
Gegenwart zu beglücken.

Er erwähnt endlich auch am Schlusse seines Vortrags der Erweiterung
der Handelsverhältnisse Galliziens, der Erleich-
terung des Absatzes für die Produzenten, der Verminderung der für die ärmeren Klassen der Unterthanen so
sehr drückenden Vorspannlast, endlich auch der Sistierung der gegen die
unbefugten Auswanderer in den Jahren 1805 - 1807 erlassenen Strafurtheile
als eben so vieler Mittel um die günstige Stimmung zu vermehren, worüber
wohl im Ganzen kein Zweifel obwalten kann und ich mir nur die ge-
horsamste Bemerkung erlaube, daß ein Theil dieser patriotischen Wünsche
durch den oben erwähnten nächstens mit Rußland und Preußen abzu-
schließenden Traktat in wirkliche Erfüllung gehen wird.

Ein Umstand, welcher gegenwärtig ganz vorzüglich berücksichtiget werden zu müssen scheint, ist jener, daß E. M. in Ihrer Weisheit für angemessen befunden haben, d a s n e u e L o m b a r d i s c h - V e n e z i a n i s c h e K ö n i g r e i c h d u r c h m a n c h e r l e y B e g ü n s t i g u n g e n u n d B e w e i s e d e s A l l e r h ö c h s t e n W o h l w o l l e n s a u s z u - z e i c h n e n , d a ß d a h e r u m s o s o r g f ä l t i g e r d a r ü b e r z u w a c h e n w ä r e , d a ß d e n G a l l i z i e r n a u c h n i c h t e i n S c h e i n g r u n d v e r b l e i b e , s i c h a l s m i n d e r b e g ü n s t i g t o d e r w o h l g a r z u r ü c k g e s e t z t z u b e t r a c h t e n , b e - s o n d e r s b e i V e r t h e i l u n g v o n G n a d e n b e z e u g u n - g e n , d a m i t e n d l i c h e i m a l a u c h d o r t d i e s o s e h r e r - w ü n s c h l i c h e l e b h a f t e Überzeugung entstehe, daß bei dem ge- rechtesten Monarchen g l e i c h e E r g e b e n h e i t und Treue immer auf gleiche väterliche Sorgfalt, Huld und Milde mit voller Zuversicht rechnen dürfen.

F. v. Metternich

Wien, den 18. April 1815

Ich behalte den Vorschlag des Grafen Goëss zurück, und erlasse die in dieser Hinsicht nötigen Befehle unter einem an Meinen Präsidenten der Polizei-Hofstelle, und an Meinen Obersten Kanzler.

Franz m. p.

Wien, den 26. April 1815

StK. Vortr. 291, 5, 644.

No. 3

MEMOIRE AN DIE STAATSKANZLEI — (FRHR. V. SARDAGNA)

(SUMMER 1815)

ÜBER DIE EINFÜHRUNG DER ÖSTERREICHISCHEN CIVIL-
UND CRIMINAL-GESETZBÜCHER IN ITALIEN

... Der Österreicher v o r 5 0 J a h r e n h e r, und der jetzt lebende,
sind aller Erfahrungen, die seither die Generazionen belehren, und jener
überaus großen Fortschritte in der Kultur, deren die Geschichte keines
Volkes ein ähnliches Beispiel aufzustellen vermag, ungeachtet, von ein-
ander noch immer weniger verschieden, als z u r S t u n d e d e r
I t a l i e n e r u n d d e r D e u t s c h e. ... Unmöglich kann eine Regierung, die so väterlich das Wohl ihrer Völker will, die Wichtigkeit dieser
so einfachen Bemerkung verkennen, unmöglich kann es unter dem milden
Zepter des gütigsten Monarchen geschehen, daß auf die Eigenheiten und auf
die Bedürfnisse der Völker Italiens bei der Einführung unserer Gesetz-
gebung gar keine Rücksicht genommen und vorzügliche Justizmänner aus
ihrer Mitte — als ob es sich um die Organisierung einer Kolonie oder um
die Civilisierung eines ganz rohen Volkes handelte — hierüber gar nicht
vernommen oder die gemachten Bemerkungen unbeachtet gelassen werden
sollten.

... Wenn aber es wahr seyn sollte, daß in einigen, ja sogar in Haupt-
städten deutscher Provinzen, Inquisiten Monate lang auf Verhör warten,
daß bei Landgerichten Beamte es wagen dürfen und wagen können, die
Heuärnte der Untersuchung eines Verbrechens vorzuziehen, wenn unbedeu-
tende Processe ohne Verletzung der Form in Jahre hinausgezogen werden
können, wovon der Verfasser dieses Aufsatzes allerdings selbst Beispiele
erlebt hat — und dies bey einer rechtlichen Nation teutonischen Stammes
vorfällt — und wenn hingegen seit Einführung der napoleonischen
Processordnung die Justiz bei einem ränkevollen Volke lateinischen Stammes ungleich schneller als je vorher administriert wurde, so ist es schwer
sich der Überzeugung hinzugeben, daß die österreichische Form hierlands
die passendste sey!!

Wir schließen diese Bögen mit einer uns sich in der österreichischen
Monarchie häufig aufdringenden Betrachtung, daß nämlich die Absicht
durch Gleichförmigkeit in der Verfassung und in den Gesetzen ein A m a l -

g a m der so vielen und so verschiedenen Nationen aus welchen der österreichische Kaiserstaat besteht, zu bilden, wohl nimmermehr, sondern vielleicht gerade eine fortwährende Divergenz unter denselben erzweckt werden dürfte.

Keines der Völker, die dem sanften Zepter des erlauchten Habsburg-
Lothringischen Erzhauses unterworfen sind, ist zahlreich und mächtig
genug, um m i t R e c h t, auf das Vorherrschen Anspruch machen zu
können, und gerade die Deutschen, welche die Hauptstadt besitzen, sind es
weniger noch als die Übrigen.

Die Erfahrung lehrt uns, daß die bezweckte A s s i m i l a t i o n der
Stämme nur dann möglich ist, wenn kleine Provinzen einem großen homo-
genen Körper, wie etwa Elsaß mit Frankreich, vereiniget werden.

Liebe zum Herrscher-Stamme auf milde Regierung und Völkerglück
begründet, ist das wahre Band, das den österreichischen Staaten-Verein so
innig verkettet, und das sich in Zeiten von Gefahr stets bewährt hat — die
Nichtrespektierung der Herkunft, der Bildung, der Sitten und Gewohn-
heiten, die man den Franzosen in allen Manifesten vorwarf, und eine
eherne Form, die uns g l e i c h ist, o h n e A l l e n g l e i c h p a s s e n d
z u s e y n, scheint das Mittel nicht, um diesen so ganz in den Absichten
des gütigsten Monarchen liegenden Zweck, zu erreichen.

In Ländern wo noch Roheit und gänzlicher Mangel an wissenschaftlicher
Ausbildung herrscht, kann hierin leichter durchgegriffen werden, dahingegen
ist um so mehr Vorsicht in jenen Provinzen nöthig, die in der Aufklärung
wenigstens gleichen Schritt mit den deutschen gehalten haben, deren Litera-
tur aber und vorzüglich die juridische, fünf Jahrhunderte des Fortschreitens
zählt, dessen wir uns nicht erfreuen können. . . .

StK. Prov/LV 40, 80.

No. 4

LORD STEWART TO THE VISCOUNT CASTLEREAGH K.G.

Dispatch No. 13   Milan, 4th of February, 1816

My Lord!

Since my Dispatch No. 8 relating to the arrangements in contemplation for the Formation of the new Government for the Austrian states in Italy, some progress has been made, and I understand the following Appointments are immediately to take place.

His Imperial Highness The Arch Duke Antony is to be named Viceroy, and Marshal Bellegarde hitherto acting as Lieutenant of the Viceroy returns to Vienna, where He is to be placed with His Imperial Highness the Hereditary Prince as a Councillor and Companion. The separate Establishment of His Imperial Highness will be formed under the Marshal's Superintendance, and His Imperial Highness's Education being terminated He will enter upon a new plan of Life; The removal of Marshal Bellegarde is sincerely regretted here, as He is much more popular than the Civil Governor the Count Saurau who remains (I understand) in his actual Capacity as the Chief Confidential Individual in this Government: Count Saurau has been very marked in his civilities and attentions to all the English, but He is reported to be a corrupt and profligate Character and generally unpopular. He pleases the Emperor however by his strict and regid Austrian Ideas, and has contrived to seat himself in his present Situation to the banishment of the other contending Interest. . . . I am inclined to believe if Prince Metternich's long Indisposition [a severe eye ailment] had not impeded His active Exertions, he would have brought about a greater Liberality in the Arrangements for the Emperor's Italian Subjects and have prevented much of the ill Temper and dissatisfaction that exists. A strong party in the Austrian Government are endeavouring to germanize every Concern here, and His Imperial Majesty is too apt to listen to his Vienna Subjects. The brilliant Court that was held here by the Viceroy Eugene has been succeeded by a System of Ceremony so regid and seclusion so absolute, that the Italians who pay nearly the same *Impôts* are discontented not to receive the same Enjoyments and Festivities, and conceive all their Money as well as every Thing else that is precious is carried into the Austrian Dominions. The Discontented Spirit manifests itself in a thousand ways; The Languages of the Women of the First Families, the placards that appear on the Walls, and the Squibs that are in distribution, a specimen of which I enclose, and last of all the general *Gêne* that prevails between the Austrians and the Italians clearly denote to the most common Observer the Animosity and Discontent that exist. All this however need not alarm for it is evident the most animating and vivid Blaze will in the end expire, if fuel is not at hand, and the present peevishness and vomiting [sic] of the Milanese is perfectly impotent almost unworthy of Note and very certain of speedily subsiding. At the same time it would have been more agreeable to have witnessed a liberal and enlightened System of Arrangement; to reduce nearly all the former Offices of the State, to pay them at one third of their former Receipts; to try to transfer the Law Decisions on the most trifling Questions to Vienna under immense Expences to the parties; to establish an Arch Duke for a Viceroy without Influence, without Power, without Credit, and without Money, thus placing him in the most painful Situation after a very popular predecessor who commanded every Resource that is now withheld; to keep up at the same time the same Contributions and Taxes; to do nothing in a liberal Sense for the people at large who have been looking for Acts of Beneficence and Grace. All These Proceedings are certainly impolitick and unwise, but, I believe, are really more to be attributed to the particular turn of mind of the Emperor's Mind and Habits, and to the slow uniform, unchangeable and unchanged Mode in which the Austrians conduct their publick Affairs, than to any despotical or improper feelings towards this Country.

Prince Metternich, as I have already said, is disposed to see Things in a point of View infinitely more liberal and congenial to the Sentiments of this Nation, but he has a party to manage whom He cannot always overcome, and who are so blind as not to see that a Volatile advanced and enlightened people as these are become by rapid Strides under the Controul of the French will not with patience bear to see all their Concerns regulated by an Aulick Council at Vienna or in the Bureau of the Affaires Etrangères in that Capital where, as Your Lordship knows, Business is not very rapid, and above all without their own Countrymen having Office, Post, Employment, or Emolument.

The Count Lazansky who is the Austrian Minister especially for the Affairs of Italy is extremely disliked. The new Arrangement it is hoped, will take from him much of the power and influence He has lately had.

Although these Renseignemens may not be of much Moment, I have deemed it as well to give Your Lordship a Sketch of the common Conversation of the place.

Some Changes are taking place in the Austrian Disposition of their Troops in Italy. I understand all the Grenadiers are to be taken now permanently from their former Regiments and formed into the Emperor's Guard always to be kept together and to have no Establishments of Grenadier Companies even in time of peace with their Regiments.

I have the Honor to be with the greatest truth and Respect,

My Lord!

Your Lordship's most Obedient Humble Servant

Stewart,
Lt. Genl.

PRO, FO 7, 126.

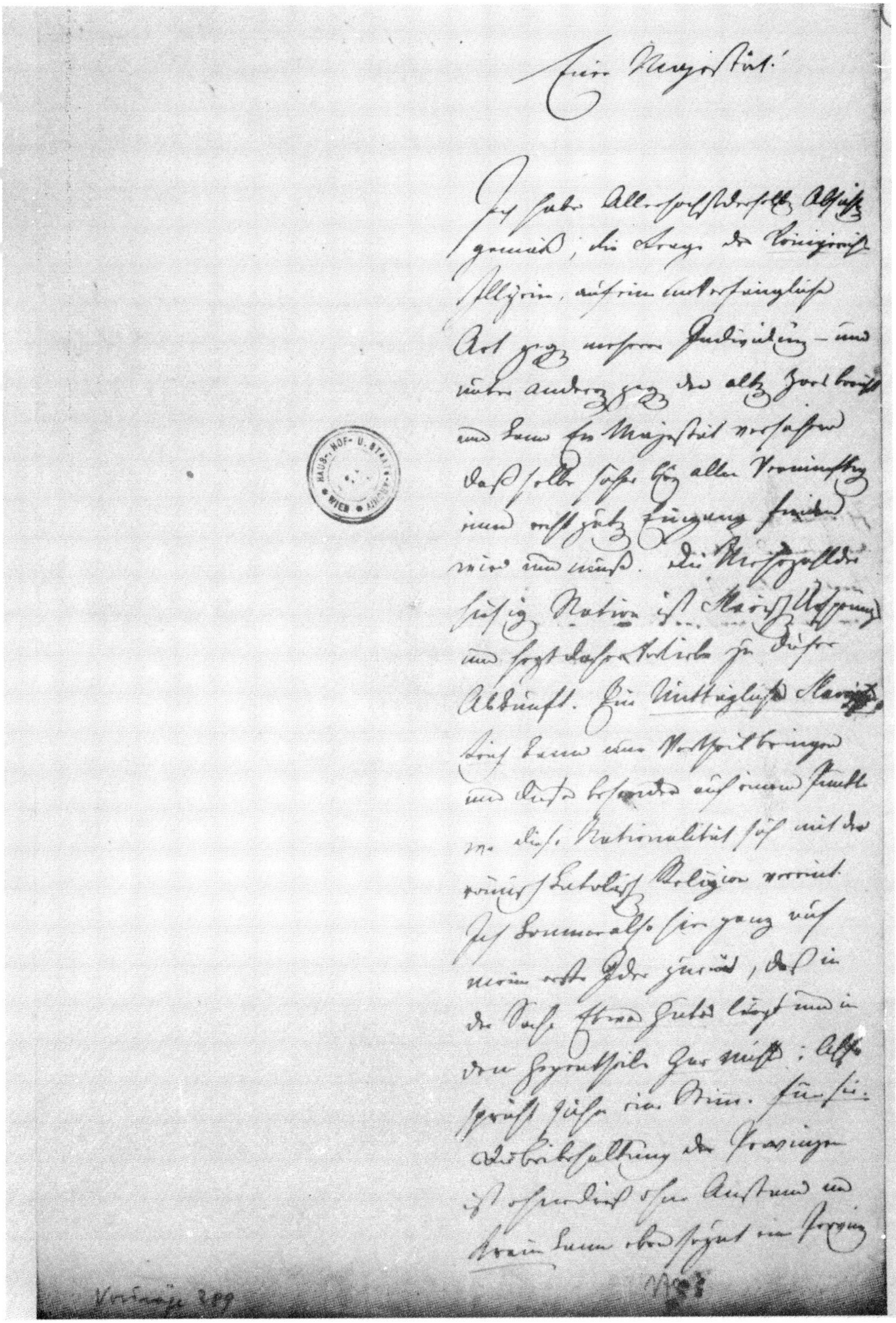

METTERNICH TO KAISER FRANZ, MAY 24, 1816

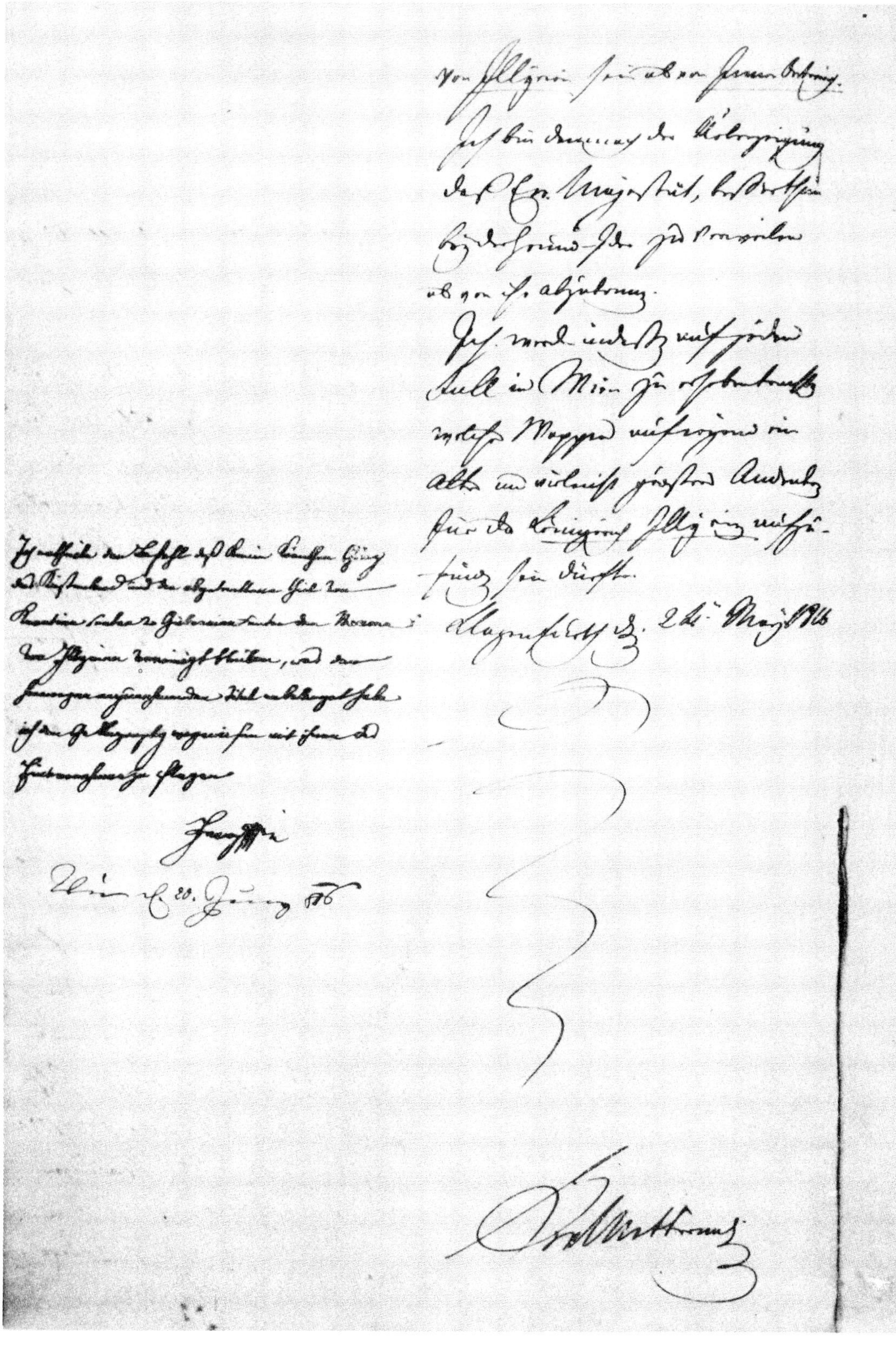

METTERNICH TO KAISER FRANZ, MAY 24, 1816

No. 5

VORTRAG DES FÜRSTEN METTERNICH AN KAISER FRANZ,
DIE BILDUNG DES ILLYRISCHEN KÖNIGREICHS BETREFFEND.

Eure Majestät!

Ich habe allerhöchstderselben Absichten gemäß, die Frage des K ö n i g - r e i c h s I l l y r i e n , auf eine unverfängliche Art gegen mehrere Individuen — und unter anderen gegen den alten Goes berührt und kann Ew. Majestät versichern, daß selbe sicher bey allen Vernünftigen einen recht guten Eingang finden wird und muß. Die Mehrzahl der hiesigen Nation ist Slavischen Ursprungs und hegt daher Vorliebe zu dieser Abkunft. Ein M i t t ä g l i c h e s S l a v i s c h e s R e i c h kann nur Vortheil bringen, und dieses besonders auf einem Punkte wo diese Nationalität sich mit der römisch katholischen Religion vereint. Ich komme also hier ganz auf meine erste Idee zurück, daß in der Sache E t w a s G u t e s liegt und in dem Gegentheile G a r N i c h t s . Also spricht sicher eine Stimme f ü r s i e . Die Beibehaltung der Provinzen ist ohnedieß ohne Anstand und K r a i n kann ebensogut eine Provinz von I l l y r i e n sein als von I n n e r - O e s t e r r e i c h . Ich bin demnach der Ueberzeugung, daß Ew. Majestät, besser thun bey der Grund-Idee zu verweilen als von ihr abzukommen.

Ich werde indessen auf jeden Fall in Wien zu erheben trachten, welches Wappen auf irgendein altes und vielleicht größeres Andenken für das K ö n i g r e i c h I l l y r i e n aufzufinden sein dürfte.

Klagenfurth, den 24. May 1816

F. v. Metternich

Ich ertheile den Befehl daß Krain, Kärnthen, Görz, das Küstenland und der abgetrettene Theil von Kroatien unter 2 Gubernien unter dem Namen von Illyrien vereinigt bleiben, was den hierwegen anzunehmenden Titel anbelanget, habe ich den Gr. Lazansky angewiesen, mit ihnen das Einvernehmen zu pflegen.

Franz   m. p.

Wien, den 20. Juny 1816

StK. Vortr. 298, 1, 70.

No. 6

FÜRST DIETRICHSTEIN AN METTERNICH

27. Okt. 1817

Lieber Freund!

Ich konnte letzthin deinen gehaltvollen Vortrag nur h ö r e n , nicht aber mich darüber ä u ß e r n . Ich habe nun sehr darüber nachgedacht und glaube dir das Resultat davon mittheilen zu müssen. Ich bin mit dir über d i e S a c h e ganz einverstanden, nicht so aber über ein und anderen T h e i l derselben, auch nicht über das eine M o t i v das du beim Vater wegen dem Sohne geltend machen willst. Dieses Motiv ist in meinen Augen nur in votis, aber — leider! — höchst unwahrscheinlich in der Zukunft als begründet zu erwarten. D e m Unglück das uns bevorsteht, könnte nur etwas steuern das d a n n nicht abgeändert werden könnte, indeß zur Abänderung einer solchen G e s c h ä f t s verfassung nur ein Wort — durch wen immer veranlaßt — nöthig wäre. Allen aus jenem Unglück drohenden Folgen könnte n i c h t s entgegenstehn, als eine V e r f a s s u n g, die weder du noch ich vorschlagen werden und mit welchem Vorschlage man uns auch spatzieren schicken würde. Deshalb bleibt auf jeden Fall unsere Zukunft ganz der Willkür des Schicksals überlassen. Was du aber für die Zeit von nun bis dahin thun kannst, wird immer ein großes Verdienst seyn, je größer, je länger wir bis dahin haben werden, weil es uns und andere fähiger machen wird Stürmen zu trotzen und sie zu beschwören.

Deine Idee ist vortrefflich, aber hüte dich die Rechnung ohne den Wirth zu machen! In dem vorliegenden Fall sind d i e P e r s o n e n nicht minder wichtig als die Sache, und die beste Sache kann durch die Personen s c h l e c h t werden. Ich kann nicht für archiducal gelten: j'ai fait mes preuves contre; doch aber habe ich dir vor 4 Monaten schon gesagt: daß ich, um die Sache a n z u f a n g e n , niemanden als den E[rz] H[erzog] R[ainer] sähe: du selbst fandest die ingeniöse Modalität — Min[isteri]um des Innern — Minister vacat — einstweilen dirigiert durch S[eine] K[aiserliche] H[oheit] den E.H.R. Indeß will ich glauben daß, da man einmal den Italienern einen E.H. zum V[ize] K[önig] v e r s p r o c h e n hat, statt ihnen Bellegarde zu lassen, und da man sie seitdem s c h l e c h t behandelt hat, itzt nichts anderes erübrigt als den E.H.R. hinzuschicken. Cela posé, glaube ich auch daß Strassoldo bei ihm, und Mellerio als ital. Kanzler hier, gut thun wird.

Aber den Titel O b e r s t k a n z l e r würde ich ganz eingehen lassen und sehe dies als u n u m g ä n g l i c h   n ö t h i g an: denn er ist a l t und die ung[arischen], siebenb[ürgischen], ital[ienischen] Kanzler n i c h t ge-wohnt unter i h m zu stehen; wogegen der M i n i s t e r   d e s   I n n e r n tout court n e u ist, folglich die anderen leichter unter ihn zu rangiren.

Aber wer soll es seyn? U g a r t e wäre lächerlich und eine Satire auf die ganze Organisation, die keinen guten Lappen, — was er vielleicht nicht einmal ist—sondern un homme à poil d'ongle braucht. W a l l i s , Gottlob, soll es nicht werden. S a u r a u hätte wohl e i n i g e Eigenschaften dazu, aber nicht a l l e   p o u r   l e   c o m m e n c e m e n t . L a z a n s k y hat zu wenig Bildung. K o l o w r a t zu wenig Kraft — eine in unserem Zeit-alter überhaupt sehr seltene Eigenschaft. Du denkst wohl nicht an B a l - d a c c i , M i t r o f s k y , G o ë s s , u[nd] d[er]g[leichen]. H a u e r dürfte i n   z e h n   J a h r e n vielleicht dazu taugen, itzt aber noch nicht. Ich sage dir auch nicht: qui, moi: moi, vous dis-je, denn ich zweifle allmälig bei uns an allem Guten und ich sage was der Kaiser selbst einst sagte als — ich weiß nicht wer — mich, und — ich weiß nicht zu was — vorschlug: "Jo, aber das wär'n G'schrey!" Vielleicht meinte er aber auch mein eigenes, statt dem der anderen gegen mich. Aber, ohne Scherz, je n'ai pas la routine de ces misères intérieures. Auch S t a d i o n wäre nicht dazu, wenn du ihm auch einen Nachfolger en finances wüßtest. Z y c h y wäre nicht viel besser als Ugarte. An C h o t e k wird wohl nicht gedacht.

An deiner Stelle würde ich, wenn ich einen dazu wüßte, auf einen M i n i s t e r   d e s   I n n e r n sans un mot de plus dans le titre, antragen, und unter ihm auf 1. einen böhm. mähr. schlesischen, 2. einen ungarischen, 3. einen galizischen, 4. einen siebenbürgischen, 5. einen öst. (Ober- und Niederöst., Salzburg, Tirol, Steiermark), 6. einen ital. (Lomb. und Vened.), 7. einen illirischen (Kärnten, Krain, Croatien, Littorale, Dalmatien, Alb.), denn 1. mit 3. zusammen wäre lächerlich groß, und ihm entgegen 7. lächer-lich klein, und dies umso mehr als ich nicht glaube daß das so lächerlich getaufte Königreich Illirien contre le serment du roi d'Hongrie, contre l'intérêt de l'état et contre le sens commun Fiume und Croatien behalten wird.

Ich an deiner Stelle würde antragen auf:
1. einen Min. des Auswärt.
2. einen Min. des Innern
3. einen Min. des Kriegs
4. einen Min. der Finanzen
5. einen Min. der Justiz (ohne Gnadensachen)
6. einen Min. des Kultus und öffentl. Unterrichts
7. einen Min. der Polizei.

12 Metternich

Denn 6. und 7. sollte n i c h t unter 1. stehen, am wenigsten 7. — was durchaus s e l b s t ä n d i g seyn sollte — seiner Wichtigkeit in einem verfassungslosen Staate wegen. Und 6. ist nun bei uns wichtig g e n u g , um a u c h selbständig zu seyn. Übrigens bin ich mit deiner diesem Ministerium untergeordneten G e n e r a l d i r e k t i o n einverstanden, würde aber den P r e s i d e n t e n Titel ausschließend aus den ersten Hofräten aller Ministerien so wie den Gerichtsstellen reservieren.

Auf m i c h mußt du für keine Generaldirektion und für kein Presidium rechnen: je suis trop vieux et trop avancé pour cela. Du siehst daß ich auf 2. so wenig als auf 1. und 3. Anspruch mache, und, was eine der sieben —oder deinige sechs — Kanzlerstellen betrifft, möchte gegen mich eben das, wie gegen das Min.-um des Innern einzuwenden seyn und müßte ich vor allem wissen: w e r Min.r des Innern ist, bevor ich mich entschlösse einer seiner Kanzler zu werden, so wie: wer mir noch in dieser Kategorie v o r g e h e n sollte; car, quelque humble que je sois individuellement dès qu'il s'agit de comparaison je me souviens dans quel pays nous sommes.

Ebenso werde ich stets für jeden Hofdienst, jedes Landesgubernium, und jede ambassade unzugängig bleiben, wie ich dir schon längst sagte.

Ich schließe hier mit der Bitte daß du über diese meine Marginalien zu deinem Vortrage unpartheiisch nachdenken mögest, denn vielleicht habe ich doch nicht Unrecht.

Ich höre du gehst erst Donnerstag und werde dir noch vorher meinen Brief nach Florenz schicken.

Dein alter Dietrich

GK 481, 6, 50.

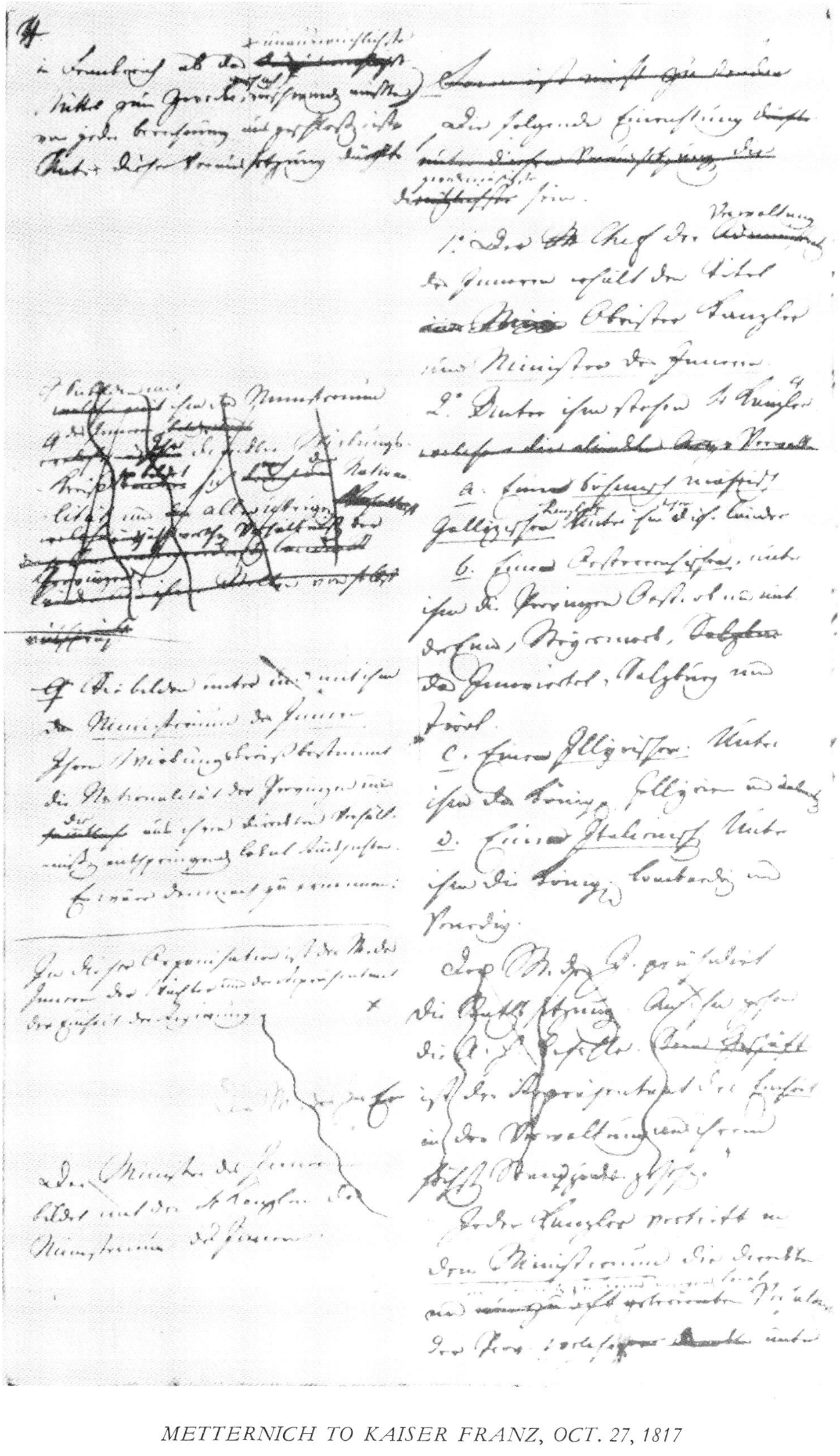

METTERNICH TO KAISER FRANZ, OCT. 27, 1817

No. 7

(From)

VORTRAG DES FÜRSTEN METTERNICH AN KAISER FRANZ
27. OKTOBER, 1817.

Ich gehe von dem Urbegriffe aus, daß das Fusions System, bei welchem als erste Maßregel die Benennung der Königreiche und Provinzen, wie es im Anfang der Revolution in Frankreich als das unausweichlichste Mittel zum Zwecke geschah, verschwinden müßte, von jeder Berechnung ausgeschlossen ist. Unter dieser Voraussetzung dürfte die folgende Einrichtung die zweckmäßigste sein:

1. Der Chef der Verwaltung des Innern erhält den Titel: O b e r - s t e r K a n z l e r und M i n i s t e r d e s I n n e r n.
2. Unter ihm stehen 4 Kanzler. Sie bilden unter und mit ihm das M i n i s t e r i u m d e s I n n e r n. Ihren Wirkungskreis bestimmen die Nationalität der Provinzen und die aus ihren directen Verhältnissen entspringenden Localrücksichten.

Es wäre demnach zu ernennen:

a) Ein b ö h m i s c h - m ä h r i s c h e r K a n z l e r. Unter ihm stehen diese Länder.

b) Ein Ö s t e r r e i c h i s c h e r [Kanzler]. Unter ihm stehen die Provinzen Oest[erreich] ob und unter der Enns, Steiermark, das Innviertel, Salzburg und Tirol.

c) Ein I l l y r i s c h e r [Kanzler]. Unter ihm das Königreich Illyrien und Dalmatien.

d) Ein I t a l i e n i s c h e r [Kanzler]. Unter ihm die Königreiche Lombardei und Venedig.

In dieser Organisation ist der M[inister] des Innern der Wächter und der Repräsentant der Einheit der Regierung.

Jeder Kanzler vertritt i n d e m M i n i s t e r i u m die direkten und nothwendig zu berücksichtigenden Localverhältnisse der Prov[inzen], welche unter seinem Wirkungskreise stehen.

StK. Vortr. 308, 70-138.

No. 8

(From the)

WIENER ZEITUNG

Mittewoche   den 24. Dezember 1817

Wien. Se. k.k. Majestät, deren väterliche Sorgfalt stäts auf das Wohl Ihrer geliebten Unterthanen gerichtet ist, haben in der Ueberzeugung, daß bey der großen Ausdehnung Ihres Reiches der allgemein nützliche Zweck der Regierung nur durch Einheit in den Anordnungen erreicht, und sie nur hierdurch die nöthige Kraft erhalten kann, doch bey Anwendung dieser Anordnung auf die Einzelnen den Kaiserstaat bildenden Bestandtheile die nöthige Rücksicht auf ihre besondere Lage und Verhältnisse, und die aus selben hervorgehende Verschiedenheit der Bedürfnisse, nie aus den Augen gelassen werden dürfe, sich bewogen gefunden, die bisher, unter der Benennung: Vereinigte Böhmisch-Oesterreichische und Galizische Hofkanzley und Zentral-Organisierungs-Hofkommission bestandenen obersten politischen Behörden, in ein eigenes Ministerium und Hofkanzley, unter der Benennung: Ministerium des Innern, zu vereinigen; welche Zentral-Stelle, unter einem Obersten Kanzler, Minister des Innern, aus drey Kanzlern, nemlich:

einem Böhmisch-Galizischen,

einem Oesterreichisch-Illyrischen, und

einem Lombardisch-Venezianischen, bestehen wird.

Diese Oberste politische Zentral-Stelle ist berufen, in den bisher in Hinsicht auf die innere Administrazion unter der Leitung der vereinigten Hofkanzley und Zentral-Organisirungs-Hofkommission gestandenen Provinzen und Ländern, die Wohlfahrt dieser Provinzen im ausgedehntesten Sinne zu befördern, die öffentlichen Lasten nach einem richtigen Ausmaße zu vertheilen, Bildung und Unterricht nach gleichförmigen Grundsätzen zu verbreiten, zugleich aber nicht minder Sorge zu tragen, daß unter steter Berücksichtigung des Grundbegriffes der Einheit des Kaiserthums, die Eigenthümlichkeiten der verschiedenen Bestandtheile desselben überall, wo es deren Lage und Verhältnisse erheischen, erhoben, erwogen und beachtet werden.

Eines der vorzüglichsten Augenmerke Sr. k.k. Majestät war dahin gerichtet, daß die für Ihre geliebten Unterthanen und deren Verhältnisse wohlthätig und schonend erprobte Einrichtung, in Folge welcher die Geschäfte ihren Zug von den Kreisämtern oder Delegazionen an die Gubernien oder Regierungen, und von diesen an die Oberste Zentral-Behörde nehmen,

auch fernerhin unverändert beybehalten werde, so daß sämmtliche Unterthanen, in administrativer Hinsicht eben so, wie in der Justiz-Verwaltung,
der Wohlthat dreyer Instanzen genießen, und ihr Verhältniß gegen die
politische Oberste Zentral-Behörde das bisherige bleibe.

Se. k.k. Majestät haben sonach ernannt:

Zum Obersten Kanzler und Minister des Innern, Allerhöchstihren Staats-
und Konferenz-Minister, Grafen Franz von Saurau.

Zum Böhmisch-Galizischen Kanzler, den Hofkanzler Grafen Prokop
v. Lazansky.

Zum zeitweiligen Stellvertreter des Oesterreichisch-Illyrischen Kanzlers,
den Vize-Kanzler Freyherrn Johann Nep. von Geißlern.

Zum Lombardisch-Venezianischen Kanzler, den Grafen Jakob Mellerio.

Se. k.k. Majestät haben geruhet, den Präsidenten der Obersten Justiz-
Stelle, Grafen v. Oettingen, von der bisher von ihm begleiteten Stelle aller-
gnädigst zu entheben, und zum Beweise Allerhöchstihrer Zufriedenheit mit
dessen treu geleisteten langjährigen Diensten, zu Allerhöchstihrem Staats-
und Konferenzminister zu ernennen.

Zum Präsidenten der Obersten Justizstelle, haben Se. k.k. Majestät den
Staats- und Konferenz-Minister, Grafen Wallis, ernannt, und demselben
unter Enthebung seiner bisherigen Dienstleistung beym Staatsrath, zugleich
das Präsidium der Hofkommission in Justiz-Gesetzsachen so wie Jenes der
Hofkommission in politischen Gesetzsachen zu übertragen geruhet.

DATA ON AUSTRIAN OFFICIALS APPEARING IN THIS WORK

(Occasionally the various sources, from which the information given here was gathered, contradict each other on particular items. Moreover, for lesser-known personalities, exact information is sometimes scarce. Thus, it is hoped that the reader will be understanding, should he come across some errors in these short biographies — which are meant to be no more than a convenience. For brevity's sake, I have used, as part of a lexicon style, a good many abbreviations; they are explained in the list preceding the Notes.)

APPONYI, Anton Rudolf, Gf., 1782-1852. From old Hungarian nobility. Long and varied dipl. career. Envoy in Stuttgart, then Karlsruhe. 1815 Florence. 1816 Rome. 1825 Naples. 1826-48 ambass. in Paris. Confidant of Mett., became after 1815 one of the most influential diplomats of his time. Patron of the arts as well as industry. His diaries provide a good source for the history of the Restoration Period (*Vingt-cinq Ans à Paris*, 4 vls, 1913-4).

BALDACCI, Anton Maximilian, Frhr. v., 1762-1841. Of an ancient Corsican family. Known for his reorganization plans of 1805-6. In the following years he demanded a *national* war ag. Napoleon. 1810 2nd vice-chancellor of the *Vereinigte Hofkanzlei*. 1811 Pres. of the *General Rechnungsdirektorium*. Responsible for the first real use of statistics. 1813 *Armeeminister*. He became a confidant of KF, was often occupied with administrative problems and was the author of various reform plans, some of which have been described by Krones. Cf. Bibliography: Krones.

BELLEGARDE, Heinr. Jos. Joh., Gf., 1756-1846. RGV. Son of the Saxon war minister, he began a distinguished military career in Habsburg service in 1771. 1788 col. in the Turkish war, 1796-9 FML in the campaigns ag. the French. 1800 GdC. 1801-5 Cmdr. in Venetia; 1806 in Galicia; 1809 fought ag. the French. Made FM and then *Hofkommissair* in Galicia. 1810, as Pres. of the HKR, reorganized Austrian army. His merits during the Rearmament Program earned him the praise of KF, who is said to have remarked, "Bellegarde is accomplishing the impossible." At the same time, Mett. won the high opinion of Bllg. which he was to hold henceforth. Describing the year 1811, Mett. wrote in his autobiography: "I have to mention here one man, in whose perspicacity, ability, and devotion, the emperor had a firm support and I an enlightened as faithful helper in the shaping of the empire's fortunes. This man was the then serving president of the *Hofkriegsrat*, Count Bellegarde. He possessed a most solid knowledge of the art of war, was well acquainted with my way of thinking, and was in complete agreement with my political views. His concern was not just to maintain the armed forces of the empire but, inconspicuously, to strengthen them for every possible test. He alone knew my intentions completely and he, as I, was not to be misled by those illusions sometimes taken to be public opinion; he understood, as I did, the value of letting someone else do the talking." (NP I, p. 119). 1813 he took command of the Italian army, CinC. in LV; 1815 representative of the non-existent viceroy. Left Italy 1816, after having repeatedly advised Vienna to grant the Italian provinces meaningful autonomy. 1820 again Pres. of the HKR. Retired from active service in 1826. He is described as having been of middle height, slender, of straight but not stiff military bearing, of giving the impression of calmness, kindliness, gallantry, and charm. He was a man of wide knowledge and proven ability. Cf. Bibliography: Smola.

BOMBELLES, Ludwig, Gf., 1780-1843. Raised in Naples, entered diplomatic service in Vienna. 1813 in Berlin; 1814 in Copenhagen; then with KF in Paris; then once more in Copenhagen. 1816 in Dresden; accompanied the emperor to Galicia in 1817. With Mett. in Karlsbad. 1820 envoy to Naples until the revolution; thereafter, Florence, Modena, Turin, and finally, Bern. In 1834 he married Marie Louise, the widow of Napoleon and Neipperg.

BUBNA v. Littiz, Ferd., Gf., 1768-1825. From ancient Bohemian nobility. 1784 entered military service. Distinguished career both as officer and diplomat. Participated in Turkish and all of the French wars. 1809 advanced to FML. 1813 div. cmdr. at Battle of Leipzig. 1814 mil. gov. in Turin. 1815 marched to Lyon, late in the year mil. cmdr. in Milan. From there crushed the revolt in Piedmont in 1821. Died suddenly in 1825. At his funeral, the Milanese municipality had had inscribed the words "Civis integer, Bellator fortis, Moderator sapiens" — words which were, acc. to the Italian historian Pedrotti, "spontaneous and heartfelt and not imposed as one might think" and which "mirrored the sincere feelings of the whole population." Pedrotti's judgment may serve as a suitable characterization: "Innumerable would be the proofs of Bubna's humaneness, of his affection for the Lombards . . . he never ceased to desire justice instead of arbitrariness, discipline instead of corruption and police methods. Stately of person, distinguished in manner, mundane in the better sense of the word, he frequented assiduously Milanese society which, in turn, was well disposed towards him, appreciating his conciliatory moderate spirit and his integrity of character. All of our historians, from Gualterio and Cusani to Tivaroni and Salata, acknowledge unanimously General Bubna's energy, instinct of command and inflexible firmness in pursuit of duty, while they remember simultaneously his respect for national rights, his condescension and loyalty towards his subordinates — qualities which never failed him, be it in the face of conspirations, political life, or war. Thus [his] name should pass on to posterity free from that legitimate rancor which accompanied the disappearance of so many other representatives of foreign rule." Cf. Bibliography: Pedrotti.

CHOTEK, Karl, Gf., 1783-1868. 1805 *Kreishauptmann* in Moravia; 1811 *Gubernialrat;* 1815 *Generalintendant* of the Austrian army in Italy. Then gov. in Trieste from where he conducted excavations in Aquileia and Pola; 1818 Tyrol; 1825 Pres. of *Studien-Hofkommission;* 1826 *Oberstburggf.* of Bohemia, in whose cultural renaissance he played an important part. Retired 1843.

DIETRICHSTEIN-Proskau-Leslie, Franz Jos. Joh., Fst., 1767-1854. At the age of 21, a captain, he was mentioned for bravery in the army reports of Gen. Laudon during the War ag. the Turks. Valor during the War ag. the French resulted in being decorated, in 1793, by the young KF. A major general at 29, he was sent on diplomatic missions to Berlin, then St. Petersburg. An exponent of Thugut's policies, he resigned his offices upon the latter's dismissal in 1805 and reputedly refused the offer to take over the foreign ministry. He retired to private life at the age of 34 and began to turn his keen mind to the study of statecraft and political theory; at the same time he devoted a great deal of time to the arts and sciences. In his many writings, most of which appear to be lost, he demonstrated versatility as well as vision. In 1817 he proposed an Education Ministry and seven national chancelleries for the seven major regions of the empire. In the 1820s, Metternich finally found a use for D., who had repeatedly asked his friend for some suitable employment in state service, by sending him on diplomatic missions to Paris and London (Letters to Mett., MAP, AC 6). For his humanity and philanthropy, the city of Vienna made him, in 1850, an honorary citizen. Somewhat typical of his individuality was his last wish: to be buried in the common cemetery of St. Marx — where, incidentally, Mozart is also buried. He was a close friend and unofficial advisor of Mett. as well as of Goëss. As much as Mett. valued D.'s opinion, he could become quite ungracious should such "outsiders' " views challenge or criticize his own. Something of this sort occurred in the summer of 1820, as a self-assured but severely annoyed Mett. urged KF to pay absolutely no attention to a tract D. had composed on the state of Austria's finances (Mett. Vortr. June 20, 1820, 327, 1, 106). Perhaps it was just the close friendship which brought Mett. to a rarely found outburst. His characterization of D. was on this occasion quite unkind although essentially correct. The tone of bitterness accompanying it may be attributed to Mett.'s deep disappointment with D.'s brilliant but fully impractical mind: "Prince D. writes yearly hundreds of sheets on all sorts of issues regarding public and private administration. In the meantime, one of the biggest fortunes of the Monarchy has flown through his hands. He has neither *Haus noch Hof* — he could not even hold on to his honor. He was a soldier and a diplomat and yet is nothing. He would have been a Field Marshal or a minister if he had just one bit of practicality. On the other hand, he is a good faithful man with vast theoretical knowledge, a true friend and full of the best intentions. His one need is writing. One has to let him write as long as he makes no misuse of his productions. If this should be the case, then I shall take it upon myself to bring him back on the right path in the friendliest possible manner."

ESTERHAZY v. Galantha, Paul Anton III, Fst., 1786-1866. RGV. Entered diplomatic service 1806; London and then Paris, where he came to assist ambassador Metternich. Returned to Vienna with Mett.; thence to Dresden. Again with Mett. in Allied headquarters and in Paris and London. Distinguished himself in the various negotiations of the 5th Coalition. 1815, upon the wish of the Prince Regent, appointed ambassador to London, to which post he was esp. suited through his knowledge of the land and its language. One of Mett.'s most trusted friends; his "eyes and ears" in Britain. Played important part in the London Conference of 1830. Illness prevented his return to England in 1842. Played a role in 1848, attempting to reconcile Habsburg and Hungarian interests. Sent in 1856 on his last mission, to Moscow. His last years were marred by the continuous and ever-worsening condition of his family fortune, which sumptuous living had fully dissipated. Died in Bavaria, where he had "exiled" himself after the complete bankruptcy of his enormous estates.

FICQUELMONT, Karl Ludwig, Gf., 1777-1857. Entered military service at 15, participated in 12 campaigns between 1795 and 1815. 1813 adjutant of Bllg. in Italy. 1814 named major gen. During the Hundred Days advanced to Lyon. Then joined the emperor and Mett. in Paris. In September, on Metternich's suggestion, he was named envoy to Stockholm. 1820 to Tuscany and Lucca; 1821 envoy to the restored Naples. Before that, he was attached to the exiled Neapolitan king — a very important post, especially during the campaign. Nevertheless, he was a sharp critic of Neapolitan reaction. In 1829 sent to St. Petersburg. The following year he received the rank of FML. 1839 returned to Vienna and represented Mett. during the latter's serious illness; 1840 named *St. und Konf. Minister;* 1843 GdC; 1847 *Adlatus* of Viceroy Rainer in Milan. On March 1, 1848, Pres. of the HKR; on the 18th, succeeded Mett. as foreign minister. However, as a close friend and associate of Mett., he soon was also suspect and forced to resign. Thereafter in retirement; he died in Venice. He was the author of numerous works on political and diplomatic affairs. Cf. Bibliography: Kantor.

FLORET, Engelbert Jos., Frhr. v., 1776-1827. "The faithful Floret" — most of his active life in the service of Mett. — accompanied the latter to Hungary in 1809; 1812 with Napoleon to Wilna. 1813 *Hofrat*; a friend of Hudelist, in frequent use at the Congr. of Vienna. Accompanied Mett. on his journey to Italy in 1815-16, again in 1817 and 1819. Also with him to Aachen in 1818, to Laibach in 1821. He often handled Mett.'s most intimate or delicate correspondence.

FRIMONT, Joh. Maria, Gf. v. Palota, Fst. v. Antrodocco, 1759-1831. Entered military service 1776. Participated in Bavarian, Turkish, and French campaigns. Won highest decorations. 1801 major gen.; 1805 in Italy; 1809 made FML and again served in Italy. 1813 GdC; 1814 gov. in Mainz, then 1815 in Italy, as Cmdr. against Murat, and thereupon in So. France. 1819 com. general in Venetia; 1821 headed the army against the revolution in Naples. 1825 CinC. in LV as successor of Bubna; however, he remained in Padua and later made his headquarters in Verona, not in Milan. 1831 suppressed revolt in Modena; thereupon Pres. of HKR shortly before his death.

GENTZ, Friedr. v., 1764-1832. A brilliant publicist of tireless energy, a remarkable capacity for political analysis, called "Secretary of Europe" for his work at the Congr. of Vienna. Mett.'s right-hand man in external affairs, esp. in regard to such questions as revolution, constitution, and the German states. Prepared protocols and drew up drafts at innumerable conferences. Subj. of biographies by Golo Mann and Paul Sweet. Cf. in Bibliography, further: Kircheisen, Rantzau, Wittichen.

GHISILIERI-Calderini, Filippo Carlo, Marchese. Originally from Bologna. He lost his property and was imprisoned by the French for his pro-Austrian activities. Entered Austrian service in 1814, becoming a member, somewhat later, of the COHC. Wrote several important memoranda for the StK on the situation in LV.

GOËSS, Peter, Gf., 1774-1846. RGV. Born in Florence, of a noble family from the southern Netherlands (orig. it had come from Portugal). Raised in Vienna; he entered state service at an early age. 1797 *Kreiskommissair,* assigned to supply Austrian troops retreating from Italy. Later similar services with Russian troops crossing Carinthia on the way to Italy. 1802 he participated in the organization of the former Venetian territories which had been granted to Austria after Campoformio (*Dalmatinische Hofstelle*). 1803 *Ajo* of the 9 yr. old crown prince Ferdinand. Then appointed *Hofrat* and pres. of the *gubernium* of Dalmatia in Zara. As was his practice throughout his career, he went to great pains to gather first-hand knowledge of the areas for which he was responsible. This, his enlightened administration in general, as well as his repeatedly demonstrated magnanimity earned him the affection of the inhabitants — a feeling reflected even in the writings of one modern historian from Dalmatia (Voinovitch). During a famine he distributed large quantities of grain which he paid for (supposedly an enormous price of 300,000 Gulden) out of his own pocket. 1804 also pres. of the Carinthian *Landrat.* 1805 held as hostage by the French for a refusal of the Carinthians to pay exorbitant war tributes. 1808 gov. in Trieste where he had to deal with the difficulties ensuing from Napoleon's continental system. 1809 Quartermaster Gen. of the army in Italy and Tyrol. Captured by the French but soon released after the Peace of Schönbrunn. 1812 gov. of Galicia in Lemberg. 1815 gov. of Venetia. Applied unsuccessfully for the post of Illyrian chancellor in 1818 (KF never named any one to this post). 1819 appointed Lombardo-Venetian chancellor with the ministry of interior in Vienna. 1823 also pres. of the *Studien-Hofkommission*. Received a series of honorary high positions in the later years of his life. 1845 chancellor of the Order of the Iron Crown. Cf. Bibliography: Schulz.

GUICCIARDI, Diego, Gf., 1756-1837. Originally from the Val Tellin. Participated in local politics, then served in the Cisalpine Republic and then in the Napoleonic Kingdom of Italy as police director of Milan. He was appointed member of the Italian Senate, of which he became chancellor in 1814. In that capacity, he opposed the attempt to keep Eugene Beauharnais as King of Italy. Retained in service by Bellegarde. 1816 he helped organize the CBA, although reluctantly. As the new organization of LV went into effect in 1818, he became v.pres. of the Milanese *gubernium*. Later he was appointed chancellor of the Order of the Iron Crown.

GUICCIARDI, Francesco Giuseppe, Gf., 1806-1807 pres. of the Carniolan dept. of the *Vereinigten Hofkanzlei*. Although one of the more important members of the COHC (he signed, along with Lazansky, many of its proclamations), and one of its experts on Italian affairs, his influence was apparently limited.

HAAGER v. Altensteig, Franz, Frhr., 1750-1816. An injury suffered from a fall from his horse ended his career as an officer; 1786 entered state service. At first in Vienna; 1803 *Hofrat*. 1809 helped establish armed militia (*Landwehr*) and became v.pres. of the police, then 1813 pres., a post which he held until his death.

HAUER, Franz Seraph, Frhr. v., 1777-1822. An expert administrator, he began his career in 1797 at the Galician dept. of the *Hofkanzlei*. 1807 *Hofrat* and *Referent* for Galicia. Friend of Baldacci, whom he accompanied in the campaign of 1813. 1815 succeeded Goëss as gov. of Galicia. His knowledge of and sympathy for the land in which he served, as well as his humane manner, were long remembered there.

HILLER, Joh., Frhr. v., 1748-1819. Military career. 1789 colonel. 1794 Italian campaign; 1796 on the Rhine; 1801 Croatia; 1805 Cmdr. in Tyrol; 1807 again in Croatia; 1809 Cmdr. of all Austrian forces west of the Enns; commanded right wing at Aspern, thereupon made FZM; 1810 Cmdr. in Croatia; 1811 in Slavonia-Syrmia; 1813 Cmdr. of Inner-Austrian army which soon was called the Italian army. Replaced by Bellegarde in Dec., 1813. 1814 Cmdr. in Transylvania, then in Galicia, until his death.

HOPPÉ, Friedr. v., 1760-1821. As a confidant of Metternich, he was often used by the StK. for special and secret missions. As a young man, in 1783, to Paris; he handled secret corr. of Marie Antoinette. Came to StK. in 1796; 1816 became chancellery director of the foreign section of the StK.

HUDELIST, Jos. v., 1759-1818. Born and raised in Carinthia, studied at the Univ. of Vienna; he began a diplomatic career as priv. secr. of Cardinal Hrzan in Rome. After four years, he moved on to Naples in 1791. 1798 embassy secr. in Berlin with functions of envoy. 1801 with the embassy in St. Petersburg where he distinguished himself in the difficult negotiations aimed at winning the Russian court to an Austrian alliance. 1803 made *Hofrat* and assigned to the StK. 1809 he saved the papers and the payroll of the StK from the invading French. 1813 became *Staats- und Konferenzrat*. He had already become, through his ability and activity, the StK's unofficial guide, especially in the first years of Metternich's tenure. During the latter's long and frequent absences in 1813-14, he practically ran the department. He himself headed the interior section and helped in reorganizing the state chancellery. His sudden death, while Mett. was at the Congress of Aachen, left a vacancy difficult to fill. Metternich's own appraisal was the following: "He had essential qualities not to be found any better and merits not to be replaced. My own work will double or even triple for some time, as a result. I've been so used to lean upon him in relegating to him interior matters and details, so that I'll always regret not being able any longer to have all these things done by him; certainly there won't be a suitable replacement for a while" (NP III, 126). His correspondence with Metternich is valuable for the richness of views and insights on all the issues of the day. Cf. Bibliography: Skokan. An obituary can be found in the *Wiener Zeitung*, Dec. 21, 1818.

HÜGEL, Clemens Wenzel, Frhr. v., 1792-1849. Diplomat and writer. Son of an Austrian diplomat, he studied at Heidelberg and Göttingen. He began his dipl. career as assistant to his father in 1810. 1812 in Paris, then accompanied Bellegarde on the Italian campaign of 1813-1814, during which he kept a journal which still lies in the Vienna archives. 1815 to Madrid. 1817 member of the party which escorted Archduchess Leopoldine to Brazil. 1818 again in Madrid. Experienced the revolution there, events which he described in a book (*Spanien und die Revolution*, Leipzig, 1821). 1821 to Berlin, 1828 on to Paris. 1840 returned to Vienna, as *Hofrat* became asst. to Mett. in the StK. 1846 appointed director of the *HH&St. Archiv*. Arrested but soon released during the revolution of 1848. The excesses during the autumn of that year severely depressed him and led to a mental breakdown. He died soon thereafter. The author of various tracts, including one on a conservative position in regard to the freedom of the press (1847), he was well known in literary circles. He was a patron of the arts, a man of cosmopolitan outlook, fine taste and vast knowledge.

INZAGHI, Karl Borromäus, Gf., 1777-1856. Administrator, served in Galicia but also in the army during various Napoleonic campaigns. 1818 became gov. in Laibach, then one year later moved on to Venice, replacing Goëss. Some years later, in Brünn. Then became *Hofkanzler*; upon the death of Mittrowski, he was given the post of *Oberster Kanzler*, which he held until 1848. He was also pres. of the *Studien-Hof-kommission*. He founded various schools and hospitals, esp. in Graz. Like many members of noble families, he devoted much of his private life to a study of the humanities.

KAUNITZ, Alois Wenzel, Fst., 1774-1848. Last prince of that line, a brother-in-law of Mett. and grandson of the great *Staatskanzler*. Diplomat, envoy in Dresden, Copenhagen, Naples, and Madrid.

KÜBECK v. Kübau, Karl Friedr., Frhr., 1780-1855. A man of remarkable ability and talent and of a wide range of interests. Already as a boy he attracted the attention of the young Kaiser Franz. Various members of the aristocracy recognized the possibilities of the gifted youth and he became the protegé of Gf. Dietrichstein and Gf. Wallis. Despite his humble origins (his father was a tailor) he advanced rapidly to the highest circles and positions. His career, as described in his autobiography (*Tagebücher*), makes for fascinating reading and gives valuable sidelights on the history of Austria for that time. His diaries contain especially colorful portraits of many Austrian officials, such as Wallis, Chorinsky, Zichy, and Ugarte. Already at 32 he was *Hofrat*. 1814 he was employed by the COHC to make the basic proposals regarding the future administration of LV. Although an independent and perceptive worker, he followed in this case the rather specific instructions of the emperor, not being able to do much else under the circumstances. Later he made a name for himself as a financial expert, and helped in organizing the Austrian National Bank. In 1826 he was raised to the *Freiherrnstand*. He

also earned the trust of Mett.; there exists an extensive corr. between them, also published in K.'s *Tagebücher*. He played an important part in the building of Austria's rail-
roads. He is a good example of a man able to reconcile his early ardor for reform
with the realities of a successful state service career, without, however, compromising
away his ideals. He did what he could in helping Austria along toward modernization.

LATTERMANN, Christoph, Frhr. v., 1753-1835. Officer in Bavarian and Turkish
campaigns. 1793-4 with the army on the Rhine; 1796 earned high decorations for
bravery; 1797 major gen. in Italy. Severely wounded at Marengo. 1805 cmdr. in
Bohemia; 1807 in Hungary; 1809 on Croatian mil. frontier; 1810 with HKR; 1813
FZM and provisional mil. gov. in Illyria; 1814 to Venice, then pres. of the Mil. Court
of Appeals; 1833 raised to rank of FM.

LAZANSKY, Prokop, Gf., 1771-1823. 1813 *Hofkanzler;* July 1814 became pres. of
the COHC; 1817 Bohemian-Galician chancellor, also pres. of the *Studien-Hofkommission*.
His Josephinistic tendencies, esp. his desire for centralization, often stood in conflict
with Mett.'s ideas on administration.

MERVELDT, Maximilian, Gf., 1764-1815. Of Westphalian nobility. An officer and
diplomat, he served in the Turkish and various French wars. 1800 FML. 1805 envoy to
the king of Prussia, in an attempt to win him to the Coalition ag. Napoleon. 1806-1808
amb. in St. Petersburg. 1813 GdC. 1814 amb. to London, where he died.

METTERNICH-Winneburg, Clemens Lothar Wenzel, Gf., then Fst., 1773-1859. RGV.
Born in Koblenz, educated in Mainz and Strassburg; through a fortunate marriage with
the granddaughter of the great Kaunitz, he established for the displaced Metternichs a
good social position in Vienna. 1801 envoy in Dresden; 1803 in Berlin; 1805, 32 years
old, ambassador to Napoleon in Paris; 1809, after the unsuccessful rising of Austria
against the French, he was summoned to take over the Office of Foreign Affairs (*Dirigieren-
der Minister der Auswärtigen Geschäfte*). His extraordinarily successful diplomacy lead
to Austria's remarkable recovery and to its becoming the decisive weight against Napoleon. At the Congress of Vienna, with the aid of Castlereagh, he successfully blocked
the designs of Prussia and Russia to appropriate all of Saxony and Poland respectively.
His external policy envisioned a long recuperation of Europe through repose based on
acceptance of legitimacy. The German difficulties of 1819 and the Mediterranean Revolutions of 1820-1822 forced him to reappraise his previously somewhat lenient views
on internal policy, esp. regarding Italy. In 1821 he became *HH&St. Kanzler*, but was
not able to gain the influence over Kaiser Franz on internal affairs which he had
regarding external ones. Also, after 1826, the increasing rivalry with Kolowrat made
his position ever more difficult and prevented him from following a course as he might
have wished and done with the aging emperor. During the reign of Ferdinand he
formed, along with Kolowrat and Archduke Ludwig, the so-called ruling "triumvirate".
A prolific writer, there exists an enormous correspondence with various individuals.
Mett. never tired of explaining his political theories, and even in the days prior to
1848, these are sometimes remarkably openminded and advanced in their positions.
Nevertheless, his dogmatizing led more and more to the view that progress is natural
and can not be forced, that innovations must wait upon quiet conditions (which never
came), and that under no circumstances might concessions be extracted from authority
through threat or force. His rigidity meant a rigidity of the whole Austrian state —
unfortunately, some of his essentially correct principles and prognoses were thrown
onto the heap in 1848. After an exile in England (where he renewed old acquaintances)
and Belgium, he was allowed to return to Vienna in 1851. He spent the last years of

his life as a daily-consulted elder statesman, active until the end. He died in 1859, just before the defeat of Austria in Lombardy, which meant the loss of that land which had cost him so much concern.

MITTROWSKI v. Mittrowitz, Anton Friedr., Gf., 1770-1842. RGV. Administration expert, began career 1791 with Austrian-Boh. chancellery. 1796-1799 *Kreishauptmann* in Bohemia and Galicia. Then, *Stadthauptmann* in Vienna. 1801 *Hofrat* with the *Polizei-Hofstelle*. 1802 v. pres. of Lower Austrian *gubernium*. 1804 he held the same post in Prag. 1815-27 gov. of Moravia and Austrian Silesia. In Brünn he is especially remembered for his activity in all sorts of cultural endeavors. He financed the publication of several important document collections. 1827 *Hofkanzler* and pres. of the *Studien-Hofkommission*. 1830 until his death, *Oberster Kanzler der Vereinigten Hofkanzlei*. His special interests were devoted to schools, libraries and to the development of modern transportation.

NEIPPERG, Adam Albert, Gf., 1775-1829. A dashing officer, he distinguished himself in many campaigns, during one of which he acquired his famous eye-patch. He rose to FML; in 1814 he escorted the Empress Marie Louise from France, via Geneva and Savoy, to Vienna, and then to Parma. His presence, and undoubtedly his charm, helped Marie Louise to forget all too quickly her husband Napoleon. She became Duchess of Parma, and there, Neipperg — by this time her acknowledged lover — became virtual ruler. They had several children, the first (the later Fürst Montenuovo = Neuberg = Neipperg) being illegitimate. Mett. nevertheless praised Marie Louise to her father for her "impeccable *political* behavior". Upon the death of Napoleon, she and Neipperg were married. He was an able administrator and an effective proponent for Habsburg might on the Italian peninsula.

NUGENT of Westmeath, Laval, Gf., 1777-1862. Born in Ireland, of an old noble family. He entered Habsburg military service on the Continent at an early age, participated in the Allied siege of Mainz in 1793, fought at Turin and various other battlefields of Italy, then with the English in Spain in 1812. 1813 he made the suggestion to appeal to Croatian national feeling and thus to bring about an insurrection against the French. He turned this project into reality with a small force of 2000 men. He took the citadel of Trieste on Oct. 30, 1813, and then proceeded, along with English troops, into Italy. There he commanded the Austrian western corps, often acting somewhat independently. 1815 he rose to the rank of FML in the campaign against Murat. He occupied Rome and then advanced to Naples, where he remained in the service of the restored Bourbon king until the revolution of 1820. Later, he resumed his service with the Austrian army and served in various parts of the Monarchy. In 1848 he took part in action against Hungarian insurgents. He fought under Radetzky; his last battle was Solferino, where he held the rank of FM.

PILAT, Jos. Anton, Edler v., 1782-1865. Mett.'s private secretary in 1811; accompanied him to London in 1814. A well educated man, always interested in the arts, literature and the humanities, he was one of the leading figures in a circle of Catholic intellectuals in Vienna. He was one of Mett.'s most loyal friends. 1815 he became editor of the *Österreichischer Beobachter*, at which post he remained until 1848. Cf. Bibliography: Baxa, Zechner.

PORCIA, Alfons Gabriel, Fst., 1761-1835. Member of an ancient Italian noble family which had served the House of Austria for centuries; he too made a career of state service. 1819 gov. in Trieste. He applied unsuccessfully for the post left vacant by Goëss' departure to Vienna in 1819. Instead, he did become v.pres. of the *gubernium* of Venice in 1820. He devoted much of his time to the study of the natural sciences.

REUSS-PLAUEN, Heinrich, Fst., 1751-1825. Long and successful mil. career. Fought in Turkish and French wars. 1797 FML with army of Archduke Charles. 1813 signed the convention of Ried, whereby Bavaria deserted Napoleon and joined the Allies. 1814 FZM and temp. mil. gov. of Venice, a post which he relinquished in 1815. Cmdr. in Galicia 1819. FM upon his retirement in 1824.

REVICZKY v. Revisnye, Adam, Gf., 1786-1862. As bright young man, he quickly advanced to the rank of *Gubernialrat*, then *Hofrat;* in 1820 *Sektionschef* of Viceroy Rainer's chancellery in Milan. 1822 v.pres. of the Galician *gubernium* in Lemberg. There he compiled the information and the statistics comprising the "White Paper" issued by Austria on the government in LV, in response to a request of Lord Aberdeen of the British Parliament.

ROSCHMANN, Anton Leopold, Frhr. v., 1771-1830. Of a renowned Tyrolean family, he entered Austrian state service in 1800. 1809 land commissioner for Tyrol. Misunderstood for the mediatory role which he had to play during the Tyrolean uprising under Andreas Hofer, he earned the lifelong hatred of many involved, esp. the "patriotic" historian Hormayr. In Dec. 1813, he became provisional *Landeschef* for the "Italian and Illyrian" parts of Tyrol. He had soon thereafter — in 1814 — responsibility for organizing the entire province. However, suspicious Tyroleans made loud their lack of confidence and he was replaced in 1815. Not true is the charge that he followed a centralization policy and tried to prevent an estates-constitution. He had close contacts with Gentz and Adam Müller.

SARDAGNA v. Meanberg und Hohenstein, Jos., Frhr., 1774-1832. Born in Innsbruck of a South Tyrolean family. He studied at various Austrian universities and began his career serving with various courts and agencies concerned with judicial affairs. 1814 became *"Hofrath bei der Obersten Justizstelle und Referent für Justizsachen".* 1815-1817 he played an important part in the introduction of the Austrian law code into the Italian provinces — a measure ag. which he pleaded in vain. Nevertheless, his excellent services were rewarded in 1817 with the v.presidency of the High Court of Appeals in Verona. Because of illness, he returned to Vienna in 1819, but even before that he indicated that he was not happy with his post, applying unsuccessfully for the position of dipl. secretary to the viceroy in Milan. KF had turned down this application with the reason that the viceroy would not indulge in such activity. 1821-1822, during the conspiracy trials (Confalonieri, Andryane *et al.*), he was Mett.'s confidential investigator and coordinator of judicial procedure among various Italian states. He recommended clemency. 1828 v.pres., shortly thereafter, pres. of the *Hofkommission in Justizsachen.*

SAURAU, Franz Jos., Gf., 1760-1832. RGV. From Styrian nobility. Began his career at municipal posts. 1789 *Stadthauptmann* in Vienna. After 1790, assisted Thugut in matters of internal administration. Then *Regierungspres.* of Lower Austria, further, *Finanz- und Polizeiminister;* in latter activity won the admiration of KF for his zeal in discovering conspiracies. 1797 organized Styrian militia ag. the French and raised 37,000 men in eight days. As finance minister he tried to prevent the threatening state bankruptcy. 1801 resigned with the cabinet of Thugut. Thereupon amb. to St. Petersburg where he tried unsuccessfully to win Russia's alliance. 1805 *Hofkommissair* in Styria; organized the Landwehr of Inner Austria. 1810 pres. of the *gubernium* of Lower Austria (plus what was left of Upper Austria). 1814 *Hofkommissair* for the organization of the Illyrian Provinces. In the following year, special commissioner in Italy during the campaign ag. Murat. Then became civil gov. in Milan, where he remained, despite

Mett.'s efforts to have him sent as amb. to Spain, until Dec. 1817. Then he was appointed *Oberster Kanzler* of the new ministry of the interior. This post he held until his retirement shortly before his death. He was a capable and efficient organizer, strongly influenced by rationalistic principles; perhaps in his anticlericalism were his Josephinistic attitudes most apparent. Like many of his colleagues, he was widely-read and took an intense interest in the arts and sciences.

SEDLNITZKY v. Choltic, Jos., Gf., 1778-1855. Member of a Moravian family (originally from Poland). A university graduate, he became *Kreiskommissair* in Brünn and shortly thereafter assistant of Gf. Wallis (*Presidialsekretär*). Held various administrative posts. 1815 vice pres. of the *Polizei Hofstelle*; he advanced to the presidency upon Haager's death in 1816. He held this post until 1848. The fiercest villain for the liberal and nationalistic critics of *Vormärz* Austria, he actually was a many-sided and probably misunderstood personality. His ideas on organization and administration tended to be centralistic. His police apparatus, compared with modern ones, was more of an instrument of harassment than one of brutal suppression. Those who plotted ag. the state, esp. in LV, had less an argument ag. him than those whose letters were consistently opened or those who felt their right of free expression was stifled by his ridiculous and petty-minded censors. All this seemed necessary in his holding up dutifully a patriarchal absolute system which was increasingly submerged by the stream of the times. Thus he was an unfortunate tool. Ironically, as a private person he was kind and gentle. After his retirement in 1848, he was able to devote himself fully to philanthropy and patronage, thereby, as the ADB puts it, rounding his life out on a good note. Cf. Bibliography: Marx.

SOMMARIVA, Annibale, Marchese, 1755-1829. Of an old Lombard noble stock. Began military career 1771. Fought in Turkish war. 1800 mil. gov. of Tuscany. 1807 FML. 1811 Inspector Gen. of troops. 1812 in Hungary. 1813-1814 in No. Italy. In April, 1814, entered Milan as representative of Allied powers. There he did much to calm a tense situation. Reorganized Austrian-Italian regiments. 1817 GdC. 1820 made commanding general. 1825 commanded the guards at the imperial palace in Vienna.

STADION, Joh. Philipp Karl Jos., Gf., 1763-1824. A statesman distinguished for his part in the patriotic war against the French in 1809. His role therein is best described in Rössler's *Österreichs Kampf um Deutschlands Befreiung*. From 1805 to 1809 he was *Min. für Auswärtige Angelegenheiten*; replaced by Mett. as the failure of his policy was made apparent by defeat. He returned in 1813 as Finance Minister and held this post for the rest of his life. He is responsible for a strict economy; the first Austrian national bank is largely his and Kübeck's work. Cf. Bibliography: Rössler, Langsam.

STRASSOLDO, Julius Jos., Gf., 1773-1830. 1814 imperial commissioner in Parma, which he took over in the name of Marie Louise. After the defeat of Murat in 1815, he headed a provisional commission in Bologna. Became member of the COHC. 1816 he was appointed Police Director in Milan. 1818 became *Regierungspres.* (gov.) of Lombardy, where he remained until his death. Like Sedlnitzky he was a target for Italian historians; according to his biography in *Wurzbach*, he, like so many other Austrian public figures, devoted the last years of his life to works of charity, founded schools and libraries, and even raised endowment funds for widows and orphans. He was a true and yet critical servant of the Habsburg cause. Although gallant and gentle, he had serious differences with some Austrian officials in Milan. He protested ag. Vienna's conformity policy much as Bellegarde and Bubna had done. Cf. Bibliography: Stern.

STÜRMER, Ignaz Lorenz, Frhr. v., 1752-1829. A former Jesuit, he began the study of jurisprudence after his order had been dissolved. 1780 served with the *Internuntius* (amb.) in Constantinople, rendering esp. valuable service as interpreter (capitulation of Belgrade 1789). Under Thugut, he was briefly in the StK. For a short period in the Netherlands. 1801 *Hofrat*, 1802-1818 himself Internuntius in Constantinople. 1819 became Hudelist's successor and took over the interior section of the StK. He had been made Frhr. in 1813 and later became a magnate of Hungary.

TOMMASICH, Franz, Frhr. v., 1761-1831. Spent most of his mil. career as a cmdr. in various Croatian and Dalmatian areas. He rose to the rank of FML, conquered Dalmatia in 1813. He was mil. cmdr. in Zara for the last 18 years of his life.

UGARTE, Alois, Gf., 1749-1817. RGV. Of a noble family originally from Spain. 1769 *Appellationsrat* in Bohemia, then *Gubernialrat* in Galicia. 1786 *Hofrat* in Vienna. Governor of Moravia before becoming, in 1802, chancellor of the *Vereinigten Hofkanzlei*. 1813 *Staats- und Konferenz Minister* and *Oberster Kanzler*. He was one of the emperor's advisors on interior policy. KF bestowed the Order of the Golden Fleece upon him, as a last act of favor, on his deathbed.

WALLIS, Jos., Gf., 1767-1818. RGV. Of a Bohemian family originally from Ireland. Administrative and legal expert. 1798 *Hofrat* with the *Vereinigten Hofkanzlei's* Bohemian dept. Then various judicial positions. 1805 gov. of Moravia then gov. (*Oberstburggraf*) of Bohemia. 1810 Pres. of the *Hofkammer* (finances). Effected the notorious state bankruptcy of 1811. 1813 *St. und Konf. Min.* 1817 *Pres. der Obersten Justizstelle und Gesetzgebungs-Hofkommission.* In Bohemia he showed an active interest in charities, schools and agricultural projects. Kübeck's *Tagebücher* cast some light on his strange character. He was a close advisor of KF.

WESSENBERG, Joh. Phil., Frhr. v., 1773-1858. Since 1801 he served at various diplomatic posts in Germany. 1813 to London, where he participated in all sorts of negotiations. In June of 1814 he was sent to LV to investigate economic conditions and to make some proposals in regard to Austrian organization policy there. He came out strongly against any attempt to make the Italian Provinces into "German" ones. Upon Mett.'s request he was made v.pres. of the COHC in order to give the StK a better voice in reorganization proceedings. However, he had little opportunity to take advantage of this position since he, along with Gentz and Mett. made up the Austrian team at the Congress of Vienna; he was second Austrian plenipotentiary there. Esp. recognized was his work on German affairs and on the organization of the German Confederation. After the Congress he seems to have developed views not in conformity with those of Metternich, esp. in regard to the Karlsbad Decrees. He retired temporarily and undertook private journeys — a journal of his trip to Provence in 1822 still lies in the St.K. archives. In 1830 he was envoy to the Kingdom of the Netherlands. His position on the Belgian secession aroused the displeasure of Mett. and caused his leaving state service once again. In 1848 the turn of events brought him back as Mett.'s successor as head of the Foreign Office, and as Pres. of the new cabinet. For the 2 vol. biography by A. Arneth, cf. Bibliography; also: Wittichen.

ZICHY-Vasonykeö, Karl, Gf., 1753-1826. RGV. As a young man he held various administrative posts in Illyria and Hungary. 1790 pres. of a *Hofkommission* concerned with financial troubles. 1808 *St. und Konf. Min.* 1809 *Armeemin.* in charge of the army's pay. 1813 undertook supervision of internal affairs directly from the emperor. Made proposals for the organization of the Illyrian Provinces which were accepted for the most part by KF. He was a good speaker, a man of fine taste, a patriot devoted to Hungarian interests within the Monarchy, and a close friend and advisor of the emperor.

ABBREVIATIONS

A full listing of archives collections and sections in proper order can be found in the Bibliography, under the heading "Unpublished Primary Sources". Full names as well as biographical data on various Austrian officials can be found in Appendix B. Book and article titles and authors' names abbreviated in the Notes are cited, when possible, in full in the Bibliography. The numerals after an abbreviated archives collection designation are always, first, the carton or fascicle number; second, the convolute or folder number (if any); and third, the folio or page number. If only two sets of numerals appear (e.g. Vortr. 381, 51), then they are the carton/fascicle and page/folio numbers. With the Kaiser-Franz-Akten (KFA), the first set of numerals is followed by another in parentheses — the former is the new, the latter the old (prior to 1955) numeration.

AGENCIES, ARCHIVES, AND DOCUMENTS

StK = Staatskanzlei
StR = Staatsrat
HKR = Hofkriegsrat
HKz = Hofkanzlei
COHC = Central-Organisierungs-Hof-Commission
CBA = Central-Beobachtungs-Anstalt
PRO = Public Record Office
FO = Foreign Office
ASM = Archivio di Stato, Milano
MAP = Metternich Familien-Archiv, Plass/Prag
VA&AMI = Verwaltungsarchiv und Archiv des Ministeriums des Innern
WHHStA = Wiener Haus-, Hof- und Staatsarchiv
Vortr. = Vorträge
Nw = Notenwechsel
Int. Korr. = Interiora, Korrespondenzen
Prov. = Provinzen
Böh. = Böhmen
Dalm. = Dalmatien
Gal. = Galizien
Ill. = Illyrien
KKG = Kärnten, Krain, Görz

KS = Kroatien-Slavonien
Sb. = Siebenbürgen
Ung. = Ungarn
LV = Lombardo-Venetien
Geh. Korr. = Geheime Korrespondenz
GK = Große Korrespondenz
FA = Friedens-Akten
St. Abt. = Staaten-Abteilungen
Eng. = England
Lond. = London
Frank. = Frankreich
Russ. = Rußland
St. Pbg. = Sankt Petersburg
Sard. = Sardinien
Tos. = Toscana
Weis. or W/ = Weisungen
GA = Gesandtschafts-Archiv
Ber. = Berichte
KArch. = Kabinettsarchiv
KFA = Kaiser-Franz-Akten
KA = Kabinetts-Akten
AKA = Alte Kabinetts-Akten
KK = Kabinettskanzlei
Konf. A-a = Konferenz-Akten, Serie a
StRA = Staatsrats-Akten

Prot. = Protokoll Band
Ind. = Indices Band
Bill. = Billetten/Billetts
AC = Acta Clementina
COHCA = Central-Organisierungs-Hof-
  Commissions-Akten
HKzA = Hofkanzlei-Akten
AhH = Allerhöchstes Handschreiben
AhR = Allerhöchste Resolution
AhE = Allerhöchster Entschluß

AhK = Allerhöchstes Kabinettsschreiben
Res. aug. = Resolutio augustissimi
Kais. Pat. = Kaiserliches Patent
Gut. = Gutachten
a-m = Aide-memoire
Prokl. = Proklamation
Prom. = Promemoria
fasc. = fascicle
conv. = convolute
f. = folio

PERSONS AND RANK

KF = Kaiser Franz
Mett. = Metternich
Bllg. = Bellegarde
Latt. = Lattermann
Bub. = Bubna
Wess. = Wessenberg
Guicc. = Guicciardi
Strass. = Strassoldo
Est. = Esterhazy
Castl. = Castlereagh
App. = Apponyi
Bald. = Baldacci
Hud. = Hudelist
Stürm. = Stürmer
Lebz. = Lebzeltern
Laz. = Lazansky

D. = Dietrichstein

FM = Feldmarschall
FML = Feldmarschall Leutnant
FZM = Feldzeugmeister
GdC = General der Cavallerie
Gen. = General
Cmdr. = Commander
CinC. = Commander in chief
Gov. = Governor
Gouv. = Gouverneur
VK = Vizekönig
RGV = Ritter des Goldenen Vliess
Ehzg. = Erzherzog
Fst. = Fürst
Gf. = Graf
Frhr. = Freiherr

PERIODICALS AND PUBLISHED COLLECTIONS

ADB = Allgemeine Deutsche Biographie
AHR = American Historical Review
AÖG = Archiv für österreichische
  Geschichte
AÖR = Archiv für öffentliches Recht
AS = Archivio Storico
ASL = Archivio Storico Lombardo
AWC = Akten des Wiener Congresses
AV = Archiv des Völkerrechts
AZ = Archivalische Zeitschrift
BSIR = Biblioteca di Storia Italiana
  Recente
DALV = Deutsches Archiv für Landes-
  und Volksforschung

DLZ = Deutsche Literaturzeitung
DR = Deutsche Revue
EHR = English Historical Review
GWU = Geschichte in Wissenschaft und
  Unterricht
HJb = Historisches Jahrbuch
HV = Historische Vierteljahresschrift
HZ = Historische Zeitschrift
JCEA = Journal of Central European
  Affairs
JHI = Journal of the History of Ideas
JKGS = Jahrbuch für Kultur und
  Geschichte der Slawen
JMH = Journal of Modern History

JVGSW = Jahrbuch des Vereines für die Geschichte der Stadt Wien

MIÖG = Mitteilungen des Instituts für österreichische Geschichtsforschung

MÖIG = Mitteilungen des österreichischen Instituts für Geschichtsforschung

MÖStA = Mitteilungen des österreichischen Staatsarchivs

NP = Nachgelassene Papiere

NRS = Nuova Rivista Storica

NR = Neue Rundschau

ÖR = Österreichische Rundschau

ÖUR = Österreichisch-Ungarische Revue

ÖZÖR = Österreichische Zeitschrift für Öffentliches Recht

PJb = Preußische Jahrbücher

RH = Revue Historique

RHD = Revue d'Histoire Diplomatique

RP = Review of Politics.

RSI = Rivista Storica Italiana

RSR· = Rassegna Storica del Risorgimento

RSRI = Rivista Storica del Risorgimento Italiano

UJb = Ungarisches Jahrbuch

WP = World Politics

ZG = Zeitschrift für Geschichtswissenschaft

ZO = Zeitschrift für Ostforschung

ZÖR = Zeitschrift für öffentliches Recht

ZPG = Zeitschrift für Preußische Geschichte

ZRGG = Zeitschrift für Religions- und Geistesgeschichte

NOTES

INTRODUCTION

[1] For a fuller discussion of this point, the reader may refer to the bibliographic note at the end of this study.

[2] Metternich to Lieven, Dec. 28, 1818, *Geist und Herz verbündet, Metternichs Briefe an die Gräfin Lieven*, (Mika ed.); also, Nov. 16, 1820, E.C.C. Corti, *Metternich und die Frauen*, II, p. 147.

[3] Some biographical information on a number of Austrian officials with whom Metternich had to deal can be found in Appendix B.

[4] Especially Gentz and Metternich made it a point to distinguish carefully between an estates-constitution (*Landesständische Verfassung*), which they favored, and one based on popular representation (*Repräsentative Verfassung*), which they felt would spell the ruin of a multinational state held together by an absolute monarch.

[5] Metternich, NP III, p. 77.

[6] Karl Othmar Frhr. v. Aretin, "Metternich's Verfassungspläne, 1817/1818", *HJb*, LXXIV (1955), pp. 718-725.

[7] Golo Mann, *Gentz — Secretary of Europe* (London, 1946), p. 280.

CHAPTER I

[1] "Voici que les forces anglaises et autrichiennes se dirigent vers ce pays pour lui rendre la liberté et l'indépendance! . . . Souvenez-vous que vous portez un nom glorieux et combattez, comme ont fait les Espagnols et les Russes pour recouvrer votre indépendance." Proclamation of Adm. Lowen, Oct. 10, 1813, to the Ragusans. Voinovitch, *Histoire de Dalmatie*, II, p. 683.

[2] Correspondence between the Austrian general Millotinovich and the Russian Colonel Nikitsch, Apr. 1814, Prov/Dalm. 7. Further the negotiations between Gen. Tommasich and Capt. Hoste: Vortr. Colloredo to the HKR, Feb. 12, 1814, *ibid.*

[3] StK to the "k.k. Kommandierenden" in Slavonia, FZM Baron Hiller, Jan. 12, 1813, Prov/KS 1.

[4] Ehzg. Franz Ferdinand v. Österreich-Este to Mett., Jan. 23, 1814; to Hud., Mar. 16, 1814, Prov/Dalm. 7, special folder.

[5] Notes to Castlereagh and Nesselrode, also correspondence regarding Col. Nikitsch and the Montenegrin disorders, as well as a letter of Emperor Alexander to the Metropolitan of Montenegro, *ibid.*

[6] FZM Baron Lattermann to Mett., May 5, 1814, Prov/Ill. 15.

[7] A German translation of this really interesting proclamation is given in Johann Sporschil's *Feldzug der Österreicher in Italien und Illyrien in den Jahren 1813-1814*,

p. 95, and a French translation in M.H. Weil's *Le Prince Eugène et Murat*, III, p. 647; cf. also, Anton Springer, *Geschichte Österreichs*, I, 242-3; also, R. John Rath, *The Fall of the Napoleonic Kingdom of Italy*, pp. 48, 54.

[8] Castl. to Bentinck, Mar. 30, 1814. Cf. Mett. to Bllg. of the same date, Prov/LV 3, 3, 21-25.

[9] Arthur G. Haas, "Kaiser Franz, Metternich und die Stellung Illyriens", *MÖStA*, XI (1958), pp. 377-381.

[10] Vortr. of Baron Haager, May 19, 1814 and June 19, 1814, Konf. A-b, 8, No. 1064, and 10, No. 1187.

[11] "Anrede der illyrischen Deputierten an S.M. den Kayser", Prov/Ill. 16. The document bears no date but probably was submitted at the end of July, 1814.

[12] *Loc. cit.*; cf. also, "*Österreichischer Beobachter*", Aug. 28 and 29, 1814.

[13] Laz. note, March 10, 1814, Konf. A-b, 8, No. 576.

[14] Hermann Wendel, *Der Kampf der Südslawen um Freiheit und Einheit*, p. 138.

[15] Laz. note, *loc. cit.*; Haager notes, Dec. 1 and 26, 1813, Konf. A-b, Prot. 2, Nos. 791 and 941.

[16] Laz. note, loc. cit., No. 577.

[17] Bald. note, Nov. 29, 1813, Konf. A-b, Prot. 2, No. 797.

[18] Saurau to KF, Apr. 25, 1814, Prov/Ill. 16, 1; Laz. note, Apr. 28, 1814, Konf. A-b, Prot. 3, No. 898; Haager Vortr. and Konf. note to Ugarte, June 1814, Konf. A-b, 10, No. 1219, and Prot. 3, No. 1233. Also, HKzA, IIA1, 232.

[19] F.R. Freiherr v. Krones, *Zur Geschichte Österreichs, 1792-1816, mit besonderer Rücksicht auf das Berufsleben des Staatsmannes Freiherrn von Baldacci*, p. 368 ff.

[20] Rath, *Fall*, pp. 22-26; for a thorough discussion of the economic problems in LV, cf. by the same author, "The Habsburgs and the great Depression in Lombardy-Venetia, 1814-1818", *JMH*, XIII, No. 3 (Sept. 1941), p. 305.

[21] This fact is confirmed by the interesting contemporary report of the Austrian Lt. Col. Frhr. Ludwig v. Welden, a member of Bellegarde's staff. He had been chosen to conduct the restoration of order in Milan following the disorders of April 20, 1814, still in the name of Eugene but with Austrian approval (Capitulation of Mantua, April 16; Eugene's final abdication on the 26th). Cf. Aretin, "Eugen Beauharnais' Königreich Italien beim Übergang zur österreichischen Herrschaft", *MÖStA*, XII (1959), p. 288.

[22] "[Das] italienische Volk schmeichelt sich in der Hoffnung, daß der Eintritt der österreichischen Waffen in Italien in gleichzeitigen großen Reformen zum Vortheile der Bewohner bezeichnet seyn wird." Fürst Reuss to Count Ugarte, Feb. 28, 1814, KFA 26 (27), 1, 17-30.

[23] For example, from the year 1812: cf. Edith Kotasek's "Ein Einigungsplan für Italien aus dem Jahre 1812", *MÖStA*, VII (1954), p. 208. A plan for confederation from 1804: *Hermes*, Vol. II (1820) [cf. Gentz to Mett., Aug. 1, 1820, in Wittichen, Carl Friedrich (ed.), *Briefe an und von Friedrich von Gentz*, vol. III: *Schriftwechsel mit Metternich*, part 2, p. 25]. From 1811: for a plan of Marshal de la Tour of Piedmont for a unified Italian Kingdom under Franz d'Este of Modena, see Domenico Spadoni's "Federazione e Re d'Italia mancati nel 1814-1815", *NRS*, X (1931), pp. 398-433. For projects, whose main theme was often that unification must come from the Italians themselves, cf. Rath, *Fall*, p. 29 ff., who cites Melchiore Gioia's "Dissertazione su quale dei governi liberi meglio convenga all'Italia" (1797), and others by such well-known figures as Monti, Alfieri, and Foscolo. Cf. further, A. Solmi's "L'idea dell' unità italiana nell' età napoleonica", *RSR*, XX (1933), p. 1.

²⁴ Aretin, "Eugen Beauharnais", p. 285.

²⁵ Josef Alexander Freiherr von Helfert, "Der Ausgang der französischen Herrschaft in Oberitalien und die Brescia-Mailänder Militär-Verschwörung", AÖG, LXXVI (1890), p. 440.

²⁶ In the Kingdom of Italy, the members of the Senate were appointed directly by King *Napoleone*. The electoral colleges were composed of members of the proprietory and commercial classes as well as of academicians and representatives of the intellectual pursuits. They had the duty of supervising the constitutionality of the Senate's transactions and the conduct of public officials. On the outspoken public support for the colleges against the Senate, as well as for a fine account of the April events in Milan, cf. Rath, *Fall*, p. 96 ff.

²⁷ The Treaty of Prag, July 27, 1813.

²⁸ Immediately before the uprising, Bllg. had reported to Mett. of disorder and an inflammable public mood in Milan, as well as of a strong sentiment for independence among the Italian army: Apr. 20, 1814, Prov/LV 3, 1, 172. Further, Strassoldo reports enclosed with reports of Bllg. to KF on May 4 and 9, 1814, KFA 26 (27), 1, 32-84. Also, Spadoni, "Federazione e Re d'Italia mancati".

²⁹ Strassoldo to Bllg., Apr. 26, 1814, KFA 26 (27), 1, 32; cf. also Aretin, "Eugen Beauharnais", p. 268.

³⁰ Bllg. to KF, Apr. 28, 1814, Prov/LV 3, 1, 188.

³¹ Bllg. to KF, May 9, 1814, with enclosed copy of proclamation, KFA 26 (27), 1, 60-81. The exact date on which Lombardy was allotted to Austria is in dispute. After a careful checking, Rath supposes it to have been during the fourth week of April. On Apr. 21, Mett. wrote to Hud.: "Wahrscheinlich werden wir unsere Gränze bis an den Ticino ausdehnen, wodurch selbe sehr schön wird, und die Monarchie in Italien in Verbindung mit Modena, Parma, und Toscana einen sehr festen Fuß erhält . . ." Int. Korr. 78.

³² Federico Confalonieri, *Memorie e Lettere*, ed. by Gabrio Casati, vol. II, p. 8.

³³ Bllg. to KF, May 4, 1814, KFA 26 (27), 1, 47-48.

³⁴ Ettore Verga, "La deputazione dei collegi elletorali del Regno d'Italia a Parigi nel 1814", ASL XXXI (1904), p. 318. For this and the following reference I am indebted to Prof. Rath (*Fall, pp. 189-194*).

³⁵ Mett. in a conversation with Cardinal Consalvi: Consalvi to Card. Pacca, Sept. 8, 1814. P. Ilario Rinieri, *Corrispondenza inedita dei cardinali Consalvi e Pacca nel tempo del Congresso di Vienna, (1814-1815)*, p. 5.

³⁶ Confalonieri to his wife, May 8, 1814, *op. cit.*, p. 9; cf. further, Helfert, "Ausgang", p. 473.

³⁷ The delegation of the Electoral Colleges included Count Giacomo Mellerio, whom we shall encounter again in a quite different capacity.

³⁸ Letters of Verri to Paris deputation; cf. further the observation of Baron Hügel, cited in note 68.

³⁹ AhRes. June 27, 1814, Konf. A-b, Prot. 3, Nos. 638 and 1233.

⁴⁰ KF to Bllg. May 14, 1814, Int. Korr. 78; also Konf. A-b, Prot. 3, No. 996.

⁴¹ Mett. to Hud., Mar. 14, 1814, Int. Korr. 77.

⁴² Mett. to Hud., Dec. 16, 1813, Int. Korr. 76.

⁴³ Gentz to Mett., Apr. 25, 1814, Wittichen, *op. cit.*, III, part 1, p. 298.

⁴⁴ Hud. to Mett., Dec. 24, 1813, Int. Korr. 76.

⁴⁵ Gentz to Mett., Apr. 24, 1814, Wittichen, *op. cit.*, III, part 1, p. 296.

⁴⁶ Mett. to Hud., Mar. 25, 1814, Int. Korr. 77.

⁴⁷ Even if sometimes in a somewhat deprecatory manner: "deutschthümelnde Gelüste", NP I, p. 207; "In einem Moment in welchem so viele Schwindelköpfe nach·Constitutionen seufzen. . . .", Mett. to Hud., May, 25, 1814, Int. Korr. 78.

⁴⁸ Diary of Baron Hügel, Mar. 25 and 30, 1814; original autographed manuscript in Prov/LV 45.

⁴⁹ Mett. to Hud., Oct. 31, 1813, Int. Korr. 76. At a time when Napoleon's collapse was by no means certain, Mett. apparently hoped that at least Venetia might be torn from his grip, observing thereby, "It is just as impossible for Napoleon to reconquer what he has lost as for him to surrender what he still has in his hands . . ."

⁵⁰ Bllg. to Count Mier, Jan. 28, 1814, Prov/LV 3, 1, 39.

⁵¹ Bllg. procl. to his troops, Feb. 4, 1814, Prov/LV 3, 1, 54: "Die Völker Italiens sind unsere Freunde; wir kommen sie von dem Druck fremder Gewalt zu erlösen", published in French in Weil, *Eugène et Murat*, III, p. 646.

⁵² Hud. to Mett., Nov. 8, 1813, Int. Korr. 76.

⁵³ Hud. to Mett., Feb. 28, 1814, Int. Korr. 77; Mier to Mett., Apr. 6, 1814, Rath, *Fall*, p. 51.

⁵⁴ Bllg. to Mett., Mar. 21, 1814, enclosing report from Mier, Prov/LV 3, 1, 89.

⁵⁵ "For the purpose of promoting union and putting aside every minor consideration, you will do the utmost to conform with the views of Marshal Bellegarde, regulating at the same time your conduct toward Marshal [sic] Murat upon principles of cordiality and confidence. . . . You will studiously abstain from encouraging any measure which might commit your Court or its Allies with respect to the ultimate disposition of any of the other territories in the heart of Italy, the destination of which must remain to be discussed upon a peace." Castl. to Bentinck, Mar. 30, 1814; a copy of the original English text is enclosed with the communication of Mett. to Bllg., same date, Prov/LV 3, 3, 21-25.

⁵⁶ For Mett.'s repeated glowing accounts of Castlereagh, see Mett. to Hud., Jan. 20, 21, 23, 27, and 30, 1814, Int. Korr. 77.

⁵⁷ Mett. to Bllg., Mar. 30, Apr. 3, 1814, Prov/LV 3, 3, 21-39.

⁵⁸ Hügel's diary, Mar. 25, 1814.

⁵⁹ Actually, unofficial British impulses, often abetted by the Opposition at home, never stopped. Apparently there was still some hope attached to the outcome of the Congress of Vienna. Reports continued to occupy the StK regarding the questionable behavior of various British nationals; especially did the conduct of Gen. Wilson incur Austrian displeasure. Later, during the Murat crisis of 1815, the complaints multiplied. Cf. on this issue, Bllg. to KF, May 4, 1814, KFA 26 (27), 1, 32 ff; Mett. to Bllg., May 15, 1814, Prov/LV 3, 3, 50-56; Mett. to Hud., May 17, 1814, Int. Korr. 78; Bllg. to Mett., July 5, 1814, Prov/LV 3, 4, 1; Bllg. to Mett., Sept. 22, 1814, Prov/LV 3, 4, 105; Strass. to Haager, Oct. 16, 1814, KK, Polizei Hofstelle Vortr. 6, 1, 356; Bllg. to Wess., Oct. 28, 1814, GK, 482; Mett. Vortr. Dec. 15, 1814, Feb. 4, 1815, Vortr. 290, 2, 116, and 291, 2, 192; Mett. to Merveldt, Apr. 21, 1815, St. Abt. Eng. Weis. 203. An instructive description of English activity during the first part of 1814 can be found in Rath, *Fall*, above all in the chapter entitled "The English and Public Opinion".

⁶⁰ Mett. to Hud., May, 17, 1814, Int. Korr. 78.

⁶¹ Mett. to Hud., Apr. 3, 1814, Int. Korr. 78; Mett. to Bllg., same date, Prov/LV 3, 3, 27-39.

⁶² Mett. to Hud., Apr. 21, 1814, Int. Korr. 78.

⁶³ Mett. to Bllg., Apr. 26, 1814, Prov/LV 3, 3, 48-49.

⁶⁴ Mett. to Hud., May 17, 1814, Int. Korr. 78.

[65] KF to Bllg., May 15, 1814; Mett. to Bllg., same date; Mett. to Hud., May 17, 1814, Int. Korr. 78; also Prov/LV 3, 3, 50-56; Konf. A-b, No. 996. A further reference to these instructions as well as to attending events can' be found in a chronology of Mett.'s career, written by Floret, MAP, AC 26. Cf. Appendix A, No. 1.

[66] According to Hügel, *op. cit.*, the news had reached Bllg. on May 24, 1814.

[67] It is interesting to note here the remark of the well-known Ugo Foscolo, one of the "Italici puri" and compatriot of Confalonieri, written in the spring of 1814: "The Italians now are of a sort that no 1000 Lycurgi, 10,000 Timoleons, 100,000 Washingtons and one million Spartan warriors could be capable of constituting them into a nation." Helfert, "Ausgang", p. 463. Also, Mett. to Gentz, May 7, 1819, NP III, p. 244.

[68] Hügel's diary, May 18, 1814: "On dit ici que Notre Empereur alloit prendre le titre de Roi des Lombards ou Langobards. Il n'y auroit pas de mal qu'il se fît le chef d'une ligue italienne. Egalement, on dit, que l'Italie alloit former un royaume séparé des états héréditaires."

[69] At the same time, KF had ordered Reuß to investigate this issue. Konf. A-b, Prot. 3, No. 996.

[70] As in their replies to the Italian delegations; also, Bllg. to Mett., June 4, 1814. Prov/LV 3, 1, 206.

[71] Mett. to Bub., June 2, 1814, in regard to Sardinia. ASM, Bub. 1.

[72] Reports of Gen. Tommasich, Jan. 4, 1814, KFA 28 (29), 1. Cf. also, Latt. to Enge Konf., May 2, 1814, HKzA IIA1, 16.

[73] Some examples (in translation) from the end of 1813 and the beginning of 1814: Hud. to Mett., Int. Korr. 76 and 77: On Oct. 20, "If nothing is done right away [regarding the regulation of financial questions in the conquered areas] then the right moment is lost and we'll have nothing to expect but the discontent of the inhabitants." On Oct. 28, "In the districts of Illyria occupied by us, the confusion due to a lack of any government grows daily. Pretty soon one will finally be convinced that things just won't go as one thought." On Nov. 14, "There exists in the newly occupied Italian and Illyrian districts grand disorder in the administration, and this has dissatisfaction as a natural consequence." One week later: more of the same, and as an additional thought, "Neither Illyria nor the Italian Provinces nor Croatia should be incorporated into the Monarchy before a peace — which would not prevent them, however, from being administered advantageously now. But just the opposite seems to be happening." On Dec. 5, on the instructions finally issued by KF: "Had they been issued two months ago, they would have avoided all the disorder under which these provinces are now sighing" but then, "*il vaut mieux tard que jamais.*" On Feb. 26, "One doesn't know a thing around here about the state of things in Italy." On the same subject, cf. note of Hingenau on administrative delay, Dec. 24, 1813, Konf. A-b, Prot. 2, No. 955; Haager notes of Dec. 1 and 26, 1813, and Jan. 22, 1814, Konf. A-b, Prot. 2, Nos. 791 and 941, fasc. 8, No. 201.

[74] Hud. to Mett., Nov. 21, 1813, Int. Korr. 76.

[75] KF to Zichy, Nov. 14, 1813, Konf. A-b, 6, No. 711.

[76] Already twenty years earlier, Bald. had been — then only twenty-nine years old — secretary with the former Illyrian *Hofkanzlei*.

[77] Krones, *Geschichte Österreichs*, p. 265 ff.

[78] AhE, Nov. 28, 1813, Konf. A-a, 3; also HKzA IIIA4, 343, 2.

[79] KF to Reuss, Nov. 9, 1813, Konf. A-b, 6, No. 789.

[80] AhE of Nov. 28, 1813: ". . . so viel wie möglich, eine Gleichförmigkeit zwischen

den verschiedenen Bestandtheilen der Gouvernements durch successives Hinarbeiten auf das was in Meinen deutschen Ländern allgemein besteht, in so weit es ohne übermäßige Schwierigkeiten ausgeführt werden kann, zu bewirken." Further, KF to Zichy, Apr. 1, 1814, Prov/Ill. 16, 1; also, Hud. to Mett., Apr. 8, and 9, 1914, Int. Korr. 78.

[81] AhE of Nov. 28, 1813; further, Hingenau note of Dec. 24, 1813, *loc. cit.;* KF to Latt., Jan. 7, 1814, Konf. A-b, Prot. 3, No. 115.

[82] AhE, May 12, 1814, Konf. A-b, 9, No. 832.

[83] AhE, May 14, 1814, *ibid.* Prot. 3, No. 996.

[84] Öttingen note, Mar. 5, 1814, Konf. A-b, Prot. 3, No. 539. This was to be, expectedly, a slow business. On Oct. 11, 1814, KF repeated this order in regard to the Italian provinces. Nearly two years after the original provision, the "Illyrian" project still dragged on: Öttingen note, Dec. 29, 1815, StR Prot. and Ind., 275, No. 9.

[85] "Ich will das Schul- und Studienwesen in den neu-acquirierten Illyrischen und Italienischen Provinzen, deren Einverleibung in Meine Staaten schon bestimmt ist, so schnell wie möglich, nach den in Meinen deutschen Staaten bestehenden Vorschriften organisiert wissen." KF to Ugarte, July 11, 1814, Konf. A-b, Prot. 10, No. 1164.

[86] Procl. of Latt., June 23, 1814, HKzA IIA1, 16.

[87] KF to Ött., Mar. 15, 1814, and again Mar. 12, 1815, StR Prot. 3, No. 3666. The question of language and the administration in general was not that simple. Whereas Austrian civil servants in Italy were from the beginning fairly proficient in the Italian language, this was not the case with the *Hofstellen* in Vienna, where there was no "Italian department", and therefore never a sufficient number of individuals who could process the reports from Italy. Consequently, there were requests from the various agencies in Vienna that the reports should be drawn up in German, since otherwise they were not understood (HKzA IIIA4, 356, Prot. of June 3, 1814). The emperor could well appreciate such a point of view, and originally seems even to have acquiesced to it — at least he intended to have Reuss submit his reports from Italy in German. However, perhaps under some advice from Mett., he came to see the problem from the other side; on Aug. 2, 1814, he wrote in his own hand that he did not intend to force the many persons in the Italian gubernia who did not know German to submit their reports in that language (AhRes., Konf. A-b 11, No. 1394). By Apr. 13, 1815, he even expressed his desire that in the Italian gubernia the local language be used as much as possible (StR Prot., 1815, 2, No. 2154).

[88] Beamten Listen, Dec., 1814. HKzA IIIA4, 343 and 356. Also KFA 12 (13).

[89] Especially non-Italian court officials: for example, the emperor crossed out with his own hand the name of a well-known Milanese candidate (Patroni) for the post of *Justiz-Einrichtungs-Hofkommissair* for Austrian Lombardy on the grounds that in a land such as Lombardy, passion and personality could easily come to dominate an issue, and that memories of the "recent excitement" might well incite to some sort of partisanship. It would be wiser, thus, to choose a German with the same qualifications under whom Patroni could then serve as second commissar (AhRes., June 30, 1814, Konf. A-b 10, No 1286). Ultimately, the emperor named to this post Count Enzenberg (who was reluctant to go) and as his assistant not Patroni but *Appelazionsrath* v. Brenner (Konf. A-b 10, No. 1313).

[90] For example: Prov/Ill. 16, and Dalm 7; KFA 28 (29) and 30 (31) and 34 (36a).

[91] More or less detailed accounts of administrative organizing in the areas south of the Alps may be found in: Helfert, *Kaiser Franz und die Stiftung des Lombardo-Venetianischen Königreiches;* Krones, *op. cit.;* Rath, *Fall,* and by the same author, "The

Austrian Provisional Government in Lombardy-Venetia, 1814-1815", *JCEA*, II, No. 3 (Oct. 1942), p. 249; also Stjepan Antoljak, "Prekosavska Hrvatska i pitanje njene rein-korporacije (1813-1822)", *Starine*, XLV (1955), pp. 91-150.

[92] Reuss to KF, Jan. 9, 1814, KFA 26 (27), 1, 3-16; Bllg. to Mett., Dec. 18 and 21, 1813, Jan. 3, 1814, Prov/LV 3, 1, 1-12; also, Saurau in regard to Illyria, cf. below, footnote No. 99.

[93] According to a French historian, soon the malicious slogan appeared: "Langue in-intelligible, monnaie inutilisable, bâton infatigable, promesses interminables." A. Pingaud, "La Lombardie en 1814", *RHD*, XLI (1927), pp. 434-467.

[94] Tarvis Deputation to Latt., Dec. 11, 1813; Latt. to Ugarte, Dec. 16, 1813; Konf. Vortrag, Jan. 26, 1814; AhE, Mar. 30, 1814, HKzA IIA3, 26, No. 309.

[95] Ugarte note to the Hofkanzlei, July 6, 1814, *ibid.*, No. 856.

[96] KF to Saurau, Mar. 9, 1814, Prov/Ill. 16, 1.

[97] KF to Zichy, Mar. 9, 1814, Prov/Ill. 16, 1.

[98] How unsatisfactory and confusing the situation had in the meantime become, one can surmise from a report from Hud. to Mett., Apr. 9, 1814: "Heute abends reiset Gf. Saurau von hier nach dem k.k. Feldhoflager um seine Instruktionen als Einrichtungs-Hofkommissair für Illyrien, das heißt, für Krain Görz, Gradisca, zu empfangen. Wir haben also jetzt *Roschmann* exclusiv für Tirol, unter unmittelbarer Oberleitung des Herrn Präsidenten *von Baldacci*, so daß wir hier nicht wissen was dort geschieht. Italien administriert vom *Fürsten Reuss*, erstattet seine Berichte an die hiesigen Hofstellen und an S.M.. Illyrien administriert vom *Gen. Lattermann*, welcher, wie Fürst Reuss an die Hofstellen in Wien berichtet; dann jetzt *Gf. Saurau*, welcher vermuthlich unmittelbare Befehle von S.M., und ausgedehntere Vollmachten erhalten wird, um in vielen Stücken nach Gutbefinden zu handeln: Kroatien unter dem *Vice-gouverneur von Giurkovich*, welcher an Lattermann gewiesen ist: Istrien von dem *Intendanten Baron Lederer* in Triest administriert. Dalmatien unter dem *General Tommasich*, welcher an die Hofstellen nach Wien berichtet: die Bocche di Cattaro in den Händen des Metro-politen von Montenegro; die Inseln Lissa, Curzola, Angusta, etc., in den Händen der Engelländer, und Ragusa von Intriguen aller Art bearbeitet: endlich das militärische Kroatien unter dem *Hofkriegsrath*. In allen diesen wieder-eroberten Provinzen theils französische, theils deutsche, theils hungarische, theils italienische Gesetze, theils Willkühr, oder gar nichts. Eine Menge von hier dahin geschickter Beamten, welche aus Mangel an Oberleitung wenig oder nichts leisten. Beträchtliche Summen klingender Münze, und fast der ganze Bedarf der Armeen an Fleisch und Früchten, welche alle Monate dahin ge-schickt werden müssen! Dabei allgemeine Unzufriedenheit in jenen Provinzen. Dies ist das keinesmegs übertriebene und eben darum höchst traurige Bild einer für die öster-reichische Monarchie in politischer, militärischer und finanzieller Hinsicht gleich inter-essanten Strecke Landes, welche unter einer einsichtsvollen, auf den Karakter der ver-schiedenen Nationen berechneten, energischen Zentral-Leitung glücklich seyn, dem Staat, so lange der Krieg dauert, nichts kosten, nach hergestelltem Frieden aber reichliche Früchte bringen müßte. Gf. Saurau als General-Gouverneur in Laibach, wenn ihm nach den beiden dort herrschenden Hauptsprachen, ein italienischer und ein illirischer Senat — jeder aus 4 oder 5 Personen bestehend — beigegeben würde, um die Hauptadministrations-zweige zu leiten, würde als oberste politische Behörde hinreichen, wenn man einmal weiß was man will, und ihm der Zweck und die Gränzen bestimmt vorgezeichnet sind, so daß er nicht nöthig hat, wegen jeder einzelnen Verfügung erst in der Ferne anzufragen sondern auf eigene schwere Verantwortlichkeit handeln darf." Int. Korr. 78.

[99] Saurau to KF, Apr. 25, 1814, Prov/Ill. 16, 1.

[100] Cf. above, footnote No. 18.

[101] Saurau to KF, Apr. 25, 1814, Prov/Ill. 16, 1.

[102] KF to Saurau, May 2, 1814, *loc. cit.*, and KFA 26 (27), 1. Saurau's authority did not please everyone. Gentz's opinion was singularly negative. Gentz to Mett., May 17, 1814, *Wittichen*, III, part 1, p. 302.

[103] "Wir werden sämtliche Bewohner dieser Provinzen als Unterthanen mit der Liebe umfangen, von welcher der größte Theil bereits in älteren Zeiten so viele Beweise erhielt." *Carinthia*, 99, 1909, p. 203.

[104] KF to Laz., July 31, 1814, AKA, Sep. Bill. Prot., 258, No. 331.

[105] Helfert, *Stiftung*, p. 19 ff.

[106] Hud. to Mett., May 1, 1814, Int. Korr., 78.

[107] Mett. to Hud., May 24, 1814, Int. Korr., 78.

[108] Hud. to Mett., July 11, 1814, Int. Korr. 78.

[109] Mett. to KF, July 30, 1814, Vortr. 288, 1.

[110] On June 28, July 5 and 12, 1814.

CHAPTER II

[1] Mett. to Hud., May 24, 1814, Int. Korr. 78.

[2] Cf. Joseph Rossi, *Denkbuch für Fürst und Vaterland*, 2 vols. (Vienna, 1814).

[3] Mett. to Bllg., June 2, 1814, Prov/LV 3, 3, 57.

[4] *Ibid.* The emperor was informed of the purpose of Wess.' mission on the following day. Mett. to KF, June 3, 1814, Vortr. 287.

[5] Wess. to Mett., July 4, 1814, *ibid.*

[6] Wess. to Mett., "Einige kurze Betrachtungen über die Organisierung der Italienischen Provinzen", Aug. 13, 1814. Report in German, accompanying letter in French. Prov/LV 40, 161.

[7] An untitled memorandum and "Betrachtungen über die Erwerbungen des Hauses Österreich in Italien", Aug. 9, 1814, Kongreß A. 25. Arneth gives the date as Aug. 9, but Archivbehelf No. 188 of the WHHStA indicates the date as Oct. 9. The difficulty may have arisen from the practice of that time of writing October as "8bre". However, Aug. 9, is the more logical date. Cf. Alfred Ritter v. Arneth, *Johann Freiherr von Wessenberg. Ein österreichischer Staatsmann des neunzehnten Jahrhunderts*, Vol. I, p. 201 ff.

[8] Although this document lacks signature and date, as was customary for confidential reports, external as well as internal features correspond too closely to the report of Aug. 13 to leave any doubt as to its authorship. One has only to compare the words quoted at the end of the previous paragraph with the following sentence from the anonymous memorandum: "Whether in view of the disparity between the Italian Provinces and the German hereditary lands, a complete conformity is now advisable, I must doubt all the more, since such would require considerable time, during which a great many of the advantages which the present moment offers, and some of the good now existing, would be lost to the future." It was probably submitted in July or August of 1815.

[9] Helfert, "Ausgang", p. 475.

[10] *Ibid.*, p. 495.

[11] *Ibid.*, p. 475.

[12] Wess. was notified of his appointment on Aug. 9: Prov/LV 43, 226.

[13] AhH, Nov. 1, 1814, AKK Prot. (1814), 258, No. 2908, Billett No. 689; also, HKzA IIA1, 16, No. 159.

[14] Bllg. to Wess., July 31, 1814, GK 482, conv. *Bellegarde.*

[15] Wess. to Mett., Aug. 13, 1814, Prov/LV 40, 161.

[16] To be sure, this remark was meant for the Austrian embassy in London and perhaps some ears beyond it, and thus would be not too specific in regard to the question of blame. In the same letter, Mett. again felt it necessary to call for a chastising of Lord Bentinck. Mett. to Merveldt, Aug. 18, 1814, St. Abt. Eng. Weis., 203.

[17] Mett. to KF, Aug. 29, Sept. 5, Nov. 3, 1814, resp. Vortr. 288, 2, 200; 289, 1, 50; 290, 1, 17.

[18] Mett. to KF, Oct. 9, 1814, Vortr. 289, 2, 16.

[19] Bllg. to Mett., Dec. 12, 1814, Prov/LV 3, 4, 198; thereupon, Mett. to KF, Dec. 27, 1814, and Jan. 1, 1815, resp. Vortr. 290, 4, 12; 291, 6, 748.

[20] AhR July 8, 1815, *ibid.*; thereupon, Mett. to Bllg., July 26, 1815, Prov/LV 4, 1, 66.

[21] Haager Vortr. Sept. 13, 1814, Konf. A-b, 12, No. 1651.

[22] Bllg. to KF, July 31, 1814, Prov/LV 3, 4, 9-20, in answer to the emperor's communication of July 14, *loc. cit.* KF further informed the marshal of his intent to disperse Italian troops throughout various caserns in the German provinces: KF to Bllg., July 31, 1814, Konf. A-b, 10, No. 1249.

[23] Bllg. to Mett., Sept. 22, 1814, Prov/LV, 3, 4, 105.

[24] Regarding resumed activities of English agents, cf. esp. Strass. to Haager, Oct. 16, 1814, KK-Polizeihofstelle: Vortr. 6, 356.

[25] Circulation of leaflets calling for Italian independence, *loc. cit.*

[26] Bllg. to Wess., Oct. 28, 1814, GK 482, conv. *Bellegarde.*

[27] Bllg. to Mett., Dec. 5, 1814, Jan. 4 and 25, 1815, resp. Prov/LV 3, 4, 192; 4, 1, 1; 4, 2, 7.

[28] Bllg. to KF, Bllg. to Mett., Jan. 20, 1815, Prov/LV 4, 3, 11. A secret report to KF by a Chev. Freddi — an agent of Haager responsible for Italian matters — illustrates in a highly interesting manner Bllg.'s difficulties as well as the reason for Mme. Bllg.'s popularity in Milan: "La nouvelle des arrestations de Rasori, de Théodore Lecchi, de Gasparinetti suivies à Milan fournit une ample matière à la conversation. Mme. de Belle-garde désapprouva hautement ces mesures d'une sévérité déplacée; elle assura que son mari était bien loin d'exercer l'empire de la force, de la violence et du despotisme, mais que les ordres souverains le forcent, malgré lui, à ces malheureuses démarches qui ont le sceau de la violence et de la persécution et qui éteignent le peu de partisans qui restent encore en Italie à l'Autriche. 'On emploie ici', dit-elle, 'tous les moyens possibles pour éteindre le feu sacré dont les coeurs italiens étaient allumés pour la cause de notre souverain chéri, et pour embraser l'Italie d'une horrible révolte qui ôtera enfin à l'empire autrichien ces belles et riches provinces. Mon mari me fait craindre toujours de ses jours. MM. de Zichy, Baldacci et Lazansky, qui ne connaissent pas ce pays et qui ont même des préventions injustes, donnent à l'empereur de bien mauvais conseils. Pauvre empereur! Ecoutez, ma, chère comtesse' — Mme. de Bellegarde adressait la parole à Mme. de Crenneville — 'on choisissait ici des Allemands, et récemment des Hongrois, pour aller à (!) gouverner les Italiens. Peut-on se prendre plus maladroitement et plus impolitiquement que de confier à des gens inexperts, ignorants de la langue et des moeurs, le régime des provinces jadis si florissantes? Est-ce que Bonaparte avait en-

voyé des Français gouverner l'Italie? Il n'y avait que le Vice-roi Eugène et son secrétaire Méjan qui fussent Français. Tous les autres fonctionnaires étaient nationaux Italiens, et Bonaparte, malgré son sceptre de fer, malgré sa conscription, malgré la gravité de ses impôts, fut obéï et craint jusqu'au dernier moment. Il faut avouer le vrai: Il y a bien ici des têtes imbéciles qui ne se connaissent point du tout dans l'art de gouverner . . .' " Everyone, according to the report, applauded "the liberal principles" which Mme. Bellegarde had so ardently and eloquently put forth. Encl. in Haager Vortr. to KF, Dec. 28, 1814; published in Fournier, *Geheimpolizei*, p. 316.

[29] Mett. to KF, Dec. 15, 1814, Vortr. 290, 2, 116.

[30] Mett. to KF, Feb. 4, 1815, Vortr. 291, 2, 192.

[31] For the reorganization of the Staatskanzlei and the formation of ministries, cf. among others, Mett. to Hud., July 28, 1814, Int. Korr. 78; Mett. to KF, Aug. 15, 1814, MAP, AC 10, *Stadion*, 278; for the Staatsrat: NP I, 120 II, 444; Mett. to KF, Sept. 26, 1814, Vortr. 289, 170; Zichy to Mett., Aug. 30, 1814, Int. Korr. 78; further, Srbik, *Metternich*, I, 458; Friedrich Walter, *Die Geschichte der österreichischen Zentralverwaltung in der Zeit Franz II. (I.) und Ferdinand I.; 1792 bis 1848*, vol. I, Chap. II, sec. 2: "Das entscheidende Problem der franziszeischen Verwaltung"; also, re the StR: "*Grundsätze*", KK Sep. Prot. 258, Aug. 27, 1814, No. 394; further, instructions for Wallis and *Hofstellenchefs*, Nov. 29, 1814, KK Sep. Prot. 258, No. 3061. Article I of the "*Grundsätze*" was: "Der Staatsrath ist Mein Rath und hat keine ausübende Gewalt irgend einer Art."

[32] For this problem, see esp. Walter, *op. cit.*

[33] HKzA IIIA4, 357.

[34] Bllg. to COHC, Oct. 25, 1814, "Statistische Auskünfte über die österreichisch-italienischen Provinzen nach den Leitfäden der Hohen Central-Organisierungs-Hofcommission vom 18. August 1814", *loc. cit.*; synopsis in Helfert, *Stiftung*, p. 56 ff.

[35] Reuss-Plauen to Hud., July 17, 1814, Int. Korr. 78.

[36] KF to Bald., Oct. 15, 1814. The Baldacci report was among the now lost *Staatsrath* collection; cf. Helfert, *Stiftung*, p. 56 ff.

[37] The new *gubernium* in Laibach was to function as of Jan. 1, 1815. Latt. to Mett., Dec. 7, 1814, Prov/Ill 15, 1, 55.

[38] Kübeck to COHC, Dec. 8, 1814. "Über die zukünftige Verwaltung Italiens." HKzA IIIA4, 357.

[39] Here Helfert seems to have skirted the main point. According to him, "Die erste Frage, jene um die es sich vor allem handelte, war die der staatsrechtlichen Eigenschaft der reaquirirten Gebiete und deren Einführung in den Rahmen des Gesamtstaates". *Stiftung*, p. 58.

[40] On July 31, 1814, at the creation of the COHC.

[41] The deputies were sent home on Feb. 9, 1815, save Mellerio and Porcia, who — as a special sign of imperial confidence — were requested to remain for the time being in the capital. Later, both received high posts.

[42] COHC Vortr. to KF, Jan. 3, 1815. Damaged originals, HKzA IIIA4, 357; also KFA 12 (15), 1, 77-90. Six days later, the emperor passed on the *Vortrag* to the president of the *Hofkammer*; on Feb. 20, it was turned over to the Staatsrat where it circulated one week among its members before a general discussion. Then it was returned, along with an approving opinion, to KF. The Vortrag itself contained two chief sections: "A. Organische Staatsverwaltung", and "B. Ständische Provinzialverfassung".

[43] *Loc. cit.*; also printed in Helfert, *Stiftung*, p. 117.

44 Decree of appointment: HKzA IIIA4, 357.

45 Helfert, *ibid.*

46 Ironically enough, only a few days before Napoleon's escape from Elba, Metternich had to insist to Talleyrand that Austria would not tolerate French interference in Italy under any circumstances, even for the purpose of a Bourbon restoration in Naples. Mett. to Tall., Feb. 25, 1815, ASM, Geh. Korr. Bubna 1. On the same day, he could still feel optimistic about the regulation of Italian affairs. Mett. to Bub., *ibid.* The reproach of Archduke John that Mett. treated the whole escape-from-Elba affair as a joke indicated how outward appearances could mislead even shrewd observers. Erzherzog Johann, *Tagebuch,* Mar. 4, 1815.

47 Freiherr vom Stein, *Tagebuch,* Mar. 8, 1815.

48 Bllg. to Mett., Mar. 11, 1815, Prov/LV 4, 2, 11.

49 Thus Bllg. continued to represent mutual Austro-Italian interests. He even made a case for the famous Italian poet Ugo Foscolo and thought of using his literary services in order to gain for Austria public opinion "in a nation which had been educated and formed through a literature of four centuries." Bllg. to Haager, Mar. 20, 1815, Helfert, *Stiftung,* p. 560.

50 Bllg. to Mett., Mar. 28, 1815, Prov/LV 4, 3, 122.

51 Notenwechsel, HKz to StK, 79, Feb. 28, 1815; also, COHC Vortr. of Mar. 17 and 26, 1815, HKzA IIIA4, 357.

52 Mett. to Hud., Mar. 12, 1815, Prov/LV 38, conv. *Besitznahme 1814-1815.*

53 In regard to the viceroy, there followed in the first draft the words "ohne jedoch an der administration theil zu nehmen", which were later prudently omitted, in "Hauptgrundsätze nach welchen das Königreich Langobardien besteht", *loc. cit.*

54 Draft of Mett. Vortr. in Hudelist's hand. Mar. 31, 1815, *loc. cit.*; further, Helfert, *Stiftung,* p. 206 ff.

55 *Ibid.,* p. 207.

56 HKzA IIIA4, 357, Apr. 3, 1815.

57 Draft in Mett.'s hand, added corrections from that of KF, Apr. 5, 1815. Vortr. 291, 4, 504.

58 Damaged Italian-language originals, signed by "Francesco", Ugarte, Laz. and Guicc., HKzA IIIA4, 357.

59 Helfert, *Stiftung,* p. 209.

60 Here Murat was simply dusting off some of the high-sounding phrases used in the campaign of the previous year, during which he also spread this idea. Cf. Hud. to Mett., Feb. 28, 1814, Int. Korr. 77.

61 Freely translated and paraphrased. Murat proclamation, Rimini, Mar. 30, 1815, enclosed with letter of Bllg. to Mett., Apr. 17, 1815, Prov/LV 4, 3, 130-135.

62 Freely translated and paraphrased. Bllg. proclamation, Milan, Apr. 5, 1815, *loc. cit.*

63 Proclamation of the Lombardo-Venetian Kingdom, Apr. 16, 1815, Prov/LV 4, 3, 145: "SUA MAESTÀ l'Augusto nostro Sovrano, fermo in quei sentimenti di predilezione per i suoi Stati in Italia che già manifestò fin dai primi momenti del reingresso ne'medesimi delle sue Truppe, ora che le solenni transazioni politiche hanno fissato i certi limiti di detti Stati, si è degnato compiere le intenzioni benefiche fin d'allor dimostrate, e formar de'suoi Stati in Italia un REGNO LOMBARDO-VENETO. Una tale Determinazione che conserva ad ogni Città tutti i vantaggi de'quali godeva, e ai Sudditi Italiani di SUA MAESTÀ quella nazionalità che a ragion tanto apprezzano, non può non essere riconosciuta universalmente come una delle prove più luminose del paterno affetto con cui

l'Augusta Casa d'Austria ha sempre riguardato gl'Italiani. Un Vicerè, di cui SUA MAESTÀ si riserva la nomina, rappresenterà in questo Regno la sua Augusta Persona, e l'organizzazione del Regno sarà conforme anche all'indole e alle abitudini degl'Italiani. L'onorevole incarico, impostomi da grazioso Decreto di SUA MAESTÀ, di essere Luogotenente del Vicerè, mi riesce doppiamente grato per poter a Popolazioni che nelle relazioni avute per più anni con loro mi hanno sempre inspirato stima e affezione, annunziare, anche in prevenzione della imminente proclamazione solenne del nuovo Regno e delle relative disposizioni, tali sovrane beneficenze, base sicura della loro durevole felicità."

64 Bllg. to Mett., Apr. 13, 1815, Prov/LV 4, sp. conv. 2, 13-16.

65 On Apr. 24, 1815, Helfert, *Stiftung*, p. 225.

66 AhK, Apr. 27, 1815, Prov/LV 6, 2, 1.

67 Vortr. Laz., May 4, 1815, Konf. A-a, 4, No. 264.

68 Mett. to Saurau, May 3, 1815, Prov/LV 6, 2, 5-13.

69 For example: "Idee der Einrichtung einer italienischen Confederation mit Österreich an der Spitze"; further, "Antwort eines Italieners auf die in Paris erschienene Broschüre — 'Note d'un Italien aux puissances alliées sur la nécessité d'une confédération italienne pour la paix de l'Europe' ", dated Dec. 12, 1814, Kongreß A. 25, and Hügel's diary, Mar. 24, 1814. Prov/LV 45. Further, the diary of Archduke John, *op. cit.*, Dec. 21, 1814. In 1799, the Directory negated the question "Is it in the interest of the Republic to form a league in Italy to resist its enemies outside and to maintain peace within?" Hermann Hüffer and Friedrich Luckwaldt, *Der Frieden von Campoformio, Urkunden und Aktenstücke zur Geschichte der Beziehungen zwischen Österreich und Frankreich in den Jahren 1795-1797.* Furthermore, cf. an anonymous work, sometimes erroneously attributed to Friedr. v. Gentz, entitled *Ideen über die Bildung eines freien germanischen Staatenbundes nebst Anhang über einen ähnlichen Italienischen Bund* (Leipzig, 1814).

70 Domenico Spadoni, "Federazione e Re d'Italia mancati", p. 420.

71 Mett. to Bllg., June 12, 1815: ". . . occupé depuis longtemps du projet de former sous notre égide un système fédératif de défense en Italie, qui puisse assurer à cette partie intéressante de l'Europe une paix solide et durable au dehors et la tranquillité dans l'intérieur, je n'attendais que la première circonstance favorable pour y donner suite." Prov/LV 4, 1, 60. For an interesting comparison with thoughts of Mett. apropos a related subject, expressed at a much later period (1840s), cf. Ilda Gabardini's article: "L'unificazione politica italiana nel pensiero del Principe di Metternich", *RSR* XIII (1926), pp. 466-476.

72 Mett. to KF, June 20, 1815, Vortr. 292, 3, 143; further, on June 30, *loc. cit.*, f. 231; Aug. 3, suggesting now Bourbon Naples as a principal participant, Vortr. 293, 2, 18.

73 For an accounting of the exasperating and ultimately futile efforts of Starhemberg and Metternich, cf. Karl Grossmann's article, "Metternichs Plan eines italienischen Bundes", *Historische Blätter, im Auftrage der Beamten des WHHStA*, Vienna, 1931, Heft 4, pp. 37-76; also Spadoni, *op cit.*; further, Antonio Bettanini, "Un disegno di confederazione italiana etc." in *Studi di storia dei trattati e politica internazionale*, Padua, 1939.

74 For example, Bllg. to Mett., June 23, 1815, Prov/LV 4, 4, 20. Nevertheless, Mett. persisted for over a year in the hope that Sardinia might yet be brought to reason — even through gentle pressure. The project was briefly revived in 1821-22, following the restoration of order in revolution-torn Italy, but by then Mett.'s interest seemed to have waned.

75 The thoughts of Bllg. expressed here and in the following several paragraphs are

taken from two documents: Bllg. to Mett., July 13, 1815, Prov/LV 4, 4, 32; Bllg. to Haager, Aug. 10, 1815, published in Helfert, *Stiftung*, appendix, pp. 572-579.

[76] Bllg. to Laz., Jan. 9, 1815 (Helfert, *Stiftung*, p. 31): "Daß diese Provinzen seit undenklichen Zeiten gewohnt sind, und es als ein Privilegium ansehen, eine eigene Oberste Justiz-Behörde zu besitzen, wie das vordem von Wail. Sr. Maj. Kaiser Joseph II. höchst sel. Andenkens im Jahre 1786 eingeführte Supremo Tribunale di Giustizia, der ehemalige Senato war."

[77] Joseph Freiherr v. Sardagna had been Bellegarde's secretary and apparently the two were of one view on the Italian situation. "Nous aimons de nous appuyer à l'autorité de M. le Maréchal de Bellegarde et à vous référer différentes dépêches qu'il a écrites sur ce sujet." The two documents are: "Mémoire sur l'État des Provinces Italiennes", sine dat.; and "Promemoria über die Einführung der österreichischen civil- und -criminal Gesetzbücher in Italien", sine nom. et dat., Prov/LV 40, 790-801.

[78] Cf. Appendix A, No. 3.

[79] Mett. to Hud., Sept. 7, 1815, Int. Korr. 79.

[80] Hud. to Mett., July 12, Sept. 23, Oct. 3, 1815, *ibid.*

[81] Mett. to Hud., Sept. 7, 1815, *ibid.*

[82] Mett. to Merveldt, July 6, 1814. St. Abt. Eng. Weis. 203.

[83] The above-mentioned notes and the protocol of the meeting of Feb. 21, 1815, are reproduced in Johann Ludwig Klüber, *Acten des Wiener Congresses in den Jahren 1814 und 1815* (AWC), vol IX, p. 40 ff. Mett.'s note was apparently based on his verbal explanations given at a meeting on Jan. 9, 1815, *ibid.*, p. 24; cf. further, Kongr. A. 12, for various memoirs on the Polish question.

[84] Mett. to KF, Apr. 18, 1815, Vortr. 291, 5, 644. KF's answer was a simple and typical resort to the police. Cf. Appendix A, No. 2.

[85] AWC, VI, 97-119; V, 121-137. Also copies in Konf. A-a, 4; further, Kongr. A. 12.

[86] Klüber, *Schlußacte des Wiener Congresses vom 9. Juni 1815*, Art. I, par. 2, p. 27: "Les Polonois, sujets respectifs de la Russie, de l'Autriche et de la Prusse, obtiendront une représentation et des institutions nationales, réglées d'après le mode d'existence politique que chacun des gouvernements, auxquels ils appartiennent, jugera utile et convenable de leur accorder."

[87] Hud. to Mett., July 25, 1815, Int. Korr. 79.

[88] Hud. to Mett., July 20, 1815, Int. Korr. 79; cf. also, Hud. on "Gährung in Galizien", Kongr. A. 14.

[89] Hud. to Mett., Aug. 31, 1815, Int. Korr. 79.

[90] Hud. to Mett., Aug. 26, 1815, Int. Korr. 79.

[91] Mett. to Hud., Sept. 16, 1815, *ibid.*

[92] ". . . jamais la tranquillité publique n'a été sérieusement troublée un seul instant. Chose de fait, qui, si l'on veut être juste, n'est pas sans mérite, ce me semble, pour le gouvernement dans les temps aussi difficiles et parle en sa faveur." Bellegarde to Mett., Sept. 20, 1815, MAP, AC 6, Corr. polit. Autriche II, conv. *Bellegarde.*

[93] *Ibid.*

[94] Mett. to Hud., Sept. 16, 1815, Int. Korr. 79.

[95] Laz. to KF, Aug. 15, 1815 — a long Vortrag on the problems of the LVn adm.: AhR, Sept. 13; Saurau to Bllg., Oct. 14, further a note from Rosetti emphasizing the confusion in Milan at that time to the point of saying that no real government exists, all burnt fragments, COHCA, 171. Further, Helfert, *Stiftung*, p. 283.

[96] Bllg. to Mett., Oct. 14, 1815, MAP, AC, *loc. cit.*; it is strange that just these two

communications of Bellegarde, expressing such frank and protesting attitudes, should never have been filed with the Staatskanzlei correspondence. Instead, they turned up in the private archives of the Metternich family. Metternich simply pocketed them, although it is anyone's guess whether he did so intentionally or whether, as sometimes happened, correspondence received on journeys occasionally was placed in separate folders and then erroneously wound up some place other than originally destined.

[97] Mett. to Hud., Oct. 4, 1815, Int. Korr. 79.

[98] Mett. to Hud., Sept. 16, 1815, *ibid.*

CHAPTER III

[1] Mett. to Hud., Dec. 8, 1815, Int. Korr. 79. The British ambassador wrote from Venice, before Metternich's arrival, of the severe economic situation (unbearable port taxes, officials appointed by the French still serving but at half pay etc.) and of a "want of capacity and vigor to make the necessary Reforms" and further, "I do not apprehend much has been done as yet in placing the Government on a better footing. Probably Prince Metternich's Arrival and Assistance is waited for." Stewart to Castl., Nov. 29, 1815, FO 7, 120.

[2] Mett. to Bub., Dec. 17, 1815, Prov/LV 37, 2, 7.

[3] Hoppé to Mett., Jan. 13, 1816, Int. Korr. 81, 2, 71. A similar comment: "Not much enthusiasm nor joy shewn at the arrival of their Majesties." Stewart to Castl., Jan. 1, 1816, FO 7, 126.

[4] Hoppé to Mett., Apr. 27, 1816, Int. Korr. 81, 2, 96. These extremes of feeling were also reported by Stewart in commenting on Kaiser Franz's concessions to the Venetians "whom the Emperor has taken as great a partiality for, as I hear He has, dislike to His Milanese Subjects." Stewart to Castl., Dec. 31, 1815, FO 7, 120.

[5] Mett. to KF, Dec. 29, 1815, Vortr. 295, 3, 83.

[6] Mett. to KF, Jan. 21, 1816, Vortr. 296, 2, 50-62.

[7] Metternich continued, "Ich unterfange mich E.M. allerunterthänigst zu bitten, den gegenwärtigen Vortrag zu allerhöchstderoselben ausschließlichen Wissenschaft vorzubehalten. . . . In der vorliegenden Frage ist es leider noch kaum möglich, daß nicht Fehler der Personen ebenso sehr als der Sache in Anrechnung gebracht werden. E.M. hegen keinen Zweifel, daß es bei mir nur um die Sache zu thun ist . . . Ich würde den gegenwärtigen Vortrag, wenn ich nicht platterdings daran verhindert wäre [eye ailment] eigenhändig geschrieben haben, da mir doch dieses nicht möglich war, so habe ich mich der Feder des H. v. Floret bedient, für dessen unverbrüchliche Verschwiegenheit und Diskretion ich bürge."

[8] Jan. 23, 1816, AKA Prot. 282, No. 149.

[9] These comments are taken chiefly from two dispatches: Stewart to Castl., Jan. 18 and Feb. 4, 1816, FO 7, 126. For the latter document, cf. Appendix A, No. 4.

[10] Similar sentiments were expressed by Stewart in regard to the Bavarian question: "Prince Metternich's turn of Mind would lead Him to a more liberal System and to more enlightened Views, but the circle surrounding the Emperor usurps so much influence in upholding a Stiff, close, littleminded Stile of Action, that Prince Metternich has not power or Means to resist this Side that overwhelms him." Stewart to Castl., April 7, 1816, FO 7, 127.

[11] Stewart to Castl., Mar. 15, 1816, FO 7, 126.

[12] Marchese Filipo Carlo Ghisilieri, "Pensées d'un sujet fidèle à l'occasion de l'arrivée en Italie de S.M. l'Empereur François Premier, et surtout à l'époque de son entrée solennelle à Milan", Prov/LV 40, 167-186.

[13] Bllg. to Wssbg., Dec. 16, 1815, GK 482, *Bellegarde*.

[14] KF to Trauttmansdorff, Mar. 7, 1816, StR Prot. 246, No. 1603.

[15] More recent Italian historians are inclined to exculpate Bellegarde from blame for the shortcomings of the Austrian administration in LV. Cf. for ex. Spadoni, *op. cit.* p. 430.

[16] The secrecy may be explained by the contained disclosures which practically amount to counter-intelligence reports. The double correspondence's deceptive art resulted in occasional duplication since not always was there a strict line drawn in the secret correspondence between routine details and confidential information, but all routine details had to appear in the regular correspondence. Also, since it was expected that Bubna would take a stand now and then on certain issues within the normal correspondence, phrases are sometimes repeated. Until recently, the Metternich originals and Bubna drafts were kept in Milan. They are now in Vienna where are the Bubna originals and the Metternich drafts.

[17] Saurau to Mett., Jan. 6, 1816, NW, Hkz to Stk, 81.

[18] In informing Metternich of his promotion, Sardagna recalled his past services with Bellegarde and cast thereby a very interesting light upon his relationship to the marshal: he had partially conducted the correspondence of the marshal with Metternich and many of the most important pieces and elaborations had come from his pen. His special qualifications had been, as he claimed, that he was the only one associated with the provisional government as versed in Italian as in German language and forms and, moreover, acquainted with most of the leading figures of the previous government. Sard. to StK., Jan. 20, 1816, Prov/LV 21, 1, 2.

[19] In this, he felt certain of Metternich's support before the emperor. Bllg. to Mett., Mar. 25, 1816, Prov/LV 4, 4, 127.

[20] Signed original proclamations, Mar. 7, 1816, HKzA IIIA4, 358; also, NW, HKz to StK, 81.

[21] Saurau to KF, Mar. 16, 1816, KFA 12 (15), 1, 174; also AKA Prot. 281, No. 675.

[22] Imperial comment, *loc. cit.*

[23] "Ernennung eines blos zur Repräsentazion und höherem Glanze bestimmten Vizekönigs", AhK, June 21, 1816, HKzA IIIA4, 358. Publ. by Helfert, *Stiftung*, p. 494.

[24] P.S., dated Aug. 22, 1816, to above mentioned Ghisilieri memoir, Prov/LV 40, 167-186.

[25] KF to Wallis, undated, KFA 12 (15), 1, 6.

[26] Mar. 29, 1816, AKA Prot. 282, No. 494.

[27] AhE, Apr. 15, 1816, Helfert, *Stiftung*, pp. 388-393.

[28] For example, on Nov. 1, 1815, KFA 14 (16), 1, 218; cf. Chapt. I, note 87. This very definite attitude was reiterated by Erzherzog Rainer on June 19, 1816, KFA 30 (31), 2.

[29] COHC Vortr. Nov. 27, 1815, KFA 30 (31), 3, 108.

[30] COHC Vortr. Dec. 25, 1815, approved by the emperor, Jan. 23, 1816, KFA 15 (17), 1, 8; also, StR Prot. 245, No. 30. Ironically, the professor appointed to the chair for German at Padua some four years hence had the name Angelo Ridolfi.

[31] StR Prot. 262, No. 8159, Nov. 14, 1817.

[32] "Vorträge der COHC in Studienangelegenheiten", based on the work of Hofrat

Jüstel: on universities, Aug. 21 (deliberations Sept. 20 and Oct. 23), and imperial resolution on Dec. 7, 1816; on *lyceums*, Sept. 11, resolved on Nov. 9, 1816; on *gymnasiums*
and public schools, Sept. 28 and Oct. 22, resolved on Dec. 17, 1816. KFA 14 (16),
6, 5-84.

³³ Cf. above, Chapt. I, note 85.

³⁴ Jüstel Vortrag, Dec. 19, 1815. KF solemnly noted (in translation) upon the report:
"The habit of cursing in Venice must be made to disappear through an application of
earnestness, shrewdness, and gentleness." KFA 16 (18), 1, 13-18.

³⁵ Bllg. to Haager, 1815. Helfert, *Stiftung*, p. 301.

³⁶ Saurau to Mett., Mar. 9, 1816, Prov/LV 6, 3, 90.

³⁷ Mett. to KF, July 19, 1816, Vortr. 299, 2, 23-37; publ. by A. Luzio (cf. Bibl.).

³⁸ KF to Mett., Oct. 10, 1815: ". . . das schon längere Zeit bei Ihnen haftende Stück
'Illyrien und seine Verfassung' . . . zurückzuschicken, da eine Entscheidung hierüber dringend
ist." Vortr. 294, 2.

³⁹ Hud. to Mett., Apr. 8, 1814, Int. Korr. 78.

⁴⁰ Mett. Gutachten, Feb. 1, 1816, Vortr. 296, 3; KFA 30 (31), 1.

⁴¹ Protocol of the COHC's session of Feb. 17, 1816, and of Lazansky's Vortrag of
Feb. 28, 1816, KFA 30 (31), 1.

⁴² The endless troubles arising from the persistent strife and fierce local allegiances
within the Dalmatian coastal cities led Mett. to urge "sie als Mitglieder eines und desselben Staatenbundes mehr und mehr ineinander zu verschmelzen und alle älteren Unter-
schiede unter einem gemeinschaftlichen Namen verschwinden zu machen." Mett. to KF,
May 21, 1815, Vortr. 292, 2.

⁴³ For example, in the case of Galicia, Mett. to KF, Apr. 18, 1815, Vortr. 291, 5, 644.

⁴⁴ Count Peter Goëss, at that time governor in Venice, previously governor of Dalmatia — a man well acquainted with Illyrian matters.

⁴⁵ Mett. to KF, Klagenfurt, May 24, 1816, Vortr. 298, 1, 70. Cf. Appendix A, No. 5.

⁴⁶ AhRes. to Laz. Vortr. of Feb. 28 followed on June 13, 1816; to Mett.'s Vortr. of
May 24, on June 20, 1816, with the following words: "Ich ertheile den Befehl, daß
Krain, Kärnten, Görz, das Küstenland und der abgetretene Theil von Kroatien unter
zwey Gubernien unter dem Namen von Illyrien vereinigt bleiben, was den hinwegen
anzunehmenden Titel anbelangt, habe Ich den Gr. Lazansky angewiesen, mit Ihnen das
Einvernehmen zu pflegen." KFA 30 (31), 1; Vortr. 298, 1, 70.

⁴⁷ AhRes., June 13, 1816, *loc. cit.*

⁴⁸ Laz. to StK., June 22, 1816; StK (Bretfeld) to Laz., July 10, 1816, Prov/Ill., 16.

⁴⁹ Laz. Vortr., Jul. 13, 1816, KFA 30 (31), 1.

⁵⁰ Res. aug. and imperial patent, Aug. 3, 1816, *ibid.*

⁵¹ Mett. to Est., Jan. 17, 1816, St. Abt. Engl., Weis. 205, 1, 42-55 and 55-65; Mett. to
Est., Mar. 9, 1816, *ibid.*, 3, 4. Cf. further, Mett. to Steigentesch, May 1816 (with Stewart
to Castl., June 10, 1816, FO 7, 127), in which he claimed the *esprit public* in Germany
and Italy gave less cause for worry than in France.

⁵² Hud. to Mett., Jan. 6, and March 13, 1816, MAP, AC 16, 2, 126 and 292. Soon
Hud. came closer to Mett.'s views and called for a protectorate of limited nature not
necessarily based on expensive military might. Nevertheless, he was convinced that not
to have a protectorate at all would cost Austria even more in the long run, especially if
Austria should suddenly be occupied by a crisis elsewhere.

⁵³ Mett. to KF, Feb. 3, 1816, Vortr. 296, 3, 23-100. Cf. further, Feb. 23, and the
beginning of May, 1816, *ibid.*, 4, 67 ff, and Vortr. 298, 1.

[54] Hud. to Mett., Jan. 6, 1816, MAP, AC, 16, 2, 126; Mett. to KF, Dec. 10, 1815, Vortr. 295, 2, 62 ff and 107 ff.

[55] In Germany, not even in partnership with Prussia — Mett. to Buol, Jul. 2, 1816, GA Lond. W/5, 97.

[56] Mett. to Saurau, July 1, 1816, Prov/LV 20, 1, 491; Mett. to Guicc., July 7, 1816, ASM, Geh. Corr. Guicc. 1.

[57] Mett. to Hud., Apr. 11, 1816, Int. Korr. 80 ("Richelieu's present situation is one of the saddest because it is an impossible one.")

[58] Mett. to KF, June 2 and July 20, 1816, Vortr. 298, 2, 61, and 299, 2, 40.

[59] "L'Empereur et Metternich me paraissent dans une ivresse complète. Les flagorneries des Italiens et l'enthousiasme, vrai ou factice, qu'ils professent, leur ont fait tourner les têtes à un point incroyable. Metternich écrit à une personne de sa famille, 'qu'enfin il se trouvait dans un pays, où on savait rendre justice au mérite, et où ceux qui avaient perdu les provinces de la Monarchie n'étaient pas, comme cela se faisait ailleurs, mieux traités que ceux qui les avaient reconquises.' Ce sera encore autre chose à Milan, où, d'après les personnes qui connaissent le terrain, on est beaucoup plus fort, même en belles phrases et flatterie habile qu'à Venise." Gentz to Wessenberg, December 26, 1815, *Gentz und Wessenberg*, p. 97.

[60] Mett. to Hud., Dec. 16, 1815, Int. Korr. 79.

[61] General instructions to Est., Nov. 7, 1815, GA Lond. W/3, 15; further, Mett. to Est., Feb. 29, 1816, St. Abt. Engl. Weis. 205, 2, 44. This problem was also one of those which never ceased: Mett. to Est., Feb. 18, 1817, GA Lond. W/7, 1, 263. The Italian colony in London now counted Ugo Foscolo among its members. Helfert, *Stiftung*, p. 454. Later, as Russian agents entered the picture and took an interest in the Italian independence matter, correspondence on this issue increased accordingly.

[62] Gentz to Mett., Jan. 18, 1816, *Wittichen*, III 1, p. 321, referring to Dominique Dufour Baron de Pradt's *Du Congrès de Vienne*, published in 1815.

[63] A futile endeavor: cf. StK to HKz, Jan. 20, and Laz. Vortr., Jan. 8 and Laz. note of Mar. 10, 1816, NW, StK to HKz 28.

[64] Mett. to Est., Feb. 6, 1816, St. Abt. Engl. Weis. 205, 2, 9.

[65] Mett. to Est., July 29, 1816, *ibid.*, 6, 59. This thought was already expressed at an earlier opportunity by Stewart (perhaps he had heard it then from Mett.): "That Austria trembles at the very name of a constitution founded on national representation in Italy is clear" because if established once anywhere on the peninsula, the whole would be in danger. Stewart to Castl., Feb. 17, 1816, FO 7, 126. Re Metternich's fear of the Sicilian constitution, cf. further: Stewart to Castl., June 23, 1816, FO 7, 127.

[66] Hud. to Mett., MAP, AC 16, 2, 113.

[67] Mett. to Est., July 29, 1816, St. Abt. Engl. Weis. 205, 6, 56.

[68] Saurau to Mett., Jan. 26, 1816, Prov/LV 6, 5, 1, along with the draft of the proposed article.

[69] Mett. to Saurau, Feb. 4, 1816, *loc. cit.* Apropos this matter, Stewart reported that the Milanese, inspired by what Alexander had done for his Polish subjects, compared their monarch quite unfavorably with the Russian ruler. Stewart to Castl., Mar. 2, 1816, FO 7, 126.

[70] Haager and Sedl., Polizei Vortr., Feb. 26, 1816, Polizei A., No. 556; Helfert, *Stiftung*, p. 415.

[71] Mett. to Saurau, Feb. 29, 1816, Prov/LV 20, 3, 477.

[72] For example, in answer to Mett.'s Vortr., Febr. 5, 1816, Vortr. 296, 3, 105.

[73] App. to Mett., Apr. 1 and 5, 1816, ASM, Geh. Corr. Guicc. 1. Giuseppe Antinori, il duca di Brindisi, 1773-1856, is the subject of a recent Italian study by A. Cutolo (cf. Bibliography), which is esp. explicit for the period 1816-1822.

[74] Mett. to App., Apr. 8, 1816, ASM, Geh. Corr. Guicc. 1; for a report on activities of a committee of the independence party in Milan, cf. Bub., to Mett., July 3, 1816, ASM, Geh. Corr. Bub. 1.

[75] Still in May, Metternich began to play down the idea of a real threat to Italy, although already emphasizing the need for close scrutiny: "L'Italie a dû nous fournir le sujet de graves et de profondes observations. L'Esprit de ce pays ne peut être reconnu et jugé de loin, et il mérite de ne pas l'être superficiellement." But after having scrutinized in a most secret manner the *esprit* of the peninsula, "je n'hésite pas d'affirmer positivement, que ce pays ne doit offrir nul sujet d'inquiétude." Mett. to Steigentesch, May 1816, enclosed with Stewart to Castl., June 10, 1816, FO 7, 127.

[76] Mett. to Bub., Aug. 16, 1816, ASM, Geh. Corr. Bub. 1; Mett. to KF, Oct. 8 and 22, 1816, Vortr. 302, 1, 38-46 and 166-172. Metternich was convinced: ". . . daß nähmlich eine allgemeine Verschwörung zur Erlangung der Unabhängigkeit, ein ganz Italien umfassender, nach bestimmten Gesetzen geregelter, nach einem gemeinschaftlichen Plane handelnder Bund der Guelfen, unter Englischem oder irgend einem anderen fremden Einfluß gegenwärtig durchaus nicht besteht, daß dies ein bloßes Hirngespinst sey. . ."

[77] Mett. to Guicc., in regard to the establishment of the CBA, May 10, 1816, Prov/LV 6, 1, 1.

[78] Mett. to Guicc., June 16, 1816, *loc. cit.*; further, Mett. to KF, June 17 and July 5, 1816, Vortr. 298, 2, 176 and 299, 1, 35.

[79] Mett. to Saurau, July 12, 1816, Prov/LV 20. In autumn, Mett. suggested to the emperor that Saurau might make a good ambassador to Spain: Oct. 28, 1816, Vortr. 302, 1, 213. However, Saurau did not particularly want to go: Saurau to Mett., Jan. 4, 1817, Prov/LV 6, 4, 39. A comment of Stewart in regard to Saurau's planned transfer and possible replacement by Goëss provides an interesting sidelight: "M. de Saurau has been for a long period, as my letters from Italy will have announced to your Lordship, obnoxious to the people at Milan, and, although by his administration, great vigor and activity were exerted, and the German system rigidly enforced, still, in the long run, it has been deemed expedient to remove him." Stewart to Castl., Dec. 21, 1816, FO 7, 129. Metternich's obvious effort was not successful and Saurau stayed for the time being in Milan.

[80] Mett. to Bub., Aug. 16, 1816, ASM, Geh. Corr. Bub. 1.

[81] Mett. to KF, Oct. 22, 1816, Vortr. 302, 1, 176. Mett. to Guicc., Prov/LV 6, 1, 64, Dec. 10, 1816; Mett. to Bub., Dec. 10, 1816, ASM, Geh. Corr. Bub. 1.

[82] These are taken from — among others — the following letters: Mett. to Guicc.: 1.) May 10, 1816, Prov/LV, 6, 1; 2.) June 16, 1816, *ibid.*; 3.) July 7, 1816, ASM Guicc. 1; 4.) Dec. 10, 1816, Prov/LV 6, 1; 5.) Feb. 12, 1817, *ibid.*; 6.) Apr. 6, 1818, Prov/LV 7, 1; 7.) July 14, 1819, Prov/LV 26, 1. Guicc. to Mett.: 8.) Jan. 17, 1817, Prov/LV 6, 1; Mett. to Bub.: 9.) June 16, 1816, Prov/LV 25, 1; 10.) July 7, 1816, ASM Bub. 1; 11.) Aug. 16, 1816, *ibid.*; 12.) Oct. 3, 1816, *ibid.*; 13.) Dec. 10, 1816, *ibid.*; 14.) Feb. 17, 1817, *ibid.*; 15.) July 25, 1817, *ibid.* Bubna to Mett.: 16.) July 3, 1816, *ibid.* Mett. to Saurau; 17.) June 14, 1816, Prov/LV 20, 3; 18.) July 1, 1816, *ibid.* Mett. to KF: 19.) Oct. 8, 1816, Vortr. 302, 1; 20.) Oct. 22, 1816, *ibid.*; 21.) May 5, 1819, Vortr. 319, 1; 22.) Oct. 12, 1819, Vortr. 322, 2. KF (Mett.) to Czar Alexander: 23.) Apr. 23, 1819,

GA Lond. W/11, 2. Mett. to Gentz: 24.) May 7, 1819, *Wittichen,* III 1, p. 425. Mett. to Est.: 25.) Nov. 23, 1816, GA Lond., W/6, 2; 26.) July 26, 1817, *ibid.,* 8, 1; 27.) Feb. 15, 1819, *ibid.,* 11, 1; 28.) Apr. 30, 1819, *ibid.,* 11, 2; 29.) July 9, 1819, *ibid.,* 12, 1; 30.) Mar. 19, 1821, *ibid.,* 17, 2. Mett. to Lebz.: 31.) May 24, 1820 *ibid.,* 14, 1. In the following paragraphs, each thought carries the number of the particular source as listed above.

[83] 1, 2, 3, 5, 16, 21, 22.

[84] 2, 3, 5, 8, 19, 25, 26, 27, 28, 29.

[85] 2, 3, 15, 18.

[86] 1, 2, 3, 4, 9, 10, 12, 14, 17, 20 etc.

[87] 2, 3, 5, 6, 7, 9, 11, 13, 17, 23, 24, 30, 31.

[88] Reports appear almost regularly; cf. esp. Guicc. to Mett., Dec. 24, 1816, ASM Guicc. 1.

[89] Mett. to Guicc., 2, 5 (as numbered in note 82).

[90] Bub. to Mett., Nov. 18, 1816, ASM Bub. 1.

[91] Sedl. report to Mett., contained in Vortr. of Mett. to KF, Mar. 15, 1817, Vortr. 305, 1, 142.

CHAPTER IV

[1] Mett. to his wife, Eleonora, Aug. 29, 1817, NP III, p. 46; Mett. to Goëss, Dec. 24, 1817, Prov/LV 18, 2, 50. Significantly, Mett. had wanted, as in the autumn of 1815, to have Ld. Stewart accompany him to Italy. However, Stewart did not succeed in obtaining permission from London. Stewart to Castl., Apr. 18, 1817, FO 7, 136.

[2] Mett. to Bub., July 25, 1817, ASM, Geh. Corr. Bub. 1.

[3] Mett. to Hud., June 26, 1817, Int. Korr. 80; Mett. to Lebz., June 28, 1817, NP III, p. 50; Mett. to Est., July 26, 1817, GA Lond. W/8, 1, 151.

[4] Mett. to KF, July 1 and 5, 1817, Vortr. 307, 2, 6, 24.

[5] Sedl. Vortr., Mar. 28, 1817, KA, Polizei Vortr., 43, No. 947.

[6] Bub. to Mett., Aug. 19, 1817, ASM, Bub. 1.

[7] Mett. to Bub., July 25, 1817, *loc. cit.* Further, "Il ne faut jamais oublier que notre position ne ressemble à nulle autre, car nous sommes entièrement *centraux*; nous formons un île comme vous, mais avec la grande différence, que vous avez des remparts inexpugnables autour de vous, tandis que nous n'offrons que des points d'attaque. Notre grande force doit être morale", Mett. to Stewart, May 30, 1816, ad No. 46, FO 7, 127.

[8] Mett. to KF, July 1 and Aug. 8, 1817, Vortr. 307, 2, 6, and 3, 45.

[9] Mett. to Bub., July 25, 1817, *loc. cit.*

[10] Mett. to KF, Aug. 8, 1817, *loc. cit.*

[11] Ehzg. Rainer to KF, Aug. 30, 1817, Nachlass Rainer, 3, 850.

[12] Sard. to Mett., Feb. 14, 1817, Prov/LV 21, 2, 134.

[13] Mett. to Bub., July 25, 1817, *loc. cit.*

[14] Bub. to Mett., Oct. 12, 1817, ASM, Bub. 1.

[15] Mett. to Bub., Apr. 12, 1817, ASM, Bub. 1; Mett. to KF, May 17, 1817, Vortr. 306, 2, 4; further, Aug. 4, 1817, Vortr. 307, 2, 6; Saurau to Mett., June 1, 1817, Prov/LV 20, 2, 218: Saurau had denied Manzi a passport to Vienna and called him a revolutionary.

[16] Mett. to KF, Nov. 3, 1817, with Manzi reports, Vortr. 309, 1, 35-243: "Ausarbeitungen über Italien mit neun Beilagen — Nr. 9 v. S. Maj. zurück behalten. (Der

Stand der Dinge in Italien)." These various pieces include: "Bemerkungen über den inneren Stand von Italien", part of which is published, along with the accompanying introductory *Vortrag* in NP III, p. 91 ff; further, "Bemerkungen über die Ausarbeitung Bartholdy's über Italien" — an interesting comparison of the views of this Prussian official with those of Manzi as well as the report of Bartholdy himself; further, "Notizen über die Carbonari, vorzüglich im Königreich Neapel", "Zustand von Neapel", and finally an additional *Vortrag* of Mett., also of Nov. 3, pleading for a lifting of the ban on studying outside of Austria — at least in regard to Tuscany — a land ruled by the emperor's brother and which, according to the minister, could not really be considered as *Ausland*. This plea was made in consideration for the Lombardo-Venetian students who had long been accustomed to round out their humanistic studies in the south — especially Florence, and who were now prevented from following this tradition. KF's answer was that absolutely everything would remain as it was. The section within the Manzi report dealing with Naples has just been published by N. Nada, "Il Regno di Napoli nell'Età della Restaurazione secondo i Giudizi di Tito Manzi", *RSR*, XLVIII-IV (Oct. — Dec. 1961), pp. 627-645.

[17] Arthur G. Haas, "Kaiser Franz, Metternich und die Stellung Illyriens", *MÖStA*, XI (1958), pp. 373-375. The word "Illyria" was loosely applied prior to Napoleonic times. Within the Habsburg lands it usually referred to the so-called Kingdom of Croatia-Slavonia and the Serb-speaking districts along the southern frontier rather than to Carinthia, Carniola, and Austrian Istria or to Venetian Istria and Dalmatia — all of which belonged later either to the French Illyrian Provinces or to the Kingdom of Illyria.

[18] Josef Karl Mayr, "Zur Geschichte der italienischen Hofkanzlei und der dalmatinisch-albanesischen Hofstelle, 1793-1809", *MIÖG*, extra vol. XI (1929), pp. 662-675.

[19] Hermann Meynert, *Kaiser Franz I. Zur Geschichte seiner Regierung und seiner Zeit*, p. 235 ff. The memorandum dates from the first half of 1815 — about the same time in which Sardagna presented his memoir to Metternich. It is not improbable that a relation exists between the two pieces. The former is partially cited by Meynert.

[20] Dietrichstein to Mett., Oct. 27, 1817, GK 481, 6, 50. Cf. Appendix A, No. 6. Unfortunately, scarcely any of the numerous tracts D. must have written are to be found today. The letter cited above, attesting well to his remarkable perception, is one of the few I have been able to uncover in the archives. Cf., further, in Appendix B: "Data on Austrian Officials", under Dietrichstein.

[21] The proverb cited by Dietrichstein: "Hüte Dich die Rechnung ohne den Wirt zu machen" applies in this instance not to KF but to the personnel available for the new posts — specifically to the intended minister of the interior.

[22] Mett. to Bub., July 25, 1817, *loc. cit.* That KF had had Rainer in mind for this post for some time can be gathered from the fact that the archduke was sent to Italy for a "get-acquainted" visit in 1816-1817. Cf. Helfert, *Casati und Pillersdorf*, p. 15.

[23] Mett. to KF, Oct. 27, 1817, Vortr. 308, 3, 70-138. The introductory *Vortrag* and that containing the proposals themselves used here, are drafts in Metternich's own hand. A neater version, used by Klinkowström, is among the Metternich collection in Prag. This copy, showing slight divergences, is printed — some paragraphs on activities properly belonging to the ministry of the interior are omitted — in the NP, vol. III. Still another copy exists in the KFA 91 (82); it was copied by a secretary but contains corrections and additions in Metternich's hand which are not to be found elsewhere — on the distinction between a minister and a "Hofstellen" president. The additions in this

third copy were written subsequent to Oct. 27; it was an enclosure of a communication of Saurau to KF, dated Dec. 18, 1817. Along with the Metternich drafts in the *Vorträge,* there are, furthermore, a *Vortrag* of Stadion on financial matters, a draft of the imperial patent, and two versions of an article for the *Wiener Zeitung* in regard to the new regulations of the interior administration and, finally, a *Vortrag* on the erection of a ministry of justice under Count Wallis. Cf. Appendix A, No. 7.

[24] Much points to the assumption that Metternich had D.'s letter before him as the second copy — at least — was finished on Oct. 27: all documents — the Metternich pieces as well as the D. letter — carry the same date; furthermore, the Palais Dietrichstein almost adjoins the Palais Kaunitz (the Staatskanzlei and Metternich's residence). It is quite likely that the D. letter was brought over during the course of the day; the second Metternich copy must have been finished during the later part of the day, since a first draft carrying the same date preceded it.

[25] From the third version of Metternich's *Vortrag* of Oct. 27, KFA 91 (82).

[26] Cf. editor's note, NP III, pp. 74-75. Further: Alfred Stern, "L'idée d'une représentation centrale de l'Autriche conçue par le Prince de Metternich", *RH,* XXXI (1886), pp. 313-326. Also, Mett. to Kübeck, Feb. 14, 1851, NP VIII, p. 509 ff.

[27] Aretin, "Metternichs Verfassungspläne, 1817-1818" *HJb,* LXXIV (1955), pp. 718-725.

[28] *Tagebücher* von Friedrich von Gentz, II, p. 180, Nov. 17, 1817.

[29] These documents are part of the convolute containing the Mett. drafts of his Oct. 27 *Vortrag.*

[30] *Wiener Zeitung,* Dec. 24, 1817, *loc. cit.,* cf. Appendix A, No. 8; KF to Wallis, Dec. 23, 1817, AKA Prot. 291.

[31] This version was erroneously published by the editors of the NP as the official version; we may forgive them for not knowing better the details of this new but short-lived organization some sixty years after it had lost all significance.

[32] KFA 91 (82), 163-177. Saurau to KF, Dec. 18, 1817.

[33] Among others: certain revenue matters, property matters, charities, commerce, communications, road construction, public works, civil service appointments, public education, disciplinary measures, police excesses, penal institutions, sanitation, tolerance and affairs dealing with the clergy, Jews, and the estates. Issues dealing with "national" matters were not mentioned, presumably because these fell under the competence of the chancellors. Most of the activities listed, Mett. thought, should be handled by special subordinate bureaus within the ministry.

[34] KF to Saurau, Dec. 23, 1817, a) StR Prot., 1817, 263, No. 10345; b) AKA Prot., 291, Sep. Bill. Prot., No. 821. Shortly before, Saurau had been named ambassador to Madrid at Metternich's urging. This appointment was, of course, now cancelled.

[35] b) *loc. cit.,* No. 824.

[36] a) *loc. cit.,* No. 10346; b) *loc. cit.,* No. 823; further, Dec. 25, 1817, NW, HKz to StK, 86, 753.

[37] KF to Colloredo, Dec. 25, 1817, a) No. 10176. Copies of the oaths and other documents relating to the oathtaking ceremony are to be found in HKzA IIIA2, cart. 299. An oath abjuring membership in forbidden organizations drawn up by the HKz was not used because the StK insisted that only it had the prerogative of drawing up such an oath, which it then did.

[38] All dated Dec. 24, 1817: to Bub., two letters, ASM, Bub. 1 and Prov/LV 37, 2, 27; to Guicc., two letters, Prov/LV 6, 1, 185-192; to Goëss, Prov/LV 18, 2, 50; to Mell., Prov/LV 6, 2, 206.

[39] Goëss to Mett., Dec. 30, 1817, Prov/LV 18, 4, 105-108. Goëss' application was the reply to Mett.'s letter of Dec. 24. He proudly cited his long experience. In a second letter of the same date, written in French, he praised the new measures as being in line with the spirit of the times.

[40] Mett. to Bub., July 25, 1817, ASM, Bub. 1.

[41] Signed originals, HKzA IIIA4, cart. 359.

[42] KF to Mett. and Saurau, Dec. 23, 1817, StR Prot. 1817, 263, No. 10347. Thereupon the notification from the HKz to the StK, Dec. 25, 1817, NW 86, 753.

[43] AhH. Billett, Dec. 27, 1817, AKA Curr. Prot. 287, No. 8472; Saurau's draft, same date, StR Prot. 1817, 263, No. 10178.

[44] Bub. to Mett., Jan. 4 and 5, 1818, Prov/LV 26, 2, 115 and 124; ASM, Bub. 2.

[45] The grumblers further pointed to Guicc.'s non-Milanese origin (Val Tellin), a fact which Bubna mentioned only in his confidential French letter to Metternich, but omitted from the German one which went through regular channels.

[46] Bub. to Mett., Dec. 26, 1817, Prov/LV 25, 2, 447. In regard to the personnel arrangements of the new administrative system, both Guicc. and Bub. requested Mett. to seek the emperor's approval to employ Tito Manzi as go-between of their respective offices: Guicc. to Mett., Jan. 1, 1818 (acknowledgment of Mett.'s Dec. 24 letter), Prov/LV 7, 1, 1; Bub. to Mett., Jan. 4, 1818, Prov/LV 26, 2, 115, as well as ASM, Bub. 2.

[47] Bub. to Mett., Dec. 26, 1817, loc. cit.; Bub. to Mett., Jan. 13, 1818, Prov/LV 26, 2, 128; ASM, Bub. 2.

[48] Guicc. to Mett., Jan. 20, 1818, Prov/LV 7, 3, 15.

[49] Bub. to Mett., Jan. 4, 1818, loc. cit.; further, Bub. to Mett., Feb. 11, 1818, Prov/LV 26, 2, 142, as well as ASM, Bub. 2.

[50] Mett. to KF, Jan. 11, 1818, Vortr. 310, 1, 41.

[51] Mett. to KF, Jan. 24, ibid., 2, 43.

[52] In submitting to KF the dispatches from LV, Mett. had also put in a good word for Tito Manzi. He labelled him a talented and capable servant of Austria despite the republican leanings which made KF suspicious (as Saurau had already been). What endeared Manzi to Mett. was that he disliked the nobility and the clergy as well as the other Italian governments. Bub. was to treat him kindly and to take care that M. would not get the idea that he was doing police work. Mett. to Bub., two letters, Jan. 27, 1818, ASM, Bub. 2; Prov/LV 37, 7, 3.

[53] Mett. to KF, Jan. 28, 1818, Vortr. 310, 2, 75.

[54] Bub. to Mett., Feb. 11, 1818, loc. cit.

[55] Mett. to KF, Mar. 24, 1818, Vortr. 311, 2, 46. (The German word is "Oberleitung"; emphasis is my own.)

[56] Loc. cit.

[57] Guicc. to Mett., Apr. 1, 1818, Prov/LV 7, 1, 16-23.

[58] Mett. to Guicc., Apr. 6, 1818, ibid., 23-26.

[59] Mett. to Bub., Apr. 6, 1818 (confidential), ASM, Bub. 2.

[60] Bub. to Mett., Apr. 24, 1818, Prov/LV 26, 2, 196.

[61] AhKS, Apr. 5, 1818, Konf. A-a 6.

[62] Bllg. to KF, Jan. 23, 1816, burnt fragment, HKzA IIIA4, 359.

[63] "Instructions to the Viceroy", Konf. A-a 6, Nos. 111 and 159. They are cited in final form, bearing the date June 22, 1818, by Sandonà, Il Regno Lombardo Veneto, pp. 92-95; cf. further, R. J. Rath, "L'amministrazione austriaca nel Lombardo Veneto (1814-1821)", Archivio Economico dell'Unificazione Italiana, Serie I, Vol. IX, p. 18.

[64] AhKS to Saur., May 2, 1818, HKzA IIIA4, 359.

[65] Prot. of the Min. of the Int., May 21, 1818, *ibid.*

[66] Guicc. to Mett., May 11, 1818, Prov/LV 7, 1, 27-51.

[67] Bub. to Mett., May 14, 1818, Prov/LV 26, 2, 204.

[68] Bub. to Mett., May 26, 1818, Prov/LV 26, 2, 212; ASM, Bub. 2. Previous mention on Apr. 24.

[69] Mett. to KF, June 26, 1818, Vortr. 313, 2, 30. One happy sidelight: Mett.'s intercession for Sard. had effect, since the latter found employment in Milan to probe public opinion, as Mett. so nicely put it, "called here, at Your Majesty's command."

[70] Mett. to Bub., June 13, 1818, ASM, Bub. 2.

[71] KF to Mett., June 11, 1818, Vortr. 313, 2, 31.

[72] Stewart to Castl., Sept. 8, 1818, FO 7, 139.

[73] Mett. to KF, Aug. 10, 1818, Vortr. 314, 2, 87-90.

[74] Bub. to Mett., July 3, 1818, Prov/LV 26, 2, 248.

[75] Bub. to Mett., Aug. 21 and 31, 1818, MAP, AC 16, 2, 611-670.

[76] Hud. to Mett., Aug. 17, 1818, *ibid.*

CONCLUSION AND EPILOGUE

[1] The relationship of European powers toward *nationalism* as a new historical force and toward German, Italian, and Polish nationalism in particular, is something else again. Under this aspect come most judgments on the Congress of Vienna's sins of omission: cf. Hannah Straus, *The Attitude of the Congress of Vienna toward Nationalism in Germany, Italy and Poland*, especially the preface and conclusion.

[2] This was a belief of some elder-generation Lombards in the Restoration period and is an opinion of some contemporary historians. Cf. R.J. Rath, "L'amministrazione austriaca nel Lombardo Veneto (1814-1821)", p. 30. However, police reports on an Italian dissatisfaction at the slow replacement of the French administrative system must be taken with some caution. A natural rancor at conscription and harsh wartime taxes imposed by the French accounted for many such statements, especially in Venetia. Indeed, criticism was more often directed against disliked appointees of the French still in office than at the administrative system as such. Moreover, an uncritical police dutifully passed on every rumor and plaint. The numerous statements of Wess., Bllg., Mett., and Sard. and even Bubna testify to the contrary; they insisted on a general admiration for and even superiority of Franco-Italian methods.

[3] Ct. Kolowrat's occasional requests to be relieved, which a solicitous KF always "successfully" persuaded him to reconsider, are a completely different matter. These requests were a tactic in a power struggle with Metternich and were protests directed against the chancellor rather than against the emperor. On this issue, cf. Srbik, *Metternich*, I, p. 454, and R. W. Seton-Watson, "Metternich and internal Austrian Policy", *Slavonic and East European Review*, XVII and XVIII (1939), p. 541.

[4] *Re* Bohemia: Mett. to KF, Feb. 5, 1818, Vortr. 310, 2, 40-56; *re* LV: Mett. to Hardenberg, May 31, 1817, Vortr. 306, 2, 174-186.

[5] Cf. chapter II, notes 84 and 86; Hud. to Mett., April 4, 1816, MAP, AC 16, 2, 333.

[6] Ugarte to the governor, Hauer, quoted by Hermann Meynert, *Kaiser Franz I. Zur Geschichte Seiner Regierung und Seiner Zeit*, p. 241.

[7] *Loc. cit.*

[8] KF to Mett., Aug. 25, 1817, Vortr. 307, 3, 45.

[9] "Représentants du Royaume de Pologne! Vos espérances et mes voeux s'accomplissent. Le peuple que Vous êtes appelés à représenter jouit enfin d'une existence nationale, garantie par les institutions que le temps a mûries et sanctionnées . . .; en mettant en pratique les principes de ces institutions libérales qui n'ont cessé de faire l'objet de ma solicitude etc. . . ." Finally: "Polonais, c'est à Vous à consolider votre renaissance . . . elle est indissolublement liée aux destinées de la Russie . . . [laquelle] assure désormais à la Pologne un rang honorable parmi les nations de l'Europe." Speech of Czar Alexander at the opening of the Polish Diet, March 27, 1818, GA Lond. W/9, 2.

[10] Mett. to KF, April 20, 1818, Vortr. 312, 2, 167-171.

[11] Mett. to KF, April 18, 1815, Vortr. 291, 5, 644; cf. Appendix B, No. 2.

[12] For Russian subversion in Galicia: Mett. to KF, Oct. 21, 1818, Vortr. 315, 2, 167.

[13] Mett. to Bub., Jan. 28, 1819, ASM, Bub. 2.

[14] Goëss to Archd. Rainer, Feb. 15, 1819, KFA 71 (73), 2, 70; Bub. to Mett., April 24, 1819, Prov/LV 26, 409.

[15] Mett. to KF, May 5, 1819, Vortr. 319, 1, 48 ff.

[16] Mett. to his wife Eleonora, June 9, 1819, NP III, p. 213.

[17] Bub. to Mett., Sept. 1, 1819, Prov/LV 26, 3, 467 ff.

[18] Mett. to Est., July 9, 1819, GA Lond. W/12, 1; Mett. to KF, Aug. 1, 1819, Vortr. 321, 1.

[19] Mett. to Lebz., Feb. 20, 1820, GA Lond. W/13, 1.

[20] Mett. to Strass., Sept. 22, 1819, Prov/LV 7, 2, 48-51.

[21] Bub. to Mett., Sept. 1, 1819, *loc. cit.;* Mett. to KF, Oct. 12, 1819, Vortr. 322, 2, 123 ff.

[22] Bub. to Mett., Sept. 1, 1819, *loc. cit.;* Mett. to Guicc., July 14, 1819, Prov/LV 26, 1, 79. Incidentally, Mett. again made a strong plea for Tito Manzi, whom he suggested employing with a new CBA.

[23] Mett. to Bub., Mar. 31, 1820, enclosing imperial resolution of Mar. 13; further, Mett. to Bub., Apr. 19, 1820: Bub. was to continue his activity. KF turned Manzi down, later however, again at Mett.'s request, appointed him *Regierungsrat.* ASM, Bub. 3.

[24] Mett. to KF, June 22, 1820, Vortr. 327, 1, 141; further, Dec. 22, 1820, Vortr. 329, 3, 118; Mett. to Bub., July 22, 1820, ASM, Bub. 3, enclosing intercepted letters of Confalonieri as proof.

[25] Bub. to Mett., May 11, 1820, Prov/LV 27, 1, 121; encloses Sard. report. This report probably formed the basis for Strassoldo's report to Mett. on July 29, 1820. (Cf. Stern, *Geschichte Europas,* I, p. 245, and *RSRI,* I [1895], in which the Strassoldo report is published.) Actually, Strass. had nothing new to offer, and merely repeated, what Mett. had so often heard from Bllg., Sard., and others as he wrote that whatever advantages the Austrian administration might offer were offset by the injuries done to Italian national pride and that "Les Lombards n'ont pu, ne peuvent et ne pourront jamais s'accoutumer aux formes germaniques empreintes à l'administration de leur pays; ils les abhorrent et ils détestent le système d'une uniformité par lequel on les a mis au pair des Allemands, des Bohèmes et des Galliciens."

[26] Mett. to Bub., Aug. 9, 1820, Prov/LV 37, 2, 10.

[27] "I can't recommend half-measures; only with total ones can one save anything. Had I been Your Majesty's counselor between the years 1792 and 1812, then we probably would not have come to any of the wars which we waged in that time or we would

have beaten our foe with double the might and half the cost." (In translation) Mett. to KF, Sept. 15, 1820, Vortr. 328, 2, 154.

[28] Mett. to KF, Sept. 24, 1820; also, Mar. 8, 1821, Vortr. 328, 3, 99 and 331, 1, 38.

[29] Mett. to Est., May 10, 1821, GA Lond. W/18, 1; Mett. to Vincent, Mar. 7, 1822, Prov/LV 43, 326.

[30] Mett. to KF, Sept. 30, 1822, Vortr. 341, 2, 69-73.

[31] Mett. to Stadion, July 21, 1822, Prov/LV 56, 217, enclosing a copy of the original English questions of Aberdeen. The *Referent* entrusted with compiling the report was Adam Reviczky; there were three versions, the first in German, the others in French, submitted in November, 1822. The final version, published in engraved script, Prov/LV 40. Mett. continued this method of presenting Austria's case by bringing out a "White Book" on the Confalonieri and Andryane trials in January, 1824.

[32] Bub., Strass., Neipperg, Ficquelmont, and Bombelles. Their collective memoir plus individual reports, Nov. 25, 1822, Prov/LV 40. With these documents is also a very interesting and extensive recommendation by Tito Manzi for an Italian Confederation (Manzi to Lebz., Nov. 4, 1822, *ibid.*), to be prepared at the Congress of Verona.

[33] ˌKFA 211 (226), 2, 354-475.

[34] For example, a *Vortrag* of the Hungarian chancellery of December 12, 1817, designated as a "wiederholte Bitte" was acknowledged with the remark: "Ist bei den Acten des Staatsraths zu hinterlegen". StR Prot. 263, No. 10, 134.

[35] This despite the fact that he ordered the Austrian law code translated into "Illyrian" in 1814 (cf. Chapt. I, n. 84); Hofdecret to the *Küstenländische Appellationsgericht,* February 9, 1822: no language other than the privileged three, or at least a translation in one of them. Alfred Fischel, *Das österreichische Sprachenrecht,* p. 130.

[36] "Um den getreuen Unterthanen Meines Königreiches Ungarn einen neuen Beweis Meiner Huld und Gnade zu geben, und Ihnen die Vortheile des Handels mit dem Auslande zu erweitern, habe Ich beschlossen, den jenseits der Save gelegenen Theil von Civil-Kroatien und das ehemalige ungarische Küstenland, welche Bezirke bisher einen integrierenden Theil Meines Königreiches Illyrien ausmachten, von nun an dem Königreiche Ungarn einzuverleiben." AhH. to Mett., July 1, 1822, StK Prov/Ill. 16, *Einverleibung.*

[37] For the various documents pertaining to this matter, cf. Haas, "Kaiser Franz, Metternich und die Stellung Illyriens", *MÖStA,* XI, pp. 396-397; further, Antoljak, "Prekosavska Hrvatska i pitanje njene reinkorporacije", *Starine,* XLV (1955).

[38] *Haus-, Hof- und Staatsschematismus,* 1825.

[39] "Mais est-ce par la révolte et par la guerre civile que [les Grecs] peuvent se flatter d'atteindre ce but éminent? Est-ce par d'obscures menées, par de ténébreux complots qu'une nation peut espérer de revivre et de s'élever au rang des nations indépendantes?" Neither Metternich, nor the Austrian or Russian emperors thought so. Mett. to Prince Alexander Ypsilanti, March 25, 1821, GA Lond. W/17, 2. Of Y. Mett. commented (in translation) to Princess Lieven: "This Ypsilanti, for example, this insane absolute liberal, this Hellenist lacking every judgment but not fear, plays me the trick to place me into the most frightful dilemma and to force me to a decision which shall be tightly bound to my whole life's fate." Original version in Corti, *Metternich und die Frauen,* II, p. 169; strongly toned down, NP III, p. 438, May 6, 1821.

BIBLIOGRAPHY

A NOTE TO THE BIBLIOGRAPHY

The unpublished archives material upon which this investigation is primarily and principally based consists for the most part of Metternich's official and private correspondence and the relevant records of various governmental agencies and departments. Much of Metternich's private correspondence still lies in the Plass Metternich Family Archives now available in a limited manner through the courtesy of the Czech National Archives in Prag. Metternich's confidential exchange of letters with General Bubna has recently been put at the disposal of the Vienna Archives by the Archivio di Stato in Milan. The bulk of Metternich pieces remains in the files and collections of the particular state organs in Vienna. These again are concentrated in several archives; almost all of the Vienna material used for this work is located in the Verwaltungs-Archiv and the Wiener Haus-, Hof- und Staatsarchiv. Fortunately, a good part of the collections is fairly intact; damage was suffered during the 1927 riot and burning of the *Justizpalast* (COHCA and HKzA) and during 1945. Ironically, losses in 1945 occurred precisely among those papers removed from the city for supposed safekeeping in the surrounding countryside; some collections were scattered or burned by Russian troops (*Staatsrats-Akten* up to 1832).

A word about the form of the material itself: Metternich's *Vorträge to Kaiser Franz* — that is, all business which the minister presented in writing to the monarch —, as is the case with most transactions of governmental agencies, are in German and written in German script. Much of the private and almost all of the diplomatic correspondence is in French and written in Latin script. *Denkschriften* are apt to be composed in either language, sometimes in Italian. The police reports from Illyria and other hereditary provinces are in German; those from Lombardy-Venetia are Italian, sometimes in condensed form in German or accompanied by German commentaries (possibly with letters in French) when sent on to Vienna. For most official correspondence conducted through a *Kanzlei* or a governmental agency, rough drafts or copies exist or did exist; an exception are Metternich's *Vorträge* to the emperor, which were returned with (usually autographed) imperial comment and resolutions to the Staatskanzlei's files. Thus, the user of the archives might avoid some time-consuming deciphering of nearly illegible drafts when neater final versions are also available. Furthermore, only the final copies contain sometimes important enclosures. For example, use of the often scrawled drafts of diplomatic instructions to ambassadors found in the *Staatenabteilungen* is made unnecessary when one knows that the clean final copies are in the *Gesandtschaftsarchiv* — ordered according to the respective embassies. Similarly, all the imperial *Handbilletts* and resolutions are carefully copied in the AKA Protocolls. Further, in the Bubna — Metternich correspondence, the final copies of the Bubna letters are to be found in *Provinzen/Lombardei-Venedig* along with the Metternich drafts; conversely, the Metternich final copies and the Bubna drafts are in the Milanese Secret Correspondence fascicles. In the same way, in London, the letters of the British ambassador in Vienna, Stewart, to the foreign minister, his half-brother Castlereagh, are kept along with the

Castlereagh drafts in the Foreign Office collection *Austria;* the Stewart drafts and Castlereagh originals are to be found in the Embassy Archives, under the heading *Vienna.*

A collection as unique as interesting are the hundreds of cartons comprising the *Kaiser-Franz-Akten.* They might be characterized as the spilled-over contents of the imperial desk-drawer. They grew out of the emperor's habits of requesting written opinions on every conceivable subject and then of keeping on hand for further reference such memoranda, special reports and *Vorträge* (which eventually should have been returned to the proper agencies) of a particular interest. But because Kaiser Franz could devote as much attention to the regulation of a rural post-office in Bukowina or to lists of candidates for Istrian subaltern posts as he could to proposals for internal re-organization, the cartons' contents are of a highly variable quality.

Some agency collections have their protocols (invaluable in the case of the *Staatsrats-Akten,* since the original pieces up to the year 1832 are lost); others, such as the *Kongress-Akten,* have fairly good indices of pieces. For various collections there are valuable aids (*Archivsbehelfe*). Detailed information on the various collections, their histories, and their make-up can be gathered from the following volumes of the *Gesamt-inventare österreichischer Archive:*

I.   *Inventar des Allgemeinen Archivs des Ministeriums des Innern.*

V.   *Inventar des Wiener Haus-, Hof- und Staatsarchivs:*

       vol.   2:   Josef Karl Mayr, *Geschichte der österreichischen Staats-kanzlei im Zeitalter des Fürsten Metternich.*

       vol.   3.   Josef Karl Mayr, *Mettternichs Geheimer Briefdienst.*

       vols. 4-8:   Ludwig Bittner, *Gesamtinventar des Wiener Haus,- Hof- und Staatsarchivs.* 5 volumes.

VII.   *Inventar des Wiener Hofkammer Archivs.*

Furthermore, the Plass Metternich Family Archives are described by Ottokar Weber in *Archivalien zur Neueren Geschichte Österreichs,* I, "Bericht über die Bestände des fürstlich Metternichschen Familienarchivs in Plass."

The archives' material listed in this bibliography covers the decade 1812-1822. The numbers following the collections are those of cartons or fascicles. Each contains, on the average, 400-500 folios.

The chief published primary source is, of course, the eight volumes of Metternich's *Nachgelassene Papiere* (NP). They offer a mass of significant and revealing documents from private and public life as well as autobiographical sketches; but actually, they encompass only a small fraction of the Metternich papers. In the matter of selection, one can hardly deny their editor — Metternich's son Richard — feelings of filial loyalty. The younger Metternich and his arranger — the archivist and historian Klinkowström — are guilty of frequent deletions and of some remarkable remolding, especially with the undesignated letters to Princess Lieven (as recent researches of Corti and de Bertier in Prag have borne out). In an investigation of just this issue, Karl Obermann has come to some very harsh conclusions (ZG, VI [1958], p. 1330 ff.) — at any rate, it is at times difficult to distinguish, among the editor's motives, between well-meant discretion and intended falsification. Most of Metternich's autobiographical segments were written in distant retrospect and, especially those subsequent to the events of 1848, can be expected to contain a flavoring of self-justification. Intriguing disparities which appear more than once between the autobiographical pieces and the presented documents in-dicate the care called for in the use of the autobiographical material; however, these segments are not very important for this work. They immediately became, as Metternich himself, subject of controversy among historians. A severe critic of these segments was Paul Bailleu; a balanced, even well-thought-out criticism of the *Nachgelassene Papiere* as a whole, recognizing positive as well as negative elements, can be found in Ottokar Lorenz's *Staatsmänner und Geschichtsschreiber des neunzehnten Jahrhunderts*. The memoirs' chief value lies in the documents presented, which provide a usually usable sampling of the tens of thousands of pieces scattered throughout various archives collections. Of course, in any serious study of any *particular* issue in Metternich's career, the NP do not suffice and recourse to the archives is as mandatory as unavoidable. Incidentally, there are French and English editions of parts of the NP. The French version is condensed; the English version comprises only the first half of the eight volume set and is so faultily translated that it can not be relied upon.

In general, other published collections of correspondence for the years from 1812 to 1822 are lean on interior matters; in later years, occasional references to earlier issues as well as reflections on "what could have been done" sometimes appear. Important primary material can also be found in various secondary works (Helfert, Krones, Corti, among others).

Acquaintance with secondary literature on Metternich and his period is a time-consuming task of sometimes questionable reward. I have not bothered to include here all biographies written in a popular vein — they are all pretty much on the same level of entertainment. Frequently, motives and prejudices of authors are apt to draw wider interest than their scholarship; all such aspects receive ample treatment in Srbik's biography of Metternich — especially in the third volume, published posthumously in 1954. Moreover, recent articles by Schroeder and Zywczynski (and, before them — in 1943 —, by Rieben) have brought up to date the survey of Metternich scholarship since the publication of Srbik's biography.

It is somewhat puzzling that to this day some historians still take the works of Viktor Bibl to be a proper antidote to those of Srbik. Unfortunately, Bibl's insight, style and scholarship are marred by his penchant for polemic, a fact which a glance at the foreword (especially to the fourth edition) of Bibl's *Metternich, der Dämon Österreichs*, will adequately illustrate. Perhaps his admiration for "history written with the blood of one's heart in the service of one's fellow-countrymen" offends less than his recurrent rancor — not only at Metternich but at Srbik and all those who did not take him earnestly enough; this rancor led to such extremes in his work *Lügen der Geschichte* that a number of noted historians (among them Dopsch, J. K. Mayr, Kretschmayr, Brunner, Bittner and Bauer) found it necessary to publish a protest in Austria's leading historical journal (MIÖG XLV-1931). Nevertheless, Bibl did not mind the accusation of historical bias if it meant being put on the same line as his idol, Treitschke. Like the Prussian historian, Bibl had nothing but contempt for a cosmopolitan statesman who "disregarded" the interests of his people and who let himself be "used" by the Jews — as he interpreted the connections of Metternich with the Rothschilds. A nationalist with some populist sentiments, Bibl saw in Metternich a political dilettante and haughty grand seigneur hostile to all that was noble in a true German. For that reason he regarded Metternich's inclusion into the biographic series *Die Grossen Deutschen* as "a wonderful joke designed to produce a relieving laughter throughout the German land". It is grotesque that in the search of a scapegoat for the disaster of 1918, a supposedly serious historian should come up with Metternich. Bibl concluded his *Metternich, Dämon* with the exclamation: "The rubble-field left after the collapse of November 1918 is in the last resort the work of Metternich. Indeed, he was — the demon of Austria."

Certainly, Bibl's all-too-simple thesis that Metternich enjoyed nearly unlimited power (Dämon, p. 8) seems contradicted by all that the archives have to offer. Although Bibl justified his publication of Metternich studies (after Srbik's publication) on the grounds of revealing new information found in the archives, references to new material in his *Dämon* are surprisingly scarce. The very few citations from the *Vorträge* (only once for the period 1813-1822) in earlier works (*Der Zerfall Österreichs* and *Metternich in Neuer Beleuchtung*) would indicate that Bibl did not go through the *Vorträge* — the most important single source collection for Metternich. But, unlike Srbik, he also liked to disparage the *Nachgelassene Papiere*. One can not help suspecting that Bibl overrated his own use of the archives and that this use merely served to underscore his prejudices.

That Srbik's almost overly-profound Metternich biography relied extensively on the NP and other published sources should not be surprising. Srbik felt that such material, and an occasional check into the archives, would suffice for a more than adequate documentation as well as for valid conclusions. Indeed, the particular issue of Metternich and the idea of nationality Srbik recognized and interpreted quite correctly on the basis of the *Vorträge* of October 27 and November 3, 1817, published in the NP. On the other hand, as Srbik was the first to admit, "a systematic checking through of the nearly immeasurable collections" of the HHStA was simply not within his possibilities. To sort all that a man as deft with a pen as Metternich had written or signed within a half-century would be a life-long project for which, as yet, there have been no volunteers.

Although one might not agree with all of Srbik's opinions, one can hardly deny the depth of his analysis of Metternich's political philosophy. But where the fundamentals of this philosophy are spelled out, set down and fixed with such conviction — probably more specifically than Metternich himself would have dared —, considerations due to evolution and change are bound to suffer. From a reputed agility to a rigidity in Metternich's statecraft is a long process for which age alone can not account. At least one can ask: how did Metternich come to the so-called "system"? Srbik seemingly went along with Metternich's oft-voiced contention that his principles remained the same throughout his lifetime — a contention which Bibl at least had criticized. Srbik maintained that there is "no strict distinction between the Metternich before and after 1815" ("Der Ideengehalt des Metternichschen Systems", *HZ*, CXXXI, p. 243) and thus left the question unanswered. In due time however, Srbik came to feel that he had overvalued the "system" and in the posthumously published bibliographic volume of his *Metternich* he indicated a retreat from his previous emphasis.

This bibliography is concentrated on the topics of Austrian internal development, Metternich, and the problem of nationality — all during the Congress Era. For completeness' sake, it includes some works of, at most, marginal value for this book, but which might perhaps be of greater use to a reader interested in related subjects. It also includes some works dealing with topics subsequent to 1818 because they contain references to previous events or because they offer either parallels in nationality issues or interesting contrasts to Metternich's position of earlier years. Coverage of works pertaining exclusively to foreign policy or to European Congresses from Châtillon to Verona — which deal largely with international or German concerns of no bearing on the problems of reorganization and nationality — is not intended in this bibliography.

UNPUBLISHED PRIMARY SOURCES

I. Public Record Office, London: Foreign Office:
   No. 7— Austria: 117—120, 127—129, 134—136, 139, 143, 144, 149—154.
   No. 120— Embassies/*Vienna*: 3—47

II. Archivio di Stato, Milano: Geheime Correspondenz Guicciardi: 1; Geheime Correspondenz Bubna: 1—4 (now in Vienna).

III. Státní Archiv Zemědělský, Praha: Metternichsches Familien-Archiv/Plass, Acta
   Clementina: 6, 9, 10, 11, 13, 16—19, 26—30, 49—50.

IV. Verwaltungsarchiv und Archiv des Ministeriums des Innern, Wien:
   1. Central-Organisierungs-Hofkommissions-Akten: 158—184. (Partly burned
      or water-damaged fragments.)
   2. Hofkanzlei-Akten: 16, 26, 228 b, 298—302, 308, 309 a, 309 b, 340, 341, 343,
      354, 356—360.

V. Wiener Hofkammer-Archiv:
   59. Illyrisch-Italienische Akten (1813—1814): 16; Prot.: 1—4.

VI. Wiener Haus-, Hof- und Staatsarchiv:
   A. Staatskanzlei:
      1. Vorträge: 285—343.
      2. Notenwechsel:
         a) Staatskanzlei to Hofkanzlei: 26—35.
         b) Hofkanzlei to Staatskanzlei: 77—91.
      3. Interiora:
         a) Korrespondenzen: 76—82, 91, 94.
         b) Organisierung: 2.
      4. Provinzen:
         a) Böhmen: 7, 8.
         b) Dalmatien: 7, 8.
         c) Galizien: 1—6.
         d) Illyrien: 14—16.
         e) Kärnten, Krain, Görz: 1.
         f) Kroatien, Slavonien: 1.
         g) Siebenbürgen: 1.
         h) Ungarn: 1.
         i) Lombardei-Venetien: 3—9, 18, 20, 21, 25—28, 33—40, 43—45, 56, 73.
      5. Friedens-Akten: 158.
      6. Verträge betreffende Akten: 7, 8.

7. Kongress-Akten: 10, 12, 14, 25, 37, 41, 44, 45.
8. Große Korrespondenz: 481, 482.
9. Staatenabteilungen. England/Weisungen: 203, 205, 208, 210, 213.

B. Kabinettsarchiv:
1. Kabinetts-Akten: 33—52; Prot.: 13—17; Indices: 33—37.
2. Alte Kabinettskanzlei-Akten: 256—336. Separat-, Current- und Reise-Protokolle und Indices. (StK material only in Sep. Prot. and Reise-Prot.)
3. Kaiser-Franz-Akten (new numeration): 12—19, 26, 28, 30, 31, 34, 71, 72, 87—91, 164—170, 174, 175, 209—211.
4. Staatskonferenz-Akten: Serie A: 3—10; Prot.: 2—6; Ind.: 28—30. Serie B: 6—12; Prot.: 2, 3; Ind.: 4, 5.
5. Staatsrats-Akten-Protokolle: 228—316.
6. Allerhöchste Handbilletts: 2—8.
7. Vertrauliche Akten: 72.
8. Nachlass-Akten
   a) Baldacci: 7.
   b) Erzherzog Ludwig: 1.
   c) Erzherzog Rainer: 1, 2.
9. Kabinettskanzlei-Akten: Polizei Hofstelle — Vorträge Baldacci: 6.

C. Gesandtschaftsarchiv:
1. Botschafter-Archiv. London/Weisungen: 1—24.

PUBLISHED PRIMARY SOURCES

ANONYMOUS: (the same as the author of *Ideen über das politische Gleichgewicht Europas,* Leipzig, 1814. Erroneously taken by some to be Friedr. v. Gentz). *Ideen über die Bildung eines freien germanischen Staatenbundes. Nebst Anhang über einen ähnlichen italienischen Bund.* Leipzig, 1814.

CHROUST, ANTON, ed.: *Gesandtschaftsberichte aus München.* Abteilung II: *Die Berichte der österreichischen Gesandten.* Munich, 1939.

CONFALONIERI, FEDERICO: *Memorie e Lettere.* Edited by Gabrio Casati. 2 vols. Milan, 1889.

CONSALVI, HERCULE CARDINAL: *Correspondance du Cardinal Hercule Consalvi avec le Prince Clemens de Metternich, 1815—1823.* Edited by Ch. van Duerm. Brussels, 1899.

GENTZ, FRIEDRICH VON: *Tagebücher von Friedrich von Gentz. Aus dem Nachlaß Varnhagens von Ense.* Edition and introduction by Ludmilla Assing. 5 vols. Leipzig, 1873.

— *Staatsschriften und Briefe, 1815—1832.* Edited by Hans von Eckardt. 2 vols. Munich, 1921.

— *Österreichs Theilnahme an den Befreiungskriegen. Ein Beitrag zur Geschichte der Jahre 1813 bis 1815, nach Aufzeichnungen von Friedrich von Gentz, nebst einem Anhang: "Briefwechsel zwischen den Fürsten Schwarzenberg und Metternich."* Ed. by Prince Richard Metternich, arranged by Alfons Freiherr von Klinkowström. Vienna, 1887.

— *Briefe von und an Friedrich von Gentz.* Ed. by Friedrich Carl Wittichen. 3 vols. in 4 parts (the last two parts: Gentz and Metternich). Munich, 1909—1913.

— *Dépêches inédites aux Hospodars de Valachie.* Paris, 1876.

— *Gentz und Wessenberg. Briefe des Ersten an den Zweiten.* Ed. by August Fournier. Vienna, 1907.

H . . . ., R. v. (Joseph Max Friedr. v. Liechtenstern): *Reisen durch das österreichische Illyrien, Dalmatien und Albanien im Jahre 1818.* Meißen, 1822.

HANSARD, T. C.: *The Parliamentary Debates from the Year 1813 to the Present Time.* Vols. 28—30. London, 1815.

Haus-, Hof- und Staats-Schematismus des Kaiserthums Österreich. Vols. for the years 1813—1823.

HORMAYR, JOSEF FRHR. V., ERZHERZOG JOHANN V. ÖSTERREICH: *Aus Österreichs stillen und bewegten Tagen. 1813—1815 und 1810—1812. I. Zeitgeschichtliche Studien aus dem Tagebuche Erzherzogs Johann von Österreich, 1810—1812; II. Hormayrs Lebensgang bis 1816 und seine Briefe an den Vorgenannten 1813—1816.* Ed. by Frhr. von Krones. Vienna, 1892.

JOHANN, ERZHERZOG VON ÖSTERREICH: *Aus dem Tagebuch des Erzherzogs Johann von Österreich, 1810—1815.* Ed. by Franz v. Krones. Innsbruck, 1891.

KLÜBER, JOHANN LUDWIG: *Acten des Wiener Congresses in den Jahren 1814—1815.* Vienna, 1816.

— *Schlußacte des Wiener Congresses vom 9. Juni 1815.* Vienna, 1815.

KÜBECK, CARL FRIEDRICH FRHR. V.: *Tagebücher des Carl Friedrich Freiherrn Kübeck von*

Kübau. Herausgegeben und eingeleitet von seinem Sohne Max Freiherrn von Kübeck. Vienna, 1909.

LIEVEN, DOROTHEA PRINCESS: *The Private Letters of Princess Lieven to Prince Metternich, 1820—1826.* Ed. by Peter Quennell. London, 1937.

MARMONT (MARÉCHAL): *Mémoires du duc de Raguse.* 9 vols. Paris, 1857.

METTERNICH, CLEMENS LOTHAR FÜRST VON: *Aus Metternichs Nachgelassenen Papieren.* (Published under the auspices of the son of the state chancellor, Prince Richard Metternich; ed. by Alfons von Klinkowström). 8 vols. Vienna, 1881—1884.

— *Bericht an Kaiser Franz über die Unterhaltung mit dem Grafen Federigo Confalonieri* (dated March 3, 1824). Published by Klinkowström in the *Wiener Volksfreund,* 1 and 2 March, 1869.

— *Geist und Herz verbündet. Metternichs Briefe an die Gräfin Lieven.* German edition of the French version (ed. by Hanoteau) with introduction by Emil Mika. Vienna, 1947.

NEUMANN, PHILIPP VON: *The Diary of Philipp von Neumann, 1819—1850.* Translated and ed. by E. Beresford Chancellor. London, 1928.

NOSTIZ, KARL VON: *Leben und Briefwechsel.* Dresden, 1848.

ROSSI, JOSEPH: *Denkbuch für Fürst und Vaterland.* 2 vols. Vienna, 1814.

SCHMIDT, OTTO EDUARD, ed.: *87 Briefe aus der Zeit des Freiheitskrieges und des Wiener Kongresses.* Berlin, 1914.

SCHWARZENBERG, FÜRST VON: *Briefe Schwarzenbergs an seine Frau.* Ed. by Joh. Friedr. Novack. Vienna, 1913.

STEIN, HEINRICH FRIEDRICH KARL, FREIHERR VOM UND ZUM: *Freiherr vom Stein, Briefwechsel, Denkschriften und Aufzeichnungen.* Ed. by Erich Botzenhart, vol. V, part III, "Tagebuchaufzeichnungen Steins während des Wiener Kongresses", pp. 173—238. Berlin, 1933.

VARNHAGEN VON ENSE, K. A.: *Denkwürdigkeiten des Eignen Lebens.* Introduction by Joachim Kühn. 2 vols. Berlin, 1923.

VAUDONCOURT, F. GUILLAUME DE: *Histoire des campagnes d'Italie en 1813 et 1814.* 2 vols. London, 1817.

— *Histoire politique et militaire du Prince Eugène Napoléon, Viceroi d'Italie,* 2 vols. Paris, 1828.

WILSON, SIR ROBERT: *Private Diary of Travels, Personal Services, and Publick Events, during mission and employment with the European armies in the campaigns of 1812, 1813, and 1814.* 2 vols. London, 1861.

WOLTMANN, KARL LUDWIG V.: *Grundlinien der Politik der österreichischen Monarchie.* Frankfurt, 1815.

SECONDARY SOURCES

ALBERTI, ANNIBALE: "La teorica di Metternich sull'intervento al congresso di Troppau", *RSR*, XXI (1934), pp. 19—30.

ALISON, SIR ARCHIBALD: *Lives of Lord Castlereagh and Sir Charles Stewart*. Edinburgh, 1861.

ANDEREGG, P.: *Metternichs Urteil über die politischen Verhältnisse Englands*. Diss. Bern, 1954.

ANTOLJAK, STJEPAN: "Transavian Croatia and the Question of its Re-incorporation (1813—1822)" [Prekosavska Hrvatska i pitanje njene reinkorporatije (1813—1822)], *Starine*, XLV (1955), pp. 91—150.

ARESE, FRANCO: "La Lombardia e la politica dell'Austria", *ASL*, LXXVII (1950), pp. 5—57.

ARETIN, KARL OTHMAR FRHR. VON: "Metternichs Verfassungspläne, 1817/18", *HJb*, LXXIV (1955), pp. 718—725.

— "Eugen Beauharnais' Königreich Italien beim Übergang zur österreichischen Herrschaft im April 1814. Aus den nachgelassenen Papieren des k. k. Feldzeugmeister Ludwig Frhr. v. Welden", *MÖStA*, XII (1959), pp. 257—288.

ARNETH, ALFRED V.: *Johann Freiherr von Wessenberg. Ein österreichischer Staatsmann des neunzehnten Jahrhunderts*. 2 vols. Vienna, 1898.

AUERBACH, BERTRAND: *Les races et les nationalités en Autriche-Hongrie*. Paris, 1898.

BAILLEU, PAUL: "Metternichs Teplitzer Denkschrift", *HZ*, L (1883). pp. 190—192.

BASCH, ISABELLA: *Klemens von Hügel, 1792—1849*. Diss. Vienna, 1946.

BAUER, W.: *Die öffentliche Meinung und ihre geschichtlichen Grundlagen*. Tübingen, 1914.

BAXA, JAKOB: "Josef Anton Pilat". *Jahrbuch der österreichischen Leogesellschaft*, 1929, pp. 82—92.

— *Adam Müller: Ein Lebensbild aus den Befreiungskriegen und aus der deutschen Restauration*. Jena, 1930.

BEIDTEL, IGNAZ: *Geschichte der österreichischen Staatsverwaltung*. Vols. 1 and 2. Breslau, 1913,

BENNA, ANNA: "Organisierung und Personalstand der Polizei Hofstelle, 1793—1848". *MÖStA*, VI (1953), pp. 99—104, 134—141.

BERKELEY, G. F. H.: *Italy in the Making*. Cambridge, 1932.

BERTIER DE SAUVIGNY, GUILLAUME DE: *Metternich et son temps*. Paris, 1959.

— *France and the European Alliance, 1816—1821. The Private Correspondence between Metternich and Richelieu*. Notre Dame, 1958.

— "Sainte Alliance et Alliance dans les conceptions de Metternich", *RH*, CCXXIII (1960), pp. 249—274.

BETTANINI, ANTONIO: "Un disegno di confederazione italiana nella politica internazionale della restaurazione", in *Studi di storia dei trattati e politica internazionale*, Padua, 1939.

BIANCHI, NICOMEDE: *Storia documentata della diplomazia europea in Italia dall'anno 1814 all'anno 1861*. Turin, 1865—1872.

BIBL, VIKTOR: *Der Zerfall Österreichs. Kaiser Franz und sein Erbe.* Vienna, 1922.

– *Metternich in Neuer Beleuchtung. Sein Geheimer Briefwechsel mit dem bayerischen Staatsminister Wrede.* Vienna, 1928.

– *Metternich. Der Dämon Österreichs.* Vienna, Leipzig, 1936.

– *Kaiser Franz.* Vienna, Leipzig, 1938.

BIRKE, ERNST: *Frankreich und Ostmitteleuropa.* Cologne, 1960.

BLACK, CYRIL E.: "Fouché in Illyria: 1813", *JCEA*, II (January, 1943), pp. 386—395,

BUCKLAND, C. S. B.: *Metternich and the British Government, 1809—1813.* London, 1932.

BÜDINGER, M.: "Zu den Verwaltungsgrundsätzen des Kaiser Franz", *ÖUR*, New Series. IV (1887), pp. 257—284.

BURCKHARDT, CARL J.: *Gestalten und Mächte* (Chapter on Gentz). Zürich, 1945.

CAPOGRASSI, ANTONIO: "L'unità d'Italia nel pensiero di Lord William Bentinck", *RSR*, XXI (1934), pp. 227—258.

CASTRO, GIOVANNI DE: "La restaurazione austriaca in Milano (1814—1817). Notizie desunte da diari e testimonianze contemporanee", *ASL*, XV (1888), pp. 591—658, 905—979.

— *Milano e le cospirazioni Lombarde, 1814—1820.* Milan, 1892.

CECIL, ALGERNON: *Metternich.* New York, 1933.

CORTI, EGON CAESAR CONTE: *Metternich und die Frauen. Nach meist bisher unveröffentlichten Dokumenten.* 2 vols. Vienna, 1948.

CRESSON, W. P.: *The Holy Alliance.* New York, 1922.

CUTOLO, ALESSANDRO: *Il Duca di Brindisi*, Milan, 1960.

CZOERNIG, C. VON: *Die Alten Völker Oberitaliens.* Vienna, 1885.

DEMELITSCH, FEDOR VON: *Metternich und seine auswärtige Politik.* Stuttgart, 1898.

DEUTSCH, W.: *Das Werden des italienischen Staates.* Vienna, 1936.

DIWALD, HELLMUT: "Deutschböhmen, die Deutschen Prags und das tschechische Wiedererwachen", *ZRGG*, X (1958), pp. 124—142.

DRIAULT, J. E.: *Napoléon en Italie (1800—1812).* Paris, 1906.

DU COUDRAY, HELENE: *Metternich.* New Haven, 1936.

EDER, KARL: *Der Liberalismus in Altösterreich. (Wiener Historische Studien,* ed. by Hantsch, Eder and Kramer.) Vienna, 1955.

ENGEL-JANOSI, FRIEDRICH: "Zur Genesis der Revolution von 1848. Die Verfassungsfrage im deutschen Österreich, 1815—1848." *ZÖR*, III (1922—3).

— "Über die Entwicklung der sozialen und staatswirtschaftlichen Verhältnisse im deutschen Österreich, 1815—1848". *Vierteljahrsschrift für Sozial- und Wirtschaftsgeschichte*, XVII (1924), pp. 95—108.

ERBER, T.: "Storia della Dalmazia dal 1797 al 1814", *Archivio storico per la Dalmazia*, vols. VI—VIII (1928—1930).

ERDMANN, KARL DIETRICH: "Nationale und übernationale Ordnung in der deutschen Geschichte", *GWU*, January, 1956.

FALCIONELLI, ALBERT: *Les sociétés secrètes italiennes.* Paris, 1936.

FERRERO, GUGLIELMO: "L'effet de la révolution française sur l'Italie", *Revue Bleue*, February, 1928, p. 65.

FISCHBACH, MENDEL: *Die Stellung Österreichs zur polnischen Frage vor und auf dem Wiener Kongreß.* Diss. Vienna, 1923.

FISCHEL, A.: *Österreichische Sprachenpolitik und Sprachenrecht. Eine Quellensammlung.* Brünn, 1901.

FORST DE BATTAGLIA, OTTO: "Fürst Metternich — Weltbürger und Europäer", *Universitas*, IX (1954), pp. 743—748.

FOURNIER, AUGUST: "Die europäische Politik von 1812 bis zum ersten Pariser Frieden", *Historische Blätter*, I (1921), pp. 97—132.

— "Zur Vorgeschichte des Wiener Kongresses", *Historische Studien und Skizzen*, II, (chap. 9, pp. 290—327), Vienna 1908.

— *Die Geheimpolizei auf dem Wiener Kongreß. Eine Auswahl aus ihren Papieren.* Vienna, 1913.

FRANCHETTI, AUGUSTO: "Della Rivoluzione francese e della coscienza politica nazionale in Italia", *Nuova Antologia*, CIV, CV (1889), pp. 417—429, 672—694.

FRANKE, ELISABETH: *Metternich und die politische Tagespresse von 1809 bis 1813.* Diss. Vienna, 1919.

FRANZ, GEORG: *Liberalismus. Die deutschliberale Bewegung in der habsburgischen Monarchie.* Munich, 1955.

FRAUENDIENST, WERNER: "Preußisches Staatsbewußtsein und polnischer Nationalismus. Preußisch-Deutsche Polenpolitik 1815 bis 1890", in *Das östliche Deutschland, Ein Handbuch aus dem Göttinger Arbeitskreis,* Würzburg 1959.

GABARDINI, ILDA: "L'unificazione politica italiana nel pensiero del Principe di Metternich", *RSR*, XIII (1926), pp. 466—476.

GELCICH, J.: "Die letzten Tage der Republik Ragusa und ihre Einverleibung in Österreich", *ÖUR*, New Series, V (1888), pp. 311—321.

GERHARD, DIETRICH: "Regionalismus und ständisches Wesen", *HZ*, CLXXIV (1952), pp. 307—337.

GHISALBERTI, CARLO: "Sulle amministrazioni locali in Italia nel periodo napoleonico", *RSR*, XLVII (1960), pp. 33—54.

GLOSSY, KARL: "Berichte Metternichs an Kaiser Franz aus Karlsbad", *ÖR*, LX (1919), pp. 128—136.

GODECHOT, JACQUES: "Les Français et l'Unité italienne sous le Directoire", *Revue internationale d'Histoire Politique et Constitutionelle.* New Series, II (1952), pp. 96—110, 193—204.

GREENFIELD, K. R.: *Economic Liberalism in the Risorgimento. A study of nationalism in Lombardy, 1814—1848.* Oxford, 1934.

GRIEWANK, KARL: *Der Wiener Kongreß und die Neuordnung Europas.* Leipzig, 1942.

GROOS, KARL: *Fürst Metternich. Eine Studie zur Psychologie der Eitelkeit.* Stuttgart, Berlin, 1922.

GROSSMANN, KARL: "Metternichs Plan eines italienischen Bundes", *Historische Blätter.* IV (1931), pp. 37—76.

GRUNWALD, CONSTANTIN DE: *La Vie de Metternich.* Paris, 1939.

HAAS, ARTHUR G.: "Kaiser Franz, Metternich und die Stellung Illyriens", *MÖStA*, XI (1958), pp. 373—398.

HANTSCH, HUGO: *Die Nationalitätenfrage im alten Österreich. (Wiener Historische Studien,* ed. by Hantsch, Eder, and Kramer.) Vienna, 1953.

HAUER, J. v.: *Beiträge zur Geschichte der österreichischen Finanzen.* Vienna, 1848.

HAYES, CARLTON J.: *Essays on Nationalism.* New York, 1935.

— *The Historical Evolution of Modern Nationalism.* New York, 1931.

HELFERT, JOSEF ALEXANDER FREIHERR VON: *Österreich und die Nationalitäten. Ein offenes Wort an Herrn Franz Palacky.* Vienna, 1850.

— *Kaiser Franz und die europäischen Befreiungskriege gegen Napoleon I.* Vienna, 1867.

— *Joachim Murat, seine letzten Kämpfe und sein Ende.* Vienna, 1878.

— "Der Ausgang der französischen Herrschaft in Oberitalien, und die Brescia-Mailänder Militär-Verschwörung", *AÖG*, LXXVI (1890), pp. 407—555.

— "Zur Geschichte des Lombardo-Venezianischen Königreichs", *AÖG*, XCVIII (1908), pp. 1—382.

— *Kaiser Franz von Österreich und die Stiftung des Lombardisch-Venezianischen Königreiches.* Innsbruck, 1901.

— *Casati und Pillersdorf, und die Anfänge der italienischen Einheitsbewegung.* Vienna, 1902.

HERMANEK, GERTRUDE: *Die Staatsauffassung Metternichs.* Diss. Vienna, 1947.

HERMANN, ARTHUR: *Metternich.* New York, 1932.

HINTZE, OTTO: "Das monarchische Prinzip und die constitutionelle Verfassung", *PJb*, CXL (1911), pp. 381—412.

HOCHBAUM, JUL.: *Metternich und der ungarische Landtag, 1811—1812.* Diss. Vienna, 1935.

HOCK, CARL FREIHERR V., and BIDERMANN, HERMANN IGNATIUS: *Der österreichische Staatsrat. 1760—1848.* Vienna, 1879.

HOFFMANN, VIKTOR: *Die Devaluierung des österreichischen Papiergeldes im Jahre 1811.* Munich, 1923.

HORMAYR ZU HORTENBURG, JOSEF: *Kaiser Franz und Metternich.* Leipzig, 1848.

HUCH, RICARDA: *Das Risorgimento.* (Chapters on Confalonieri, Pellico, Salvotti, Kaiser Franz, and Karl Albert von Savoyen.) Leipzig, 1908.

— *Das Leben des Grafen Federigo Confalonieri.* Leipzig, 1925.

HUGELMANN, K. G.: *Volk und Staat im Wandel deutschen Schicksals.* Essen, 1941.

JÄGER, A.: *Die Wiedervereinigung Tirols mit Österreich in den Jahren 1813—1816.* Vienna, 1856.

JETTEL, FREIHERR V.: "Die polnische Frage auf dem Wiener Kongreß", *DR*, XLII (1917), p. 70.

JOHNSTON, R. M.: "Lord William Bentinck and Murat", *EHR*, XIX (1904), pp. 263—280.

KAINZ, F.: "Grillparzers Stellung im österreichischen Sprachen- und Nationalitäten-kampf", *HZ*, CLXI (1940), pp. 485—531.

KANN, ROBERT A.: *The Multinational Empire.* 2 vols. New York, 1950.

— "Metternich, a Reappraisal of his Impact on International Relations", *JMH*, XXXII (1960), p. 333.

— *A Study in Austrian Intellectual History. From Late Baroque to Romanticism.* New York, 1960.

KANTOR, VERA: *Karl Ludwig Ficquelmont. Ein Lebensbild mit besonderer Rücksicht auf seine diplomatische Mitarbeit bei Metternich.* Diss. Vienna, 1948.

KARELL, V.: *Der Karlsbader Kongreß.* Karlsbad, 1937.

KING, BOLTON: *A History of Italian Unity. 1814—1871.* London, 1899.

KIRCHEISEN, FRIEDRICH M.: "Eine bibliographische Übersicht der Schriften von und über Friedrich von Gentz", (plus an addition by Wittichen), *MIÖG*, XXVII (1906), pp. 91—146.

— *Bibliographie des napoleonischen Zeitalters.* 2 vols. Berlin, 1908.

KIRCHHOFF, A.: *Zur Verständigung über die Begriffe Nation und Nationalität.* Halle, 1905.

KISSINGER, HENRY A.: "The Congress of Vienna; A Reappraisal", *WP*, January 1956, pp. 264—280.

— *A World Restored. Metternich, Castlereagh, and the Problems of Peace, 1812—1822.* Boston, 1957.

KISZLING, RUDOLF: *Die Kroaten. Der Schicksalsweg eines Südslawenvolkes.* Graz, 1956.

KITTEL, ERICH: "Metternichs politische Grundanschauungen", *HV*, XXIV (1928), pp. 443—483.

KOENIG, SAMUEL: "Land and People of Galicia", *JCEA*, I (1941), pp. 55—65.

KOHN, HANS: "Romanticism and the Rise of German Nationalism", *RP*, XII (1950), pp. 443—472,

— *The Idea of Nationalism*. New York, 1946.

— *Die Slawen und der Westen. Eine Geschichte des Panslawismus*. Vienna, 1956.

KOLNAI, AUREL: "The Problem of Austrian Nationhood", *JCEA*, II (1942), p. 290.

KÖRNER, J.: "August Wilhelm Schlegel und Metternich", *MIÖG*, XLIII (1929), pp. 123—125.

KOTASEK, EDITH: "Ein Einigungsplan für Italien aus dem Jahre 1812", *MÖStA*, VII (1954), pp. 208—218.

KRAMER, HANS: *Die Italiener unter der österreichisch-ungarischen Monarchie. (Wiener Historische Studien*, ed. by Hantsch, Eder, and Kramer.) Vienna, 1954.

KRONES, FRANZ VON: "Freiherr von Baldacci über die inneren Zustände Österreichs. Eine Denkschrift aus dem Jahre 1816". (ed. and introduced by F. R. von Krones), *AÖG*, LXXIV (1889), pp. 1—160.

— *Zur Geschichte Österreichs im Zeitalter der französischen Kriege und der Restauration. 1792 bis 1816. Mit besonderer Rücksicht auf das Berufsleben des Staatsmannes Freiherr von Baldacci.* Gotha, 1886.

LACKLAND, (Miss) H. M.: "Lord William Bentinck in Sicily, 1811—1812", *EHR*, XLII (1927), p. 371.

— "The Failure of the Constitutional Experiment in Sicily, 1813—1814", *EHR*, XLI (1926), p. 210.

LANGSAM, WALTER C.: "Count Stadion and Archduke Charles", *JCEA*, VI (1946), pp. 147—151.

— "The Principles of Government of Emperor Francis II", *Fordham University Studies, Burke Society Series No. II: Centenary Charter Lectures in Modern Political History, 1945—1946.* New York, 1946.

— *The Napoleonic Wars and German Nationalism in Austria.* New York, 1932.

— *Francis the Good.* New York, 1955.

LAPTER, DOROTHEA: *Die Wiener politische Journalistik unter Metternich.* Diss. Vienna, 1950.

LAUBER, EMIL: *Metternichs Kampf um die europäische Mitte, 1809, 1815.* Vienna, Leipzig, 1939.

LEONARDELLI, F.: *Der Kampf gegen die pressepolitischen Maßnahmen der österreichischen Regierung in Lombardia-Venezia, 1815—1848.* Diss. Vienna, 1955.

LEMBERG, EUGEN: "Grundlagen des nationalen Erwachens in Böhmen, 1773—1844", *Veröffentlichungen der Slawistischen Arbeitsgemeinschaft an der deutschen Universität Prag*, X, (Reichenberg, 1932).

— *Geschichte des Nationalismus in Europa.* Stuttgart, 1950.

LEMMI, FRANCESCO: *La Restaurazione austriaca a Milano nel 1814.* Bologna, 1902.

— *Le origini del Risorgimento italiano, 1748—1815.* Milan, 1924.

LEVIS-MIREPOIX, EMMAN. DE: *Un collaborateur de Metternich. Mémoires et papiers de Lebzeltern.* Paris, 1949.

LIMOLI, DONALD A.: "Pietro Verri, a Lombard Reformer under Enlightened Absolutism and the French Revolution", *JCEA*, XVIII (1958), pp. 254—280.

LOCHER, TH. J. G.: *Die nationale Differenzierung und Integrierung der Slovaken und Tschechen in ihrem geschichtlichen Verlauf bis 1848.* Haarlem, 1931.

LORENZ, OTTOKAR: *Staatsmänner und Geschichtsschreiber des neunzehnten Jahrhunderts. Ausgewählte Bilder.* Berlin, 1896.

LUZIO, ALESSANDRO: "La 'Biblioteca Italiana' e il Governo Austriaco (Documenti)", *RSRI*, I (1895—96), pp. 650—711.

MAASS, FERDINAND: *Der Spätjosephinismus. 1790—1820.* Vienna, Munich, 1957.

MACARTNEY, CARLISLE AYLMER: *National States and National Minorities.* London, 1937.

MALLESON, GEORGE BRUCE: *Life of Prince Metternich.* London, 1888.

MANN, GOLO: *Gentz — Secretary of Europe.* London, 1946.

MARKERT, WERNER: "Metternich und Alexander I. Die Rivalität der Mächte in der europäischen Allianz", *Schicksalswege deutscher Vergangenheit.* Festschrift für S. A. Kaehler, pp. 147—176. Düsseldorf, 1950.

MARX, JULIUS: "Die Amtslaufbahn des Grafen Sedlnitzky bis 1817", *Jahrbuch für Landeskunde von Niederösterreich*, XXVII (1938).

— "Neuer Beitrag . . ." (to above named article), *ibid.*, XXXII (1955—56), pp. 181—191.

— "Metternich als Zensor", *JVGSW*, XI (1954).

— "Die Zensur der Kanzlei Metternichs", *ÖZÖR*, IV (1951).

— *Die österreichische Zensur im Vormärz*, Vienna, 1959.

MATL, J.: "Materialen zur Entstehungsgeschichte des südslawischen Staates", *JKGS*, New Series II (1926), pp. 53—80.

— "Das politische und kulturelle Werden der Südslawen", *PJb*, CCXVI (1929), pp. 152—174.

MAYR, JOSEF KARL: *Geschichte der österreichischen Staatskanzlei im Zeitalter des Fürsten Metternich.* (Volume II of the eight volume set: *Gesamtinventar des WHHStA*). Vienna, 1935.

— "Aufbau und Arbeitsweise des Wiener Kongresses", *AZ*, XII (Munich, 1939).

— *Metternichs geheimer Briefdienst. Postlogen und Postkurse.* (Volume III of *Gesamtinventar des WHHStA*.) Vienna, 1935.

— "Zur Geschichte der italienischen Hofkanzlei und der dalmatinisch-albanesischen Hofstelle. (1793—1809)", *MIÖG*, supplementary volume, XI (1929), pp. 662—675.

MAYR, MICHAEL: *Der italienische Irredentismus. Sein Entstehen und seine Entwicklung vornehmlich in Tirol.* Innsbruck, 1917.

MAZADE, CHARLES DE: *Un chancelier d'ancien régime. Le règne diplomatique de Metternich.* Paris, 1889.

MEHRING, FRANZ: *1813 bis 1819. Von Kalisch nach Karlsbad.* Stuttgart, 1913.

MEINECKE, FRIEDRICH: *Weltbürgertum und Nationalstaat. Studien zur Genesis des deutschen Nationalstaats (7th ed.)* Munich, 1928.

MEISSNER, H. O.: *Die Lehre vom Monarchischen Prinzip im Zeitalter der Restauration und des Deutschen Bundes. (Untersuchungen zur deutschen Staats- und Rechtsgeschichte*, ed. by Gierke, No. 122.) Breslau, 1913.

MEYER, ARNOLD OSKAR: *Fürst Metternich. (Einzelschriften zur Politik und Geschichte*, No. 5.) Berlin, 1924.

— "Der Streit um Metternich", *HZ*, CLVII (1937), pp. 75—84.

MEYNERT, HERMANN: *Franz I., Kaiser von Österreich und sein Zeitalter.* Leipzig, 1834.

— *Kaiser Franz I., Zur Geschichte seiner Regierung und seiner Zeit.* Vienna, 1872.

MISKOLCZY, JULIUS: *Ungarn in der Habsburger Monarchie.* Vienna, 1959.

— "Metternich und die ungarischen Stände", *MÖStA*, XII (1959), pp. 240—256.

MONTI, A.: *L'idea federalistica nel Risorgimento italiano.* Bari, 1922.

MURKO, MATT. V.: *Die Bedeutung der Reformation und Gegenreformation für das geistige Leben der Südslaven.* Prag, Heidelberg, 1925.

MÜSEBECK, ERNST: *Die ursprünglichen Grundlagen des Conservativismus und Liberalismus in Deutschland.* Berlin, 1915.

NADA, NARCISO: *Metternich e le riforme nello Stato Pontifico. La missione Sebregondi a Roma 1832—1836. (BSIR,* New Series, III.) Turin, 1957.

— "Il Regno di Napoli nell'Età della Restaurazione secondo i Giudici di Tito Manzi", *RSR,* XLVIII (1961), pp. 627—645.

NÄF, WERNER: *Staat und Staatsgedanke.* Bern, 1935.

NAGLER, HERBERT: *Regierung, Publizistik und öffentliche Meinung in den Jahren 1809—1815 in Österreich.* Diss. Vienna, 1926.

NOACK, U.: "Das Metternich-Problem", *UJb,* XI (1931), pp. 206—223.

NOETHER, EMILIANA PASCA: *Seeds of Italian Nationalism. 1700—1815.* New York, 1951.

OBERMANN, KARL: "Bemerkungen über die bürgerliche Metternich-Forschung", *Zeitschrift für Geschichtswissenschaft,* VI (1958), pp. 1327—1342.

OMODEO, ADOLFO: *Die Erneuerung Italiens und die Geschichte Europas. 1700—1920.* Zürich, 1951.

PEDROTTI, PIETRO: "I rapporti di Tito Manzi col governo austriaco in alcuni documenti viennesi", *RSR,* XXIX (1942), pp. 3—45.

— "Il Generale Bubna in Lombardia", *RSR,* XXIII (1936), pp. 1564—1568.

PERONI, BALDO: "La passione dell'independenza nella Lombardia occupata dai Francesi", *NRS,* XV (1931), pp. 60—104.

PINGAUD, ALBERT: "La Lombardie en 1814", *RHD,* XLI, (1927), pp. 434—467.

— "La politique italienne de Napoléon Ier", *RH,* CLIV (1927), pp. 20—33.

POSCH, ANDREAS: "Staatsrat Josef Jüstel", *Zeitschrift des historischen Vereins für Steiermark,* XLIV (1953), pp. 99—110.

RAAB, HEINRICH: *Kaiser Franz und sein Verhältnis zu den Deutschen in Österreich.* Diss. Vienna, 1919.

RAGER, FRIEDRICH A.: "National Autonomy in Austria-Hungary", *JCEA,* I (1942), pp. 417—428.

RANTZAU, J. A. VON: "Friedrich von Gentz und dessen Politik", *MIÖG,* XLIII (1929), pp. 77—112.

RATH, R. JOHN: *The Fall of the Napoleonic Kingdom of Italy. 1814.* New York, 1941.

— "The Habsburgs and the Great Depression in Lombardy-Venetia, 1814—1818", *JMH,* XIII (1941), pp. 305—320.

— "The Austrian Provisional Government in Lombardy-Venetia, 1814—1815", *JCEA,* II (1942), pp. 249—266.

— "The Habsburgs and Public Opinion in Lombardy-Venetia, 1814—1815", *Nationalism and Internationalism. Essays inscribed to Carlton J. Hayes,* pp. 303—335. New York, 1950.

— "L'amministrazione austriaca nel Lombardo Veneto (1814—1821)", *Archivio Economico dell'Unificazione Italiana,* IX (1959), fasc. 1.

— "Teaching for citizenship in the Austrian elementary schools during the reign of Francis I", *JCEA,* IV (1944), p. 147.

RAUPACH, THEODOR: *Der tschechische Frühnationalismus. Ein Beitrag zur Gesellschafts- und Ideengeschichte des Vormärz in Böhmen.* Essen, 1939.

RECKE, WALTER: *Die Polnische Frage als Problem der Europäischen Politik.* Berlin, 1927.

REINÖHL, FRITZ V.: "Das politische Vermächtnis des Kaisers Franz I.", *Historische Blätter*, VII (1937), pp. 71—78.

REUCHLIN, H.: *Geschichte Italiens von der Gründung der regierenden Dynastien bis zur Gegenwart*. Leipzig, 1859.

RIE, ROBERT: "Das Legitimitätsprinzip des Wiener Kongresses", *AV*, V (1955), pp. 272—283.

RIEBEN, HANS: *Prinzipiengrundlage und Diplomatie in Metternichs Europapolitik. 1815—1848. (Berner Untersuchungen zur Allgemeinen Geschichte*, XII.) 1942.

— "Die Metternichforschung seit 1925", *Schweizer Beiträge zur allgemeinen Geschichte*, I (1943) p. 268.

RIEDWEG, F.: *Aufbruch zur Freiheit. 1813—1815. Aus zeitgenössischen Schriften*. Berlin, 1941.

ROBERT, A.: *L'idée nationale autrichienne et les guerres de Napoléon*. Paris, 1933.

ROHDEN, PETER RICHARD: "Metternichs Kampf um Europa", *NR*, LI (Berlin, 1940), pp. 271—282.

— *Die klassische Diplomatie. Von Kaunitz bis Metternich*. Leipzig, 1939.

RÖSSLER, HELLMUTH: *Österreichs Kampf um Deutschlands Befreiung. Die deutsche Politik der nationalen Führer Österreichs. 1805—1815*. Hamburg, 1940.

— *Zwischen Revolution und Reaktion. Ein Lebensbild des Reichsfreiherrn Hans Christoph von Gagern, 1766—1852*. Frankfurt, 1958.

ROTA, E.: *Il problema italiano dal 1700 al 1815. (L'idea unitaria)*. Milan. 1941.

— *Questioni di storia del Risorgimento e dell'Unità d'Italia*. Milan, 1951.

ROTHFELS, HANS: "Grundsätzliches zum Problem der Nationalität", *HZ*, CLXXIV (1952), pp. 339—358.

— Review of Heinrich Srbik's *Metternich, Der Staatsmann und der Mensch. DLZ*, XLVI (1925), 2193—2203; 2397—2400.

SANDEMANN, GEORGE AEMILIUS C.: *Metternich*. London, 1911.

SANDONÀ, A.: *Il regno Lombardo-Veneto. 1814—1859; la costituzione e l'amministrazione*. Milan, 1912.

SCHENK, H. G.: *The Aftermath of the Napoleonic Wars. The Concert of Europe — an Experiment*. London, 1947.

SCHIEDER, THEODOR: "Idee und Gestalt des übernationalen Staates seit dem 19. Jahrhundert", *HZ*, CLXXXIV (1957), pp. 336—366.

— "Nationalstaat und Nationalitätenproblem", *ZO*, I (1952), pp. 161—181.

SCHLITTER, HANS: *Aus Österreichs Vormärz*. Vienna, 1920.

SCHMALZ, H. W.: *Versuche einer gesamteuropäischen Organisation, 1815—1820, (Berner Untersuchungen zur Allgemeinen Geschichte*, X) 1940.

SCHMIDT, W. A.: *Geschichte der deutschen Verfassungsfrage während des Befreiungskrieges und des Wiener Kongresses*. Stuttgart, 1890.

SCHMIDT-WEISSENFELS, EDUARD: *Fürst Metternich*. Prag, 1860.

SCHROEDER, PAUL: *Metternich's diplomacy at its zenith: Austria and the congresses of Troppau, Laibach and Verona*. Diss., University of Texas, 1958.

— "Metternich Studies since 1925", *JMH*, XXXIII (1961), pp. 237—260.

SCHULZ, JOSEPH: *Peter Graf von Goëss als Mensch und Staatsmann*. Vienna, 1853.

SCHUMACHER, RUPERT VON: *Des Reiches Hofzaun. Die Geschichte der Militärgrenze*. Darmstadt, 1942.

— "Das Schrifttum über die österreichische Militärgrenze", *Deutsches Archiv für Landes- und Volksforschung*, No. 1/2, (Leipzig, 1942), pp. 207—240.

SCHÜSSLER, WILHELM: *Deutsche Einheit und gesamtdeutsche Geschichtsbetrachtung. Aufsätze und Reden*. (Chapter on Metternich.) Stuttgart, 1937.

SCHWICKER, JOH. HEINRICH: *Geschichte der österreichischen Militärgrenze*. Teschen, 1883.

— *Politische Geschichte der Serben in Ungarn*. Budapest, 1880.

SETON-WATSON, ROBERT WILLIAM: *The Southern Slav Question and the Habsburg Monarchy*. London, 1911.

— "Metternich and internal Austrian Policy", *Slavonic and East European Review*, XVII (1939), pp. 539—555 and XVIII (1939), pp. 129—141.

SKOKAN, JOSEFINE SELMA: *Die Korrespondenz des Fürsten Metternich mit dem Staatsrat Hudelist. Ein Beitrag zur Lebensgeschichte Hudelists*. Diss. Vienna, 1946.

SMOLA, KARL FREIHERR VON: *Das Leben des Feldmarschall Grafen Heinrich von Bellegarde*. Vienna, 1847.

SOLMI, A.: "L'idea dell'unità italiana nell'età napoleonica", *RSR*, XX (1933), p. 1.

SPADONI, DOMENICO: "Il sogno unitario e wilsoniano d'un patriota nel 1814—1815", *RSR*, XIII (1926), pp. 341—355.

— "Federazione e Re d'Italia mancati nel 1814—1815", *NRS*, XV (1931), pp. 398—433.

— "Aspirazioni unitarie d'un austriacante nel 1814", *La Lombardia nel Risorgimento Italiano*, XVIII (1933), p. 71.

— "La Conversione italiana di Murat", *NRS*, XIV (1930), p. 232.

SPELLANZON, C.: *Storia del Risorgimento e dell'unità d'Italia della pace d'Aquisgrano (1748) al Vittorio-Veneto (1918)*. Vols. II and III. Milan, 1932—1938.

SPOHR, LUDWIG: *Die geistigen Grundlagen des Nationalismus in Ungarn*. (*Ungarische Bibliothek*, vol. XXIII.) Berlin, 1936.

SPORSCHIL, JOH.: *Der Feldzug der Österreicher in Illyrien und Italien in den Jahren 1813 und 1814*. Brunswick, 1844.

SRBIK, HEINRICH RITTER VON: "Die Bedeutung der Naturwissenschaften für die Weltanschauung Metternichs", (Lecture held at the meeting of the *Akademie der Wissenschaften* in Vienna on May 31, 1924), Vienna. 1925.

— "Der Ideengehalt des Metternichschen Systems", *HZ*, CXXXI (1925), pp. 240—262.

— "Metternichs mitteleuropäische Idee", *Volk und Reich*, II (1926), pp. 341—355.

— "Metternichs Plan der Neuordnung Europas, 1814—1815", *MIÖG*, XL (1925), pp. 109—126.

— "Metternich". Chapter in *Meister der Politik*. (Republished as a small book, Munich 1956.)

— *Metternich. Der Staatsmann und der Mensch*. 2 vols. Munich, 1925. Volume III (a bibliographical essay posthumously published), Munich, 1954.

— *Österreich in deutscher Geschichte*. Munich, 1936.

STEINACKER, HAROLD: "Die geschichtlichen Voraussetzungen des österreichische Nationalitätenproblems und seine Entwicklung bis 1867", chapter I in *Das Nationalitätenrecht des alten Österreich*, ed. by K. G. Hugelmann, Vienna, 1934.

STERN, ALFRED: "L'idée d'une représentation centrale de l'Autriche conçue par le Prince de Metternich", *RH*, XXXI (1886), pp. 313—326.

— *Geschichte Europas seit den Verträgen von 1815 bis zum Frankfurter Frieden von 1871*. Vol. I. Berlin, 1894.

— "Memoriale del Conte Strassoldo al Principe di Metternich sulle condizioni e i sentimenti della Lombardia nel 1820", *RSRI*, I (1895—1896), pp. 570—576.

STIMMEDER, HANS: *Die Auffassung Österreichs als Vielvölkerstaat. 1818—1918*. Diss. Vienna, 1948.

STIX, F.: "Zur Geschichte und Organisierung der Wiener Geheimen Ziffernkanzlei", *MIÖG*, LI (1937), pp. 131—160.

STOLBERG-WERNIGERODE, O.: "Stein und das System Metternichs", *Süddeutsche Monatshefte*, XXIX (1932), p. 323.

STRAUSS, HANNAH A.: *The Attitude of the Congress of Vienna toward Nationalism in Germany, Italy and Poland*. New York, 1949.

STROBL VON RAVELSBERG, FERDINAND: *Metternich und seine Zeit*. Vienna, 1906—1907.

SWEET, PAUL: *Friedrich von Gentz, Defender of the Old Order*. Madison, 1941.

SWOBODA, VALERIE: *Fürstin von Lieven und Fürst Metternich*. Diss. Vienna, 1945.

TAMARO, A.: *La Vénétie Julienne et la Dalmatie*. Rome, 1919.

THOMPSON, S. HARRISON: "The Germans in Bohemia to 1918", *JCEA*, II (1942), pp. 161—179.

TKALAC, E. VON: *Jugenderinnerungen*. Laibach, 1894.

TRITSCH, WALTHER: *Metternich und sein Monarch. Biographie eines seltsamen Doppelgestirns*. Darmstadt, 1952.

UHLIRZ, KARL and MATILDE: *Handbuch der Geschichte Österreichs und seiner Nachbarländer Böhmen und Ungarn*, vol. II, 1810—1914. Vienna, 1941.

VALJAVEC, FRITZ: *Die Entstehung der politischen Strömungen in Deutschland. 1770—1815.* Munich, 1955.

— "Die josefinischen Wurzeln des österreichischen Konservativismus", *Südost-Forschungen*, XIV (1955), pp. 166—175.

— *Der Josephinismus. Zur geistigen Entwicklung Österreichs im 18. und 19. Jahrhundert.* (2nd ed.) Munich, 1945.

VERGA, ETTORE: "La deputazione dei collegi elettorali del Regno d'Italia a Parigi nel 1814", *ASL*, XXXI (1904), pp. 308—333.

VIERECK, PETER: "New Views on Metternich", *RP*, XIII (1951), pp. 211—228.

— *Conservatism Revisited*. New York, 1950.

VOINOVITCH, COUNT L.: *Histoire de Dalmatie*. Vol. II. Paris, 1934.

WALTER, FRIEDRICH: *Die Österreichische Zentralverwaltung*. Vol. V. Vienna, 1936.

WALTER, FRIEDRICH, and STEINACKER, HAROLD: *Die Nationalitätenfrage im alten Ungarn und die Südostpolitik Wiens*. (Buchreihe der Südostdeutschen historischen Kommission, 3) Vienna, 1959.

WANDRUSZKA, ADAM: "Der Kutscher Europas. Fürst Metternich im Urteil der Historiker von heute." *Wort und Wahrheit*, XIV (1959), pp. 459—461.

WEBER, OTTOKAR: "Bericht über die Bestände des fürstlich Metternichschen Familienarchivs in Plass", in *Archivalien zur Neueren Geschichte Österreichs*, I, pp. 140—157. Vienna, 1913.

WEIL, GEORGES: *L'éveil des nationalités et le mouvement libéral, 1815—1848*. (Peuples et civilisations) Paris, 1930.

WEIL, M.-H.: *Le Prince Eugène et Murat (1813—1814). Opérations militaires, Négociations diplomatiques*. 5 vols. Paris, 1901—1902.

— *Joachim Murat, Roi de Naples. La Dernière Année de Règne (Mai 1814—Mai 1815)*. 5 vols. Paris, 1909—1910.

WELDEN, LUDWIG FREIHERR VON: *Der Krieg der Österreicher in Italien gegen die Franzosen in den Jahren 1813 und 1814*. Graz, 1853.

WENDEL, HERMANN: *Aus dem südslavischen Risorgimento*. Gotha, 1921.

— *Der Kampf der Südslaven um Freiheit und Einheit*. Frankfurt, 1925.

WESTPHAL, OTTO: "Metternich und sein Staat", *ÖR*, 19th year, (1923), pp. 901—917.

WIEDEMANN-WARNHELM, ADOLF: *Die Wiederherstellung der österreichischen Vorherrschaft in Italien*. 1813—1815. Vienna, 1912.

WINTER, EDUARD: *Der Josefinismus und seine Geschichte. Ein Beitrag zur Geistesgeschichte Österreichs: 1740—1848*. Brünn, 1943.

WITTICHEN, CARL: "Gentz und Metternich", *MIÖG*, XXXI (1910), pp. 88—111.

— "Johann von Wessenberg über Friedrich von Gentz", *MIÖG*, XXVIII (1907).

WITTRAM, REINHARD: *Das Nationale als europäisches Problem*. Göttingen, 1954.

WOLFF, K.: *Die deutsche Publizistik in der Zeit der Freiheitskämpfe und des Wiener Kongresses. 1813—1815*. Diss. Leipzig, 1934.

WURZBACH, C. V.: *Biographisches Lexikon des Kaiserthums Österreich*. 60 vols. Vienna 1855—1891.

WUSTEL, RICHARDIS: *Der Begriff des Vaterlandes im politischen Denken Österreichs in der Zeit des ausklingenden Barock bis zum Biedermeier*. Diss. Vienna, 1940.

YPSILANTI, HELENE: *Metternichs Stellung zum griechischen Freiheitskampf*. Diss. Vienna, 1927.

ZECHNER, WOLFGANG: *Josef Anton Pilat*. Diss. Vienna, 1954.

ZÖLLNER, ERICH: *Die Angeblichen Memoiren Metternichs*. Vienna, 1946.

— *Geschichte Österreichs*, Munich, 1961.

ZWITTER FRAN: "Illyrisme et sentiment yougoslave", *Le Monde Slave*. Paris, 1933.

— en collaboration avec Jaroslav Sidak et Vaso Bogdanov: *Les Problèmes Nationaux dans la Monarchie des Habsbourgs*. Belgrad, 1960.

ZYWCZYNSKI, MIECZYSLAW: "Metternich w swietle nowszej historiografii", *Kwartalnik Historyczny*, LXVIII (1961), pp. 423—434.

INDEX

Names appearing solely as references in the Notes are not included. Pages in bold type refer to a specific inclusion in Appendix B.

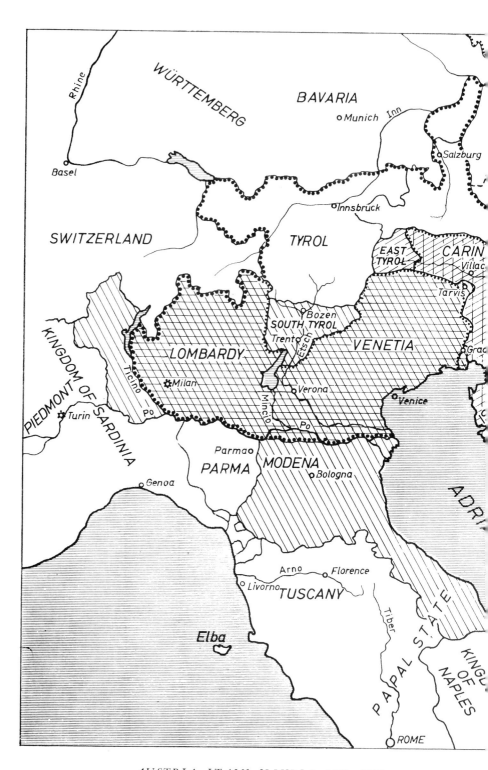

AUSTRIA, ITALY, ILLYRIA: 1813—1822

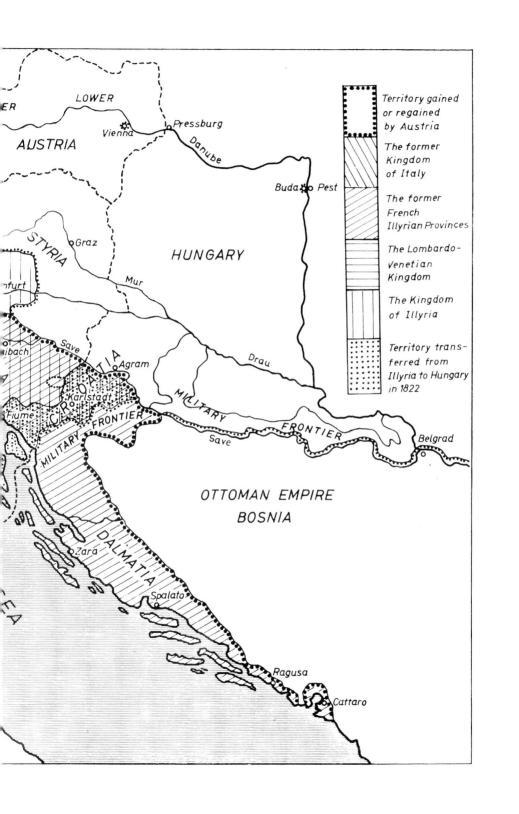

LOWER
ER
AUSTRIA
Vienna
Pressburg
Danube

Buda Pest

STYRIA
Graz
HUNGARY
Mur
nfurt
Drau
Save
CROATIA
Agram
ibach
Karlstadt
MILITARY
FRONTIER
Fiume
MILITARY
FRONTIER
Save
Belgrad

OTTOMAN EMPIRE
BOSNIA

DALMATIA
Zara

Spalato

EA

Ragusa

Cattaro

Territory gained
or regained
by Austria

The former
Kingdom
of Italy

The former
French
Illyrian Provinces

The Lombardo-
Venetian
Kingdom

The Kingdom
of Illyria

Territory trans-
ferred from
Illyria to Hungary
in 1822

VERZEICHNIS DER VERÖFFENTLICHUNGEN

DES INSTITUTS

FÜR EUROPÄISCHE GESCHICHTE MAINZ, ABTEILUNG UNIVERSALGESCHICHTE

HERAUSGEGEBEN VON MARTIN GÖHRING

Die nicht aufgeführten Bände dieser Reihe sind Veröffentlichungen
der Religionsgeschichtlichen Abteilung des gleichen Instituts.

21 Dr. Helmuth K. G. Rönnefarth, *Die Sudetenkrise in der internationalen Politik.* Entstehung · Verlauf · Auswirkung. Teil I, XII und 775 Seiten; Teil II, 358 Seiten. Mit 45 Abb. auf 5 Tafeln sowie 1 Falttafel und 3 Karten, Ln. zus. 40,— DM, 1961

22 Dr. Werner G. Zimmermann, *Valtazar Bogišić 1834—1908.* Ein Beitrag zur südslavischen Geistes- und Rechtsgeschichte im 19. Jahrhundert. X u. 530 Seiten mit 1 Tafel, Ln. 52,— DM, 1962

23 Dr. Ingeborg Streitberger, *Der königliche Prätor von Straßburg 1685—1789.* Freie Stadt im absoluten Staat. VI und 402 Seiten, Ln. 38,— DM, 1961

27 Dr. Donald S. Detwiler, *Hitler, Franco und Gibraltar.* Die Frage des spanischen Eintritts in den Zweiten Weltkrieg. XI und 185 Seiten mit 1 Tafel und 1 Kartenskizze, Ln. 20,— DM, 1962

28 Dr. Arthur G. Haas, *Metternich, Reorganization and Nationality 1813—1818.* A Story of Foresight and Frustration in the Rebuilding of the Austrian Empire. VIII und 244 Seiten mit 9 Tafeln und 1 Kartenskizze, Ln. 28,— DM, 1963

IN VORBEREITUNG BEFINDEN SICH FOLGENDE BÄNDE

Dr. Kurt Jürgensen, *Lamennais und die Gestaltung des belgischen Staates.* Der liberale Katholizismus in der Verfassungsbewegung des 19. Jahrhunderts.

Dr. Lothar Gall, *Benjamin Constant.* Seine politische Ideenwelt und der deutsche Vormärz.

Dr. Karl Otmar Freiherr von Aretin, *Heiliges Römisches Reich 1776—1806.* Reichsverfassung und Staatssouveränität.

Dr. Fritz Kallenberg, *Die Fürstentümer Hohenzollern am Ausgang des Alten Reiches.* Ein Beitrag zur politischen und sozialen Formation des deutschen Südwestens.

Dr. Beate Baumanns, *Die neuere deutsche Geschichte in der französischen Geschichtsschreibung zwischen 1870 und 1918.*